CHANGING OF THE GUARDS

CHANGING OF THE GUARDS

Private Influences, Privatization, and Criminal Justice in Canada

EDITED BY
Alex Luscombe, Kevin Walby, and Derek Silva

UBCPress · Vancouver · Toronto

© UBC Press 2022

All rights reserved. No part of this publication may be reproduced, stored in a retrieval system, or transmitted, in any form or by any means, without prior written permission of the publisher, or, in Canada, in the case of photocopying or other reprographic copying, a licence from Access Copyright, www.accesscopyright.ca.

31 30 29 28 27 26 25 24 23 22   5 4 3 2 1

Printed in Canada on FSC-certified ancient-forest-free paper (100% post-consumer recycled) that is processed chlorine- and acid-free.

Library and Archives Canada Cataloguing in Publication

Title: Changing of the guards : private influences, privatization, and criminal justice in Canada / edited by Alex Luscombe, Kevin Walby, and Derek Silva.
Other titles: Changing of the guards (2022)
Names: Luscombe, Alex, 1990- editor. | Walby, Kevin, 1981- editor. | Silva, Derek M. D., editor.
Description: Includes bibliographical references and index.
Identifiers: Canadiana (print) 20220214786 | Canadiana (ebook) 20220214832 | ISBN 9780774866842 (hardcover) | ISBN 9780774866866 (PDF) | ISBN 9780774866873 (EPUB)
Subjects: LCSH: Corrections—Contracting out—Canada. | LCSH: Privatization—Canada.
Classification: LCC HV9506 .C53 2022 | DDC 365/.971—dc23

Canada

UBC Press gratefully acknowledges the financial support for our publishing program of the Government of Canada (through the Canada Book Fund), the Canada Council for the Arts, and the British Columbia Arts Council.

Printed and bound in Canada by Friesens
Set in Segoe and Warnock by Artegraphica Design Co.
Copy editor: Dallas Harrison
Proofreader: Judith Earnshaw
Cover designer: Will Brown

UBC Press
The University of British Columbia
2029 West Mall
Vancouver, BC V6T 1Z2
www.ubcpress.ca

Contents

Foreword: The Privatization of Criminal Justice: Emotional, Intellectual, and Political Responses / vii
ADAM WHITE

Acknowledgments / xi

Introduction: Canadian Perspectives on Private Influences and Privatization in Criminal Justice / 3
ALEX LUSCOMBE, KEVIN WALBY, and DEREK SILVA

Part 1 Private Provision and Purchase of Security

1 Police, Private Security, and Institutional Isomorphism / 27
MASSIMILIANO MULONE

2 Private Policing of Images in Canada / 48
STEVEN KOHM

3 Postsecondary Security in the Canadian Context / 74
ERIN GIBBS VAN BRUNSCHOT

Part 2 Private Actors in City Spaces and Surveillance

4 Policing Canadian Smart Cities: Technology, Race, and Private Influence in Canadian Law Enforcement / 99
JAMIE DUNCAN and DANIELLA BARRETO

5 Platforms and Privatizing Lines: Business Improvement Areas, Municipal Apps, and the Marketization of Public Service / 126
DEBRA MACKINNON

Part 3 Private Influences and Privatization in Courts, Prisons, and Jails

6 Private Risk Assessment Instruments and Artificial Intelligence in Canada's Criminal Justice System / 153
NICHOLAS POPE and REBECCA JAREMKO BROMWICH

7 The Implications of Food Privatization in Jails: A Case Study of the Ottawa-Carleton Detention Centre / 176
KAITLIN MacKENZIE

8 Shape Shifting: The Penal Voluntary Sector and the Governance of Domestic Violence / 198
RASHMEE SINGH

Part 4 Private Actors in National Security and Border Control

9 Evidence of High Policing Pluralization in Canada / 221
ALEX LUSCOMBE

10 The Creeping Privatization of Immigration Detention in Canada / 247
JONA ZYFI and AUDREY MACKLIN

Postscript: Privatization Cultures and the Racial Order: A Dispatch from the United States / 290
TORIN MONAHAN

Contributors / 295

Index / 300

Foreword

The Privatization of Criminal Justice: Emotional, Intellectual, and Political Responses

ADAM WHITE

The privatization of criminal justice is fast becoming a hallmark of twenty-first-century capitalism. Functions once considered the exclusive preserve of the state – maintaining public order, investigating crimes, managing offenders – are increasingly being undertaken by, modelled on, or otherwise coming under the influence of market providers. Proponents of this trend argue that the private sector offers much-needed value for money, flexibility, and expertise to consumers in a variety of contexts – from neighbourhood groups requiring additional patrols on their streets, to multinational corporations searching for fraudulent transactions on their books, to cash-strapped governments seeking to reduce expenditures in their carceral systems. Yet, far from quietly passing by as "plain good business sense," these transactions frequently take on an air of controversy. They cause politicians to make impassioned speeches, journalists to pen front-page headlines, and of course academics to perform in-depth inquiries – like those in this volume. Why is this? What lies behind these animated responses?

For many, the first response on encountering the privatization of criminal justice is a kind of emotional disorientation, a sense of the familiar order being shaken up. Over the past couple of centuries, the criminal justice system has been at the heart of the modern state-building project in all of its forms. Spin the globe, land your finger on any country, and you can expect to find state-run police forces, prisons, and courts reproducing some kind of law and order within a defined territorial boundary. Sometimes these institutions are forces for good, sometimes not. But they are almost always there. As Migdal (2001, p. 137) remarks, most people consider this "image" of the state "to be as natural as the landscape around them; they cannot imagine their lives without it." So when the logic of the market enters into and begins to break apart this taken-for-granted landscape, it can generate a hard-to-define feeling of something not being quite right, an uncomfortable reshuffling of the furniture of state. Just at first glance, then, the privatization of criminal justice tends to elicit a basic emotional response.

Another response, which often follows from this initial discombobulation, is a kind of intellectual unease. On thinking through the implications arising from this trend, among the first questions that come to mind are those related to democracy, equality, justice, and human rights. In more recent decades, state elites have tended to make a similar set of distinctly liberal claims when justifying the criminal justice system to their citizens: police forces, prisons, courts, and the like exist to protect the life and liberty of everyone, regardless of wealth, influence, or fame and irrespective of race, gender, or social class. Part of the endurance of the modern state-building project lies in the fact that in many countries – particularly in the Global North and Canada certainly among them – everyday practices regularly make good on these claims. Definitely not always. But often enough to persuade the majority of citizens to consent to these sharp-edged institutions. If these claims were pure liberal fantasy, then the whole edifice surely would have fallen apart long ago. This means, however, that when private interests find their way into the criminal justice system and present a challenge to the non-rivalrous, non-excludable nature of these goods, they grate against a widely accepted set of liberal principles. As Loader et al. (2014, p. 477) put it, "once this presumption of equal treatment is made, the market becomes inappropriate as a mechanism for distributing basic protective resources and criminal justice disposals. Allowing money to reign in this sphere would be to subvert and destroy the democratic promise of security." As such, emotional disorientation can soon morph into intellectual unease.

For some, a third type of response then kicks in – political resistance. Journalists regularly decry the privatization of criminal justice with rich hyperbole, not just because they believe that it is the right thing to do, but also because they know that it finds resonance with similarly minded readers and viewers. Politicians translate these messages into policy debates, from both ideological conviction and desire to score political points and win votes. On the front line, criminal justice workers are known to contest and subvert the process of privatization with uncooperative behaviour, making

Foreword

life difficult for their private sector counterparts. Equally, though, these private sector counterparts can be found subtly challenging the very trend that they embody, adopting a "whatever it takes" attitude to the vulnerable victim standing in front of them when their contract stipulates a tightly defined, resource-specific, fully commodified service. In my research on the politics and practices of the Lincolnshire Police–G4S Strategic Partnership – by some distance the largest police outsourcing initiative in UK history – I found all of these acts of resistance in motion at the same time (White, 2014, 2015). What is more, together they can make a big difference. Lincolnshire Police, for instance, recently announced that they will not be extending their contract with G4S at the ten-year renewal point in March 2022, bringing to an end this notable chapter in the chronicles of criminal justice privatization.

In short, these emotional, intellectual, and political responses illustrate that there is a great deal at stake when it comes to the privatization of criminal justice. It is not a trivial matter that plays out under the radar. It is intimately connected to how we understand the world around us and what we want it to look like. It thus invites in-depth inquiry. Yet, while over the past few decades criminologists, sociologists, political scientists, historians, lawyers, and anthropologists (among others) have readily answered this call, there remain many gaps in our knowledge. This is why this volume is such a welcome addition. It not only addresses an under-researched area – the privatization of criminal justice in Canada – but an under-researched area that, for me at least, is somewhat surprising to find. Some of the early classics in this field, dating back forty years now, were acutely concerned with developments unfolding in Canada (Shearing & Stenning, 1981, 1983). Curiously, though, this early momentum did not carry forward – at least when compared with the amount of research subsequently produced elsewhere in the Anglosphere. In recent years, the authors of the following chapters have made significant steps toward redressing this imbalance with their excellent and insightful scholarship, which not only provides an illuminating look at current affairs in Canada but also sheds light on the privatization of criminal justice more broadly. This volume stands as a testament to these important contributions.

Adam White
School of Law
University of Sheffield
United Kingdom

References

Loader, I., Goold, B., & Thumala, A. (2014). The moral economy of security. *Theoretical Criminology, 18*(4), 469–488.

Migdal, J. S. (2001). *State in society: Studying how states and societies transform and constitute one another.* Cambridge University Press.

Shearing, C., & Stenning, P. (1981). Modern private security: Its growth and implications. *Crime and Justice, 3,* 193–245.

Shearing, C., & Stenning, P. (1983). Private security: Implications for social control. *Social Problems, 30*(5), 493–506.

White, A. (2014). Post-crisis policing and public-private partnerships: The case of Lincolnshire Police and G4S. *British Journal of Criminology, 54*(6), 1002–1022.

White, A. (2015). The politics of police "privatization": A multiple streams approach. *Criminology and Criminal Justice, 15*(3), 283–299.

Acknowledgments

We owe an enormous debt of gratitude to Randy Schmidt and colleagues at UBC Press for their hard work and assistance throughout the preparation of this book.

On behalf of the contributors to this volume, we would like to thank the three anonymous reviewers who took the time to review an earlier draft of the volume. Your critical feedback, without question, has made this a much stronger work of scholarship.

Alex Luscombe is grateful for the support of his colleagues at the University of Toronto, whose feedback and words of encouragement during the preparation of this volume were invaluable. Kevin Walby wishes to thank his colleagues in the Department of Criminal Justice at the University of Winnipeg. Derek Silva thanks his colleagues in the Department of Sociology at King's University College at Western University.

This work would not have been possible without the generous financial support of the Social Sciences and Humanities Research Council and the Centre for Criminology and Sociolegal Studies at the University of Toronto.

CHANGING OF THE GUARDS

Introduction

Canadian Perspectives on Private Influences and Privatization in Criminal Justice

ALEX LUSCOMBE, KEVIN WALBY, and DEREK SILVA

Private actors play an increasingly central role in the administration of criminal justice around the world. Although one might be tempted to suggest that this is a simple matter of cost-cutting and efficiency, a growing body of scholarship over the past two decades consistently casts privatization in a negative light, and with good reason. Privatization tends to reshape criminal justice institutions and procedures in ways that are frequently antidemocratic and often cause more harm than good (Ericson & Doyle, 2003; Feeley, 2002; Fitzgibbon & Lea, 2018; Hucklesby & Lister, 2017; Loader, 1999, 2000; Mulone, 2011; Verkuil, 2007; White, 2010). Although research on privatization and criminal justice has blossomed in recent decades, most research has focused on the United States and United Kingdom (Blesset, 2012; Burkhardt, 2019; Fulcher, 2011; Hucklesby & Lister, 2017; Rappaport, 2018; Saldivar & Price, 2015; Selman & Leighton, 2010; Shapiro, 2011; Shichor & Gilbert, 2001), even if some scholars are beginning to adopt a more global perspective (Byrne et al., 2019; Daems & Belen, 2018; Singh & Light, 2019; White, 2016). There is a dearth of research on how issues of privatization become manifest in Canada's unique cultural and political contexts. Criminal justice–related research from countries such as the United States and United Kingdom might be generalizable to Canada, but this is an empirical question rather than an assumption to be taken at face value (Dorn & Levi, 2007; Meerts, 2013; Meerts & Dorn, 2009; van Calster, 2011; van Steden & de Waard, 2013; van Steden & Sarre, 2007). This leads us to the central questions posed in this volume. What role do private actors play in the administration of criminal justice in Canada? What are the major motivations and driving forces behind developments pertaining to the involvement of private actors in the Canadian criminal justice system?

Although privatization of criminal justice is not new (Harding, 2019; Simmons, 2007; Zedner, 2006a), in recent decades we have witnessed an apparent return of private actors in criminal justice throughout much of the world. This includes not only the "rebirth" of private security guarding, a well-documented trend since the 1980s (Johnston, 1992; Jones & Newburn, 1998; Shearing & Stenning, 1983, 1987), but other forms of private influence and privatization, affecting a broad range of institutions, from prisons and jails, to courts, to national security agencies, to border police. Yet, for the vast literature on privatization that now exists in criminology, sociology, and criminal justice studies, most of it focuses on reconfigurations affecting the police without much regard for other sectors of the criminal justice system. The question of how privatization is affecting other aspects of that system, such as sentencing and incarceration, has received comparatively little attention, both in Canada and beyond (Hucklesby & Lister, 2017; Joh, 2004; Kraska & Brent, 2011; Selman & Leighton, 2010).

There are many motivations and driving forces behind the privatization of criminal justice. As argued in some of the original writings on private policing (Shearing & Stenning, 1983; Stenning & Shearing, 1979), private, for-profit security services are often purchased because they are flexible and offer a wider array of sanctions over which the client maintains a greater degree of control. Private contractors can also be appealing for their relative lack of transparency and, in some cases, their willingness to engage in dirty work to get the job done (Hansen Löfstrand et al., 2016; Thumala et al., 2011). In the field of forensic accounting and corporate investigation, Williams (2005) found that private firms are preferred in large part for the relative gains in secrecy that clients obtain, allowing them to retain a greater degree of control over the investigative process than they would have if the job was handled exclusively by the state. Although arguments about these and other motivations and driving forces behind the involvement of private actors in criminal justice figure centrally in the chapters of this volume, these are difficult questions that scholars will grapple with for a long time to come.

Changing of the Guards: Private Influences, Privatization, and Criminal Justice in Canada is a step toward filling these gaps in the literature by providing both in-depth and wide-angle looks at some of the major developments in the involvement of private actors in the Canadian criminal justice system today. Although private security figures centrally in several of the chapters of the volume, it also contains chapters on the impacts of privatization in more neglected sectors of the criminal justice system in Canada, such as prosecution, imprisonment, and security intelligence. The chapters illuminate the impacts of both private influence and privatization on democratic law and policy, transparency, accountability, administration of justice, and public debate. The volume extends foundational scholarship on the role of private actors and agencies in criminal justice (Davis et al., 1991; Henry, 2015; Loader, 1999; Shearing & Stenning, 1983; Stenning & Shearing, 1979; Zedner, 2006a, 2006b) through a detailed examination of key trends and developments in Canada.

Private Influence and Privatization in Canadian Criminal Justice
As Hucklesby and Lister (2017, p. 4) observe, privatization is a "broad, container concept, the precise meaning of which is subject to debate." Privatization can be total, but it can also be partial, as in the form of public-private partnerships (White, 2015). Although there are many excellent conceptual frameworks available (see, e.g., Crawford, 2006; Diphoorn, 2016; Jones & Newburn, 1998; Loader, 1999, 2000; Newburn, 2001; Tomczak & Buck, 2019), the main conceptual distinction that we draw in this volume is between private influence and privatization, although we describe some specific instantiations of these concepts below. By *privatization*, we refer to the whole or partial outsourcing of public services to private entities. In contrast, what we call *private influence* involves cases of private actors who bend the actions and outcomes of some agency in their favour, such as at the level of law and policy (Condon, 1998; Lippert, 2002, 2007). Private influence does not always emanate from corporations and for-profit businesses. Private voluntary groups, non-profit organizations, and charitable entities can also influence criminal justice practices, laws, and policies (Maguire et al., 2019; Tomczak & Buck, 2019). The high number of calls for police services made by private entities such as corporations could also be conceived of as a form of private influence that shapes the allocation of criminal justice resources (Rappaport, 2018).

Beyond this crude distinction between private influence and privatization, we did not impose a rigid definition of these terms on chapter contributors (indeed, they were not required to use these terms if they did not wish to do so). Contributors were invited to engage creatively with their areas of study using whatever theoretical and conceptual tools that they thought appropriate. We did this for two reasons. First, intending this to be an interdisciplinary volume, we have avoided imposing any one theoretical framework on chapter contributors, which inevitably would come with disciplinary baggage. Second, we have not sought to impose a high level of theoretical integration and agreement across the chapters because we do not believe that this is what the study of private influence and privatization in Canada, an exploratory field in the early stages of development, currently needs.

Bringing together leading researchers from sociology, criminology, criminal justice, socio-legal studies, and law, we invited contributors to examine themes of private influence, privatization, and criminal justice in their respective subareas. The authors build upon previous inquiries in Canada that examine private entities that do criminal justice work (Baar, 1999; Brodeur, 2010; Ericson & Doyle, 2003; Sanders, 2005; Schneider, 2006; Williams, 2005) by investigating how human and other resources circulate across the public/private divide. Consistent with findings in other countries (Ayling & Shearing, 2008; Joh, 2004; Löfstrand et al., 2018; Stenning, 2000), many of the chapters argue that private influence and privatization are making the Canadian criminal justice system less transparent, equitable, and accountable by transforming public goods into commodities to be bought, sold, and marketed. Many of the chapters further demonstrate how the market logics of private influence and privatization in criminal justice intersect with other aspects of power and inequality, including systemic racism and sexism (see also Fosten, 2017; Simmons, 2007).

Before discussing the layout of the volume and the focus of each chapter, we present an overview of key developments pertaining to private influence and privatization in the Canadian criminal justice system. We organize the discussion in terms of eight overarching themes that we identified in our reading of existing academic literature (including the chapters of this volume) and current events in Canada. Although many of these themes overlap empirically, we have chosen to separate them analytically. The eight themes discussed below are (1) de-governmentalization versus load-shedding, (2) procurement of goods and services, (3) operational networks, (4) donations and sponsorships, (5) stakeholder engagement, (6) corporatization, (7) commercialization, and (8) revolving doors and directorates. The chapters engage with these and other core themes relevant to the study of private influence and privatization of criminal justice.

De-Governmentalization versus Load-Shedding

De-governmentalization refers to cases in which government agencies outsource total responsibility for a core criminal justice function to the private sector. In the United States, the quintessential example of criminal justice de-governmentalization is the fully privatized prison (Burkhardt & Connor, 2016; Enns & Ramirez, 2018; Sparks & Gacek, 2019), owned and operated by corporate giants such as CoreCivic. This kind of wholesale privatization has been exceptionally rare in the Canadian penal system, occurring only once before being overturned in the early 2000s. From 2001 to 2006, Central North Correctional Centre, a maximum-security prison located in Penetanguishene, Ontario, was Canada's first and only privately run prison (Buitenhuis, 2013). Facing significant backlash from prison activists and labour unions, among others, the then newly appointed Liberal government of Ontario terminated its contract with Management and Training Corporation, the company running the facility, and reclaimed public ownership and operation of it. Private jails similarly have had a limited history in Canada (McElligott, 2007). In other sectors of the criminal justice system, such as policing, evidence of de-governmentalization is similarly slim. To our knowledge, Canadian governments have contemplated de-governmentalization in the policing sector, but they have never achieved it. During the 1990s in Quinte West, Ontario, there was a sustained discussion about contracting Intelligarde, an Ontario-based private security company, for policing in the city (Rigakos, 2002). Intelligarde was asked to submit a proposal detailing how it would replace the Ontario Provincial Police (OPP) as the main police service in the region. In the end, the decision was made not to replace the OPP with Intelligarde.

In Canada, de-governmentalization appears to have happened more on the edges of the criminal justice system than at the core, which we refer to here as *load-shedding*. It occurs when governments involve private actors in criminal justice operations without handing over complete ownership or responsibility. In contrast to de-governmentalization, akin to handing over the keys to the car, load-shedding results in a more hybrid, public-private institutional form or "partnership" (typically referred to as a public-private partnership, PPP, or P3 in government parlance). The work of MacKenzie (this volume) on the privatization of food provision in the Ottawa-Carleton Detention Centre is an example of load-shedding in the Canadian criminal justice system. Privatized food provision is an example of privatization at the periphery of Canadian criminal justice operations. Another example can be found in the work of Buitenhuis (2013) on two Ontario prisons built after the failed Central North Correctional Centre experiment via public-private partnerships. Under these arrangements, the government retained ownership of and responsibility for operating the prisons, and a private company held responsibility for designing, financing, building, and maintaining the facilities (Buitenhuis, 2013). With load-shedding, responsibility for "core government services" in the criminal justice system remains the principal domain of the state, private actors being involved in more "peripheral," but no less important, ways.

Procurement of Goods and Services
Procurement is the main mechanism through which government agencies initiate and sign formal agreements with private entities to acquire their goods and services. Through systems of procurement, government agencies put out requests for tenders on which private actors can bid and hope to secure. Requests for tenders can be competitive or non-competitive (the latter also known as sole-source contracting). In the case of competitive bidding, the government chooses a winning bidder based upon select criteria codified in law and policy. With sole-source contracting, the government agency directly contracts a private entity to provide the good or service without any formally competitive process or necessary consideration of alternative parties (though the agency may choose to do so). Sole-source contracting is justified on several grounds, the most common reasons being size of the contract (smaller contracts are often sole-sourced), urgency, existence of a private monopoly, or national security secrecy. Prior to awarding contracts, government agencies can also submit what is known as a "request for information" or RFI. RFIs are submitted to the private sector to acquire more information about potential products or services prior to launching requests for tenders. In the acquisition of artificial intelligence tools, an area where the government generally lacks in-house expertise, RFIs are commonly used (Molnar & Gill, 2018). Finally, products and services can be procured in more informal ways. Technology companies might lend or donate surveillance and other equipment (e.g., bulletproof vests) to police agencies, sometimes on the condition that they conduct a pilot project or provide user experience feedback to the company. An example of the latter occurred in 2011 in Vancouver when the company Armourworks Canada donated $20,000 in bulletproof vests to the city's police department in exchange for "professional evaluation" of its products (Fridman & Luscombe, 2017).

Through procurement processes, private agencies can gain influential footholds in government agencies. Ayling et al. (2008, p. 87) show how police procurement generates certain risks, including potential harms that result from vendor overdependence, and there is some evidence that this occurs in Canada. As Mulone (this volume) further demonstrates, public bodies not only might become dependent but also begin to operate more in accordance with the goals and procedures of the private agencies with which they are working. As a result of contracting out government work, perceptions of the role of government and what constitutes a "core government service" could also change, in theory, though as noted there is limited evidence that this is occurring (yet) in Canada, at least in the domain of criminal justice.

A growing body of research in Canada examines how companies such as Axon, Clearview AI, and ShotSpotter are supplying new technologies to police, border, and other criminal justice agencies (Bud, 2016; Côté-Boucher, 2020; Molnar & Gill, 2018; Robertson et al., 2020). Examples include predictive policing software, body cameras, and various tools for cellphone, facial recognition, and other surveillance (Duncan & Barreto, this volume). In the United States, Joh (2017) has examined the proliferation of robotics technology in public policing and the private security industry. There is some evidence that similar developments might be happening in Canada. Robotics technology can be used to automate criminal justice practices, though in ways that can have unintended consequences and harmful effects. As Joh (2017, p. 585) writes, "companies engineering the algorithms for private security robots have no obligations at all under state public records laws; they are providing a private service to private clients ... [W]e cannot know whether the algorithm used by a robot might be reliable in its ability to assess threats, or equally troubling, produce results with noticeable racial biases." The Canadian First Responders Robotics Association formed in 2020 and is becoming a more prominent organization in national discussions of policing and robots.

Operational Networks
Over the past two decades, Canadian public policing agencies, like those in most G7 countries, have been moving toward a more integrated and hybrid operational model (Brodeur, 2010; Dupont, 2004; Murphy, 2007). There is a growing body of evidence in Canada showing how public and private policing agencies are forming partnerships (Kitchin & Rygiel, 2014; Lippert & Wilkinson, 2010; Murphy, 2007; Sleiman & Lippert, 2010), which we refer to here as *operational networks*. Sometimes these networks are formal public-private partnerships and well advertised as such. At the time of writing, on the international G4S website, the first promotional page discusses

a counterterrorism relationship between G4S and the Royal Canadian Mounted Police. As the website notes, "designed by the Public Engagement Unit of the RCMP, the programme aims to harmonize the work of the Canadian law enforcement community in identifying, preventing, responding to and investigating criminal activities related to terrorism and national security threats" (G4S, 2019). Other operational networks are more covert. Luscombe and Walby (2014) show how a variety of public and private actors converged to monitor and regulate Occupy protesters in an Ottawa park. The existence of these network ties was discovered through requests under freedom of information law. Other examples of formal, covert operational networks are the many partnerships that Canadian intelligence agencies have with private entities, the details of which are difficult to obtain because of official secrecy laws (Luscombe, this volume). Public-private operational networks can also be more informal, as when police leverage their ties to access public surveillance camera footage for an investigation. Much of Canada's public video surveillance infrastructure is privately owned and operated (Haggerty & Ericson, 2000). To tap into this vast information infrastructure, public police can form informal relationships with private camera operators (Hier et al., 2007; Walby & Hier, 2013). These exchanges of information are happening, for the most part, in a legal grey zone, enabled by the existence of an informal public-private partnership between police and private companies.

Donations and Sponsorships

Many police departments across Canada, as in other countries (Ayling & Shearing, 2008), now accept corporate money, products, and services in the form of *donations and sponsorships*. Such practices appear to be on the rise in both Canada and the United States (Walby et al., 2018). Private organizations and individuals provide money, goods, and/or services to public police forces through unconventional channels and sometimes for equivocal reasons (Luscombe et al., 2018). In many of these arrangements, the private organization will transfer funds to a non-profit police foundation that acts as an arms-length broker for the police department (Fridman & Luscombe, 2017). Policing-oriented galas and other events at which police and corporate representatives meet, mingle, and dine can be a means of private influence (Luscombe et al., 2018). In the province of British Columbia, the Vancouver Police Foundation solicits, acquires, and redirects millions of dollars in individual and corporate funds to the police every year. These funds have been used for everything from funding training events, to buying new bulletproof vests, to purchasing a new mobile command vehicle (CBC News, 2013). On paper, sponsorship differs from donation in that the former often involves an explicit quid pro quo (e.g., advertisement at an event in exchange for money), whereas the latter tends to be framed as one-way transfers motivated by altruism and generosity. In practice, however, the differences between them can be less clear since donors can still reap some personal and professional benefits from their generosity (Walby et al., 2020).

Stakeholder Engagement
Meetings between government officials and industry stakeholders offer private entities a more informal means of influencing government actions in their favour, and there is evidence of this type of *stakeholder engagement* occurring in Canada (Lippert, 2007; Lippert & O'Connor, 2006). Recently, the Quebec engineering giant SNC-Lavalin sought to control the outcome of an anti-bribery case by meeting regularly with federal officials and hosting roundtables involving stakeholders from the highest levels of government. SNC-Lavalin's engagement with political officials played a significant role in the decision to amend the Criminal Code of Canada, introducing the option of deferred prosecution agreements to law (Blaze Baum & Fine, 2019). In their research on the policing of Indigenous dissent across Canada, Crosby and Monaghan (2018) show how a police-corporate nexus emerged from meetings between private and public actors about Northern Gateway pipeline activists and protesters. Beginning in August 2010, several public and private actors and agencies met at the Enbridge Northern Gateway Pipeline Project–Intelligence Production Meeting. The stakeholders included oil and gas executives, Royal Canadian Mounted Police officers, and Canadian Security Intelligence Service agents. Crosby and Monaghan provide evidence of similar police-corporate engagements at the Canadian Association of Petroleum Producers meetings.

Corporatization
Privatization involves the act or process of transferring ownership from the public sector to the private sector. *Corporatization*, in contrast, involves public sector organizations that mimic, or become more like, their private sector counterparts (Brownlee et al., 2018; McDonald, 2014; O'Malley & Hutchinson, 2007). As Brownlee et al. (2018) argue, corporatization can lead to privatization by acting as its precursor. It entails broad changes to public bodies that emulate private bodies without handing over ownership or operation to the private sector. The adoption of "new public management"

principles in policing agencies and unions in the United Kingdom, Canada, and Australia is an example of corporatization (O'Malley & Hutchinson, 2007). Police officials in Canada have been encouraged to think more like managers in private corporations (Ayling et al., 2008; Law Commission of Canada, 1999). As noted above, privatization occurs when, to varying degrees, a public body ceases to provide the service and hands it over to a private agency in whole or in part. Where opposition to privatization is strong, corporatized public entities might be viewed by political and corporate elites as preferred vehicles for transforming the public sector, enhancing corporate profit, and maintaining economic growth – ways to achieve the same goals of privatization without the political and economic risks associated with it (Brownlee et al., 2018).

Commercialization

Some public police forces in Canada are beginning to charge for services in a market-like manner, which we refer to here as *commercialization*. Mulone (2011, p. 166) argues that commercialization can be coercive or non-coercive. An example of a non-coercive commercial arrangement is police offering training services to private security companies. These activities are not required by the purchasing client but offered on a voluntary basis as a way of creating additional revenues for the public police force. Police can also be hired by private companies or individuals for guarding, escorting, and other services that the client pays for out of pocket (rather than with tax dollars) (Lippert & Walby, 2013). These arrangements go by several names in Canada, most commonly "user-pay" and "paid duty" policing. In other cases, hiring police in a user-pay arrangement can be more coercive, as in the case of major sporting events or movie filming activities in many regions of Canada. In such cases, public police are required in many cities (e.g., Toronto, Vancouver) as a condition of carrying out these activities in city spaces but must be paid for by the contracting entity rather than with public tax dollars.

Revolving Doors and Directorates

The final theme that emerged from our reading of research and current events pertaining to private influence and privatization of criminal justice in Canada is *revolving doors and directorates*. The idea of a revolving door refers to the movement of employees across the public/private divide and back again. As Marx (1987) observes, the booming private security industry in North America is made up of thousands of former officials from the military, police forces, and national security agencies. These employees "go private" for a variety of reasons, including the desire to continue working past the mandatory public sector age of retirement or because they are offered more lucrative salaries in the private sector. The door is revolving because of how these now private sector officials can leverage their connections in the public sector. In research on drone technology and policy in Canada, Bracken-Roche (2019) found evidence of a revolving door between government and industry stakeholders. Another way private sector organizations can secure access to public agencies is by appointing high-level officials to their directorates. Corporations can also get their executives onto the boards of directors of organizations that might have close ties to or involvement with a criminal justice organization. For example, Motorola, one of the major suppliers of communications technology to police forces, has placed several of its executives on the boards of directors of Canadian police foundations (Walby et al., 2020).

Chapter Overviews

The interdisciplinary scholars in this volume examine how recent institutional developments are opening up the criminal justice system in Canada to varying degrees of private influence and privatization. Although the level of private influence and privatization in Canadian criminal justice appears to be nowhere near what is occurring in other G7 countries, such as the United Kingdom, this could change. The encroachment of private security into the domain of public policing has been increasing for decades in Canada (Arsenault, 2018). Private security personnel in Canada are not only growing in number (Harris, 2016) but also appear to be taking over more of the responsibilities once exclusive to public police forces (Brodeur, 2010; Rigakos, 2002). Private prisons and jails are a recurring topic of discussion in Canada (CBC News, 2006; Roslin, 2007; Tencer, 2012). Other ongoing policy debates in Canada pertain to the privatization of national security, the acquisition of private surveillance technologies by police and at the border (Molnar & Gill, 2018; Robertson et al., 2020), the expansion of private, citizen-led policing initiatives (Wood & Mackinnon, 2019), and the implementation of private risk assessment tools in sentencing and parole decisions (Pratt, 2001; Zinger, 2004), topics that the chapters of this volume examine.

The volume is divided into four parts. Part 1, "Private Provision and Purchase of Security," examines issues of private policing. In Chapter 1, Massimiliano Mulone sets the stage by proposing a novel theoretical framework, inspired by classical works in organization studies, for examining the increasingly blurred lines between private and public policing agencies in Canada. Specifically, Mulone applies Powell and DiMaggio's (1991) theory of institutional isomorphism to the study of public-private policing partnerships and dynamics. Using their concepts of coercive, normative, and mimetic isomorphism, Mulone shows how ongoing collaborations between public and private policing agencies are blurring the lines between the two sectors, rendering them more alike over time. Highlighting several policy-related concerns about these developments, Mulone points to a number of concrete avenues for challenging and resisting this increasing homogenization of public-private policing agents in Canada.

In Chapter 2, Steven Kohm examines the work of Child Find Manitoba, a grassroots charitable organization in Winnipeg that works closely with the police. In 2002, Child Find Manitoba established Cybertip.ca as Canada's line for reporting online child sexual exploitation. Renamed the Canadian Centre for Child Protection (C3P) in 2006, the organization assumed an official role as Canada's designated reporting agency under federal legislation in 2011. Kohm uses in-depth interviews with C3P directors and board members, media stories, and reports produced by the centre to explore the private policing of images in Canada. An example of a hybrid or mixed operational network, C3P acts as a liaison among the private sector, government, and police to regulate sexual exploitation online. In 2016, C3P's mandate was expanded under Manitoba's new Intimate Image Protection Act, the so-called revenge porn law. Kohm shows how C3P, despite operating at a distance from the state, though given authority and operating funding from provincial and federal governments, has become a hub for the policing of sexual images of children and adults. Throughout the chapter, Kohm critically reflects on how C3P has framed issues of sexual exploitation online and the implications of its work for policing, accountability, and access to information in Canada.

In Chapter 3, Erin Gibbs Van Brunschot examines the management of security threats on university campuses. Postsecondary institutions across Canada are under mounting pressure to ensure the security of the campus community and campus spaces. These pressures have led to several measures undertaken on campuses in the name of security, including emergency communication systems, controlled campus access, and safe-walk programs. To implement these measures, many Canadian universities have turned to the private sector for new technologies and security services. Although postsecondary environments are considered "public," Van

Brunschot argues, more often threats to security involve "norm violations" of the culture of the postsecondary environment and the foundation of academic integrity and collegial governance. Using data from her university, Van Brunschot discusses jurisdictional issues related to norm violations, private governance of public spaces, and the dual challenges of autonomy and liability in the provision of security in the postsecondary context.

In Part 2, "Private Actors in City Spaces and Surveillance," the focus is on private security, surveillance, and governance in the urban environment. In Chapter 4, Jamie Duncan and Daniella Barreto explore the corporate logics and discourses of smart city developments in relation to the long-standing issue of racialized policing across Canada. Using the notions of privatization, platformization, and anticipation as a conceptual framework, Duncan and Barreto show how the proliferation of for-profit data-driven technologies acquired by police can amplify the overcriminalization and underprotection of racialized and marginalized people in Canada. Central to their chapter is the claim that private influence and privatization in criminal justice can further entrench patterns of racism, inequality, and exclusion in society.

In Chapter 5, Debra Mackinnon examines issues of corporatization, urban governance, and policing by business improvement areas (BIAs) using Vancouver, British Columbia, as a case study. Mackinnon shows how city governments like that of Vancouver, in collaboration with BIAs, have implemented a range of private, tech-based "solutions" and expanded public-private networks to augment urban governance and service delivery. Specifically, Mackinnon examines how five Vancouver-based BIAs have been using an app called VanConnect – a citizen-to-government or C2G application – to navigate what they conceptualize as the "splintered streetscape." Tracing the various actors and institutions involved in this work, Mackinnon adds depth and nuance to existing discussions of private influence, privatization, and corporatization through a detailed examination of the city's "clean and safe" mantra and associated policing, surveillance, and intelligence practices.

Part 3 examines issues of private influence and privatization in Canadian courts, prisons, and jails. In Chapter 6, Nicholas Pope and Rebecca Bromwich examine the use of privately owned risk assessment tools in court decision making. Comparing Canada's efforts to regulate the use of these tools with efforts in the United States, Pope and Bromwich express concern about how an increasing reliance on these new privately developed predictive tools can undermine "fundamental foundations of the common law tradition." They find that, though Canadian courts impose a higher standard of algorithmic transparency and accountability than courts in the United States, there is still considerable room for improvement as well as much about which to be concerned.

In Chapter 7, Kaitlin MacKenzie explores the privatization of food services in Canadian prisons and jails. Food service privatization was heralded as a measure that would increase efficiency and save the Ontario government money. However, not only did privatization fail to achieve the cost-saving and efficiency goals, it also led to a food crisis in Ontario prisons and jails. MacKenzie examines the human rights implications of food privatization through a case study of the Ottawa-Carleton Detention Centre. Drawing from interviews with former prisoners, they reflect on the range of impacts of food privatization on the carceral experience. MacKenzie argues that food consumption comprises both "concrete" and "symbolic" punishment and reflects on the broader moral and ethical consequences of using incarceration and punishment as opportunities for corporate profit.

In Chapter 8, Rashmee Singh investigates the implications of private influence and privatization for the governance of domestic violence in Canada. Singh draws from a case study of Toronto's specialized domestic violence plea courts. Established in the late 1990s, these courts are notable for their reliance on eleven community-based organizations to deliver provincially accredited Partner Abuse Response (PAR) programs. Drawing from ethnographic observations of the court process and interviews with PAR counsellors conducted over nearly two decades, Singh explores voluntary penal partnerships and their impacts on the prosecution and punishment of domestic violence. Singh reveals the complex and variegated ways in which penal power asserts and reasserts itself as it governs through the community.

Finally, Part 4 examines issues of private influence and privatization in Canadian national security intelligence and border control. In Chapter 9, Alex Luscombe examines how privatization affects national security or "high policing" operations in Canada. Despite the extensive literature that has now emerged documenting the rise of America's "industrial-espionage complex," Luscombe argues that it is important not simply to assume that trends in countries such as the United States generalize to Canada. In search of evidence of privatization in Canada's high-policing apparatus, Luscombe looks to procurement arrangements, accountability mechanisms, public controversies, and events and publications of non-profit associations and think tanks. Luscombe finds similarities and differences between high-policing privatization in Canada and the United States and discusses their broader implications for theories of policing, surveillance, and pluralization from a Canadian perspective.

In Chapter 10, Jona Zyfi and Audrey Macklin analyze the rise of private, for-profit actors in Canada's immigration detention regime. Once the core responsibility of the state, Canada's border agency is increasingly turning to the use of private, for-profit companies to manage detention facilities across the country. These companies are being contracted in Canada to supervise detainees and assist in the deportation process. Zyfi and Macklin further argue that emerging partnerships between federal and provincial governments in Canada are blurring the boundaries between public and private logics. They show how provincial jails are now renting out detainment facilities to Canada's federal border agency, as if they were contractors, and that drastic cuts to legal, health, and social services in publicly owned immigration detention facilities mirror the pursuit of the bottom line by private, for-profit entities. Zyfi and Macklin conclude their chapter by reflecting on how the increasing involvement of private actors and the adoption of private logics by Canada's border authority are coming at the expense of transparency and accountability in Canada's immigration system.

The volume concludes with a postscript by Torin Monahan on parallels between Canada and the United States, where racial violence and inequality are being reinforced and in some cases aggravated by the increasing involvement of private actors and institutions in criminal justice. Monahan contends that, though the United States is likely a "limit case" when it comes to the issues of racial inequality, violence, and private influence and privatization that he describes, similar patterns are present elsewhere, including Canada. As research on private influence and privatization in criminal justice in Canada continues to develop, we encourage scholars to take Monahan's call for more research on the intersections of race and inequality, private influence, and privatization seriously.

As a final word, we note that the title *Changing of the Guards* is not a rigid assertion. As we have sought to emphasize throughout this introduction, there needs to be more systematic, empirical research on the topic of private influence, privatization, and criminal justice in Canada. Whether the guards really are changing in Canadian criminal justice institutions is an empirical question that we do not yet have a definitive answer to and might not for some time to come.

References

Arsenault, C. (2018, March 2). The quiet quadrupling of Canada's private security sector. *Vice News.* https://www.vice.com/en/article/a3489z/the-quiet-quadrupling-of-canadas-private-security-sector-blackwater-academi-criminology-transparency

Ayling, J., Grabosky, P., & Shearing, C. (2008). *Lengthening the arm of the law: Enhancing police resources in the twenty-first century.* Cambridge University Press.

Ayling, J., & Shearing, C. (2008). Taking care of business: Public police as commercial security vendors. *Criminology and Criminal Justice, 8*(1), 27–50.

Baar, C. (1999). Integrated justice: Privatizing the fundamentals. *Canadian Public Administration, 42*(1), 42–68.

Blaze Baum, K., & Fine, S. (2019, July 24). A deal denied: How SNC-Lavalin spent years fighting for a deferred prosecution law, but then lost the battle to use it. *Globe and Mail.* https://www.theglobeandmail.com/politics/article-a-deal-denied-how-snc-lavalin-spent-years-fighting-for-a-deferred/

Blessett, B. (2012). Prisons for profit: The political and economic implications of private prisons. In B. E. Price & J. C. Morris (Eds.), *Prison privatization: The many facets of a controversial industry* (pp. 9–27). Praeger.

Bracken-Roche, C. (2019). Accessing information in a nascent technology industry: Tracing Canadian drone stakeholders and negotiating access. In K. Walby & A. Luscombe (Eds.), *Freedom of information and social science research design* (pp. 86–101). Routledge.

Brodeur, J. P. (2010). *The policing web.* Oxford University Press.

Brownlee, J., Hurl, C., & Walby, K. (2018). Introduction: Critical perspectives on corporatization. In J. Brownlee, C. Hurl, & K. Walby (Eds.), *Corporatizing Canada: Making business out of public service* (pp. 1–15). Between the Lines.

Bud, T. K. (2016). The rise and risks of police body-worn cameras in Canada. *Surveillance and Society, 14*(1), 117–121.

Buitenhuis, A. (2013). *Public-private partnerships and prison expansion in Ontario: Shifts in governance 1995 to 2012* [Unpublished MA thesis]. University of Toronto. https://tspace.library.utoronto.ca/bitstream/1807/42694/6/Buitenhuis_Amy_J_201311_MA_thesis.pdf

Burkhardt, B. (2019). The politics of correctional privatization in the United States. *Criminology and Public Policy, 18*(2), 401–418.

Burkhardt, B., & Connor, B. (2016). Durkheim, punishment, and prison privatization. *Social Currents, 3*(1), 84–99.

Byrne, J., Kras, K., & Marmolejo, L. (2019). International perspectives on the privatization of corrections. *Criminology and Public Policy, 18*(2), 477–503.

CBC News. (2006, November 10). Ontario to take back control of private super-jail. https://www.cbc.ca/news/canada/ontario-to-take-back-control-of-private-super-jail-1.586052

CBC News. (2013, June 13). High-tech mobile command truck rolled out by Vancouver police. https://www.cbc.ca/news/canada/british-columbia/high-tech-mobile-command-truck-rolled-out-by-vancouver-police-1.1314406

Condon, M. G. (1998). *Making disclosure: Ideas and interests in Ontario securities regulation.* University of Toronto Press.
Côté-Boucher, K. (2020). *Border frictions: Gender, generation and technology on the frontline.* Routledge.
Crawford, A. (2006). Networked governance and the post-regulatory state? Steering, rowing and anchoring the provision of policing and security. *Theoretical Criminology, 10*(4), 449–479.
Crosby, A., & Monaghan, J. (2018). *Policing indigenous movements: Dissent and the security state.* Fernwood.
Daems, T., & Belen, T. (Eds.). (2018). *Privatising punishment in Europe?* Routledge.
Davis, M., Lundman, E., & Martinez, R. (1991). Private corporate justice: Store police, shoplifters, and civil recovery. *Social Problems, 38*(3), 395–411.
Diphoorn, T. (2016). Twilight policing: Private security practices in South Africa. *British Journal of Criminology, 56*(2), 313–331.
Dorn, N., & Levi, M. (2007). European private security, corporate investigation and military services: Collective security, market regulation and structuring the public sphere. *Policing and Society, 17*(3), 213–238.
Dupont, B. (2004). Security in the age of networks. *Policing and Society, 14*(1), 76–91.
Enns, P., & Ramirez, M. (2018). Privatizing punishment: Testing theories of public support for private prison and immigration detention facilities. *Criminology, 56*(3), 546–573.
Ericson, R., & Doyle, A. (2003). The moral risks of private justice: The case of insurance fraud. In R. Ericson and A. Doyle (Eds.), *Risk and morality* (pp. 317–363). University of Toronto Press.
Feeley, M. (2002). Entrepreneurs of punishment: The legacy of privatization. *Punishment and Society, 4*(3), 321–344.
Fitzgibbon, W., & Lea, J. (2018). Privatization and coercion: The question of legitimacy. *Theoretical Criminology, 22*(4), 545–562.
Fosten, G. (2017). Profit-seeking motives and racist policy in Tennessee's criminal justice system: A triangular analysis. *Journal of Black Studies, 48*(8), 791–815.
Fridman, D., & Luscombe, A. (2017). Gift-giving, disreputable exchange, and the management of donations in a police department. *Social Forces, 96*(2), 507–528.
Fulcher, P. (2011). Hustle and flow: Prison privatization fueling the prison industrial complex. *Washburn Law Journal, 51,* 589–617.
G4S. (2019). Canadian mounties team up with G4S on counter terror programme. https://www.g4s.com/news-and-insights/insights/2019/05/09/canadian-mounties-team-up-with-g4s-on-counter-terror-programme
Haggerty, K., & Ericson, R. (2000). The surveillant assemblage. *The British Journal of Sociology, 51*(4), 605–622.
Hansen Löfstrand, C., Loftus, B., & Loader, I. (2016). Doing "dirty work": Stigma and esteem in the private security industry. *European Journal of Criminology, 13*(3), 297–314.
Harding, R. (2019). History of privatized corrections. *Criminology and Public Policy, 18*(2), 241–267.

Harris, K. (2016, November 6). "Unregulated field" of private police needs greater oversight, report warns. *CBC News.* https://www.cbc.ca/news/politics/private-security-police-industry-1.3837157

Henry, S. (2015). *Private justice: Towards integrated theorising in the sociology of law.* Routledge.

Hier, S., Greenberg, J., Walby, K., & Lett, D. (2007). Media, communication and the establishment of public camera surveillance programmes in Canada. *Media, Culture and Society, 29*(5), 727–751.

Hucklesby, A., & Lister, S. (Eds.). (2017). *The private sector and criminal justice.* Palgrave Macmillan.

Joh, E. (2004). The paradox of private policing. *Journal of Criminal Law and Criminology, 95*(1), 49–131.

Joh, E. (2017). Private security robots, artificial intelligence, and deadly force. *University of California Davis Law Review, 51,* 569–586.

Johnston, L. (1992). *The rebirth of private policing.* Taylor & Francis US.

Jones, T., & Newburn, T. (1998). *Private security and public policing.* Oxford University Press.

Kitchin, V., & Rygiel, K. (2014). Privatizing security, securitizing policing: The case of the G20 in Toronto, Canada. *International Political Sociology, 8*(2), 201–217.

Kraska, P., & Brent, J. (2011). *Theorizing criminal justice.* Waveland.

Law Commission of Canada. (1999). *In search of security: The future of policing in Canada.* Law Commission of Canada.

Lippert, R. (2002). Policing property and moral risk through promotions, anonymization, and rewards: Crime Stoppers revisited. *Social and Legal Studies, 11*(4), 475–502.

Lippert, R. (2007). Urban revitalization, security, and knowledge transfer: The case of broken windows and kiddie bars. *Canadian Journal of Law and Society, 22*(2), 29–53.

Lippert, R., & O'Connor, D. (2006). Security intelligence networks and the transformation of contract private security. *Policing and Society, 16*(1), 50–66.

Lippert, R. K., & Walby, K. (2013). Police moonlighting revisited: The case of "pay duty" in three Canadian police services. *Policing: A Journal of Policy and Practice, 7*(4), 370–378.

Lippert, R., & Wilkinson, B. (2010). Capturing crime, criminals and the public's imagination: Assembling crime stoppers and CCTV surveillance. *Crime, Media, Culture, 6*(2), 131–152.

Loader, I. (1999). Consumer culture and the commodification of policing and security. *Sociology, 33*(2), 373–392.

Loader, I. (2000). Plural policing and democratic governance. *Social and Legal Studies, 9*(3), 323–345.

Löfstrand, C., Loftus, B., & Loader, I. (2018). Private security as moral drama: A tale of two scandals. *Policing and Society, 28*(8), 968–984.

Luscombe, A., & Walby, K. (2014). Occupy Ottawa, conservation officers, and policing networks in Canada's capital city. *Canadian Journal of Criminology and Criminal Justice, 56*(3), 295–322.

Luscombe, A., Walby, K., & Lippert, R. (2018). Police-sponsorship networks: Benign ties or webs of private influence? *Policing and Society, 28*(5), 553–569.

Maguire, M., Williams, K., & Corcoran, M. (2019). "Penal drift" and the voluntary sector. *The Howard Journal of Crime and Justice, 58*(3), 430–449.

Marx, G. (1987). The interweaving of public and private police in undercover work. In C. D. Shearing & P. C. Stenning (Eds.), *Private policing* (pp. 172–193). SAGE.

McDonald, D. A. (Ed.). (2014). *Rethinking corporatization and public services in the global south*. Zed Books.

McElligott, G. (2007). Negotiating a coercive turn: Work discipline and prison reform in Ontario. *Capital and Class, 31*(1), 31–53.

Meerts, C. (2013). Corporate security – private justice? (Un)settling employer-employee troubles. *Security Journal, 26*(3), 264–279.

Meerts, C., & Dorn, N. (2009). Corporate security and private justice: Danger signs? *European Journal of Crime, Criminal Law and Criminal Justice, 17*, 97–111.

Molnar, P., & Gill, L. (2018). *Bias at the gate: A human rights analysis of automated decision-making in Canada's immigration and refugee system*. The Citizen Lab. https://citizenlab.ca/wp-content/uploads/2018/09/IHRP-Automated-Systems-Report-Web-V2.pdf

Mulone, M. (2011). When private and public policing merge: Thoughts on commercial policing. *Social Justice, 38*(1–2), 165–183.

Murphy, C. (2007). "Securitizing" Canadian policing: A new policing paradigm for the post 9/11 security state? *Canadian Journal of Sociology, 32*(4), 449–475.

Newburn, T. (2001). The commodification of policing: Security networks in the late modern city. *Urban Studies, 38*(5–6), 829–848.

O'Malley, P., & Hutchinson, S. (2007). Converging corporatization? Police management, police unionism, and the transfer of business principles. *Police Practice and Research, 8*(2), 159–174.

Powell, W. W., & DiMaggio, P. J. (1991). *The new institutionalism in organizational analysis*. University of Chicago Press.

Pratt, J. (2001). Dangerosité, risque et technologies du pouvoir. *Criminologie, 34*(1), 101–121.

Rappaport, J. (2018). Criminal justice, inc. *Columbia Law Review, 118*(8), 2251–2322.

Rigakos, G. (2002). *The new parapolice: Risk markets and commodified social control*. University of Toronto Press.

Robertson, K., Khoo, C., & Song, Y. (2020). *To surveil and predict: A human rights analysis of algorithmic policing in Canada*. The Citizen Lab. https://citizenlab.ca/wp-content/uploads/2020/09/To-Surveil-and-Predict.pdf

Roslin, A. (2007, November 21). Stephen Harper opens door to prison privatization. *The Georgia Straight*. https://www.straight.com/article-119340/stephen-harper-opens-door-to-prison-privatization

Saldivar, K., & Price, B. (2015). Private prisons and the emerging immigrant market in the US. *Central European Journal of International and Security Studies, 9*(1), 40–65.

Sanders, T. (2005). Rise of the rent-a-cop: Private security in Canada 1991–2001. *Canadian Journal of Criminology and Criminal Justice, 47*(1), 175–190.

Schneider, S. (2006). Privatizing economic crime enforcement: Exploring the role of private sector investigative agencies in combating money laundering. *Policing and Society, 16*(3), 285–312.

Selman, D., & Leighton, P. (2010). *Punishment for sale: Private prisons, big business, and the incarceration binge*. Rowman and Littlefield.

Shapiro, D. (2011). *Banking on bondage: Private prisons and mass incarceration*. American Civil Liberties Union.

Shearing, C., & Stenning, P. (1983). Private security: Implications for social control. *Social Problems, 30*(5), 493–506.

Shearing, C., & Stenning, P. (1987). *Private policing*. SAGE.

Shichor, D., & Gilbert, M. (Eds.). (2001). *Privatization in criminal justice: Past, present, and future*. Anderson Publishing.

Simmons, R. (2007). Private criminal justice. *Wake Forest Law Review, 42*, 911–990.

Singh, A., & Light, M. (2019). Constraints on the growth of private policing: A comparative international analysis. *Theoretical Criminology, 23*(3), 295–314.

Sleiman, M., & Lippert, R. (2010). Downtown ambassadors, police relations and "clean and safe" security. *Policing and Society, 20*(3), 316–335.

Sparks, R., & Gacek, J. (2019). Persistent puzzles: The philosophy and ethics of private corrections in the context of contemporary penality. *Criminology and Public Policy, 18*(2), 379–399.

Stenning, P. (2000). Powers and accountability of private police. *European Journal on Criminal Policy and Research, 8*(3), 325–352.

Stenning, P., & Shearing, C. (1979). Private security and private justice. *British Journal of Law and Society, 6*(2), 261–271.

Tencer, D. (2012). Prison privatization: Canada mulls contracting services to companies lobbying for correctional work. *Huff Post Canada*. https://www.huffpost.com/archive/ca/entry/prison-privatization-canada_n_1670755

Thumala, A., Goold, B., & Loader, I. (2011). A tainted trade? Moral ambivalence and legitimation work in the private security industry. *British Journal of Sociology, 62*(2), 283–303.

Tomczak, P., & Buck, G. (2019). The criminal justice voluntary sector: Concepts and an agenda for an emerging field. *The Howard Journal of Crime and Justice, 58*(3), 276–297.

van Calster, P. (2011). Privatising criminal justice? Shopping in the Netherlands. *The Journal of Criminal Law, 75*, 204–224.

van Steden, R., & de Waard, J. (2013). "Acting like chameleons": On the McDonaldization of private security. *Security Journal, 26*(3), 294–309.

van Steden, R., & Sarre, R. (2007). The growth of privatized policing: Some cross-national data and comparisons. *International Journal of Comparative and Applied Criminal Justice, 31*(1), 51–71.

Verkuil, P. (2007). *Outsourcing sovereignty: Why privatization of government functions threatens democracy and what we can do about it*. Cambridge University Press.

Walby, K., & Hier, S. (2013). Business improvement associations and public area video surveillance in Canadian cities. *Urban Studies, 50*(10), 2102–2117.

Walby, K., Lippert, R., & Luscombe, A. (2018). The police foundation's rise: Implications of public policing's dark money. *British Journal of Criminology, 58*(4), 824–844.

Walby, K., Lippert, R. K., & Luscombe, A. (2020). Police foundation governance and accountability: Corporate interlocks and private, nonprofit influence on public police. *Criminology and Criminal Justice, 20*(2), 131–149.

White, A. (2010). *The politics of private security: Regulation, reform and re-legitimation.* Springer.

White, A. (2015). The politics of police "privatization": A multiple streams approach. *Criminology and Criminal Justice, 15*(3), 283–299.

White, A. (2016). The market for global policing. In B. Bradford, I. Loader, B. Jauregui, & J. Steinberg (Eds.), *The SAGE handbook of global policing* (pp. 535–551). SAGE.

Williams, J. (2005). Reflections on the private versus public policing of economic crime. *British Journal of Criminology, 45*(3), 316–339.

Wood, D. M., & Mackinnon, D. (2019). Partial platforms and oligoptic surveillance in the smart city. *Surveillance and Society, 17*(1–2), 176–182.

Zedner, L. (2006a). Policing before and after the police: The historical antecedents of contemporary crime control. *British Journal of Criminology, 46*(1), 78–96.

Zedner, L. (2006b). Liquid security: Managing the market for crime control. *Criminology and Criminal Justice, 6*(3), 267–288.

Zinger, I. (2004). Actuarial risk assessment and human rights: A commentary. *Canadian Journal of Criminology and Criminal Justice, 46*(5), 607–620.

PART 1
Private Provision and Purchase of Security

1

Police, Private Security, and Institutional Isomorphism

MASSIMILIANO MULONE

Introduction

In the early 1980s, when criminologists first began to conduct research on private security, one of the main areas explored was how to identify the divergences and convergences between this "new"[1] actor and its public counterpart, the police.[2] This search for the essential characteristics that could help to distinguish between police and private security is the focus of a number of empirical studies on the activities of the private security industry (Johnston, 1992; Jones & Newburn, 1998; Prenzler, 2005; Shearing & Stenning, 1985), as is the attempt to count and classify the multiplying actors in the field to evaluate their impacts on how security is now produced, distributed, and controlled (Dupont, 2006a, 2014; Johnston & Shearing, 2003; Loader, 1999; Loader & Walker, 2001; Valverde, 2001; White, 2012; Zedner, 2006a).

Although there is no clear consensus, there are a few areas in the existing literature on the privatization of policing where there is general agreement. For example, it is agreed that the growth of the private security industry has led to a significant change in how security is produced and distributed and that these changes have had a lasting impact on citizens' relationships with security and, more generally, on the governance of security (Dupont, 2014; White, 2012; Zedner, 2006b). More important for my argument in this chapter, it is generally accepted that in the past few decades there has been a progressive blurring of the boundary between the public sector and the private sector of policing, not only because of the multiplication of hybrid actors (Johnston & Shearing, 2003) but also because of the increasing number of traditional police activities being undertaken by private security providers, whose visibility is growing as a result.

These concerns are important because the emergence of a private police force that possesses powers and privileges similar to those of a traditional police force, but whose efforts are focused only on protecting the interests of its clients, creates a potentially dangerous situation for society and the public (Rigakos, 2002; Vindevogel, 2004). Since policing and security are already unevenly distributed in society – some citizens are more targeted by the police than others, and some people live in more secure conditions than others – giving the market more influence would indubitably widen such inequities (Zedner, 2006a). Those with low resources, already in a "deficit" regarding security, indeed would be unable to invest in their own safety (and probably would be targeted by paid policing). Thus, if private security organizations come to occupy a position equivalent to that of public police forces, and the profession of providing private security becomes increasingly similar to that of police, then there is a real possibility of radical and potentially dangerous transformation in the way that security is produced in our societies.

In proposing an innovative way to understand the dynamics between private and public sectors in policing, I offer a new explanation of why the future could see more uniformity between police and private security services. I base my reflections upon the concept of institutional isomorphism found in DiMaggio and Powell (1983) and Powell and DiMaggio (1991) and establish a theoretical framework for analyzing the changes taking place in the relationships between private and public policing. DiMaggio and Powell state that there is a "natural" tendency for organizations to become increasingly similar over time: "Once disparate organizations in the same line of business are structured into an actual field ... powerful forces emerge that lead them to become more similar to one another" (1983, p. 148). They associate these "powerful forces" with three processes that can contribute to a reciprocal isomorphism among institutions (Beckert, 2010). The first process, *mimetic isomorphism*, deals with how organizations tend to imitate their counterparts, either because the practices of others are thought to be effective or because an organization confronted with a new situation chooses to deal with it by employing a technique that has been used successfully by another organization. The second process, *coercive isomorphism*, is usually imposed on an entire organizational field through legislative reform: the emergence of an organizational field pressures authorities to try to standardize practices and leads to the imposition of behavioural norms that require institutions to be more alike. The third process, *normative isomorphism*, refers to the phenomenon of professionalization and distribution of expertise. When an organizational field is taking shape, professional standards are established and gradually adopted by every actor in the field, thus promoting a certain standardization of practices.

If police and private security belong to the same organizational field, then one would expect the processes of mimetic, coercive, and normative isomorphism gradually to eliminate the distinctions between police and private security. In this chapter, I identify the elements that contribute to institutional isomorphism between police and private security, and this identification serves as the basis for a larger reflection on the relationships between the two main actors in policing (the public police and the private security companies), the overall governance of policing, as well as the potential consequences of isomorphism. I hope that this analysis will stimulate research aimed at testing my hypothesis as well as providing an innovative contribution to discussions about security governance at a time when increasing privatization seems to be the most probable future for policing (Council of Canadian Academies, 2014; Police Executive Research Forum, 2013), at least in the Anglosphere (Singh & Light, 2019).

The chapter is divided into three parts. I begin by defending my first hypothesis – that police and private security are part of the same organizational field. Then I focus on identifying signs of institutional isomorphism that are occurring as a result of the three processes of isomorphism. Finally, I conclude by discussing some sources of resistance to institutional isomorphism from both inside and outside the institution and by distinguishing between field and executive levels of operation.

Policing as an Organizational Field

To my knowledge, the first researchers to apply the concept of institutional isomorphism to the field of policing were Maguire and Mastrofski (2000) in their exploration of patterns of community policing in the United States. However, their study focused only on community policing and excluded many other forms of security, including private actors. Restriction to a single field of public police, or even to one specific model of policing, seems to be a pattern in other studies that have used Powell and DiMaggio's theory (see, e.g., Burruss & Giblin, 2014, on community policing; Cooper, 2014, on public policing practices; Giblin, 2006, on crime analysis units). My analysis is built upon the premise that private security and police are parts of the same organizational field (the field of policing), an idea that requires a supporting argument since, at first glance, police and private security seem to be different in many ways: normative rationality versus instrumental logic (Shearing & Stenning, 1985), fighting crime versus preventing loss, exclusive power versus limited authority, production of a public good versus production of a consumer good, deployment in the public space rather than the private sphere, distinct training requirements, different legal frameworks, et cetera. The list of differences between the two institutions is long and could lead one to believe that, given two such contrasting realities, it is unlikely that they have similar foundations.

Evidence of a common base can be found, however, in the vast amount of literature describing the growing role of the private security industry in the organization of contemporary policing (Johnston & Shearing, 2003; Loader & Walker, 2001; Shearing & Wood, 2000; White, 2012). DiMaggio and Powell (1983) identify four phases in the institutionalization of an organizational field (Huault, 2009).

In the first phase, there is *an increase in organizational interactions*. This is undeniable in policing. Beyond the basic observation that there has been an increase in the number of joint security initiatives (The Law Enforcement–Private Security Consortium, 2009; Morabito & Greenberg, 2005), Dupont's (2006a, 2014) analyses of security networks clearly demonstrate the density of interactions among the various security actors. My own research, which deals with security managers in private companies, has shown that increasingly relationships are being established between police and private security (Mulone & Dupont, 2008b).

In the second phase, there is *the emergence of dominant interorganizational structures*. One example is the creation of the US Department of Justice's Operation Cooperation in 2000 to support the development of partnerships between law enforcement agencies and private security organizations (Connors et al., 2000; Morabito & Greenberg, 2005). In Quebec, the Bureau de la sécurité privée (Private Security Bureau) was created in 2006 to regulate the private security industry and better coordinate private and public security efforts. In France, Le conseil national des activités privées de sécurité (The National Committee of Private Security Activities), partly inspired by the British Security Industry Authority, has a similar role (Paulin, 2017). It is perhaps a little too early to speak of the cases mentioned above as "dominant" structures in the field, but without a doubt they are becoming more important and contributing directly to how policing is structured as an organizational field.

In the third phase, there is *an increase in the amount of information that must be processed*. It is hard not to agree that this is occurring in the field of policing since the rapid development of information technology has led to exponential growth in the amount of data to be processed. For law enforcement, adoption of the intelligence-led policing model has made the use of information and intelligence even more complex. A significant amount of this information, however, is created and held by the private sector (most companies collect data on their customers), so it is no coincidence that information exchange by far is the most common activity once a public-private partnership is established (The Law Enforcement–Private Security Consortium, 2009).

And in the fourth phase, there is *awareness by actors that they belong to a common field of activity*. Such awareness is regularly noted in the literature, particularly in research that focuses on public-private partnerships in security (Council of Canadian Academies, 2014; Dupont, 2006b; Mulone & Dupont, 2008b). Indeed, public and private actors in policing increasingly acknowledge that they share a common ground and that they can help each other in their respective tasks.

These preliminary reflections make it possible to see how policing tends to be structured as an organizational field. One can thus expect the various organizations in this field – especially police forces and private security companies – to become increasingly similar, considering that "once a field becomes well established ... there is an inexorable push towards homogenization" (DiMaggio & Powell, 1983, p. 148). The rest of this chapter is devoted to discussing the elements that contribute to homogenization as well as the three processes of isomorphism (mimetic, coercive, and normative) described by DiMaggio and Powell (1983). But before going further, I would like to mention two limitations of my contribution. First, because of space constraints, I am able to deal with only two actors, police organizations and private security companies (general suppliers and corporate security). They are undoubtedly important actors but far from the only organizations in the field of policing. A more thorough analysis would include a multitude of hybrid agents whose presence is often underestimated despite their growing numbers in the field (Johnston, 1992; Jones & Newburn, 2006; Nalla & Newman, 1991). Second, as Brodeur (2010, p. 35) once said, "the public and the private sphere of policing are both highly differentiated ... Consequently, discourse that refers to the public or the private spheres of policing as a whole necessarily demonstrates a high level of generality." Some of my assertions in this chapter will be general and therefore have exceptions.

Institutional Isomorphism

My method consists of identifying the elements that contribute to each of the isomorphic processes for public and private policing and then attempting to determine if these processes are increasing for both police and private security. In doing so, I rely in part on my own research on the privatization of security (Mulone, 2012, 2013, 2016; Mulone & Dupont, 2008a, 2008b), but the majority of the discussion is based upon recent empirical studies of the development of the actors examined here. Furthermore, when I refer to homogeneity between institutions, it applies to various aspects, such as structures, processes, and behaviours. Because of limited space and to avoid creating a dry and overly rigid chapter, I will consider these three aspects as one, without necessarily distinguishing among them.

Mimetic Isomorphism: What Private Security Copies from Police

Mimetic isomorphism, as noted, deals with how organizations tend to mimic their counterparts. So which aspects of police forces are being imitated by private security companies? The most noticeable aspect of mimetic isomorphism in private security is the image that it tries to convey. Private security agents usually wear uniforms and drive vehicles that look much like those of police officers. Pants tucked into boots, belts equipped with the tools of their job (baton, walkie-talkie, sometimes a firearm or taser), dark uniforms with the name of the security company near the shoulder and/or on the chest, cars with the colours and decals of the security company – all of these elements contribute to making private security agents look like police officers. These agents not only dress like officers but also adopt the same gestures and ways of speaking. To use a Goffmanian term, it can be said that private security agents "dramatize" their professional practice in a police-like manner (Goffman, 1959). This dramatization takes place because the private security industry has relatively little legitimacy in the organizational field of policing (at least compared with police forces), and legitimacy is essential to their survival.[3] By "disguising" themselves as police officers, private security agents try to validate their existence in the eyes of the public, who might see them, through association, as a form of legitimate authority. A concrete example of this attempt at legitimacy through imitation can be seen in the practices of the Canadian firm Intelligarde, at the core of the research conducted by George Rigakos in Toronto (2002). The marketing strategy is based upon promoting the idea that Intelligarde performs the same tasks as police. It even calls itself "parapolice" and highlights its ability to act as a replacement for law enforcement (McLeod, 2002).

Mimicking often goes beyond the basic symbolic dimension and extends to practice: in some neighbourhoods in the United States and United Kingdom, groups of residents unhappy with the number of police officers on the street have decided to hire private security companies to help patrol their streets (Ransom, 2012; Salkeld, 2009). Even municipalities with budgetary constraints have enlisted the services of private security agents rather than increasing funding for police forces, whose services are considered too expensive (White, 2009). The rapid expansion of business improvement districts (BIDs) has also led to an increase in the number of security agents in public spaces (Cook & MacDonald, 2011; Huey et al., 2005; Lippert, 2012; Vindevogel, 2004). Such developments increase the visibility of private security agents in public spaces, making it more customary for citizens to see private security patrols on the streets, a task usually associated with police work. Thus, police and private security tend to look more similar to the public. I return to this point later.

Mimetic Isomorphism: What Police Copy from Private Security

Although it is clear that private security companies mimic the outward appearances – and sometimes the practices – of police forces, what about the latter? Do they imitate behaviour typical in the private sector? Two current police practices contribute to this form of mimetic isomorphism between police and private security: the commercialization of police services and the managerial rhetoric adopted by police executives.

It is becoming increasingly common, at least in the English-speaking world, to commercialize some police services. In both Canada and the United States, as well as in England and Australia, police can be hired to carry out various security tasks, like a private agency (Ayling et al., 2009). Individuals or private organizations can pay officers to patrol an area or maintain order during an event. This practice, though far from new (Reiss, 1988), is apparently becoming more frequent because of the economic crisis and resulting budget restrictions on governments (Police Executive Research Forum, 2013). In some instances, commercialization is supported by aggressive marketing tactics that lead to direct competition with the private sector. In Montreal, the municipal police bid on and won some important private contracts usually held by the private sector (Mulone, 2012). Police commercialization in Montreal at the end of the 2000s was such a mantra that one of the assistant directors of Montreal's police service/organization told journalists that their ultimate goal was to become financially independent of public funds. Possibly reflecting a global organizational strategy, this declaration, as well as its growing active participation in the market of security, made the police force look as if it wanted to become something of a private security company (Mulone, 2012).

These revenue-generating activities are often accompanied by an increase in the number of user-pay measures, in which the police organization is paid for services rendered. Examples are charges for false alarms as well as deployment of officers at certain major sporting and/or cultural events. In these situations, unlike commercial practices, "clients" have no choice but to call police, who nonetheless charge for their services. Such paid-duty schemes or new forms of police "moonlighting" are more and more common in Canada (Lippert & Walby, 2013; for a detailed explanation of why police departments choose to charge for certain services, see also Gans, 2000). These practices increase the extent to which police organizations resemble private companies by participating more actively in the security market and sometimes finding themselves in direct competition with security service providers.

This kind of mimicry is particularly apparent in the upper echelons of the police organization, where executives often have adopted elements of managerial discourse, such as consumerism, promotionalism, and managerialism, borrowed directly from the private sector (Loader, 1999). Under pressure from the currently dominant neo-liberal ideology, police institutions, like other traditional public sector organizations, such as health care and education, have embraced the idea that the management of the organization should follow the principles of the private sector (Dupont, 2006b). *The Guide to Income Generation for the Police Services in England, Wales, and Northern Ireland,* published by the Association of Chief Police Officers of England since 2004, is a prime example of this trend (Association of Chief Police Officers, 2003). More recently, after the last economic crisis, British police chiefs decided to use unprecedented contracting-out schemes as a way to meet the significant budgetary cuts imposed on them. For example, in 2012, Sussex and West Midlands police forces sent out a joint invitation to the private sector to tender for services such as patrolling, obtaining intelligence, detaining suspects, and even undertaking criminal investigations, estimated to be worth £1.5 billion over a seven-year period.

Although police officers strongly criticized these measures, police executives were overwhelmingly supportive of them and, when the call for bids was finally abandoned, concerned that the organization was not flexible enough to provide these services effectively on its own (Travis & Jowit, 2012). This growing tendency to subcontract contributes to the mimetic isomorphism between police and private security since it not only demonstrates that private security is capable of providing at least some of the same services as police but also that police, the originator of such subcontracting, recognize just how similar the two sectors are. These public and private practices and discourses provide compelling signs that gradual isomorphism is occurring. In Canada, though research on such issues is still scarce, pressure to adopt more cost-effective strategies is clearly topical. Indeed, the Council of Canadian Academies (2014) states that, to face budgetary challenges, policing in Canada inevitably will go through more collaboration with the "security network," including (but not only) more outsourcing to the private sector.

Coercive Isomorphism: Forcing Private Security to Become More like Police

Coercive isomorphism – which encompasses everything that compels institutions in an organizational field to resemble one another – is generally the exclusive domain of state authorities, which have the ability to impose regulations on an entire organizational field. In this chapter, I look not only at the legal questions this raises but also at the coercive effects of changes to the urban landscape and private property.

At first glance, there appear to be few legislative efforts to push the field of policing toward isomorphism. To my knowledge, there is no legal framework that deals with both police and private security practices – these two sectors are usually subject to distinct regulatory regimes, and their responsibilities and obligations, even the powers attributed to them, rarely if ever coincide. Most Western countries, however, recently have proposed new laws to regulate a security industry that has undergone so many changes that the previous regulations were judged obsolete (Jones & Newburn, 2006). Is it possible that these reforms, all of which deal with professionalizing the industry, are intended implicitly to turn private security agents into something that resembles public police officers? Although the full response to such a question requires a rigorous and systematic analysis of the legislation in question, a more casual reading of the literature suggests that the answer is no. Most new legislation regarding private security, though usually requiring slightly stricter training standards, remains relatively lenient and shows a shift toward self-regulation (Button, 2007; Mulone & Dupont, 2008a). Legislation does not appear, therefore, to be encouraging an increase in similarities between the private sector and police, instead leaving the former relatively unregulated, without giving it any additional powers.

There are exceptions, however. In the United Kingdom, the community safety accreditation scheme has created new security actors that stand somewhere between a private security guard and a police officer (Crawford & Lister, 2004). In Quebec, the 2004 version of the private security bill formally regulated aspects of the relationship between the private sector and police – an entire chapter in the bill dealt with requiring private security agents systematically to report certain crimes to police – though these elements were not included in the final version of the bill (Mulone & Dupont, 2008a). Spain has the most noteworthy legislation in this regard and has made some private security agents "auxiliary police" for the state. The relationship between public and private sectors is therefore far more developed and formalized there than anywhere else in the world, and it is one of the few examples of the law serving to formalize the unification of public and private security actors, thereby contributing directly to a form of coercive isomorphism. If it is difficult to determine whether the Spanish case represents an abnormality or the future, perhaps it is revealing that one of France's security representatives believes that Spain "is probably 20 years ahead of France in dealing with state/private security relations" (Délégation interministérielle à la sécurité privée, 2012, p. 3; my translation). These examples show that there is a willingness, even if not yet particularly widespread, to bring police and private security closer through a formal legal framework.

An even greater contributor to coercive isomorphism is found not in legislation but in changes taking place in the urban landscape. Security provision in cities is becoming more and more fragmented (Graham & Marvin, 2001), a result of the increasing presence of private security organizations in public spaces as well as a blurring of boundaries between private and public property (Huey et al., 2005; Kempa et al., 2004). Mass private properties, BIDs (Cook & MacDonald, 2011), communal spaces – in all of these developments, citizens and private security agents cross each other's paths in at least two ways. First, city dwellers increasingly are spending time in private spaces, such as mass private properties, naturally policed by the private sector. Second, developments such as BIDs and communal spaces mean that private security agents are operating more frequently in public spaces. By increasing their visibility in common and regularly frequented spaces, making it customary to observe and be observed by them, private security agents are becoming a normal part of the urban security landscape, thus contributing to the ever-shrinking gap between private security and police (Mulone, 2016). In other words, the fragmentation of urban space – and most notably the multiplication of private orders – "forces" citizens to be policed by private companies, in turn contributing to isomorphism between private and public policing. As already noted, "public space" (in the limited sense of the space where members of the public go), which used to be the exclusive territory of public police, is now populated by private security guards.

I should note, however, that this fragmentation of security in the urban space is largely independent of the policing sphere of influence, and the forces that it exerts on the actors of policing, for the most part, are out of their control. Because such developments have effects well beyond the field of policing, they cannot be considered part of a process of coercive isomorphism as such. Nevertheless, I believe that they contribute to increasing similarities between public and private policing.

Coercive Isomorphism: Forcing Police to Become More like Private Security

Some legislative reforms regarding police have increased their resemblance to private security agents. Although looking at all of the legislation is beyond the scope of this chapter, one easily recognizable change is that most Western countries gradually have required law enforcement to implement performance measures, a managerial technique taken directly from the private sector. Australia (Dupont, 2003; Fleming & Scott, 2008), Canada (Kiedrowski et al., 2013), France (Ocqueteau & Pichon, 2008), the Netherlands (Terpstra & Trommel, 2009), the United Kingdom (Hunton et al., 2009), and the United States (Manning, 2008) have all moved in this direction, creating systems that attempt to determine accurately the effectiveness of each organization. They also provide incentives for those who meet the established indicators, sometimes even giving bonuses to the best performers. (For a complete review of the literature, see Tiwana et al., 2015.) Such measures, which affect every level of the hierarchy, have an undeniable impact on how public policing is produced (Ocqueteau & Pichon, 2008). Although the pursuit of "numbers" is not new, present performance measures differ from more traditional crime management indicators in the degree of formalization and standardization and the importance given to economic performance figures (effectiveness). In their overview of police performance metrics in Canada, Kiedrowski et al. (2013) show that, despite a certain level of heterogeneity among Canadian police organizations, the tendency is toward the growing use of performance measures. They identify no fewer than thirty different performance indicators considered common, six of them directly linked to a financial dimension (e.g., cost of policing per citizen or data on overtime expenditures).

Normative Isomorphism: The Effect of Police on Private Security
The third and last process, normative isomorphism, can be understood in terms of professionalization and distribution of expertise. In this regard, several elements contribute to increasing similarities between police and private security. The most important is that the security industry is the preferred choice for police officers seeking a second career. As DiMaggio and Powell noted, "one important mechanism for encouraging normative isomorphism is the filtering of personnel" (1983, p. 152). By hiring a substantial number of former police officers, private security acquires police expertise and promotes the spread of police professionalization in the industry.

This exchange of knowledge and experience in dealing with security problems also happens in the more formal context of public-private partnerships (PPPs). In a survey of PPPs in security in the United States, 61 percent of partnerships had a training component (The Law Enforcement–Private Security Consortium, 2009), and such training – whether it involves information about intervening in certain emergency situations, using force, or simply writing a report that can be used immediately by law enforcement – is usually provided by police. Private security agents sometimes provide training to public law enforcement officers, particularly on specific crimes, such as technocrimes (Morabito & Greenberg, 2005). By exchanging ways of doing and seeing things, these partnerships promote a form of institutional isomorphism.

A further analysis of the development of normative isomorphism might focus on the development of professional networks – whether police and private security agents regularly take part in common associative structures (in which exchanges in expertise continue to happen) or whether it is still uncommon to see police and private security managers as members of the same professional organization. Another way to analyze the topic is to focus on the contents of the many formal educational mechanisms developed by the private sector for its members. Do these certifications and professional development programs deal with knowledge similar to that held by police? What are these programs like, and how many of them exist? What do they teach? This type of study could help us to obtain empirical evidence of the extent of isomorphism in the expertise of the contemporary private security industry.

Normative Isomorphism: The Effect of Private Security on Police
For police, things are quite different. Unlike private security companies, police organizations do not hire professionals from the private sector who want to have a second career in law enforcement. As well, the occupational role of police is characterized partly by the social isolation in which they work, leading them to be suspicious of the outside world (Reiner, 1985). Given this isolation, it is hard to imagine which aspects of police professionalization are gradually being affected by the private sector's methods.

Several elements, however, qualify this observation. First, changes, though difficult to achieve, do occur in police culture (Chan, 1996). One example is the clientelist approach, clearly taken from the entrepreneurial field, that gradually has been adopted by police organizations. It has affected field agents, too, whose relationship with the public slowly but surely has changed, to the point that they have become service providers to citizen-consumers (Clarke et al., 2007). Second, though no study has looked in depth at the potential impact of the increasing popularity of police commercialization on the professional ethos of police officers, this contractual context, in which, through the sales of services, police work for clients, drastically changes the practices of police: not only do they have to carry out routine tasks and attain their institutional objectives (fight crime, maintain order, etc.), but also they have to satisfy customers. In answering to a different type of employer, police move from the highly normative approach of the police service to the instrumental approach characteristic of the commercial sector (Shearing & Stenning, 1985). It would be important also to examine the professionalization process of the executives of police organizations, who, as we have seen, are much more affected by entrepreneurial discourse than field agents. One potential study would involve looking at the training programs required of police officers who wish to move up in their profession to see how similar these programs are to those of managers in the private security industry. For example, is it becoming more common for police chiefs to have an MBA? Measuring the similarities between police executives and private security managers in terms of professionalization is an important element in determining the private sector's effect on policing.

So far I have discussed several indicators demonstrating that a certain form of isomorphism is occurring between public and private actors in the security industry. I have sought also to identify directions for future research that would make it possible to measure more accurately how far this isomorphism has progressed.

Sources of Resistance

Having discussed the several signs of institutional isomorphism in the field of policing, it is important that we recognize the main sources of resistance to this relatively radical change, two of which I present below.

The first source of resistance, and the most important one in my opinion, is found among police officers, who will suffer the biggest loss if the divide between public and private policing decreases since most of their prestige comes from their exclusive (and centralized) position in the field. A study done by Clarke et al. (2007) compared law enforcement to health care and education and found that police officers – unlike police executives – are the least open to a clientelist approach, even if most citizens seem to find this type of relationship acceptable. Institutional isomorphism might be seen as going against the culture that characterizes field agents, notably their isolation and suspicion of the outside world (Cockcroft & Beattie, 2009).

The second source of resistance, which might come as more of a surprise, is among private security managers. Clearly, they are happy to have the chance to take over a new area in the security market: for example, when police stopped transporting detainees, the private security industry immediately stepped in to offer its services. However, my research has also shown that they want to maintain a social distinction between themselves and police (Mulone & Dupont, 2008a). In fact, rather than placing themselves directly in competition with police, most of the security managers whom I interviewed highlighted their distinct expertise as well as their inability (and unwillingness) to take on the job of police. In trying to demonstrate their uniqueness, they are attempting to preserve their distinct position in the field of policing (Mulone & Dupont, 2008b). It is also possible that they do not want to take on the public sector's responsibilities.

Resistance to institutional isomorphism seems to be situated at different levels within public and private organizations; more importantly, it is found where the power is – higher in the hierarchy for the private sector and at the level of field agents for public police. Indeed, if the majority of power in private companies is still held by senior managers, then the inverse is true for police organizations, in which field agents often possess a great deal of autonomy, what Monjardet (1996) called "hierarchical inversion." It is through this extended discretion, one of the distinctive traits of the profession, that police officers interpret and redefine the "orders" and organizational strategies presented to them, really deciding what is done as police work. On the contrary, in private security companies, as well as in house security departments, a more classical top-down power structure (from boss to employee) persists. Thus, resistance within each type of organization at the level with the most power suggests that there are major obstacles that can slow, or even potentially block, isomorphism.

That said, such resistance cannot eliminate on its own the forces pushing toward greater similarity among the various actors in policing. I have proposed a new theoretical framework that can be used to analyze the evolving relationships between police and private security and, more generally, to identify the changes taking place in the governance of security. This framework can be tested empirically through the use of indicators specific to each form of isomorphism (mimetic, coercive, normative) and for each type of actor (private or public) as well as each level of operation (executive or field). In addition, the structures, processes, and behaviours discussed above could be analyzed, as could those of other actors in the field of policing.

One of the consequences of institutional isomorphism in policing will be to weaken even more the already shaky public/private dichotomy as a tool to understand and describe the field of policing. If, in my opinion, it remains a useful distinction, this might not be the case in the future, considering that similarities should continue to grow between the sectors. Perhaps other dichotomies (normative versus instrumental logic, nature of the targeted customer, etc.) will then become more valid to analyze security in criminology. Fairly certain, however, is that the dynamics of isomorphism presented in this chapter will affect significantly the centrality of "public" police in the field of policing.

Conclusion

By applying the concept of institutional isomorphism to the vast field of policing, I have tried to put forth some new ideas about the institutional changes occurring in the field rather than describe the new configurations of contemporary security governance. My focus is on determining why (and to what extent) the similarities among the various actors in the field are likely to increase.

I hope that this chapter will encourage further research. An empirical evaluation of institutional isomorphism that establishes specific criteria and indicators, making it possible to test various aspects, is needed, as is close analysis of legislative reforms (for both police and private security industries), to evaluate trends in coercive isomorphism. Studies of training programs offered in the private sector (certifications being developed, classes being offered, new skills being marketed, etc.) could provide useful data on the normative isomorphism occurring between private security and police.

Increases in institutional isomorphism would have a profound impact on the field of policing. For example, growing similarities would tend to increase competition among the actors in this field, and such dynamics would have tremendous consequences for how security is governed, strengthening the influence of the market (Zedner, 2006a). Increased isomorphism would also affect the security of citizens, how monitored, protected, and "safe," they are – a preoccupation when discussing contemporary changes and the future of security governance.

Finally, from a theoretical perspective, there is another important question that I could not explore in this chapter because of space constraints. Institutional isomorphism theory suggests that, for any given organizational field, there is usually a central institution that all actors try to mimic, somewhat like a centre of gravity that serves as a reference point for all other objects (DiMaggio & Powell, 1983, p. 153). In the field of policing, this central institution has yet to be determined. In terms of symbolic power, public police are clearly in a desirable position, and it is tempting to see them as the "centre of gravity." However, several observations in this chapter suggest that police are also "moving" toward another model. Identifying this model, which seems to be situated somewhere between police (for their legitimacy) and private security companies (for their presumed flexibility and dependence on the market), could provide some insights into where the field of policing is headed.

Notes

1 Private security existed well before the 1980s. What was new, however, was its increasing expansion and visibility, which caught the attention of academics.
2 I employ the concepts of public and private policing in this chapter in a relatively restrictive way. By "public policing" (or simply "police"), I refer only to public law enforcement organizations (local, regional, or national). I exclude international organizations, which lead to questions outside the scope of this chapter, such as the privatization of war and private military companies. By "private policing" or "private security," I refer to both private companies that provide security products and services for a fee and security departments within companies (usually referred to as corporate security).

3 "Organizations are not only in competition for resources and clients, they are also driven by the pursuit of power and legitimacy. To gain this legitimacy, organizations invent myths about themselves, participate in symbolic activities, and create stories that contribute to their survival and institutionalization. The political components, or organizational rituals, thus outweigh the pursuit of effectiveness. The definitions of performance for these organizations are socially constructed because, to survive, they do not necessarily adopt the most appropriate practices for the economic requirements of that time but rather those that appear the most socially acceptable" (Huault, 2009, p. 123; my translation).

References
Association of Chief Police Officers. (2003). *A guide to income generation for the police in England and Wales*. Association of Chief Police Officers of England, Wales, and Northern Ireland.
Ayling, J., Grabosky, P., & Shearing, C. (2009). *Lengthening the arm of the law*. Cambridge University Press.
Beckert, J. (2010). Institutional isomorphism revisited: Convergence and divergence in institutional change. *Sociological Theory, 28*(2), 150–166.
Brodeur, J.-P. (2010). *The policing web*. Oxford University Press.
Burruss, G. W., & Giblin, M. J. (2014). Modeling isomorphism on policing innovation: The role of institutional pressures in adopting community-oriented policing. *Crime and Delinquency, 60*(3), 331–355.
Button, M. (2007). Assessing the regulation of private security across Europe. *European Journal of Criminology, 4*(1), 109–128.
Chan, J. (1996). Changing police culture. *British Journal of Criminology, 36*(1), 109–134.
Clarke, J., Newman, J., Smith, N., Vidler, E., & Westmarland, L. (2007). *Creating citizen consumers: Changing publics and changing public services*. SAGE.
Cockcroft, T., & Beattie, I. (2009). Shifting cultures: Managerialism and the rise of "performance." *Policing: An International Journal of Police Strategies and Management, 32*(3), 526–540.
Connors, E., Cunningham, W., Ohlhausen, P. E., Oliver, L., & van Meter, C. (2000). *Operation cooperation: Guidelines for partnerships between law enforcement and private security organizations*. Prepared for the Bureau of Justice Assistance, US Department of Justice. http://www.ilj.org/publications/docs/Operation_Cooperation.pdf
Cook, P. J., & MacDonald, J. (2011). Public safety through private actions: An economic assessment of BIDs. *The Economic Journal, 121*, 445–462.
Cooper, J. A. (2014). *In search of police legitimacy: Territoriality, isomorphism, and changes in policing practices*. LFB Scholarly Publishing.
Council of Canadian Academies. (2014). *Policing Canada in the 21st century: New policing for new challenges*. The Expert Panel on the Future of Canadian Policing Models, Council of Canadian Academies. https://www.scienceadvice.ca/wp-content/uploads/2018/10/policing_fullreporten.pdf
Crawford, A., & Lister, S. (2004). *The extended policing family: Visible patrols in residential areas*. Joseph Rowntree Foundation.

Délégation interministérielle à la sécurité privée. (2012). *La sécurité privée en Espagne*. Rapport de mission pour le Ministère de l'Intérieur. http://www.interieur.gouv.fr/Le-ministere/Organisation/Delegation-aux-cooperations-de-securite/La-securite-privee/Missions-de-la-delegation-a-l-etranger

DiMaggio, P. J., & Powell, W. W. (1983). The iron cage revisited: Institutional isomorphism and collective rationality in organizational fields. *American Sociological Review*, *48*(2), 147–160.

Dupont, B. (2003). Évaluer ce que fait la police: L'exemple australien. *Criminologie*, *36*(1), 103–120.

Dupont, B. (2006a). Delivering security through networks: Surveying the relational landscape of security managers in an urban setting. *Crime, Law and Social Change*, *45*(3), 165–184.

Dupont, B. (2006b). Power struggles in the field of security: Implications for democratic transformation. In J. Wood & B. Dupont (Eds.), *Democracy, society and the governance of security* (pp. 86–110). Cambridge University Press.

Dupont, B. (2014). Private security regimes: Conceptualizing the forces that shape the private delivery of security. *Theoretical Criminology*, *18*(3), 263–281.

Fleming, J., & Scott, A. (2008). Performance measurement in Australian police organizations. *Policing: A Journal of Policy and Practice*, *2*(3), 322–330.

Gans, J. (2000). Privately paid public policing: Law and practice. *Policing and Society*, *10*(2), 183–206.

Giblin, M. J. (2006). Structural elaboration and institutional isomorphism: The case of crime analysis units. *Policing: An International Journal of Police Strategies and Management*, *29*(4), 643–664.

Goffman, E. (1959). *The presentation of self in everyday life*. Doubleday.

Graham, S., & Marvin, S. (2001). *Splintering urbanism: Networked infrastructures, technological mobilities and the urban condition*. Routledge.

Huault, I. (2009). P. DiMaggio et W. Powell: Des organisations en quête de légitimité. In S. Charreire Petit & I. Huault (Eds.), *Les grands auteurs en management* (2nd ed., pp. 119–134). Éditions Management et Société.

Huey, L., Ericson, R. V., & Haggerty, K. D. (2005). Policing fantasy city. In D. Cooley (Ed.), *Re-imagining policing in Canada* (pp. 140–208). University of Toronto Press.

Hunton, P., Jones, A., & Baker, P. (2009). New development: Performance management in a UK police force. *Public Money and Management*, *29*(3), 195–200.

Johnston, L. (1992). *The rebirth of private policing*. Routledge.

Johnston, L., & Shearing, C. (2003). *Governing security: Explorations in policing and justice*. Routledge.

Jones, T., & Newburn, T. (1998). *Private security and public policing*. Clarendon Press.

Jones, T., & Newburn, T. (2006). *Plural policing: A comparative perspective*. Routledge.

Kempa, M. A., Stenning, P., & Wood, J. (2004). Policing communal spaces: A reconfiguration of the "mass private property" hypothesis. *The British Journal of Criminology*, *44*(4), 562–581.

Kiedrowski, J., Petrunik, M., MacDonald, T., & Melchers, R. (2013). *Canadian police board views on the use of police performance metrics*. Public Safety Canada.

The Law Enforcement–Private Security Consortium. (2009). *Operation Partnership: Trends and practices in law enforcement and private security collaborations*. US Department of Justice, Office of Community Oriented Policing Services.

Lippert, R. (2012). "Clean and safe" passage: Business improvement districts, urban security modes, and knowledge brokers. *European Urban and Regional Studies, 19*(2), 167–180.

Lippert, R., & Walby, K. (2013). Police moonlighting revisited: The case of "pay duty" in three Canadian police services. *Policing: A Journal of Policy and Practice, 7*(4), 370–378.

Loader, I. (1999). Consumer culture and the commodification of policing and security. *Sociology, 33*(2), 373–392.

Loader, I., & Walker, N. (2001). Policing as a public good: Reconstituting the connections between policing and the state. *Theoretical Criminology, 5*(1), 9–35.

Maguire, E., & Mastrofski, R. (2000). Patterns of community policing in the United States. *Police Quarterly, 3*(4), 4–45.

Manning, P. (2008). Performance rituals. *Policing: A Journal of Policy and Practice, 2*(3), 284–293.

McLeod, R. (2002). *Parapolice: A revolution in the business of law enforcement*. Boheme Press.

Monjardet, D. (1996). *Ce que fait la police: Sociologie de la force publique*. La Découverte.

Morabito, A., & Greenberg, S. (2005). *Engaging the private sector to promote homeland security: Law enforcement–private security partnerships*. US Department of Justice, Bureau of Justice Assistance.

Mulone, M. (2012). When private and public policing merge: Thoughts on commercial policing. *Social Justice, 38*(1–2), 165–183.

Mulone, M. (2013). Researching private security consumption. *European Journal on Criminal Policy and Research, 19*(4), 401–417.

Mulone, M. (2016). The politics of private security: No force and no legitimacy? In M. Deflem (Ed.), *The politics of policing: Between force and legitimacy* (pp. 277–293). Emerald.

Mulone, M., & Dupont, B. (2008a). Saisir la sécurité privée: Quand l'état, l'industrie et la police négocient un nouveau cadre de régulation. *Criminologie, 41*(1), 103–132.

Mulone, M., & Dupont, B. (2008b). Gouvernance de la sécurité et capital: Les gestionnaires de la sécurité privée. *Déviance et société, 32*(1), 21–42.

Nalla, M., & Newman, G. (1991). Public versus private control: A reassessment. *Journal of Criminal Justice, 19*, 537–547.

Ocqueteau, F., & Pichon, P. (2008). *La sécurité publique à l'épreuve de la LOLF*. Rapport de recherche. CERSA-CNRS.

Paulin, C. (2017). *Vers une politique publique de la sécurité privée? Réguler la sécurité privée (1983–2014)* [Unpublished PhD dissertation]. Université Paris Saclay.

Police Executive Research Forum. (2013). *Policing and the economic downturn: Striving for efficiency is the new normal.* https://www.policeforum.org/assets/docs/Critical_Issues_Series/policing%20and%20the%20economic%20downturn%20-%20striving%20for%20efficiency%20is%20the%20new%20normal%202013.pdf

Powell, W. W., & DiMaggio, P. J. (1991). *The new institutionalism in organizational analysis.* University of Chicago Press.

Prenzler, T. (2005). Mapping the Australian security industry. *Security Journal, 18*(4), 51–64.

Ransom, J. (2012, August 10). More residents hiring private security as police budgets are cut. *The Daily News.* https://www.securitymagazine.com/articles/83387-more-residents-hire-private-security-during-police-budget-cuts

Reiner, R. (1985). *The politics of the police.* Wheatsheaf.

Reiss, A. (1988). *Private employment of public police.* National Institute of Justice.

Rigakos, G. S. (2002). *The new parapolice: Risk markets and commodified social control.* University of Toronto Press.

Salkeld, L. (2009, August 7). Neighbours hire their own police force for £3 each a week. *The Daily Mail.* http://www.dailymail.co.uk/news/article-1204819/Neighbours-hire-police-force-3-week.html

Shearing, C., & Stenning, P. (1985). From the panopticon to Disney World: The development of discipline. In A. N. Doob & E. L. Greenspan (Eds.), *Perspectives in criminal law* (pp. 335–49). Canada Law Book.

Shearing, C., & Wood, J. (2000). Reflections on the governance of security: A normative inquiry. *Police Practice, 1*(4), 457–476.

Singh, A. M., & Light, M. (2019). Constraints on the growth of private policing: A comparative international analysis. *Theoretical Criminology, 23*(3), 295–314. https://doi.org/10.1177/1362480617733727

Terpstra, J., & Trommel, W. (2009). Police, managerialization and presentational strategies. *Policing: An International Journal of Police Strategies and Management, 32*(1), 128–143.

Tiwana, N., Bass, G., & Farrell, G. (2015). Police performance measurement: An annotated bibliography. *Crime Science, 4*(1), 1–28. https://doi.org/10.1186/s40163-014-0011-4

Travis, A., & Jowit, J. (2012, March 4). Police privatisation plans defended by senior officers. *The Guardian.* http://www.theguardian.com/uk/2012/mar/04/police-privatisation-plans-defend-acpo

Valverde, M. (2001). Governing security, governing through security. In R. Daniels, P. Macklem, & K. Roach (Eds.), *The security of freedom: Essays on Canada's anti-terrorism bill* (pp. 83–92). University of Toronto Press.

Vindevogel, F. (2004). Les municipalités favorisent-elles l'émergence de polices privées? *Déviance et société, 28*(4), 507–532.

White, A. (2012). The new political economy of private security. *Theoretical Criminology, 16*(1), 85–101.

White, B. (2009, April 21). Cash-strapped cities try private guards over police. *The Wall Street Journal.* http://www.wsj.com/articles/SB124027127337237011

Zedner, L. (2006a). Liquid security: Managing the market for crime control. *Criminology and Criminal Justice, 6*(3), 267–288.

Zedner, L. (2006b). Policing before and after the police. *British Journal of Criminology, 46*(1), 78–96.

2

Private Policing of Images in Canada

STEVEN KOHM

Introduction

The circulation of sexually explicit images of children online gained attention in the 1990s alongside public awareness and use of the internet (Jenkins, 2001). However, this was only the latest development in a much longer history of concerns about harms to children going back as far as the nineteenth century (Batista & Johnson, 2017). Joel Best (1987, 1990) has argued that concerns about threats to children gained new momentum through the 1970s and were well established in the 1980s; the popularization of the internet was just the latest technological development to amplify these pre-existing anxieties. Philip Jenkins (1992, 1996, 1998, 2001) has described the moral panic about exploited children that characterized this time period. In the 1980s and 1990s, dramatic stories about ritual abuse in schools and daycare centres, international pedophile rings, and abusive satanic cults were circulated in the media and propagated by politicians and moral entrepreneurs. Popular culture reflected and amplified these fears through literature, fictional film, and TV representations of these various claims about threats to children, increasing public misperceptions about so-called stranger-danger (Kohm, 2017; Kohm & Greenhill, 2011).

At the same time, the broader culture underpinning the criminal justice apparatus was shifting to emphasize risk mitigation, punishment, and control – and the shadowy figure of the pedophile as a monstrous stranger in our midst became a lightning rod within this new penal culture, spawning symbolic laws named after prominent child victims as well as sex offender registration and notification schemes (Garland, 2001). It was within this broader cultural context in the late twentieth century that a small group of predominantly white, middle-class women established a registered charity in Winnipeg, Manitoba, devoted to saving children from exploitation and harm. Premised on the idea that children were endangered by threats emanating predominantly from outside the imagined community, this group offered a means of defence against society's worst fears. In time, this group evolved into a private policing entity charged under federal and provincial legislation with responding to online sexual exploitation of children – and eventually adults – in Canada. In this chapter, I present findings from an exploratory study of this child-saving organization and its improbable rise to become a key player in Canada's national strategy for policing child sexual exploitation online.

In what follows, I present an overview of the establishment and evolution of the Canadian Centre for Child Protection (C3P[1]), its relationship with state policing agencies and corporations, and the recent expansion of its mandate to include sexually explicit images of adults under Manitoba's so-called revenge porn statute. Drawing from data collected as part of a multimethod exploratory study, including in-depth interviews with C3P directors and board members, news media stories, and reports generated by the centre itself, I reflect on how C3P has framed the issue of sexual exploitation online while acting as a powerful intermediary between the state and civil society. I argue that the activities of C3P have moved beyond simply acting as an information clearinghouse or providing support to those affected by the sexual exploitation of children. I demonstrate that C3P is engaged in activities alongside and at times in place of state agencies of law enforcement, including the proactive investigation of sexualized images of youth and, more recently, adults under Manitoba's new revenge porn statute. Interviews with directors and board members reveal an ambiguous and at times murky distinction between their activities and those of law enforcement agencies. These issues are brought to life in three distinct themes evident in interviews with key C3P informants. I describe how C3P invokes a spatial metaphor to justify its work and the continual need to expand its mandate into new areas currently underserviced by public authorities. I then describe how partnerships unfold between C3P and other societal sectors and how these partnerships sometimes involve appeals to its privileged position close to the state, whereas at other times it is framed as being at arm's length from public police. Finally, I explicate a precautionary logic of the private policing of images online that emphasizes the importance of acting in the absence of clear information about risk. This departs from the more typical risk-based, loss-prevention orientation of many other forms of private policing. I conclude the chapter by reflecting on some of the conceptual and theoretical implications of this case study.

A Brief History of Child Saving in Manitoba

Echoing nineteenth-century child-saving movements and the involvement of private charities in social welfare provision and advocacy (Batista & Johnson, 2017), C3P originated three decades ago in Winnipeg as Child Find Manitoba, a grassroots, volunteer-run, charitable organization established in the aftermath of the city's most infamous child murder. In the early 1980s, as worldwide attention was shifting to the issue of missing and exploited children (Best, 1987, 1990), Winnipeg was gripped by the disappearance of thirteen-year-old Candace Derksen. After weeks of intense media focus and fruitless searching by police and volunteers, Candace was eventually discovered bound and murdered in an industrial district near her home in November 1984. The abduction and murder of Candace by a stranger was a significant touchstone in the city's history and represented for many a collective loss of innocence.[2] Following the disappearance of her daughter, Wilma Derksen led the charge to "build an organization that can work with police and community leaders to help to protect children and to help families deal with similar tragedies" ("Centre," 2015). Child Find Manitoba was established as a registered charity and operated locally in Manitoba through the 1980s and 1990s, providing support to families of missing children, educational resources for the general public, and thousands of ID booklets for local children containing fingerprints and photographs as an aid for police in investigating an abduction. Although few could find fault with Child Find Manitoba's primary mission to prevent abductions of children, its efforts focused attention on abductions by strangers, statistically much rarer than abuse at the hands of intimates and family members. In this way, the organization emerged as a key claims maker in the social construction of child sexual abuse as a particular social problem requiring particular solutions. The activities of Child Find Manitoba (and later C3P) involved a variety of claims-making strategies via local and national media to frame the issue and assert its authority as an expert on the subject (Kohm, 2019).

The work of Child Find Manitoba took on a new level of urgency with the increasing public use of the internet in the late 1990s. In May 2001, Manitoba established the Children Online Protection Committee with the aim of developing a tip line for reporting child exploitation on the internet. The committee was chaired by Executive Director of Child Find Manitoba Lianna McDonald and reflected the grassroots, voluntary ethos of the organization. The committee was composed of "police, teachers and even computer repair specialists, who will work to find ways to combat on-line crimes against children" ("Manitoba Group," 2001). This led to the establishment of Cybertip.ca as a pilot project operated by Child Find Manitoba, "Canada's first cyber tip line" ("Canada's First," 2002).

In May 2004, Cybertip.ca was recognized in Canada's National Strategy for the Protection of Children from Sexual Exploitation on the Internet. This national-level recognition attracted increased funding and support from police and technology companies from across Canada. Child Find Manitoba was renamed the Canadian Centre for Child Protection in 2006, better positioning the charity as a national-level organization. In 2009, Manitoba amended its Child and Family Services Act to include child pornography in its definition of child abuse and made it mandatory to report child pornography to Cybertip.ca for assessment (C3P, 2012, p. 35). On December 8, 2011, Parliament passed Bill C-22, An Act Respecting the Mandatory Reporting of Internet Child Pornography by Persons Who Provide an Internet Service, and designated Cybertip.ca as the official reporting agency for online child pornography (C3P, 2012, p. 35). Under Manitoba's 2016 revenge porn statute – The Intimate Image Protection Act – C3P was authorized as the agency responsible for receiving requests for assistance and providing support. In one of the first cases litigated under the act, the lawsuit sought damages for both the alleged adult victim and C3P (Nicholson & Kubinec, 2018). Consequently, C3P has become positioned squarely between the state and civil society. Although non-profits and charities have been involved in federal and provincial corrections service delivery for several decades, C3P is emerging as a service provider for adult and child victims of internet sexual exploitation. Moreover, I argue that C3P is doing work that can be conceived broadly as the policing of online images. Its work is intimately linked with the government via federal and provincial statutes that empower C3P to act as a state agent. Before moving to my methodology and findings, I discuss scholarly perspectives and statistics on internet sex offences involving children.

Child Abuse and Exploitation on the Internet

Majid Yar (2013) points out that, of all online crimes, internet sex offences involving children generate the most political and public attention. He distinguishes between "interpersonal" and "representational" child-oriented sex offences (Yar, 2006, p. 112, 131). "Interpersonal" offences refer to sexually oriented communications between adults and minors online and can include attempts to "lure" or "groom" minors for physical sexual abuse. "Representational" offences include the production, consumption, and circulation of child pornography images online (Yar, 2013, p. 484). More recently, a number of other activities involving the online sexual exploitation of children have emerged. For example, "sextortion" – which involves individuals threatening and extorting minors for sexually explicit images – blurs the line between interpersonal and representational offences and perhaps constitutes a hybrid category. Additionally, cyber bullying, "sexting," and self/peer exploitation have gained prominence as new categories of child-oriented sex offences occurring via internet and mobile communication technologies (Karaian, 2014, 2015). Importantly, non-governmental organizations such as C3P have been at the forefront of defining and drawing public attention to these new online offences.

Child-luring offences were added to the Criminal Code of Canada in 2002. The new provisions make it "illegal to communicate with children over the internet for the purpose of committing a sexual offence" (Department of Justice, 2002, cited in Loughlin & Taylor-Butts, 2009, p. 6). Additionally, in 2002, Canada amended its Criminal Code to include specifically use of the internet for the purpose of committing child pornography offences (Loughlin & Taylor-Butts, 2009, p. 8). However, the extent of these crimes is difficult to gauge using official statistics. Rates of police-reported child luring tend to be low, "about 3 incidents of child luring per 100,000 youth under the age of 18," and clearance rates were low, with charges laid or recommended in only three of ten reported incidents (Loughlin & Taylor-Butts, 2009, p. 7). Yar (2013, p. 484) similarly notes low reported rates in the United Kingdom, with only "a few dozen" charges laid per year. Official police statistics do not necessarily reflect the true extent of the problem. Nevertheless, police reported that incidents of internet child luring in Canada rose between 2002 and 2007 (Loughlin & Taylor-Butts, 2009, p. 8), likely because of increased levels of public awareness and the establishment of Cybertip.ca in 2005. Notably, the director of Cybertip.ca told me that the vast majority (95 percent) of tips received are related to child pornography rather than online luring or grooming.

Representational offences continue to be the most common internet sex offences involving children in Canada. According to police statistics from 2017, there were 6,521 reported incidents of child pornography comprising a rate of 18 per 100,000, with no discernible increase over the previous year (Allen, 2018, p. 18). In the same year, there were 1,310 reported incidents of internet luring of children by telecommunications, a slight increase over the 1,295 incidents reported in 2016 (Allen, 2018, p. 18; Keighley, 2017, p. 20). The difference between reported online sex-oriented crimes involving children and the unknown actual volume of such offences – the so-called dark figure – has become a point of contention for child-saving advocates at C3P that plays out both in the media and in the organization's reports that raise concerns about the extent of the activity (Kohm, 2019). C3P's annual *Social Value Report* depicts the scope of the problem as "alarming":

> It is through our work in operating Cybertip.ca over the past 13 years that our agency has witnessed the growing proliferation of child sexual abuse on the internet. The misuse of technology has accelerated the propagation of child pornography, normalized the sexualization of children, and made it abundantly easier for offenders to actively participate in this illegal behaviour. Children under 12 are particularly vulnerable and the number of reports to the tip line with children in this age range continues to grow at an alarming rate. (C3P, 2014–15, p. 4)

The claims about the extent of the problem stem from the tips that the centre receives. Consequently, the framing of the problem in C3P's annual reports is a direct outcome of the organization's efforts at mobilizing the general public. C3P's role as a clearinghouse for public tips has led its directors to characterize its operations as "a neighbourhood watch for the internet" ("Manitoba Leads Fight," 2005). Invoking the idea of a police and public partnership, Cybertip.ca positioned itself as a neutral intermediary between police and the general public. Then, on January 17, 2017, C3P announced a new automated approach to gathering information about online sex abuse images. Project Arachnid is "an automated system that searches for child sexual abuse material and detects where the images and videos are publicly available on the internet" ("Online," 2017). Shifting from being an aggregator of public reports to using a high-tech web crawler or "superbot" (Martin, 2017) to search proactively for child pornography using photo DNA moves the organization conceptually closer to a policing function and ramps up the volume of incidents that it generates and presents in its annual *Social Value Report*.

C3P's *Social Value Report* for 2016–17, published prior to Project Arachnid, recorded 40,251 reports of online sexual exploitation of children, a 6 percent increase over the previous fiscal year. In the next reporting period, spanning 2017–18, C3P recorded a staggering 139,897 incidents, a 248 percent increase over the previous year. However, 70 percent (97,752) of these incidents were discovered by the proactive work of Project Arachnid, whereas in the same reporting period public reports via Cybertip.ca had increased by less than 5 percent. Although the numbers reported by C3P are characterized as large and growing, the net result of these reports – either self-generated or received from the public – is a tiny number of tangible actions by public police. The 2017–18 *Social Value Report* notes just nine arrests related to Cybertip.ca reports and five children removed from abusive environments. As a proportion of all public tips and reports generated by proactive work, this represents an extremely low clearance rate. However, such small numbers are usually buttressed by compelling personal anecdotes of children saved, inviting the view that all of this monitoring is well worth it if even just one child is saved.

None of the above is meant to suggest that the issue of child exploitation online is anything but a serious issue warranting a thorough response by state law enforcement agencies. Instead, I argue that the nature and extent of the problem of internet sex crimes involving children are contested and subject to competing constructions by groups such as C3P dedicated to raising awareness, lobbying for new laws, and seeking expanded funding for their endeavours (Kohm, 2019). Additionally, the activities of C3P have moved beyond simply providing supports or resources to those affected by the sexual exploitation of children. C3P, in fact, is carrying out activities alongside and at times in place of state agencies of law enforcement. In doing so, C3P and other organizations provide "evidence of Garland's assertion that '[t]he Central state [is] seeking to act upon crime not in a direct fashion through state agencies (police, courts, prisons, social workers) but instead by acting indirectly, seeking to activate action on the part of non-state agencies and organizations'" (Garland, 1996, p. 452, as cited in Karaian, 2014, p. 284).

Partnering to Police the Image

David Garland (2001, p. 170) suggests that the late modern criminal justice field has seen the development of a "third 'governmental' sector" concerned with prevention and security. This third sector is composed of numerous public-private partnerships involving police, community groups, non-profit organizations, and private corporations. Many grey areas of public-private policing have evolved during this period, and a range of scholarly analyses of this phenomenon has followed. For example, business improvement districts (BIDs) across North America and beyond deploy private/volunteer security teams to police public streets and sidewalks, often coordinating with public law enforcement agencies by acting as their eyes and ears (e.g., Mackinnon, this volume; Mulone, this volume; Sleiman & Lippert, 2010). Another example of this shift was provided by Shearing and Stenning (1981, 1983), who suggested that the rise of "mass private property" – shopping malls, public sporting facilities, university campuses, et cetera – has given rise to new forms of policing that fall into a murky grey zone between public and private. Policing has become more diffuse, blurs public and private forms of social control, and is informed to varying degrees by both moral (justice) and instrumental (prevention) logics/objectives (Shearing & Stenning, 1985). Stenning (2000, p. 327) argued that the rise of neo-liberal configurations of the state have significantly redefined and blurred the roles of public and private policing, so it is "fruitless and unconvincing" to draw distinctions between them. Studies of private influence in criminal justice have demonstrated that there is "hardly any police and criminal justice function imaginable that cannot be performed by a private security company" (van Steden & de Waard, 2013, p. 295). However, as Luscombe et al. note in the introduction to this volume, privatization is a "nebulous and troubling process that reshapes criminal justice institutions in ways that are antidemocratic and profit motivated." Indeed, this chapter demonstrates how private influence in the criminal justice system – even with the best of intentions – can lead to the erosion of transparency and accountability (Ayling & Shearing, 2008; Löfstrand et al., 2018; Stenning, 2000).

The case study explored in this chapter provides empirical support to the two broad conceptual concerns of this volume. First, the work of C3P in policing images online amounts to a form of *privatization*, "whole or partial outsourcing of public services to private entities" or "de-governmentalization or load-shedding" (Luscombe et al., this volume). Second, through a concerted strategy of carefully orchestrated media events, visual marketing campaigns, and political manoeuvring, C3P has also emerged as a powerful force for *private influence* in the criminal justice apparatus in Canada, affecting legal and policy changes in issues of privacy and obscenity law in Canada. This case study demonstrates that private policing extends beyond protection of private property and subsumes activities that were viewed at one time as the domain of public policing (e.g., O'Reilly, 2015; Rigakos, 2002). Moreover, the direct involvement of technology and telecommunication companies in the governance of the internet suggests that policing online sexual abuse is evidence of the corporatization of policing through public-private integration (Brownlee et al., 2018, p. 11). Although Yar (2013) contends that policing child sexual abuse remains firmly within the purview of public law enforcement, trends in the pluralized policing of child sexual abuse in Canada demonstrate increasing private influence in an activity defined by moral rather than instrumental logics.

Huey et al. (2012, p. 82) argue that much of the policing of the internet occurs through "collaborative relations" among four "nodal clusters" of actors: the government, law enforcement, private industry, and the general public. Within this collaboration, there is a significant role for members of the general public as concerned citizens or vigilante actors (Huey et al., 2012). Jewkes and Andrews (2005, pp. 42–43) describe a "joined up" approach to policing cyberspace that involves many agencies and bodies beyond state police forces, embodying "a pluralistic endeavour, encompassing a wide range of different bodies." Yar (2013, p. 488) argues that policing of internet offences has come to exemplify "a transition in the organization of policing and crime control away from state-centric and 'top down' action to a more diversified array of activity that encompasses a range of quasi- and non-state actors (including commercial bodies, charities, voluntary organisations, citizen-focused 'partnerships' and individual citizens and their families)." Campbell (2016, p. 346) similarly notes that "the policing of paedophilia involves a plethora of policing actors working across and within a multi-sited, mixed economy of sectoral interests" and that this is indicative of "a shift to 'plural,' 'nodal,' 'dispersed,' 'distributed,' 'multilateral,' 'post-regulatory' and 'networked' policing." Importantly, Campbell suggests, this shift allows for greater involvement of the general public in various ways in the policing of sex offenders on the internet. This can include a range of involvement, from concerned citizens reporting malfeasance to individuals or groups taking vigilante action to root out and punish putative offenders using tactics such as public humiliation (Kohm, 2009).

Yar (2013, p. 489) suggests that "a distributed and pluralized 'assemblage' of internet policing and crime control is evident in the configuration of responses to online sexual offences." In particular, he notes "a 'multi-tiered order maintenance assemblage of networks and nodes of security' that seek to direct, regulate, constrain and control online behavior." This unfolds in three ways.

First, telecommunication, internet, and social media providers are compelled to adopt a pre-emptive logic that seeks to identify and forestall potential risks before online offences occur. Yar (2013, p. 489) notes, as examples, that "in 2009 the US-based social networking site Myspace removed 90,000 US based users from its service, having identified them as known sex offenders," and that "in 2009 the social media platform Facebook disabled the accounts of almost 2800 registered sex offenders resident in New York alone, identifying individuals by running its user lists against official offender databases." Similarly, websites that facilitate transactions between consumers such as Craigslist and Kijiji have removed commercial sex advertisements under pressure by groups such as C3P that claim they are facilitating sexual exploitation of children (Sharkey, 2016). This sort of pre-emptive action is increasingly compelled by legal statutes that make ISPs and social media hubs responsible for the content that they host (Yar, 2013).

Second, internet users themselves are mobilized to "generate flows of information and 'actionable intelligence' about sexual offences which can then be utilized by intermediaries" (Yar, 2013, p. 489). This second "strand" of the security assemblage has been "institutionalized" in tip lines like the one operated by the Internet Watch Foundation (IWF) in the United Kingdom, a charitable organization set up by the internet industry (Yar, 2013, p. 489). In Canada, Cybertip.ca fulfills this role and operates ostensibly at arm's length from the state (Kohm, 2019). Yar (2013, p. 490) notes that this second strand is important in understanding how the security assemblage situates policing of internet crimes (and images) at a distance from the state and state agencies of law enforcement:

> This system of intervention to remove criminal content (involving users, private sector bodies and ISPs) effectively bypasses direct involvement of state actors, creating instead a crime control "assemblage" from which the public police are situated "at a distance" (at most, the police will receive information from organisations like the IWF so as to consider whether it may be possible to identify, arrest and charge those responsible for sharing the offending content online).

Third, Yar's framework of the security assemblage directly implicates individuals and potential victims of sexual crimes on the internet; this involves "the responsibilization of users themselves, especially families and parents of children deemed to be at risk from online sexual predation and harm" (2013, p. 490). The educational programs offered by C3P exemplify this strategy of responsibilization. Public information campaigns by C3P target youth and parents and focus on a range of activities, including teen sexting and self/peer exploitation, which C3P frames as harmful and "necessitating a child protectionist and criminal law response" (Karaian, 2015, p. 338). Importantly, these educational campaigns suggest that responsible personal conduct is vital to prevent child exploitation. Careless activity by parents, for example, in sharing images of their children online can lead to tragedy (Kohm, 2019). In this way, C3P attempts to activate behaviour in citizens that aligns with the state's objective to promote the watchful prevention of crimes and risky behaviours by potential victims.

An analysis of the policing of images of child sexual exploitation must therefore consider this complex, "'multi-tiered order maintenance assemblage of networks and nodes of security' that seek to direct, regulate, constrain and control online behavior." This corresponds to what Luscombe et al. (this volume) refer to as *operational networks*, a major theme characterizing the role of private actors in the criminal justice system. The work of C3P with the state, corporations, and civil society typifies a blurred or hybrid approach to criminal justice that has become more prominent in Canada in recent years (Luscombe & Walby, 2014; Murphy, 2007). I turn now to a discussion of some findings from my exploratory work with C3P.

Gaining Access to the Field

At the outset of this research project, I was interested in C3P because of my broader research agenda focusing on the representation of pedophiles and child sex abusers in visual popular culture. I was struck by the highly visual nature of public awareness campaigns by C3P and Cybertip.ca. My initial research focus was on the use of highly evocative images by C3P in its campaigns to activate behaviour by ordinary citizens. However, as the project took shape, I quickly became interested equally in the ambiguous link between the organization and state authorities. It seemed to me that C3P epitomized the type of policing and prevention activity that exists at the nexus of public and private – the embodiment of Garland's "third sector" and Yar's "multi-tiered order [security and] maintenance assemblage." As I prepared to enter the field, I narrowed my focus to the nature of the partnerships and linkages between C3P and the state to understand better the evolution of policing and security more generally as well as to contribute to our understanding of the policing of images of child sexual abuse.

I proposed a series of open-ended interviews with senior staff and board members of C3P and Cybertip.ca. I submitted an ethics protocol to my Institutional Review Board (IRB) for these key informant interviews. The IRB waived the formal ethics protocol in my case because I was seeking information about the organization rather than personal experiences or sensitive information about employees. So interviewees were simply to provide information as spokespersons for the organization with no expectation of confidentiality or anonymity. Because of the highly sensitive work of the organization and its preference for working in virtual secrecy, gaining entry was a considerable challenge. The organization's operations are situated near the University of Winnipeg in a nondescript building closed to the public. I initiated contact in early 2016 by emailing an employee inside C3P whom I'd had some contact with over the years in my capacity as chair of Criminal Justice at the University of Winnipeg. In this role, I received a number of emails over the years from C3P with information about job advertisements and invitations to workshops and events. Some years before I was chair, my department had partnered with the organization to host a speaker event related to the Holly Jones abduction and murder case in Toronto. As a result, the executive director of C3P, Lianna McDonald, met my initial inquiry with enthusiasm. She asked me to specify some days when I would be available, and she indicated that she would get her senior staff together so that we could meet and I could ask questions.

Shortly after this promising initial contact, though, I received a message from a different staff member at C3P asking for more details about the project, including my ethics clearance and my list of questions. Full disclosure being the best policy, I submitted my complete research proposal and ethics protocol outlining in full all aspects of the project and my theoretical framing of the case study along with the letter from the IRB waiving the formal ethics requirement. I thought it most ethical to let C3P know my initial thinking about the organization as part of a broader networked assemblage of prevention and policing efforts aimed at child sexual abuse and exploitation. Following the submission of these materials, there was a long break in communication before I received a response from the executive director. In short, she disagreed with my theoretical framing of C3P and its position vis-à-vis law enforcement in Canada. In her written response, the executive director expressed some concerns about my objectivity:

> It appears that you have come into this research with some preconceived notions about our work and that you have some views that are inaccurate. From what we have read, it does not appear as though you will be approaching this case study from a position of neutrality. While the questions you propose to ask are not problematic in and of themselves, it is the context and framework from which you are asking the questions that raise concerns.

In particular, McDonald expressed concern that I had referred to the activities of C3P and Cybertip.ca as constituting a type of "policing."[3] "We are a charity, and we operate as a charity, delivering programs and services that are consistent with our charitable purpose. We do not 'police' images and it is fundamentally wrong to say that we do. We are also not a 'policing organization' and we never have been."

Despite the initial concerns and skepticism expressed by the executive director, I pressed on in seeking a meeting with the organization. In a sense, it was good to have all of the cards on the table. These early conversations were illuminating in that they revealed a disjuncture between how scholars of "policing" view the term and the internalized rhetoric and justification of C3P. Although I certainly took the executive director's point that C3P is a distinct entity apart from public police, its work nevertheless involves activities that amount to a policing function. In the same way that neighbourhood block watches, citizen patrol programs, and the well-known Crime Stoppers initiative activate citizens as law enforcement partners, the activities of C3P appeared to be well connected to state law enforcement objectives and activities. Indeed, on many occasions, the executive director of C3P has described her organization as "the neighbourhood watch of the internet" or as similar in function to Crime Stoppers.

The activation of individual citizens and community groups in neighbourhood watches and citizens in patrol groups is at the heart of the reconfigured terrain of late modern criminal justice. These programs extend the eyes and ears of police while symbolically shifting responsibility for crime prevention to communities and individuals. C3P views itself as an aid to law enforcement in an era when police resources are inadequate to provide protection on the wide open internet frontier. The analogy to Crime Stoppers and Neighbourhood Watch reoccurred in my conversations with the executive director and other staff. Of course, neither Neighbourhood Watch nor Crime Stoppers has ever received official parliamentary recognition. This designation puts Cybertip.ca into a much closer and more formal relationship with the state. Although the executive director is correct in asserting that C3P is not the same as police, it nonetheless trades on the symbolic legitimacy conferred by the Canadian state in deeming it the official national reporting mechanism. Cybertip.ca could be mistaken by members of the general public for a state agency given the fact that it employs the "National Tip Line" designation prominently on its website, reports, and public education resources, and it uses visual signifiers of the Canadian state on these materials and its website (e.g., the Canadian and Manitoba government logos).

In subsequent email interactions and during in-person interviews with the executive director, it was emphasized that Cybertip.ca and C3P are independent of the state and agencies of law enforcement. Although they work closely with police and the government and receive significant funding from the state to operate, McDonald claimed that the majority of their funding comes from non-state donors – information that cannot be verified from the organization's publicly available annual reports. Nevertheless, McDonald viewed this technical independence as key to their work:

> It is and has always been fundamentally important to us that we remain neutral and arm's length from government, police and third-party funders. We have an independent Board of Directors that provides operational oversight and sets our strategic goals, and all of the decisions that we make are made independent of and free of influence from government. All of this information is clearly laid out on our website.

I will return to these concerns of C3P in the next section, where I lay out the conceptual terrain of the work of "policing" online in the virtual spaces and places of the internet.

The Private Policing of Images

In their efforts to differentiate conceptually the work of C3P from that of police and to justify their utility in the broader assemblage of online crime prevention and security, directors and board members frequently invoked a spatial metaphor. McDonald often stated that C3P occupies "a unique space."

> SK: You talk about this unique space that you occupy, you use a spatial metaphor that you're an in-between space, in a sense.
> LM: I'm looking at the way crime has moved and shifted and the role of technology in that now. Because of that transformative shift, the

original ways in which we approached crime and address crime really haven't caught up with that new reality. And so I was sort of arguing that – if you look at those who, specifically in our area, are very attuned to how crime in my *space* works, and how children are victimized, etc. – if you look at industry, and when I say industry I'm meaning technology and people who are sort of connected to it. If you look at governments, if you look at educators, parents, and police, they would all probably agree that this sort of model and structure that we've set up is actually adapting, right, in a way that makes sense because you can't do it anymore along those very traditional institutions and structures, if that makes sense.

The spatial metaphor refers to a space apart from other traditional institutions, including police, the government, and industry. C3P is able to occupy and work within this space in a way that responds to the changing nature of crime on the internet – a metaphorical space that defies regulation. A retired police officer and long-serving member of the board used the spatial metaphor to describe the differences and similarities between the work of the centre and that of public police:

Well, it's definitely in a *space* where nobody's doing anything. But having said that – I mean some of the stuff, like educational stuff and those things, … used to be done by the police, and still could be, … but the centre triages that, so that it frees police up. But I mean in that respect, could the police do it? Yeah. Yeah, they could. Could the police run a tip line? You know, with the analysts and that? Yeah, they probably could. But the question is would it be as effective?

This board member described the space occupied by C3P and Cybertip.ca as less encumbered by procedure, regulation, and red tape than the space occupied by public police. In line with the rhetoric of corporatization, it was suggested that the private organization is better able to streamline protocols and procedures that otherwise hamper the ability of public police agencies to work efficiently to detect crime online. Although very careful not to imply that C3P is subverting the procedures that bind the hands of police, this board member emphasized the efficiency of C3P and how it frees up valuable time for police.

The concept of triage was used many times to explain the value of the work of C3P in sorting criminal from non-criminal matters and delivering only the most useful intelligence to public police for follow up. This point was reaffirmed by other board members and the director of Cybertip.ca, who described the internet itself as a vast space beyond the capability of police to navigate efficiently:

> It doesn't take very long to get the buy-in once they understand that we actually in fact save police a ton of resources. And anyone at the higher ranks appreciates why that's so valuable. You know, that we can take some of that load off of police. Because, as it relates to the internet, when you're dealing with it on a global nature, the idea that, you know, police would intake absolutely everything in these *spaces* is ... it doesn't make any sense. So they quickly understand that.

The spatial metaphor was used in a different sense to denote gaps or holes in existing services provided by traditional law enforcement or government actors. For example, it was noted that police were unable to provide effective counselling services for parents or families affected by the sexual exploitation of children. In this sense, this was a space occupied by the centre because nobody else was attending to the need. In addition, McDonald identified young adults above age eighteen as an emerging area needing attention:

> Like we know that, you know, as this sort of *space* is emerging and evolving, we're stepping in where we need to step in, and we're doing things because, you know, even when we're looking, for example, eighteen- to twenty-three-year-olds, that we would even see them different, right? And we've assisted in missing children cases where twenty-two-year-olds have gone missing because, you know, the brain hasn't even developed until twenty-three ... We're seeing that population, and we're doing absolutely more for that population, because in our mind, you know, while the age of majority might be eighteen, we need to step in and provide support for that age window.

Members of C3P used spatial metaphors frequently to describe the nature and value of their work and, more importantly, to highlight gaps that they believed justified their participation in policing-related activities. Moreover, the elastic nature of the spatial metaphor was helpful in rhetorically positioning C3P as necessary. For this reason, spatial metaphors were key in C3P's claims-making strategy asserting ownership of the issue.

Public and Private Policing Partnerships

As Yar (2013) and Campbell (2016) have noted, the policing of cyberspace tends to involve an assemblage of networked entities, including public police, private industry, and non-profit organizations such as C3P. In trying to tease out the nature of C3P's role in this assemblage, I asked directors and board members about the nature of this relationship or partnership. A metaphor that several participants invoked was that of a one-way valve. Police and C3P work together, but information and reports flow one way only – from C3P analysts to public police investigators. In this way, it was suggested, a sort of firewall prevents C3P from getting too close to investigations. Consequently, it was argued, C3P cannot be involved in policing because it is insulated from formal police work. This again highlights difficulties in negotiating lay and academic conceptions of policing beyond traditional public definitions. Additionally, it highlights the importance for C3P of being seen as at arm's length from state authorities, an idea central to the symbolic value of the organization as an interlocutor among public, corporate, and state law enforcement interests. C3P must carefully balance the symbolic power that comes from being associated closely with the state (e.g., Canada's national tip line) against the need to operate informally behind the scenes to broker interactions between corporate and government bodies. The role of C3P as a mediator among tech companies, telecommunication providers, the government, and public police is at odds with the folksy image that it cultivates in the media as the neighbourhood watch of the internet. In fact, C3P plays an important role in coordinating activities within the internet prevention and security assemblage at a much higher level. It is not operating simply via a one-way valve between individual citizens and the state. This is illustrated by C3P's involvement with the Canadian Coalition against Internet Child Exploitation, "a voluntary multi-sector group of industry, government, non-governmental and law enforcement stakeholders from across the country. Chaired by Cybertip.ca, CCAICE's mandate is to devise and implement an effective national strategy to help address the problem of online child sexual exploitation" ("Canadian Coalition," n.d.). The director of Cybertip.ca elaborated on the role of C3P within this group of private and public players:

> We chair CCAICE, right? So we get around the table with ... law enforcement, the big wigs from the major telcos [telecommunication operators] ... We have crown attorneys, government officials that sit at that table. And we talk about, you know, what are some of the emerging issues? How are

particular things working? How did the *Spencer*[4] decision impact the police? What can we do now as it relates to that? It's a good open discussion where, again, we're working at the issue behind the scenes with one another.

The *Spencer* decision noted above potentially implicates the kinds of public and private interactions that C3P attempts to mediate between police and corporate ISPs. Nineteen-year-old Saskatoon university student Matthew Spencer was charged with downloading child pornography to a computer owned by his sister, with whom he lived. Police tracked the IP address and requested and received subscriber information from Shaw Communications without judicial authorization. The Supreme Court found that Spencer had a reasonable expectation of privacy in relation to subscriber information held by Shaw and that the police request amounted to a search under Section 8 of the Charter of Rights and Freedoms. This landmark ruling was seen to have important consequences for policing of online sexual offences and might underscore the need for C3P to work informally behind the scenes in the space between public police and internet providers. Furthermore, as C3P moves into proactive activities online, this provides a potential avenue to work around some of the privacy concerns voiced in *Spencer* as long as the court does not view C3P as a public policing body.

Reflecting on my initial conversation with the executive director, who expressed strong concerns about this research project and how I was framing the work of C3P as part of the policing of the internet, I asked the director of Cybertip.ca about the importance of being perceived by industry players as a charity, rather than police, and whether playing the role of intermediary between industry and police put C3P into a challenging position. The director noted that

> I think we're the linchpin that can bring everyone back together. We can always rally people back together for that common good and common purpose. And that is the charitable space behind this, and why this is so important and so needed ... We also have what no government or police entity have – the statistics and numbers that tell the picture that this is a problem.

A retired police officer serving on the board explained that for him the main value of C3P is as an intermediary between public police and private technology and telecommunication companies:

I think that's one of the biggest benefits that I saw as a senior police officer. You knew you could just phone Lianna and say ... "We got an issue with Shaw. Or we have an issue with Google or Facebook or LinkedIn or something. Do you have someone you could reach out to help out us?" And you can make those calls yourself. But if you don't have that relationship going in ... they're always leery of law enforcement. And law enforcement has to be aware that they are law enforcement. So you're not going to get the same ... as a private entity. Those connections are just invaluable.

It is easy to see why, given the comments above, C3P is keen to be seen as a non-policing entity. Much of its social capital with industry depends on being seen as independent of the state while facilitating a direct conduit for flows of information between state and industry. Additionally, the recent *Spencer* decision provides an incentive to frame the work of C3P as anything but policing.

The Logic of Private Policing of Images

Like other forms of private policing and security, the work of C3P is premised on a preventative and precautionary type of logic in which suspicion alone is a ground for action (see also Duncan & Barreto, this volume). Accordingly, the general public is encouraged to report any image that does not *feel* right. As a result, much of the material reviewed by analysts in fact is legal pornography. This sort of logic dovetails with the long-standing construction of the social problem of child sexual exploitation as the work of outsiders and strangers to the imagined community. Moreover, employees of the organization have suggested that this overriding precautionary logic has come to structure their personal lives. According to in-depth interviews with two Cybertip.ca analysts published in a recent *Toronto Star* feature about C3P, they described experiencing heightened suspicion in their day-to-day lives. A twenty-five-year-old female analyst and criminology graduate suggested that her work with the centre will have a lasting personal impact:

> Here is how her job will shape her motherhood style: her child will have very strict rules about technology. Any daycare provider will be scrutinized with deep background checks. And that includes friends and family. "With the work I do here, I really realize those are sometimes people you need to be aware of and questioning," she says. "Before I started here, I was a fairly trusting and open person. I can say I'm a lot more alert now." ("Lessons," 2015)

For a thirty-six-year-old male analyst, the logic of precaution means that any uneasy feeling must be acted on when it comes to the safety of children:

> "I remember a scenario when we went to a home daycare. As soon as we stepped in the door, alarm bells went off." The daycare provider introduced them to her husband, who she said helped out. "There was something about him ... He might be the nicest guy in the world but I didn't feel comfortable about him being there. Maybe that's a bias. But my gut instinct said no. My wife looked at my face and she knew we weren't going to send our child there." ("Lessons," 2015)

The couple ended up hiring a private nanny for their child.

Curiously, nearly all of the directors with whom I spoke described the police the police with whom they worked as an inherently and perhaps overly suspicious group. This was noted in the context of the need for C3P to earn the trust of law enforcement partners by demonstrating its value and understanding of the issue. It is telling perhaps that analysts within the centre appear to have adopted a similar culture of suspicion driven by a precautionary logic in which any imagined scenario is worth considering as a realistic possibility. The same kind of thinking characterizes the educational materials proffered by the centre for children, teens, and parents so that precautionary logic might be instilled as a way to forestall future victimization by responsibilized citizens (Karaian, 2014).

Conclusion

The work of policing images of child exploitation is complex and involves ambiguous alliances between the state and non-state organizations. The exploratory research presented in this chapter extends our empirical and conceptual knowledge of private influence in criminal justice through a case study of a largely invisible entity that has quietly taken on a key role in the policing of online sexual exploitation of children and adults in Canada. Indeed, as Stenning (2000) notes, there is scarcely any criminal justice function not currently undertaken by the private sector. In contrast to Yar's (2013) contention, even the policing of sexual abuse of children now falls largely into the hands of a private entity with low visibility and little formal accountability. Although others have noted the significant role of private players in a policing assemblage directed toward child sexual abuse (Campbell, 2016), this study reveals that C3P occupies an important role in directing and coordinating the assemblage. In this way, C3P is an exemplar not only of privatization of policing in Canada but also of how private players can exert strong influence in criminal justice at both operational and policy levels.

This study provides a rare glimpse into how key players inside the organization understand their work and their relationship with public policing and the justice system. The study reveals three distinct themes pervading the work of C3P, a private charitable entity that has grown from a grassroots support network for local families of missing children to a national player in Canada's strategy for policing online sexual exploitation and abuse of children. The first theme is that C3P has been adept at positioning itself rhetorically as an important player with specific skills and knowledge that cannot be replicated by public policing agencies. I have noted elsewhere that a part of this strategy played out in the rhetoric of claims making in the news media in the lead up to deeming C3P as Canada's official tip line in 2011 (Kohm, 2019). In wide-ranging and open-ended interviews with the directors and board members of C3P, they often used a spatial metaphor for its unique role. Often, indeed, the internet itself is ascribed a spatial quality (e.g., cyberspace), so it is not surprising that the players in C3P suggested that their work also unfolds in a unique space apart from the state and distinct from corporate and community spheres. Furthermore, the spatial metaphor is elastic and can extend to include new regions of potential activity. Most recently, C3P has extended its work to adults who have had their intimate images shared online without their consent. By framing this as a space of inaction by the state, C3P positions itself rhetorically as a logical alternative to formal police action. Indeed, the terrain of childhood itself is extended rhetorically via the spatial metaphor to encompass young adulthood. In this way, C3P can further colonize new regions of criminal justice through the expansion of its activities into adjacent spaces seen to be lacking concerted public police attention.

The second theme is the role of partnerships among the state, corporations, and civil society. C3P is positioned as an important coordinator of the various players in this networked assemblage. Although C3P was highly resistant to my framing of the organization as carrying on the work of policing, it seemed to be evident that part of its symbolic power arises from a close and privileged relationship with the state. C3P, however, works actively at times to obscure these strong linkages and associations to facilitate information exchanges among players from the different spheres. C3P therefore treads a fine line when positioning itself rhetorically within the policing network.

And the third theme is the logic that frames the work of C3P. Precautionary logic (see, e.g., Haggerty, 2003) drives the work of the organization and feeds into the way in which employees relate more broadly in the social world. In addition, this logic of precaution expressly directs citizens to take action either by reporting suspicious images or by regulating their own behaviour and the behaviour of their children (Karaian, 2014). The logic of prevention and precaution suggests a deeply negative view of the world in which feelings of unease substitute for concrete facts as a basis for action. This is exemplified by the accounts of employees as well as by the large volume of reports received by Cybertip.ca. As C3P defines new behaviours as troubling and actionable, new reports are received confirming these fears. However, low clearance rates by police call the value of public tips into question. The triage model suggested by directors and board members means that only the best tips are sent forward for further action. Yet, with only a handful of arrests after tens of thousands of tips, one might question the effectiveness of C3P's overall model. However, preventative logic suggests that, if even one child is saved, then the work is well worth it. Moreover, C3P asserts that countless children are assisted through education or prevention initiatives, a number that cannot be assessed in any real way.

It is no coincidence, perhaps, that former Conservative Prime Minister Stephen Harper linked the work of C3P with Canada's war on terrorism when he was recently honoured by the organization: "'I'm going to change topic just a little bit. I think it's just a little bit,' he said to a gala honouring the 30th anniversary of the Canadian Centre for Child Protection. 'I think it would be impossible for a prime minister today to speak about protecting children – protecting Canadians – without also addressing the threat of terrorism'" (Lambert, 2015). Elsewhere it has been noted that pedophiles stand alongside terrorists as the bogeymen of contemporary times (Kohm & Greenhill, 2011). The former prime minister's comments suggest that this link has been established firmly in part through the private policing of images by non-state organizations such as C3P that forge ambiguous alliances between the state and civil society, utilizing a preventative logic aimed at the noblest endeavour: saving children. And though it is tempting to dismiss Harper's words as a politically conservative viewpoint, child saving appears to transcend party lines. As one board member pointed out to me, C3P can rely on government support from across the political spectrum: "Really, from that sense, government wise, it doesn't really matter which government it is across Canada. You know, there's been interest, and rightfully so, because who would want to be seen as saying 'No, we're not going to do anything for kids."' Consequently, by relying on a rhetoric of child saving, C3P appears to be well positioned to withstand shifting political currents and will likely remain a key private actor in policing images online and shaping broader public policy in Canada.

Notes

1 C3P directors explained that they prefer to use the abbreviation C3P rather than CCCP, an acronym associated with the former Soviet Union.
2 The murder of Candace remains unsolved. On October 18, 2017, a verdict of not guilty was reached in the second trial of Mark Edward Grant, whose previous conviction was overturned on appeal to the Supreme Court (Pritchard, 2017).
3 Brodeur (2010) notes the complex and multiple ways that the terms "police" and "policing" can be used to denote individuals, organizations, and activities well beyond common uses. My use of the term "policing" to describe the activities of C3P clearly revealed a gap between academic and lay conceptions difficult to resolve in the course of my written and verbal interactions with the directors. In large measure, this difficulty arose because C3P believes that being associated too closely with public police would dissuade the public from reporting abuse and make it harder to function as an intermediary between corporations and state authorities. Directors were firm in asserting that their key value lies in their intermediate position between police and elements of civil society.
4 See *R v Spencer,* 2014 SCC 43, 2 SCR 212, available at https://scc-csc.lexum.com/scc-csc/scc-csc/en/item/14233/index.do.

References

Allen, M. (2018). Police-reported crime statistics in Canada 2017. Statistics Canada Catalogue 85-002-X. *Juristat, 38*(1), 1–50.

Ayling, J., & Shearing, C. (2008). Taking care of business: Public police as commercial security vendors. *Criminology and Criminal Justice, 8*(1), 27–50.

Batista, T., & Johnson, A. (2017). The Children's Aid Society: Early origins of youth empowerment in the US foster care system or paternalistic prevention? *Journal of Family History, 42*(1), 67–80.

Best, J. (1987). Rhetoric in claims-making: Constructing the missing children problem. *Social Problems, 34*(2), 101–121.

Best, J. (1990). *Threatened children: Rhetoric and concern about child-victims.* University of Chicago Press.

Brodeur, J. P. (2010). *The policing web.* Oxford University Press.

Brownlee, J., Hurl, C., & Walby, K. (Eds.). (2018). *Corporatizing Canada: Making business out of public service.* Between the Lines.

Campbell, E. (2016). Policing paedophilia: Assembling bodies, spaces and things. *Crime Media Culture, 12*(3), 345–365.

Canada's first cyber tip line being launched. (2002, September 26). *Globe and Mail.* https://www.theglobeandmail.com/technology/canadas-first-cyber-tip-line-being-launched/article20456762/

Canadian Coalition against Internet Child Exploitation. (n.d.). *Cybertip.ca.* https://www.cybertip.ca/app/en/projects-ccaice

Centre embodies "spirit of Candace." (2015, April 22). *Winnipeg Free Press.* https://www.winnipegfreepress.com/local/centre-embodies-spirit-of-candace-300892341.html

C3P (Canadian Centre for Child Protection). (2012). *Cybertip.ca: A 10-year review of Canada's tipline for reporting the online sexual exploitation of children.* https://www.cybertip.ca/pdfs/CTIP_10YearReport_en.pdf

C3P (Canadian Centre for Child Protection). (2015). *Social value report 2014–15.* https://www.protectchildren.ca/pdfs/C3P_SocialValueReport_2014-2015_en.pdf

C3P (Canadian Centre for Child Protection). (2017). *Protect we will: Social value report 2016–17.* https://www.protectchildren.ca/pdfs/C3P_SocialValueReport_2016*2017_en.pdf

C3P (Canadian Centre for Child Protection). (2018). *Stories to tell: 2017–18 social value report.* https://www.protectchildren.ca/pdfs/C3P_SocialValueReport_2017-2018_en.pdf

Garland, D. (2001). *Culture of control: Crime and social order in contemporary society.* University of Chicago Press.

Haggerty, K. (2003). From risk to precaution: The rationalities of personal crime prevention. In R. Ericson & A. Doyle (Eds.), *Risk and morality* (pp. 193–214). University of Toronto Press.

Huey, L., Nhan, J., & Broll, R. (2012). "Uppity civilians" and "cyber-vigilantes": The role of the general public in policing cyber-crime. *Criminology and Criminal Justice, 13*(1), 81–97.

Jenkins, P. (1992). *Intimate enemies: Moral panics in contemporary Great Britain.* Aldine de Gruyter.

Jenkins, P. (1996). *Pedophiles and priests: Anatomy of a contemporary crisis.* Oxford University Press.

Jenkins, P. (1998). *Moral panic: Changing conceptions of the child molester in modern America.* Yale University Press.

Jenkins, P. (2001). *Beyond tolerance: Child pornography on the internet.* New York University Press.

Jewkes, Y., & Andrews, C. (2005). Policing the filth: The problems of investigating online child pornography in England and Wales. *Policing and Society, 15*(1), 42–62.

Karaian, L. (2014). Policing "sexting": Responsibilization, respectability and sexual subjectivity in child protection/crime prevention responses to teenagers' digital sexual expression. *Theoretical Criminology, 18*(3), 282–299.

Karaian, L. (2015). What is self-exploitation? Rethinking the relationship between sexualization and "sexting" in law and order times. In E. Renold, J. Ringrose, & R. Egan (Eds.), *Children, sexuality and sexualization* (pp. 337–351). Palgrave Macmillan.

Keighley, K. (2017). Police-reported crime statistics in Canada 2016. Statistics Canada Catalogue 85-002-X. *Juristat, 37*(1), 1–49.

Kohm, S. (2009). Naming, shaming and criminal justice: Mass-mediated humiliation as entertainment and punishment. *Crime Media Culture, 5*(2), 188–205.

Kohm, S. (2017). The paedophile in popular culture: Fictional representations of sex crime. In T. Sanders (Ed.), *Oxford handbook of sex offences and sex offending* (pp. 498–516). Oxford University Press.

Kohm, S. (2019). Claims-making, child saving, and the news media. *Crime Media Culture, 16*(1), 115–137.

Kohm, S., & Greenhill, P. (2011). Pedophile crime films as popular criminology: A problem of justice? *Theoretical Criminology, 15*(2), 195–216.

Lambert, S. (2015, April 24). PM Stephen Harper talks child protection, terrorism in Winnipeg speech. *CBC News*. https://www.cbc.ca/news/canada/manitoba/pm-stephen-harper-talks-child-protection-terrorism-in-winnipeg-speech-1.3048636

Lessons from the trenches of the battle against child porn. (2015, March 26). *Toronto Star*. https://www.thestar.com/news/insight/2015/04/26/lessons-from-the-trenches-of-the-battle-against-child-porn.html

Löfstrand, C., Loftus, B., & Loader, I. (2018). Private security as moral drama: A tale of two scandals. *Policing and Society, 28*(8), 968–984.

Loughlin, J., & Taylor-Butts, A. (2009). Child luring through the internet. Statistics Canada Catalogue 85-002-X. *Juristat, 29*(1), 1–17.

Luscombe, A., & Walby, K. (2014). Occupy Ottawa, conservation officers, and policing networks in Canada's capital city. *Canadian Journal of Criminology and Criminal Justice, 56*(3), 295–322.

Manitoba group aims to protect kids on net. (2001, May 24). *Globe and Mail*. https://www.theglobeandmail.com/technology/manitoba-group-aims-to-protect-kids-on-net/article1031645/

Manitoba leads fight against child porn. (2005, June 12). *Winnipeg Free Press*. https://www.winnipegfreepress.com/historic/31584979.html

Martin, M. (2017, January 17). Blazing-fast Winnipeg-born superbot lights child-porn survivors' path out of hell. *Winnipeg Free Press*. https://www.winnipegfreepress.com/local/blazing-fast-winnipeg-born-superbot-lights-child-porn-survivors-path-out-of-hell-411005275.html

Murphy, C. (2007). "Securitizing" Canadian policing: A new policing paradigm for the post 9/11 security state? *The Canadian Journal of Sociology, 32*(4), 449–475.

Nicholson, K., & Kubinec, V. (2018, April 26). Police officer in "revenge porn" case sues over distribution of intimate images. *CBC News*. https://www.cbc.ca/news/canada/manitoba/police-officer-in-revenge-porn-case-sues-over-distribution-of-intimate-images-1.4633846

Online child sexual abuse images targeted by automated system. (2017, January 17). *CBC News*. https://www.cbc.ca/news/canada/manitoba/project-arachnid-cybertip-child-sexual-abuse-1.3938998

O'Reilly, C. (2015). The pluralization of high policing: Convergence and divergence at the public-private interface. *British Journal of Criminology, 55*(4), 688–710.

Pritchard, D. (2017, October 18). Mark Edward Grant, who was convicted of killing Candace Derksen, found not guilty at 2nd trial. *CBC News*. https://www.cbc.ca/news/canada/manitoba/mark-grant-retrial-derksen-decision-1.4360436

Rigakos, G. (2002). *The new parapolice: Risk markets and commodified social control*. University of Toronto Press.

Sharkey, J. (2016, November 21). Child exploitation often disguised as "child model" ads on Craigslist, says expert. *CBC News*. https://www.cbc.ca/news/canada/kitchener-waterloo/child-exploitation-young-models-online-1.3860055

Shearing, C., & Stenning, P. (1981). Modern private security: Its growth and implications. In M. Tonry & N. Morris (Eds.), *Crime and justice: An annual review of research* (Vol. 3, pp. 193–245). University of Chicago Press.

Shearing, C., & Stenning, P. (1983). Private security: Implications for social control. *Social Problems, 30*(5), 493–506.

Shearing, C., & Stenning, P. (1985). From the panopticon to Disney World: The development of discipline. In A. N. Doob & E. L. Greenspan (Eds.), *Perspectives in criminal law: Essays in honour of John Ll. J. Edwards* (pp. 335–349). Canada Law Book.

Sleiman, M., & Lippert, R. (2010). Downtown ambassadors, police relations and "clean and safe" security. *Policing and Society, 20*(3), 316–335.

Stenning, P. C. (2000). Powers and accountability of private police. *European Journal on Criminal Policy and Research, 8*(3), 325–352.

van Steden, R., & de Waard, J. (2013). "Acting like chameleons": On the McDonaldization of private security. *Security Journal, 26*(3), 294–309.

Yar, M. (2006). *Cybercrime and society*. SAGE.

Yar, M. (2013). The policing of internet sex offences: Pluralised governance versus hierarchies of standing. *Policing and Society, 23*(4), 482–497.

3

Postsecondary Security in the Canadian Context

ERIN GIBBS VAN BRUNSCHOT

Introduction
The security of postsecondary environments includes much more than emergency preparedness and crime control. Postsecondary campuses often contain constituents who hold a diversity of ideologies, perspectives, and experiences. A typical goal of postsecondary institutions is to support this diversity to the extent that others are not harmed – a respect for competing paradigms and opinions and the freedom to explore ideas are central to the notion of an open, secure campus. Although postsecondary environments are largely considered "public," threats to security often involve "norm violations" that contravene the "private" culture of the postsecondary environment. Such violations are undesirable behaviours that an organization deems problematic (Meerts, 2018). The creation of campus security and policing units is one means by which norms are upheld and enforced. As Joh (2004) notes, the activities that campus security units undertake are client driven, and what counts as "deviant, disorderly, or unwanted behaviour" is determined by the postsecondary institution often independently of substantial involvement by external authorities.

Complicating the provision of security in the postsecondary environment are the cultural pillars of academic freedom and collegial governance: security violations on campus are more likely to be breaches of academic integrity than criminal acts, though undesirable behaviour can run the gamut, from cheating on a test to stealing equipment. The nature and context of the behaviour often determine whether public police will be involved in responding to it, though academic and administrative norm violations typically rely on internal processes. As noted by Meerts and Dorn (2009) in their study of corporations, norm violations often are addressed by procedures internal to the organization; the provision of corporate security enables organizations to handle and manage wrongdoing on their own terms – terms that often do not involve external policing agencies. The case is much the same in the postsecondary context, with a plethora of procedures and policies governing behaviour. As Shearing and Stenning (1983) observe regarding public activities on mass private property, the provision of security on postsecondary campuses tends to fall within the domain of the postsecondary institution itself. However, in their efforts to maintain order, postsecondary security initiatives can blur the line between private policing and traditional public security (Shearing & Stenning, 1983, p. 497), with private security performing some of the same tasks as public security agencies (a form of "load-shedding," as conceptualized by Luscombe et al., this volume).

In this chapter, I consider elements of postsecondary environments that fortify the blurring between public and private security and policing in the postsecondary context (see also Mulone, this volume). My goal is to advance the conversation about the provision of security by examining the postsecondary environment and elements specific to that environment, such as academic integrity and collegial governance. The postsecondary environment, like the corporate context, leans strongly toward the internal management of security threats. I also consider issues of private policing more broadly, such as autonomy and liability, and how they figure into the postsecondary environment. First, I reflect on the broader context of postsecondary institutions, which emphasizes a market approach – competition, corporatization, and commercialization – to providing education in a secure environment. Second, I consider the range of threats to postsecondary security – from norm violations that threaten the ethos of academic integrity to criminal activities – and consider the implications of those threats for jurisdictional boundaries between private and public security efforts. Do universities have legislative authority to address criminal wrongdoing on their campuses? Who is part of the campus community, and over whom do postsecondary institutions have authority? Third, I discuss the postsecondary characteristics of collegial governance and academic freedom/integrity and the implications of this duality for security. And fourth, I consider more fully the challenges associated with security – autonomy and liability – as centrepieces of postsecondary security and policing efforts. Postsecondary security efforts appear to emulate the corporate security model, which works to safeguard public reputations through private policing and internal management of violations whenever possible.

The Twenty-First-Century Postsecondary Environment

The postsecondary environment today faces a plethora of challenges and operational pressures. According to Stoner (2019), in a world of technological and social distraction, institutions must work hard to ensure that "external trends dominating the narrative" of postsecondary education do not undermine the institution's "brand." The threats to an institution's reputation are many, including grappling with foreign interference in scholarly activities (McPherson & Coleman, 2019), dealing with the costs of higher education and pressures of enrolment (Snowdon, 2018), ensuring "access to and influence over education[al] opportunity" (Stoner, 2019), accommodating an increasingly varied academic community, and protecting freedom of expression in safe spaces. Efforts to sustain and bolster student enrolment are undertaken in the face of increasing competition among institutions for tuition dollars and decreasing public funding. The language of brand reputation goes hand in hand with a market orientation to campus life, including the notion of an integrated campus experience offering not only academic degrees but also retail, food, and shopping outlets as well as health, medical, and safety services.

The postsecondary institution faces pressure to provide expanded services along with "a safe environment, positive experience and supportive community" (Tani, 2017, p. 1866). The provision of a safe and supportive environment has led many postsecondary institutions to undertake various security initiatives, such as promoting mental health awareness and supporting campaigns against drinking, hazing, and sexual violence. Nearly every postsecondary institution in Canada has some form of "campus security," and in the United States the provision of a safe environment has resulted in campus police, many with both authority and weaponry similar to public police (Kutner, 2015). As Anderson (2015) explains, during the 1960s and 1970s campus policing took hold because of concerns about student unrest. Protests on campuses quickly led postsecondary administrators to conclude that keeping order on campuses would be imposed externally if appropriate measures were not taken by the institutions themselves (Sloan, 2020). Since that time, university and college police forces in the United States increasingly have become the norm. There is pressure on all postsecondary institutions to anticipate emergencies – preparedness for which can range from tabletop exercises for campus shooters and cyberattacks to evacuations in the case of fire, flood, or power outage. Although the provision of a safe, positive, and supportive environment is offered as part of the campus experience, achieving security is complicated by the organizational parameters of postsecondary environments and expectations regarding the consequences and management of violations within those environments.

Concerns about security on campus are fuelled by the convergence of several factors unique to the postsecondary environment. First, postsecondary campuses are populated by a large number of young adults – those most likely to participate in crime, as well as attend postsecondary institutions, are eighteen to twenty-two years old. This demographic is more risk taking and involved in a variety of behaviours, including excessive drinking, drug use, et cetera. Second, the postsecondary environment is primarily a public environment. Access to campus, for the most part, is not controlled. Members of the extended community often access services and attend events on campus, and many buildings are open to the public. Third, Tani (2017, p. 1865) describes the significant public disinvestment in higher education in the early 2000s despite the increasing demand for it. She notes that the messaging that students have received, and to a large extent have embraced, mirrors the institutional struggle to bolster brand reputation. Along with profit-oriented models of higher education and rising tuition costs, students increasingly are seen less as "recipients of a public good" and more as "private consumers," with the campus experience including not only educational content but also "a safe environment, a positive experience, and a supportive community" (Tani, 2017, p. 1866).

The complexity of the postsecondary environment is reflected in the pursuit of postsecondary security and policing. At the same time that security in the postsecondary context is premised on maintaining principles of openness and diversity, challenges to this environment often come from external pressures, such as capturing market share and responding to security as a "public good." Security and policing of the campus environment embrace a tension that Wilkinson (2016) identifies as appealing to private regulations (various internal codes of conduct) at the same time that legitimacy for security and policing is sought under the banner of security as something to which the public more generally aspires. The range of norm violations, from academic to criminal, increasingly necessitates a policing apparatus that extends beyond more traditional (public) policing pursuits as security threats to the postsecondary environment continue to grow.

Establishing Jurisdiction

Within the postsecondary environment, one might imagine a continuum of security violations, with academic or internal normative (private) violations on one end and, on the other, violations less specific to the postsecondary context, more public, and more criminal (e.g., trespassing, theft, assault, etc.). Campus security units (and campus police in the United States) tend to deal primarily with violations at the criminal or public end of the continuum. Campus security units in Canada, unlike their American counterparts (see below), have a somewhat more limited scope of duties, ranging from serving as (unarmed) first responders, to providing security for events and facilities, to undertaking parking control (Sloan, 2020). Some of these norm violations might intersect with public policing activities; there are varying degrees of external (public police) involvement depending on the violations in question. At the other end of the violation continuum are matters involving academic or organizational wrongdoing often dealt with through processes of collegial governance. "Policing" a postsecondary campus therefore involves addressing a range of possible security violations, only some of which might be considered criminal. Broadly speaking, the policing of norms and the pursuit of security are not confined exclusively to campus security/police units.

Most, if not all, postsecondary institutions have codes of conduct that define expectations regarding the behaviour of the campus community, with the immediate community typically defined as employees, academic staff (faculty), appointees, students, and volunteers. Codes of conduct reinforce that community members are required to fulfill various responsibilities that comply with both external laws and regulations (e.g., the Criminal Code of Canada and the Charter of Rights and Freedoms) and university policies. The University of Calgary website, for example, lists a number of policies under the heading "Health, Safety and Environment," including policies related to alcohol, cannabis, sexual violence, smoking, students at risk, video surveillance, and workplace violence. In addition to the external laws and internal policies to which a campus member is subject, various constituents of the campus community fall within the jurisdiction of collective agreements (governing faculty, staff, and students), which offer protection to their respective members in the face of both wrongdoing and victimization.

Although postsecondary policies spell out expectations regarding behaviour, there are issues of jurisdiction in terms of particular types of behaviour being "within the purview" of an organization as well as those to whom policies can be applied. Liivoja (2010, p. 29) explains that jurisdiction often falls into three parts: prescriptive, adjudicative, and enforcement. He describes prescriptive jurisdiction as the right to make activities and relations applicable to its rules and regulations; adjudicative jurisdiction as the capacity to subject people to the courts, tribunals, or dispute resolution mechanisms associated with its rules and regulations; and enforcement jurisdiction as the ability to induce or compel compliance with laws and regulations. Although his explanation focuses on the jurisdiction of states, his description provides insight into the issues of jurisdiction at a more local organizational level. Jurisdiction over and policing of a postsecondary campus often mean, as described by Joh (2004), a reliance on a "private [or internal] justice system" that establishes jurisdictional parameters over that which affects the organization. The jurisdiction over and handling of norm violations shift the organization away from the public police and criminal justice system and toward privatized policing and justice.

For example, postsecondary institutions apply various rules and regulations for conformity to normative expectations by way of contractual obligations. In the case of paid employees, the employer, the postsecondary institution, sets the terms of employment, and failure to follow specific rules of behaviour (usually having to do with teaching, research, and administration) constitutes a breach of the contract. In the case of students, the postsecondary institution enters a contract to provide them with a specific outcome (e.g., a degree), with payment of tuition serving as evidence of the agreement. The institution has prescribed jurisdiction over those with whom it holds a contract. With respect to adjudicative jurisdiction, the question is whether a postsecondary institution has the (internal or external) means to subject its constituents to methods of dispute resolution. Postsecondary policies often come with procedures for adjudication, but all of this might be moot if an institution is not able to enforce its policies (enforcement jurisdiction).

Above I described a continuum of violations associated with the postsecondary environment, with norm violations ranging from academic and organizational issues at one end to criminal behaviour at the other end. In the postsecondary context, the expertise available to identify, address, and manage norm violations at the "internal end" of the continuum is regarded by the courts as being well within the jurisdiction of postsecondary institutions:

Abuse of process concerns have frequently emerged in civil actions concerning universities' internal academic decisions, whether having to do with the imposition of discipline of a student or the denial of promotion of a faculty member. Case law demonstrates that courts in Ontario and across Canada have been reluctant to interfere with universities' internal academic decisions. They have held that such disputes are generally a matter to be resolved by the universities themselves, subject to judicial review. (*Said v University of Ottawa and Others*, 2013 ONSC 7186, cited in Gomery, 2013)

The courts appear to support postsecondary institutions' dealing with "internal norm violations" as part of the postsecondary policing jurisdiction. As Meerts and Dorn (2009) observe, police also appreciate less involvement in norm violations perceived to be internal to organizations, for often these violations are simply not of interest to public police. The authors provide the example of intellectual property theft as being of great concern to corporations (and to postsecondary institutions) but of less concern to public police, who do not have the resources (or will) to investigate these incidents. Meerts and Dorn further note that police are more interested in issues that affect the "public good" and less interested in issues considered to be the "private troubles" of an organization (p. 107). Increasingly, activities that violate internal normative codes of conduct are under the purview of internal policing and security units.

The continuum of security violations (academic to criminal) in the postsecondary environment oversimplifies the fact that there is a large grey area in terms of how certain issues are to be addressed and further blurs the line between public and private policing. The American context offers several examples of postsecondary institutions' efforts (and resistance) to establish jurisdiction over activities that formerly might have been dealt with by state authorities (if they were dealt with at all). Estimates are that 91 percent of public campuses in the United States have sworn campus officers, and of those 98 percent have sidearms (Sloan, 2020). Private campuses are much less likely to have armed officers (38 percent), though of those that do 82 percent carry sidearms. Many of these armed university police forces have recently gained notoriety because of their apparent increasing reach beyond their jurisdictions. For example, in 2015, Samuel Dubose was pulled over by a University of Cincinnati officer and subsequently shot to death over a minor traffic infraction (Perez-Pena, 2015). Bodyworn camera evidence confirmed that the officer in question shot Dubose without provocation, and the officer was found guilty of murder. Prosecutor Joseph Deters commented that "they're not cops ... The university does a great job educating people ... and that should be their job. Being police officers shouldn't be the role of this university" (cited in Kutner, 2015). In another instance, members of the George Washington University Police Department were suspended for "asserting their authority off-campus" by displaying weapons and badges while on public property and identifying themselves as police officers while outside the university (Gurciullo, 2013). Sloan (2020) suggests that the problems associated with many campus policing agencies can be related directly to their emulation of a standard municipal/state policing model – including efforts to be seen as legitimate by wearing military-style uniforms and carrying arms – a model increasingly seen as problematic both on and off campus. As observed by Brodeur (2010), state police often have been given a priori privileged positioning in the policing web – with less attention paid to the contexts in which policing agencies actually operate.

The desire to establish jurisdiction might be based upon external motivations that hinge on federal funding. Tani (2017) describes the incentives for American college and university campuses to adopt policies and protections regarding sexual assault to sustain public funding. According to Tani, the threat of sexual violence on campus deprives certain members of "equal access to education" (p. 1849) and is therefore a violation of their civil rights. Some surveys estimate that, during their time in college or an undergraduate institution, one in five women will experience attempted or completed sexual assault – the implication, Tani notes, is that 20 percent of postsecondary women's civil rights (entitlement to equal access to education) are violated (p. 1850). The solution to this situation was the creation of Title IX of the Education Amendments Act, which states that no person will be "excluded from participation in, be denied the benefits of, or be subjected to discrimination under any education program or activity receiving Federal financial assistance" (Department of Justice, 2015). Postsecondary institutions that failed to take measures to protect women from sexual violence would be subject to funding penalties. In the United States, these institutions became obligated legally to protect students from sexual harassment and assault or risk losing federal funding.

Tani (2017) draws a parallel to the case of workplace discrimination and observes that incentives from the outside do not necessarily mean that there is a firm commitment to the changes that might be required or a commitment to the jurisdiction that postsecondary institutions incur through legislative mandates. She notes that, though postsecondary entities, such as those regulated through Title IX provisions, might conform to legal mandates, "employers, at least, are motivated by their desire to appear legitimate and to minimize the law's encroachment on their power over employees. The result is a heavy reliance on 'symbolic structures,' policies and procedures" (p. 1889) and a superficial commitment to implementation and change. Similar issues can affect the postsecondary environment as it institutes policies and procedures that require policing to conform to externally mandated legislation (or expectations). As Wilkinson (2016) has observed, there might be some "symbolic borrowing" by private institutions from the rhetoric associated with public policing. Wilkinson notes attempts to link "private/corporate [postsecondary] security services with conceptions of security as a public good" (p. 229). In other words, policies and procedures implemented on campus appear to conform to widely held notions of security as desirable, yet these policies and procedures might serve to gloss over economic interests or problems that also underlie security policies and targets. For example, Wilkinson and Ivsins (2017) elaborate the dilemmas that certain campus policies meant to enhance security (or to provide the appearance of security) produce. They discuss the "policy environment" created with respect to on-campus drinking, with policies determining where, when, and how alcohol may be consumed. Although policies might be generated to enhance security by reducing "unwanted behaviour" on campus, Wilkinson and Ivsins note, they create other security issues, such as legal and academic problems and medical calls for intoxication or use of prohibited substances (p. 22).

The administration of various policies by those who must also conform to them, often without substantial oversight, is a jurisdictional matter of some concern and can result in the inconsistent application of policies and policing across postsecondary institutions. If the creation of Title IX provisions was meant to ensure equal protection and uniform treatment on campus, further challenges have arisen for defining who is a member of the campus community and who is not. An example of a Title IX challenge has to do with the implication that only some members of the campus population are protected through Title IX, whereas other members are not. Brenner (2018) provides the example of Michigan State University (MSU) physician Larry Nassar, who victimized a number of young women, only some of whom were students. MSU was sued since victims claimed that it was aware of Nassar's ongoing abusive activities but failed to address them; all victims sought compensation under Title IX. Lawyers defending MSU initially began by separating claims of victims according to their status as students, claiming that non-students were not entitled to the protections offered by Title IX even though they experienced the same harm as students. The lawyers argued that non-students were not eligible to receive monetary relief for damages incurred by the MSU doctor. The university argued that Title IX provisions were designed to ensure equal access to education; therefore, the creation of an environment of abuse, it maintained, was applicable only to students since they were on campus for educational purposes (as students). The crux of this challenge is who belongs on campus regardless of their status as student or non-student.

Challenges to Title IX highlight issues of jurisdiction, to whom university policies apply, and who is subject to policing on campus. As Brenner (2018, p. 97) notes, to whom policies apply is crucial when considering institutional jurisdiction and accountability. In the case of Title IX, universities and colleges are accountable to those with student status, yet the education that a campus offers often relies to a great extent on the larger communities of which the campus is a part. In the MSU case, it was determined that "access to education" included engagement with the wider community, and therefore the campus community must be considered sufficiently broad to include members of this wider community. At MSU, all victims, regardless of student status, were found to be entitled to remedies. In this determination, the community of the university was inclusive not only of those formally identified via their student status but also of those who entered the campus and used university services. Security provisions apply to all regardless of university status.

This review of Title IX is instructive for the Canadian context and highlights that the target of postsecondary security and policing can be motivated by external pressures, such as funding incentives. The target of policing measures in the postsecondary environment might be as much a product of external pressures as it is a pursuit of safety generated by internal expectations of a secure environment. As Wilkinson (2016, p. 230) observes, "appealing to the notion of security as a public good allows them [organizations] to downplay the extent to which they may be providing security in the name of private (i.e. economic) interests." Although Canadian postsecondary institutions might not have similarly explicit monetary incentives to ensure the security of their communities, the motivations to conform are the same. If a postsecondary institution fails to live up to the standards set by the Charter of Rights and Freedoms, for example, the likelihood of being found liable for associated damages is high. In the context of reduced government funding, postsecondary institutions are incentivized not to spend already limited funds on avoidable damages, such as those incurred by failing to address higher jurisdictional mandates (e.g., as dictated by the charter).

Freedom and Governance

> Reputation is an organization's most competitive asset.
> – LESLIE GAINES-ROSS, CHIEF REPUTATION STRATEGIST
> (CITED IN STONER, 2019)

There is often a great deal of anxiety on postsecondary campuses about the "corporatization" of their environments. Brownlee (2015) explains that higher education has had to grapple with corporate involvement in research, yet the academic and corporate spheres might be considered opposite: whereas academic research seeks to share knowledge, the corporate sphere is motivated by financial gain and secrecy. Turk (2017) further explains that the essence of the university is collegial governance and academic freedom. Collegial governance refers to academics who make academic decisions. In the university context, a board of governors typically addresses administrative functions of the university, whereas a senate, composed of academics, overseas academic decisions. As Turk notes, academic freedom is the notion that academics have the right to "follow their own professional judgement and not to be bound by conventional wisdom nor the dictates of governments, administrators, donors, alumni, parents or special interests" (p. 4). Corporatization, conversely, is the idea that neoliberal (market) principles are transforming postsecondary environments to function as though they are private institutions, competing in a free market and attempting to capture market share, preparing students for employment rather than for life (p. 4), and focusing research efforts on projects sponsored by funders that can generate revenue.

Although collegial governance might be the ambition, Pennock et al. (2016) surveyed senate members, who identified that one of the most pressing issues on campus is the lack of faculty engagement in governance. It appears that many academics are happy to leave administrative matters to academic managers and feel less compelled to be involved themselves (p. 77). Pennock et al. further note that the complexity of security issues that affect the postsecondary environment increasingly requires expertise in the fields of law, technology, and risk management (p. 77). In increasingly complicated internal and external environments, the need for specific types of expertise that go beyond faculty members' skill sets can undermine the capability of "collegial governance" to address effectively the evolving factors that affect the postsecondary security environment and the norm violations that are part of it. For campus security, this implies that the traditional means of dealing with threats internal to the postsecondary environment might be increasingly less capable of managing those threats through collegial governance and require specialized "corporate security units." As normative violations have become more complex, the ability of postsecondary settings to police themselves collegially is increasingly limited.

Meerts and Dorn's (2009) study of corporate security provides a framework for how we might begin to recognize and understand security and policing in the postsecondary landscape. Their analysis focuses on corporate security and how it addresses "concerns about corporate reputation" and how corporate in-house or contracted security meets "companies' needs for maintenance of privacy, discretion and reputation" (p. 97). Meerts and Dorn focus on why corporations largely have had autonomy over their security needs and been able to settle security matters privately. Essentially, this autonomy is based upon the perceptions of external authorities that norm violations inherent to the corporate environment are best addressed internally. Such autonomy echoes the desire for autonomy that the postsecondary environment has claimed is foundational (self-governance), but it also poses significant challenges given the nature of the university context as a public venue increasingly under pressure from private (internal) communities and reduced public funding and facing threats that require expert management. Although the foundational goal of the university context is academic freedom, faculty, though able to pursue academic pursuits of their choosing, might be less suited to providing expertise in domains that threaten postsecondary security.

I next consider the dual challenges of autonomy and liability as these concepts figure into the postsecondary security landscape. As noted earlier, security measures that address norm violations are both bolstered and limited by the foundations of the postsecondary context that emphasize academic freedom and collegial governance. These foundations include a desire to be autonomous in identifying and policing behaviour, yet they involve issues of liability that dictate how security is to be understood and policed.

Dual Challenges

Autonomy

The interplay between public policing agencies and private security agencies is the subject of some debate at a theoretical level. Early theorizing maintained that private policing endeavours were simply a "private adjunct" (Shearing & Stenning, 1983, p. 494) to state policing agencies seen as having a monopoly on issues of security since the nineteenth century. In this conceptualization, private security agencies behave like subcontractors of the larger state enterprise of providing security, which conforms to legislation such as the Criminal Code of Canada. Associated with this idea is the "shift thesis," which suggests that public security has shifted toward private security because of growing public demand for security beyond what can be offered by public security agencies. More recently, this shift toward private security has been referred to as "responsibilization," by which individuals and organizations increasingly take on security measures that previously might have been the domain of public policing. Again, these private entities are seen as "subcontracted" to the formal criminal justice system, reducing expectations of public police to perform security functions.

However, Meerts and Dorn (2009), drawing from their own work and that of Williams (2006), observe that private security has agendas that differ substantially from those of public security. Often private security, in contrast to public security, is substantially less concerned with external legislation than it is with issues specific to particular organizations. Private security agencies often have interests completely different from those of public security agencies: with private security, internal matters might be kept internal to organizations, whereas public security is concerned more with external issues that influence organizations.

Internal threats to postsecondary security, first and foremost, are academic misconduct that, for students, can include plagiarism, fabrication, falsification, and cheating. Although typically there are few "academic misconduct" policies in place for faculty members, there are policies that deal with research integrity, along with codes of conduct that often include references to broad normative conventions such as professional ethics. As noted by Turk (2017), academic freedom is a cornerstone of the postsecondary environment, but such freedoms are contained within disciplinary expectations and ethics – academic freedom therefore implies responsibility, the contravention of which is subject to disciplinary procedures. Upholding academic integrity is a security issue for the postsecondary environment in that academic freedom and integrity are the currency on which attendance and work at (and external reputation of) a university are based. The reputation of the institution rests on academic professionalism. The public expectation of the academic enterprise is that research is conducted within particular boundaries that uphold academic standards. Although the offence of academic misconduct, whether committed by a student or faculty member, is significant, this matter can have a less direct impact on those outside the university context, and therefore investigations of such offences fall within the purview of the postsecondary organization itself.

Issues of academic integrity threaten the institution but are not (usually) criminal and of little interest to public police. The systems in place at postsecondary institutions have drawn traditionally from the expertise of (disciplinary) experts to consider the nature of the threats and recommendations for consequences. Campus security units would have little to do with such proceedings unless the case involved a criminal act such as theft or forgery. Dealing with academic misconduct internally enables the institution to resolve such situations in ways that ensure "secrecy, discretion and control" (Meerts & Dorn, 2009, p. 103) and can reduce damage to the institution's reputation and the reputations of the individuals involved.

When it comes to dealing with issues of "non-academic misconduct," the postsecondary community calls on its security units to make decisions regarding the need for involvement of public police. This discretionary ability is central to both corporate security and postsecondary security. As Meerts and Dorn (2009, p. 103) observe, "of great importance for corporations in dealing with crime in and around their perimeters ... is control over the process and the outcome of investigations." There is a similar flexibility when dealing with crimes committed on campus, especially those that might be tied to academic misconduct. At the University of Calgary, for example, discretion is highlighted in the following passage:

> Where there is a criminal act involved in plagiarism, cheating or other academic misconduct, e.g., theft (taking another student's paper from their possession, or from the possession of a faculty member without permission), breaking and entering (forcibly entering an office to gain access to papers, grades or records), forgery, personation and conspiracy (impersonating another student by agreement and writing their paper) and other such offences under the Criminal Code of Canada, the University *may take legal advice on the appropriate response and, where appropriate, refer the matter*

to the police, in addition to or in substitution for any action taken under these regulations by the University.[1]

This passage highlights that the university has the option to add consequences to internal (and external) procedures (or substitute consequences) should *the university* choose to do so. Such discretion is pivotal – when investigations move to the public realm (and involve police), control over the investigation (and consequences) can be lost. As noted about corporate security actors, a key incentive for postsecondary institutions to retain investigations internally is how the situations might be perceived by the public – a public to which postsecondary institutions are increasingly under pressure to appeal.

Whereas matters related to academic misconduct fall more readily within the jurisdiction of postsecondary environments, instances of non-academic misconduct are not as straightforward. Policies dealing with non-academic misconduct are geared most often to student members of the campus community and include prohibitions against people and property similar to Criminal Code prohibitions. Other aspects of non-academic misconduct include behaviours specific to the university environment, such as obstructing others from carrying out legitimate activities, interfering with university functions, consuming alcohol or drugs in prohibited places, and so on. Behavioural expectations of faculty and staff are enveloped in codes of conduct that focus on maintaining environments that uphold principles such as honesty, integrity, and respect.

As with instances of wrongdoing in corporations, postsecondary institutions are motivated to deal internally with as many issues of wrongdoing as possible so as not to bring negative attention to themselves. Meerts and Dorn (2009) indicate that, once public security personnel become involved, corporate (institutional) control is lost. Yet decisions to go public with particular activities can enhance the public image of an institution, which can be seen as "doing something" about a particular problem. In their examination of corporate security actors, Meerts and Dorn found that the decision to involve public police was based upon trust. Trust was pivotal not only in terms of how internal actors might view each other but also in terms of affecting the public's trust in the corporation. Yet decisions to go public in a university environment are not necessarily made by the institution alone. In many cases, faculty and staff norm violations fall within the domain of faculty and employee collective agreements. Settlements reached through the involvement of various associations or unions can prevent disclosure of details of the "offence," thus minimizing personal damages that might result from wrongdoing. Furthermore, insurance claims for various damages can sway decisions to involve external security. Often insurers require the involvement of public police to reimburse claims for various damages.

Liability
Turk (2017) suggests that the proliferation of policies that govern behaviour undermines the foundation of the university environment by mandating civil and respectful behaviour at the same time as setting up elaborate investigatory and enforcement regimes. He suggests that policies on civility curb academic freedom by censoring free expression, yet such policies undermine collegial governance – a second foundation of the university environment – by taking control away from academics. As has become increasingly clear, however, the postsecondary context is exposed to the pressures of the external environment that emphasize security. In a situation of decreased public funding, failing to create and adopt particular policies might well reduce opportunities for whatever limited funding is available. Failing to adopt Title IX, though an American example, makes it clear that funding rests on the adoption of specific policies: American universities that fail to make provisions for Title IX – fail to secure their environments – are very likely to have their funding reduced substantially (Brenner, 2018). There is no similar government funding incentive in the Canadian context yet, though postsecondary institutions make themselves vulnerable to damages in the absence of policies governing conduct.

In the case of academic misconduct, postsecondary environments have developed clear policies that detail not only the types of offences prohibited (while often leaving some room for innovative forms of misconduct) but also the procedures to be followed in accusations of misconduct. The absence of such policies is particularly risky – universities, for example, do not want to be in the position of having to defend their actions in the face of these claims. As noted by the director of the office of student judicial affairs at a Canadian university regarding student misconduct, "if you have a clear, fair process and can show you have followed the process, it tends to stave off the lawsuits, as students feel that their concerns have been heard and they have received fair treatment" (cited in Mullens, 2008). The implication is that the absence of a process (and a relevant policy) puts the institution at risk. The risk is not only lawsuits (and the attendant costs of legal fees and settlements) but also damage to reputation, especially problematic in a competitive postsecondary market. (Beyond student enrolment, reputational risks have negative impacts on an institution's ability to hire and retain faculty and could reduce productivity [Hemel & Lund, 2018, p. 1612].)

Although policies and procedures reduce the risk of liability, the internal management of norm violations poses a risk to the organization. Postsecondary institutions do not have shareholders, but they do have stakeholders – the public – to whom they are accountable in a government-funded context. The responsibility of an organization for the activities of its members has undergone a number of revisions in the past few decades, with organizational liability for wrongdoing becoming increasingly prominent. In their article focusing on corporate liability in the United States, Hemel and Lund (2018) provide examples of corporations sued by their shareholders after executives were involved in sex scandals, with shareholders often claiming that the companies provided false and misleading statements about the nature of the work environment and withheld information from them about the scandals. Shareholders of corporations involved in sex scandals have made claims suggesting that the scandals are evidence of a failure to deliver what the companies claimed: in essence, claims about the "commitment to diversity and inclusiveness were inaccurate" (p. 1619).

The issues of organizational liability focus on three pivotal questions. Was the organization aware of the wrongdoing? How did the organization address the wrongdoing (once aware of it)? And could the organization have anticipated such wrongdoing, and were there protections in place? A 2017 decision by the Supreme Court of Canada involving a case of workplace harassment among subcontractors essentially broadened the scope of workplace harassment to include individuals beyond the more traditional employee-employer relationship. Similarly, the postsecondary institution is a workplace and involves diverse communities – again confirming that, though Canadian universities are not subject to Title IX requirements, as in the United States, the rights associated with workplaces in Canada similarly extend to individuals associated with universities. As Zaman and Rudner (2018) explain, "in light of this decision, employers should consider revising their workplace harassment, violence and anti-discrimination policies and procedures to ensure they are compliant with their legal obligations and to minimize the risk of liability." Postsecondary institutions must similarly ensure that they have policies and procedures in place to reduce their liability in the event of wrongdoing. A central aspect of policing the postsecondary context is ensuring that the institution is not vulnerable to liability issues, with at least some of the work of policing the postsecondary environment undertaken to reduce liabilities.

Conclusion

> Today, the learning environment is burdened by increasing bureaucratization, and a need to manage liabilities and find economic efficiencies.
> – RENNICK (2019, P. 84)

Part of today's "security narrative" is that threats abound, and institutions of all types must take measures to maximize the safety of their constituents. Efforts to deal with mental illness and harassment, for example, are concerns among a range of institutions beyond those of postsecondary education. As in other organizations, many of the public-facing security efforts undertaken by postsecondary institutions attempt to address threats at the crime-related or "public" end of the security violation continuum. A focus on this more public and criminal end of the continuum constitutes relatively "easy wins" for postsecondary reputational boosts: policies addressing these types of security issues bolster reputations and ensure that institutions are doing something about activities of broad concern. Public and private police are called on in various ways to secure these environments, yet the extent to which public police are involved is complicated by the specifics of the postsecondary institution, which prioritizes policing itself – a position apparently supported by the public police and judicial systems.

As Wilkinson (2016) has observed, the provision of security in the postsecondary context has been framed and legitimized as a "public good" – something that we all want. Yet our discussion highlights that incentives for creating policies and procedures might have less to do with security concerns and more to do with financial motivation and liability avoidance. Taking on jurisdiction for sexual misbehaviours that occur on campus, for example, might not have been preferred by postsecondary institutions (e.g., as per Title IX) if not for the threat of having to assume liabilities and reduced funding if found not to have addressed such misbehaviours.

I have argued that security violations comprise a continuum in the postsecondary landscape, with many violations potentially undermining an institution's reputation. As noted throughout this chapter, postsecondary institutions increasingly must position themselves as "market competitive," protecting their reputations to gain market share (more students, more funding) among their competitors. Although violations constitute a continuum, with more or less external involvement, it is to the institution's benefit to ensure that as many violations as possible are dealt with internally to maximize autonomy over security and policing issues as well as to reduce public exposure and the likelihood of liability. As suggested earlier, only in cases of serious damage to public (and to a lesser extent internal) trust is there strong motivation to reveal violations within the university to its larger communities. A postsecondary institution that presides over norm violations internally appears to be justifiable – and supported by the courts – to the extent that the violations dealt with are primarily academic. Public police as well as the criminal justice system might have limited resources to apply to private contexts that appear to be willing and able to police themselves.

Although collegial governance is foundational to the postsecondary environment, such processes represent challenges for sustaining security and policing. With the imposition of various collective agreements and protections of privacy, postsecondary institutions might condemn themselves to repeated norm violations since such violations are rarely discussed and thus offer little in terms of deterring future incidents. Internal processes often lack the transparency that might be required to deter others but also employ different thresholds for various behaviours – evidence of wrongdoing, for example, might be less (or more) stringent internally than externally. Meerts (2018) notes the problems that this poses for oversight of internally adjudicated wrongdoing – both privacy concerns and settlements can ensure that investigations and outcomes remain well hidden.

Associated with internal adjudications are the complications of twenty-first-century life – the impacts of technology and legalese, for example – that might continue to affect self-governance and addressing wrongdoing in fair and timely ways. Recent examples of student hacking involving learning management systems often require corporate computing experts to determine how systems have been hacked – circumstances that go beyond the technical capacities of internal IT specialists and administrators dealing with such cases. Technological advances and increased legal restrictions, coupled with declining faculty involvement in collegial governance (Pennock et al., 2016), suggest that traditional forms of internal security and policing might decline in the future. A corporate security model – whether in house or contracted – might be a solution to at least some of the issues with which postsecondary institutions are increasingly dealing. Brownlee (2015) underscores that there is a fundamental difference between corporate and academic institutions, suggesting that academics' focus on disinterested inquiry counters the corporate focus on profit, yet the common thread might be their desire to remain autonomous and self-policed. Despite resistance to corporate models, the notions of self-governance and autonomy that pervade the postsecondary campus parallel the corporate policing model, which also resists external policing.

Ultimately, the postsecondary environment is affected by an assortment of factors that makes security an elusive target on campus and perhaps orients security and policing to the low-hanging fruit of criminal behaviour, with less attention paid to the issues that prevail regarding internal security and the ethos of postsecondary institutions' emphasis on self-governance. The dynamic nature of twenty-first-century influences on postsecondary environments means that internal methods for dealing with security and policing issues must be revised to align the campus with the public's expectation of a "supportive and secure" environment that is now part of the market-impacted postsecondary institution.

Note

1 See https://www.ucalgary.ca/pubs/calendar/current/assets/2019_UG_CALENDAR.pdf; emphasis added.

References

Anderson, M. D. (2015, September 28). The rise of law enforcement on college campuses. *The Atlantic.* https://www.theatlantic.com/education/archive/2015/09/college-campus-policing/407659/

Brenner, H. (2018). A Title IX conundrum: Are campus visitors protected from sexual assault? *Iowa Law Review, 104*(1), 93–138.

Brodeur, J.-P. (2010). *The policing web.* Oxford University Press.

Brownlee, J. (2015). The corporate corruption of academic research. *Alternate Routes, 26*, 23–50.

Department of Justice. (2015, August 7). Overview of the Title IX of the Education Amendments of 1972, 20 U.S.C. A§ 1681 ET.SEQ. https://www.justice.gov/crt/overview-title-ix-education-amendments-1972-20-usc-1681-et-seq

Gomery, S. A. (2013, November 25). Canada: Former professor cannot sue university that refused to promote him. *Mondaq: Connecting Knowledge & People.* http://www.mondaq.com/canada/x/277298/employment+litigation+tribunals/Former+professor+cannot+sue+university+that+refused+to+promote+him

Gurciullo, B. (2013, April 22). UPD faces flak for off-campus responses. *The GW Hatchet.* https://www.gwhatchet.com/2013/04/22/upd-faces-flak-for-off-campus-responses/

Hemel, D., & Lund, D. S. (2018). Sexual harassment and corporate law. *Columbia Law Review, 118*(6), 1583–1680.

Joh, E. (2004). The paradox of private policing. *Journal of Criminal Law and Criminology, 95*(1), 49–131.

Kutner, M. (2015, August 5). Indictment of Cincinnati campus cop raises fears about armed police at schools. *Newsweek*. https://www.newsweek.com/indictment-cincinnati-campus-cop-raises-fears-about-armed-police-schools-360007

Liivoja, R. (2010). The criminal jurisdiction of states: A theoretical primer. *No Foundations: Journal of Extreme Legal Positivism, 7*(7), 25–58.

McPherson, P., & Coleman, M. S. (2019, August 5). We must have both. *Inside Higher Ed.* https://www.insidehighered.com/views/2019/08/05/research-universities-must-bolster-both-security-and-openness-opinion

Meerts, C. (2018). The organisation as the cure for its own ailments: Corporate investigators in the Netherlands. *Administrative Sciences, 8*(3), 1–15.

Meerts, C., & Dorn, N. (2009). Corporate security and private justice: Danger signs? *European Journal of Crime, Criminal Law and Criminal Justice, 17*, 97–111.

Mullens, A. (2008, April 7). When students sue. *University Affairs/Affaires universitaires*. https://www.universityaffairs.ca/features/feature-article/when-students-sue/

Pennock, L., Jones, G. A., Leclerc, J. M., & Li, S. X. (2016). Challenges and opportunities for collegial governance at Canadian universities: Reflections on a survey of academic senates. *Canadian Journal of Higher Education, 46*(3), 73–89.

Perez-Pena, R. (2015, July 30). University of Cincinnati officer indicted in shooting death of Samuel Dubose. *New York Times*. https://www.nytimes.com/2015/07/30/us/university-of-cincinnati-officer-indicted-in-shooting-death-of-motorist.html?_r=0

Rennick, J. B. (2019). Learning and teaching as emergent, standardized, and radical concepts. *Religious Studies and Theology, 38*(1–2), 80–86.

Shearing, C. D., & Stenning, P.C. (1983). Private Security: Implications for social control. *Social Problems, 30*(5): 493–506.

Sloan III, J. J. (2020, July–August). Race, violence, justice, and campus police. *Footnotes: A Publication of the American Sociological Association, 48*(4): 9–11. https://www.asanet.org/news-events/footnotes/jul-aug-2020/features/race-violence-justice-and-campus-police

Snowdon, K. (2018). *Canada's universities: Cost pressures, business models, and financial stability. Update 2018.* https://snowdonandassociates.ca/wp-content/uploads/2018/07/K.-Snowdon-2018.-Update-2018-Canadas-Universities-Cost-Pressures-Business-Models-and-Financial-Sustainability.pdf

Stoner, M. (2019, July 26). What's the reputation of your institution worth? *Inside Higher Ed.* https://www.insidehighered.com/blogs/call-action-marketing-and-communications-higher-education/what%E2%80%99s-reputation-your-institution

Tani, K. M. (2017). An administrative right to be free from sexual violence? Title IX enforcement in historical and institutional perspective. *Duke Law Journal, 66*(8), 1847–1903.

Turk, J. L. (2017). Foreword: The landscape of the contemporary university. *Canadian Journal of Communication, 42*, 3–12.

Wilkinson, B. (2016). Legitimizing security in the ivory tower: Canadian university corporate security services' public quest for legitimacy. *Canadian Review of Sociology, 53*(2), 226–243.

Wilkinson, B., & Ivsins, A. (2017). Animal house: University risk environments and the regulation of students' alcohol use. *International Journal of Drug Policy, 47,* 18–25.

Williams, J. W. (2006). Private legal orders: Professional markets and the commodification of financial governance. *Social and Legal Studies, 15*(2), 209–235.

Zaman, N., & Rudner, S. (2018, January 5). Supreme Court of Canada confirms that all workplace harassment is protected. *First Reference.* http://blog.firstreference.com/all-workplace-harassment-is-protected-even-third-parties/

PART 2

Private Actors in City Spaces and Surveillance

4

Policing Canadian Smart Cities

Technology, Race, and Private Influence in Canadian Law Enforcement

JAMIE DUNCAN and DANIELLA BARRETO

Introduction

In March 2017, Waterfront Toronto, a public development corporation with stakeholders from all levels of Canadian government (municipal, provincial, and federal) issued a request for proposals for an "innovation and funding partner" to develop Toronto's southeastern Quayside neighbourhood with "innovative, emerging technologies" (Lorinc, 2017, para. 2). Seven months later, in October, Waterfront Toronto and Alphabet-owned company Sidewalk Labs announced the Sidewalk Toronto project, pitched as a "neighbourhood built from the internet up," and garnered $50 million US from Sidewalk Labs for public consultations to take place over the following year (Scola, 2018, para. 2). The project raised significant optimism and controversy over promises to make Toronto a more sustainable, affordable, and inclusive city alongside concurrent potential to expand surveillance and cede control of public policy making to an American conglomerate. Ultimately, Sidewalk Labs pulled out of the initiative amid the COVID-19 pandemic in May 2020 (Roth & McIntyre, 2020).

Sidewalk Toronto is exemplary of the logics of corporate smart cities, but it is not alone. Increasingly, municipalities across Canada are clamouring to smarten themselves up. In 2018, almost 200 cities from every province and territory submitted applications to Infrastructure Canada's Smart Cities Challenge, for four prizes between $5 and $50 million CDN based upon population size (Infrastructure Canada, 2018e). The winning municipalities of Montreal, Quebec; Guelph, Ontario; Bridgewater, Nova Scotia; and Nunavut Communities, Nunavut, proposed data- and sensor-driven infrastructural solutions to promote food and energy security, urban mobility, and suicide prevention initiatives, respectively (Infrastructure Canada, 2018a, 2018b, 2018c, 2018d). Many smart city initiatives revolve around the pursuit of safer cities and thus often gravitate toward policing (Joh, 2019). Police departments across Canada are embracing "smart" solutions to their operations (Robertson et al., 2020). How does policing in Canada interact with the discursive logics of the corporate smart city? How do these logics interact with ongoing practices of racialized policing in Canadian cities?

In this chapter, we argue that the logics of *privatization, platformization,* and *anticipation* facilitate the amplification and obfuscation of racist policing in Canada (see Monahan, this volume, for a similar perspective regarding the United States). These discursive logics facilitate the expansion of private influence in criminal justice to the effect of eroding accountability, delegating discriminatory practices to automated systems, and eliding tensions between profit motives and the public interest. We begin by defining and detailing the entangled logics of the corporate smart city before situating them in the context of racial discrimination in Canadian policing. We then synthesize media, academic, and government sources using the logics of privatization, platformization, and anticipation as an analytical framework to identify how the proliferation of networked technology is affecting Canadian policing practices. Finally, we present a content analysis of Thunder Bay's Smart Cities Challenge application to show how the discursive logics of the corporate smart city serve to elide the contradictions of market-driven digital urbanism.

The issue of racial discrimination in policing relates to many intersections, including gender, sexuality, class, and (dis)ability. Although all are important considerations, this chapter contributes specifically to understanding how the concurrent expansion of private influence and data-driven technology interacts with the problem of racial discrimination in Canadian criminal justice. The intersection of race and technology is at the centre of many topical academic discussions. However, much of the scholarship on the impacts of predictive and data-driven technologies in criminal justice – especially in regard to race – emanates from American contexts (Byfield, 2019; Ferguson, 2017; Joh, 2017a; Richardson et al., 2019). We rely on comparisons with American policing at times; however, we add to a paucity of Canadian literature on interactions among private influence, data-driven technology, and racial discrimination in Canadian policing. Our theoretical and empirical insights will enrich domestic scholarly discourse and contribute to more robust international comparative theorizations. We begin by outlining how corporate smart city logics interact with racial discrimination in Canadian policing.

Policing the Corporate Smart City
Central to any definition of a "smart city" is the use of information and communication technologies to address common urban challenges through enhanced efficiencies. Smart city discourses often assume a capacity to tame the otherwise chaotic city by leveraging "big data" – huge quantities of rapidly accessible and varied datasets – and the "internet of things" (IoT), physical objects connected to the internet that produce data that can be used for a variety of purposes, such as monitoring traffic flows or locating the origins of a gunshot (Gold, 2015; Hajer, 2015; Kitchin, 2014b). Increasingly, ubiquitous sensors provide city officials (and the private actors to whom services and utilities are frequently outsourced) with a constant stream of data, which they can use to make decisions and automate services (Kitchin, 2014b). In smart cities, the "urban landscape and its citizenry are understood as problematic" and in need of data-driven behavioural and infrastructural solutions (Gandy & Nemorin, 2019, p. 2114).

The spectre of techno-solutionism (the notion that we can invent our way out of complex social problems) has pervaded many efforts to build purportedly smarter cities (Kitchin, 2014b; Morozov, 2013). This takes the form of discrete districts built from the ground up (e.g., Songdo in South Korea or what has been proposed by Sidewalk Toronto) and the integration of technology into pre-existing urban spaces (e.g., Rio de Janeiro's sensor-driven Intelligent Operations Centre or the London, UK, Dashboard) (Kitchin, 2014b; Morozov & Bria, 2018). There exists a clear set of often utopian discursive logics to corporate smart cities that pervades efforts to make urban spaces safer, wealthier, and more efficient (March, 2018). The overlapping logics of privatization, platformization, and anticipation feed into each other to inform a set of assumptions about urban development, optimization, and governance that prioritize profit over justice.

Privatization
Contemporary urban governance and policing are intractably entangled with privatization – a "container" concept with many meanings (Hucklesby & Lister, 2017, p. 4). We conceive of privatization as both a spectrum and a

process. As a spectrum, it can come in "weaker" forms such as outsourcing, in which a police department contracts out part of its operations to a for-profit enterprise yet retains significant control (Ayling et al., 2009; Luscombe et al., this volume). Privatization can also refer to the wholesale marketization of a previously public service in which the state cedes significant authority over the availability, quality, and cost of the marketized function to private actors (Hucklesby & Lister, 2017; Kitchin et al., 2015). Somewhere in between is the increasingly prevalent practice of public-private partnerships (P3s), which involve collaborative efforts between private and public sectors and serve as a vehicle for corporate influence in public policy making (Kitchin, 2014b; Luscombe et al., this volume; White, 2014). Across this spectrum, privatization has the effect of fostering public dependence on private solutions (Ayling et al., 2009).

Privatization is a key tenet of neo-liberalism, which since the late 1970s has blurred distinctions between public and private domains in Western liberal democracies (Starr, 1988). This process has been well studied in the context of criminal justice. The rise of managerialism and corporatization in policing is well documented in scholarship, which describes, respectively, the tendency of police to emulate and enable metric-driven corporate mentalities and organizational structures in the face of economic austerity (Ayling et al., 2009; Brownlee et al., 2018; Mulone, this volume). In this context, scholars have highlighted the multilateralization of policing, describing the emergence of a networked, pluralistic approach to governing public safety involving a multitude of actors through outsourcing and P3s (Brodeur, 2010; Zedner, 2006). Privatization thus describes enormous shifts in the form and substance of public spaces and institutions away from the assumption that liberal citizens are entitled to a government that is "public not only in its ends but also in its processes" (Starr, 1988, p. 11).

Platformization

The logic of platformization amplifies the managerialism and multilateralism characteristic of privatization through the massive proliferation of networked communication technology. Plantin et al. (2018) describe the process of platformization as the fragmentation of robust infrastructures created and regulated in the public interest in favour of mutable and programmable platforms oriented to profitability. Less critically, Egbert (2019, p. 84) defines the platformization of policing as "an organizational process in which manifold data sets and databanks – especially from police-external sources – are cross-linked, creating information retrieval and production networks designed to improve police work on numerous levels by facilitating knowledge creation." Egbert's definition does not accommodate the ambivalence that arises through attempts to justify the often competing imperatives of private profit and public good.

As Gillespie (2010) notes, the ambiguity of the word *platform* allows platform beneficiaries to elide the contradictions that arise from a platform's market-orientation. In early 2016, just months after forming Sidewalk Labs, executives Anand Babu and Craig Nevill-Manning delivered a talk entitled "Reimagining the City as a Platform." They argued that society was "poised for a revolution based on digital technology that can improve quality of life and make cities more human-focused, while using scarce resources more efficiently." In contrast to this techno-optimist managerial tone, Sadowski and Pasquale (2015, p. 1) note that "there is little escape from a seamless web of surveillance" as "government and corporate actors, often in close partnership with each other, fill cities with 'smart' technologies – turning them into platforms for the 'Internet of Things.'" Indeed, Sidewalk Labs de-emphasizes the ambivalent ends of the city as a platform by claiming that it will make cities cleaner and more affordable (thus in the public interest) while neglecting the concurrent expansion of surveillance as an organizing principle for social and economic life (Lyon, 2001; Zuboff, 2019).

Anticipation
The networked flows of communication that enable platformized surveillance generate large quantities of varied, real-time information that feed into data-driven anticipation. Platformization enables the expansion of big data and predictive analysis informed by machine-learning algorithms (recursive models used to automate tasks such as image and speech recognition and information categorization, which improve over time). The transformation of cities into a data-driven managerial project has given rise to what Kitchin (2014a) calls "anticipatory governance": that is, the trend toward prediction and deployment of increasingly automated actuarial methods to inform the workings of the city, including its law enforcement functions and sentencing practices (Pope & Bromwich, this volume; Sadowski & Pasquale, 2015). Smart city discourses often construct data and networked technologies as tools to tame otherwise chaotic and unpredictable urban environments through probabilistic logics (Hajer, 2015). The logic of anticipation is thus one of speculative risk management, which aims to optimize cost and efficiency and pre-emptively mitigate threats to public infrastructure and safety.

The logic of anticipation drives predictive policing, which leverages big data and machine-learning techniques to anticipate crime in probabilistic terms; police resources and attention are directed toward areas and individuals deemed high risk (Brayne, 2017; Robertson et al., 2020). Importantly, technologies of anticipation rely on historical data produced by police, thereby automating existing practices rather than predicting crime in and of itself (Ferguson, 2017; Joh, 2017a). Notwithstanding the demonstrable fallibility of predictive methods, Gandy and Nemorin (2019) point out that alongside prediction comes the capacity to manipulate. For example, Sadowski and Pasquale (2015) argue that the ability to track and predict protests allows authorities to discourage, prevent, and quell acts of civil disobedience and legitimate demonstrations with a variety of remote tactics, such as altering public transit routes and schedules. In Canada, efforts to monitor protests frequently target racialized groups such as Idle No More and Black Lives Matter (BLM) (Craig, 2016; Makuch, 2017; Urkosky, 2016).

White Supremacy in Canadian Policing
There is a high level of distrust between marginalized communities and Canadian police rooted in a long legacy of colonial harms and explicitly racist policing practices (National Inquiry into Missing and Murdered Indigenous Women and Girls, 2019; Wortley & Owusu-Bempah, 2009, 2011). The North West Mounted Police (NWMP) was established in 1873 to facilitate white settlement of Canada's North-West Territories (today's Manitoba, Saskatchewan, and Alberta) (Dhillon, 2017; Marquis, 2016). Although mythologized as heroic in Canada's historical imaginary and present national identity, the NWMP of the late nineteenth century was an organization engaged in prevalent sexual violence against Indigenous women (Marquis, 2016). In 1920, the NWMP evolved into the Royal Canadian Mounted Police (RCMP), which continued this legacy through the twentieth century, in part, by acting as truant officers for Canada's genocidal residential school system; the last of these institutions closed in 1996 (LeBeuf, 2011; Marquis, 2016).

Discrimination in Canadian policing has not ceased. Racist practices have been adapted and carried forward, perhaps most egregiously as "starlight tours" (common enough to have earned such a colloquialism), in which Saskatoon police drove intoxicated Indigenous men into the countryside in the middle of winter to die, as with Neil Stonechild in 1990 (Dhillon, 2017). An inquiry into the practice was called after the bodies of Rodney Naistus, Lloyd Dustyhorn, Lawrence Wegner, and Darcy Dean Ironchild were found in 2000 – and only after an unsuccessful starlight tour that Darrell Night survived to testify about (Dhillon, 2017; Roberts, 2000). More recently, police across Canada, in cities large and small, have faced a spate of reports regarding institutionalized anti-Black and anti-Indigenous racism. Cumulatively, internal-departmental, government, media, and academic research on Vancouver, Thunder Bay, Toronto, and Halifax, and on a national comparative scale, has demonstrated that marginalized communities across Canada are overcriminalized and underprotected by police (Manojlovic, 2018; Marcoux & Nicholson, 2018; McNeilly, 2018; Ontario Human Rights Commission, 2018; Owusu-Bempah et al., 2019; Rankin & Winsa, 2012; Wortley, 2019).

Black and Indigenous communities are simultaneously targeted with heightened police scrutiny and neglected by police when in need of assistance. This situation perpetuates racial inequality and amounts to a continuation of centuries of colonial violence. Among the starkest evidence comes from Winnipeg, where Indigenous people make up 10.6 percent of the population yet comprised almost two-thirds of police killings between 2000 and 2017 (Marcoux & Nicholson, 2018). And in Toronto, between 2013 and 2018, Black residents were about twenty times more likely than white residents to be killed by police, according to the Ontario Human Rights Commission (2018). Complementing a sea of damning statistics too vast for the space available here, the final report of Canada's National Inquiry into Missing and Murdered Indigenous Women and Girls (2019) contains numerous stories of gendered violence and neglect in encounters between Indigenous people and Canadian police.

Scholars have discussed the real and potential adverse impacts of privatization and the politics of austerity on community well-being and racial justice (Ayling et al., 2009; D'Alessio et al., 2005; Zedner, 2006). The logics of platformization and anticipation constitute an extension and intensification of private influence via fragmentation, managerialism, and public dependence on private sector solutions, all of which affect the everyday practices of Canadian police. In the following sections, we synthesize evidence from the Canadian context, illustrating how the discursive logics of platformization and anticipation broaden police surveillance of racialized communities and automate pre-existing discriminatory practices. Private vendors exercise influence through platformed and predictive technologies, eroding accountability and sidestepping contradictions between the stated goal of supporting public safety and tacit end of making money.

Platformization and Anticipation in Canadian Law Enforcement

Canadian police are becoming reliant on information management platforms used to bring together many disparate forms of data. This reliance often involves multiple third-party vendors and off-site cloud storage solutions. These platforms enable the use of a host of data-driven tools that Robertson et al. (2020) call algorithmic policing. Such policing is categorized into three primary forms: algorithmic mass-surveillance technologies such as social media monitoring or facial recognition; location-based technologies used to identify places where crimes are most likely to occur (often with historical enforcement data); and person-focused technologies that attempt to anticipate the likelihood of an individual's involvement in a given crime (e.g., through social network analysis).

These tools are often used concurrently by Canadian police through platform-enabled information systems and centralized command centres. Compounding the availability of powerful surveillance equipment and software to police, the platformization of urban residents' own social interactions has expanded significantly the capacities of police to collect information about individuals and communities.

In this context, private influence in policing not only contributes to a blurring of the divide between public and private but also deepens the ambiguity between high policing – driven by knowledge work and reliant on deception and circumvention to manage sophisticated forms of deviance – and low policing – which relies on threats of violence to interrupt more traditional forms of delinquency (Brodeur, 2010). In effect, platform and algorithmic policing technologies and the command centre model constitute "a private apparatus of high policing" used to facilitate low policing operations (Brodeur, 2010, p. 255).

Launched in 2016, the Ottawa Police Strategic Operations Centre (OPSOC) pulls together disparate information sources to provide officers with real-time intelligence and enhance "situational awareness": that is, details about people and places involved on a particular call (Ottawa Police Service, 2018). In addition to supporting officers on call, OPSOC is tasked with monitoring political demonstrations on social media and serving "as a 'point of contact' for various police agencies, public institutions and private companies during protests" (Munn, 2017). Little information has been disclosed about the vendors involved in OPSOC, whereas forces in western Canada have been much more open about their adoption of algorithmic policing technologies.

In 2019, the Edmonton Police Service (EPS) began rolling out a custom digital evidence management platform from IBM, allowing it to "manage and analyze a wealth of data from across its operations" ("IBM," 2018). The Operations and Intelligence Command Centre became fully operational in 2020 and connects digital evidence collection (e.g., statements or photos) with police databases, closed-circuit and traffic camera footage, and data collected from social media (Edmonton Police Service, n.d.). The system leverages advanced artificial intelligence techniques, including predictive and video analytics as well as natural language processing powered by IBM's Watson platform (Edmonton Police Service, n.d.; "IBM," 2018). The command centre "equip[s] officers with real-time situational insights" to "limit the unknowns and enable our front-line teams to make smarter, safer decisions in a timelier manner" ("IBM," 2018). The EPS is also in the process of procuring a facial recognition system to cross-reference images of suspects against a mugshot database (Robertson et al., 2020).

The Calgary Police Service (CPS) is among the keenest to experiment with smart policing technologies. In 2014, Calgary became the first city in Canada to use facial recognition with its deployment of NEC Corporation's NeoFace Reveal, which compares "photo or video of a criminal suspect" with a "master facial image database" to identify the person (Mayhew, 2014). In 2018, the city rolled out body cameras to be used by all officers responding to calls, becoming the first major Canadian city to standardize their use (Pearson, 2019). The cameras are paired with Axon's digital evidence platform to manage the footage ("Calgary Police Service," 2018). Additionally, the CPS has used controversial and secretive surveillance company Palantir's data management platform since 2013 to access and analyze "vast pools of data" in efforts to "reduce and prevent crime" (Braga, 2017, paras. 21, 22). Palantir's platform is used in concert with IBM's i2 Analyst Notebook to aggregate data from internal records "to identify central actors and key players" of interest to police using social network analysis (Robertson et al., 2020).

Like many police forces in larger cities in Canada, the RCMP, which contracts its services to many small municipalities, is "exploring options" to procure a platform for "situational awareness ... making data available for frontline operational decision-making" (Ayling et al., 2009; Royal Canadian Mounted Police, 2018). Like many local departments in Canada, "the RCMP's shifting position on cloud has ... been nudged by the vendor community, which is increasingly offering only cloud-based solutions. The migration to cloud is being shepherded by the disappearance of on-premise solutions" (Brooks, 2016, p. 3).

As in Edmonton, Calgary, and Ottawa, the RCMP leverages social networking sites for open-source intelligence. In 2019, it was reported that the RCMP had procured social media monitoring software from American security vendor Carahsoft to anticipate crimes. Project Wide Awake involved what the RCMP calls a "proactive approach" to monitoring social media in real time using the software to help predict and prevent crime; political demonstrations have been identified as a specific application of the software (Carney, 2019, para. 2). This is an expansion of more reactive social media monitoring. In 2017, internal documents were published describing the RCMP's social media surveillance of a BLM vigil (Makuch, 2017). BLM protests in Toronto were also subject to social media surveillance by the Toronto Police Service (TPS) in 2016 (Urkosky, 2016). In 2014, the RCMP's Project Sitka used a variety of networked intelligence sources, including social media, to identify over 300 and track 89 Indigenous activists, collecting "names, photographs, aliases, birthdates, phone numbers, email addresses, organizational affiliations, vehicles they drove, a five-year history of demonstrations they attended, and information on their mobility throughout Canada" (Craig, 2016, para. 5) to "map out the potential networks among Native groups" (Livesey, 2017, para. 27).

The RCMP also supports municipal departments in their efforts to monitor networked communications. One example is the deployment of cell site simulators, technically called international mobile subscriber identity (IMSI) catchers. These devices collect locational and cellular traffic data by emulating cell phone towers (Koops et al., 2019). Commonly referred to as Stingrays – the Harris Corporation's brand name for them – the devices are controlled by the RCMP and can be loaned to municipal agencies, including the police departments of Toronto and Vancouver, allowing them to monitor the cell phone traffic of suspects (Joh, 2017b; Parsons & Israel, 2016).

Toronto and Vancouver have favoured experimentation with and adoption of individual tools as opposed to the platformized command centres seen in Ottawa and Edmonton. In 2016, the Vancouver Police Department (VPD) deployed a location-based predictive policing app called GeoDASH with Latitude Geographics Group's GeoCortex machine-learning technology and Esri's ArcGIS platform (Meuse, 2017; Sohal, 2018). GeoDASH provides officers with targeted insights into areas likely to experience higher levels of crime, similar to the better-known PredPol software used in the United States (Brayne, 2017).

Other firms offer IoT solutions "built into the very fabric of urban environments" that generate data for predictive analyses (Kitchin, 2014b, p. 2). For example, ShotSpotter claims to offer the capacity automatically to detect and locate gunshots within the city using networked microphones, which after detecting a gunshot record audio and, in some cases, video of the area (Gold, 2015). The company's technology has been implemented in over 100 cities, predominantly in "high-crime" American neighbourhoods, often poor and Black ("Cities," n.d.; Coleman & Brunton, 2016).

The TPS was in the process of procuring ShotSpotter but halted in early 2019 after it became apparent that legal challenges would arise (Gray, 2019; Janus, 2019). Despite saying no to ShotSpotter, in 2018 the TPS had quietly procured a facial recognition solution from NEC (the same vendor that Calgary used) for over $450,000 CDN, which it had been using for over a year to compare images from surveillance footage and photos taken by witnesses with over 1.5 million mugshots to identify suspects (Lee-Shanok, 2019; Toronto Police Services Board, 2019).

As of the time of writing, there remain many gaps in the public record regarding the adoption and use of police platforms and algorithmic policing tools in Canada. Nonetheless, the logics of platformization and anticipation clearly pervade contemporary Canadian policing practices. Police depend on multilateral networks of private vendors to expand their surveillance capacities. Managerial discourses of efficiency are used to justify expanded surveillance and the fragmentation of policing functions produced by dependence on the private sector. The plurality of actors involved and increasingly networked flows of disparate information allow private vendors to influence the information management practices and policies of Canadian police (Luscombe et al., this volume; Mulone, this volume). In this context, we show how the discursive logics of the corporate smart city erode transparency and accountability, expand racialized surveillance, and automate pre-existing discriminatory enforcement practices while rhetorically eliding the tensions evoked by growing private influence.

Eroding Accountability

Inadequate transparency is not new in Canadian criminal justice (Ullrich, 2019). Canadian criminal justice organizations have long obfuscated discrimination by refusing to release racially disaggregated statistics (Millar & Owusu-Bempah, 2011). A growing dependence on the private sector is worsening this inadequate transparency. Joh (2017b) also discusses how vendors abuse intellectual property laws and non-disclosure agreements to help police evade surveillance accountability for their use of products such as IMSI catchers. Parsons and Israel (2016) show that Canadian agencies such as the TPS and VPD have been even less forthcoming than many American counterparts regarding their use of Stingrays. Inadequate accountability for the use of powerful surveillance technology is only worsened by the well-documented issue of racial discrimination within both forces (Manojlovic, 2018; Ontario Human Rights Commission, 2018).

Police in Canada and the United States have gone to great lengths to deny, deflect, and delay disclosure of their use of Stingrays (Joh, 2017b; Parsons & Israel, 2016). Deploying IMSI catchers in Canada requires a "tracking warrant," but details regarding use of the devices are presumed to be heavily limited by non-disclosure agreements and rarely divulged in forums accessible to the public (Koops et al., 2019; Parsons & Israel, 2016). This obfuscation benefits both the RCMP, which controls the devices, and the Harris Corporation, which sells them. It is believed that more robust accountability would negatively affect operational efficiency and sales.

Industry has also found ways to foster dependence and erode accountability through subscription business models and intellectual property laws. Increasingly, vendors offer integrated services to police departments in which control of the data and methods of analysis remain proprietary (Joh, 2017b). For example, in the case of body-worn cameras, Axon, the vendor used by the CPS, does not simply sell the hardware but also provides a cloud-based evidence management platform to maximize long-term revenue ("Calgary Police Service," 2018; Joh, 2017b). Vendors have used similar proprietary data management services to punish departments that terminate subscriptions. In 2017, the New York Police Department cancelled its contract with Palantir. Upon request, the company returned records of the department's prior analyses, though without a "translation key," making them impossible to access (Joh, 2017b, p. 120).

Despite clear issues with deepening dependence on vendors such as Axon and Palantir, departments are attracted to the powerful capacities and efficiencies of their technologies. Brayne's (2017) ethnographic study of the Los Angeles Police Department's use of Palantir's platform revealed how automated situational awareness afforded officers access to knowledge that otherwise would require a warrant and allowed for surveillance of individuals only tangentially related to a crime through the system's social network analyses – both functions constitute blatant erosions of police accountability and powerful extensions of police surveillance capacity. Unsurprisingly, these tactics disproportionately target poor and racialized communities (Ahmed, 2018; Brayne, 2017).

Similar patterns occur in Canada yet are under-documented on the public record and in scholarship. In particular, the CPS is susceptible to private influence in many of the ways documented by Joh (2017b) and Brayne (2017). The CPS relies on Palantir and Axon (among others) to integrate, analyze, and store its data, both of which sell proprietary platform-as-a-service solutions for data storage, management, and analysis (Braga, 2017; "Calgary Police Service," 2018). There is a high level of perceived profiling by the police among racialized residents of Calgary. Body cameras were introduced, in part, to improve perceived transparency and accountability, but evidence suggests that body cameras alone do not improve perceptions of police among groups subjected to police discrimination ("Calgary Police Service," 2018; Kerrison et al., 2018; Louis et al., 2019; Ngo et al., 2018). Digital evidence management solutions do little to alleviate poor relations between police and racialized communities, and they deepen CPS's dependence on third-party vendors by ceding control of how potentially sensitive information is stored, organized, and accessed to an American company.

Police agencies across Canada are embracing various digital evidence platforms and are subject to similar forms of private influence. Such multifarious dependencies established between criminal justice institutions and the private sector have been labelled "policymaking by procurement," by which standard practices of accountability and governance are displaced by and subverted through the terms and conditions of technology vendors (Crump, 2016). In this context, networked data analysis using fragmented "police-external" sources expands capacities for unaccountable surveillance. Networking disparate data sources can allow police to monitor individuals without cause and gain insights that otherwise would be prohibited. Brayne (2017) documents how police in Los Angeles were able to obtain information with Palantir's platform that otherwise would have required a warrant using methods of social network analysis similar to those deployed by the CPS.

A particularly chilling example is the revelation that over thirty Canadian police forces, including the RCMP and those in Calgary, Edmonton, Ottawa, Toronto, and Vancouver, have used technology from facial recognition company Clearview AI in their work (Aguilar, 2020). The secretive company's platform can identify images of an individual by cross-referencing billions of photos scraped from social media – a form of mass surveillance that was declared illegal by Canada's Privacy Commissioner (CBC, 2020; Office of the Privacy Commissioner of Canada, 2021). Given the propensity of Canadian police to target Indigenous and Black activists, outlined in more detail below, the data-driven forms of surveillance discussed in this section constitute powerful expansions of threats to basic civil liberties.

Intensifying Racialized Surveillance
Indeed, a proliferation of unaccountable surveillance threatens to amplify the already prevalent targeting of racialized groups by Canadian police. As Maynard (2017, p. 88) argues, "Black existence in public space is itself seen as criminal and thus subject to scrutiny, surveillance, frequent interruption and police intervention." The same might be said of Indigenous people, also disproportionately criminalized by Canadian police. Although the RCMP monitors the social media activity of white nationalist groups, it is clear that racial justice movements such as Idle No More (an anti-colonial Indigenous movement) and BLM are perceived as threats, even when engaged in legitimate public protests (Carney, 2019; Craig, 2016; Makuch, 2017; Royal Canadian Mounted Police, 2017). Associating the activities of Indigenous and Black activists with criminality ostensibly justifies invasive surveillance tactics like those deployed through Project Sitka and in surveillance of BLM. For example, BLM's peaceful vigil in Vancouver was classified as an "Unfolding Event – Serious Crime," and attempts were made to establish dubious links with radical American hate groups (Makuch, 2017). This high-level surveillance exists alongside well-documented racial disparities in the "stop-and-frisk" practices of police in Vancouver, Toronto, Halifax, and many other Canadian cities (Manojlovic, 2018; Ontario Human Rights Commission, 2018; Robertson et al., 2020; Wortley, 2019). Canadian police have given no indication that such discriminatory tactics will not simply be undertaken with greater efficiency as the technical affordances of platformized and predictive policing expand.

Delegating Discrimination and Eliding Contradiction
Predictive policing enables the obfuscation of discriminatory practices through delegation to automated systems. The automation of situational awareness in Canadian policing is one example of how this might occur. As police are nudged toward platform-as-a-service models and forced to outsource for technical expertise, they often cede control of their data –

and their role as primary analysts. As noted above, among the main consequences of outsourcing is that methods of automated analysis deployed by police are shielded from accountability through intellectual property law; companies argue that their algorithms are proprietary and cannot be released for public scrutiny (Broeders et al., 2017). Compounding deliberate obfuscation is the problem of algorithmic explainability: that is, the (in)ability to discern how and why automated determinations are made. Even if a department has full control of its digital architecture and analytical systems (unlikely in the present climate), algorithmic mediation remains a threat to accountability and stands to amplify inequality through its immanent opacity. If given access, then one may test algorithmic outputs for bias and analyze inputs for reliability, but it is not currently feasible to audit machine-learning algorithms for *why* they have produced a particular result, nor would this be especially useful since often these reasons are seemingly illogical (Broeders et al., 2017; Guidotti et al., 2018; Raji & Buolamwini, 2019).

This double black box of intellectual property protection and inexplicable algorithms allows police to complicate and obfuscate long-standing accusations of racial profiling and even claim that automation stands to reduce bias (Brayne, 2017; Ferguson, 2017; Joh, 2017a). The black box of an officer's intuition, which that officer might be forced to justify publicly, is being displaced by black-boxed, privately owned algorithms, precluded from examination on multiple levels yet simultaneously shrouded in an ethos of objectivity despite evidence of fallibility. Much as Zuboff (2019, p. 96) describes how "Google has learned to be a data-based fortune teller that replaces intuition with science at scale," predictive policing technologies are mystical in the sense that algorithmic outputs carry the "aura of truth, objectivity, and accuracy" (boyd & Crawford, 2012, p. 663) and are portrayed as "neutral and authoritative" (Hannah-Moffat, 2019, p. 260). Framing their use of technology in this way allows police to defer blame for bad decisions to purportedly objective computational tools.

The "feign[ed] impartiality and objectivity" (Noble, 2018, p. 61) of algorithms distract one from the fact that the enforcement data, which inform risk assessments, are produced in ways that reflect police culture and are therefore biased against marginalized populations (Harcourt, 2015; Joh, 2017a; Madden et al., 2017). Academics and advocates have shown how these "dirty" data sets amplify and obfuscate pre-existing inequalities through algorithmic mediation (Angwin & Larson, 2016; Ferguson, 2017; Richardson et al., 2019). The algorithms themselves are stacked against racialized populations. Facial recognition misrecognizes Black faces at a far higher rate than white ones (Raji & Buolamwini, 2019). As facial recognition creeps into police work, it stands to automate and amplify discriminatory street checks, making them at once less visible and more efficient. The logic of anticipation thus hypostatizes and obfuscates pre-existing racist tendencies (whether intentional or not) in Canadian police culture. In these multifarious ways, platformization and prediction in policing amount, in effect, to the delegation of discrimination.

Despite eroding accountability, deepening inequality, and automating discrimination, the discursive logics of platformization and anticipation allow police to elide the many tensions evoked by the intensification of private influence and the consequent convergence of public and private powers. Platform discourses accommodate the ambivalent and often contradictory ends of public interest and private profit. Platforms and algorithms are often portrayed as value neutral and apolitical yet reproduce oppressive social relations (Noble, 2018). Canadian police go one step further by framing potentially discriminatory or exclusionary policies and practices as virtuous. For example, the TPS described its use of facial recognition as a way to ensure that "witnesses and victims of crime would not be re-traumatized" by looking at mugshots (Lee-Shanok, 2019, para. 3). The RCMP emphasized that its use of Clearview AI served to identify victims of child sexual abuse (Tunney, 2020).

Although there are many examples to draw from, below we discuss a particularly rich example of how the discursive logics of the smart city help to elide the ambivalent ends of privately procured public safety technologies in a context of racial injustice. Using a content analysis of Thunder Bay's application to Infrastructure Canada's Smart Cities Challenge, we show how the logics of privatization, platformization, and anticipation facilitate the erosion of accountability, intensification of surveillance, and automation of discrimination while de-emphasizing the tensions brought to the surface by these processes.

The Case of Thunder Bay

Thunder Bay was one of almost 200 cities to apply for the Smart Cities Challenge. Its application was unsuccessful; however, it caught our attention as an exemplary case of how inclusionary language is used to exclusionary ends. The logics of platformization and anticipation help to de-emphasize tensions emergent from market-driven approaches to public safety. The application attempted to justify intensifying surveillance of Indigenous residents and automating discriminatory policing practices while framing the initiative in pseudo-humanitarian terms as a way to democratize connectivity, enhance Indigenous cultural sovereignty, and protect vulnerable populations. Specifically, the city applied for funds to support "investments in smart public safety technology and infrastructure" to tackle institutional racism and address Indigenous overrepresentation in the criminal justice system (City of Thunder Bay, 2018). Upon closer examination, the proposal effectively amounts to a request for funds to install pervasive and dystopian surveillance infrastructure throughout the city that would disproportionately affect already overcriminalized Indigenous youth.

Thunder Bay situates itself in relation to the politics of austerity by describing itself and many other municipalities as "fiscally challenged" (City of Thunder Bay, 2018, p. 29). Its bid for the $10 million prize resonates with the logic of privatization, acknowledging the trends toward multilateralization, fragmentation, and public dependence through vague references to the necessity of collaborating with "major product vendors" and a variety of "external" partners and funders (City of Thunder Bay, 2018, pp. 19, 26, 27, 29–31). The logics of platformization and anticipation are apparent throughout the proposal and, as we have argued, entrench corporate and managerial logics while eroding accountability and obfuscating discrimination through heightened multilateral private influence.

Thunder Bay proposed to spend the $10 million prize procuring a range of surveillance hardware and services. The proposed interventions centred on "smart pole" sensors and "intelligent surveillance cameras" equipped with facial recognition and motion-sensing technology, which the city claimed could be used as a crime deterrent for Indigenous youth and a way to prevent watercourse deaths, which have plagued Thunder Bay for over two decades (City of Thunder Bay, 2018, p. 2; Talaga, 2017). Smart poles would feature panic buttons and emergency lighting while extending public wi-fi and serving as public phones. Situated applications included using automated light and video tracking to discourage loitering, automating detection of emergencies near waterways via motion sensing, and tracking the movements of missing persons or criminal suspects through the city with facial recognition. The proposal was consistent with the trend of targeting poor, marginalized areas and populations with intensified surveillance and justifying it with democratizing platform rhetoric.

The document states that "a communication network is foundational to the smart city ecosystem. Providing a platform for people/machine/sensor communication will be pervasive" through the proposed technology (City of Thunder Bay, 2018, p. 5). The creation of a Public Safety Command Centre similar to those in Ottawa and Edmonton was suggested to manage data flows, and the interdependence of platformization and anticipation was made explicit. "Cameras, sensors, smart poles and access points (web portals and apps) all generate useful data that will feed an analytic engine. Data analytics will support the creation of predictive models, which can better utilize assets to respond to future needs of end users" (City of Thunder Bay, 2018, p. 17). The proposal encompassed a clear mobilization of the discursive logics of the corporate smart city; however, despite well-documented evidence to the contrary, the proposed interventions were couched in language that emphasized how smart public safety technology would reduce discrimination. The potential for the data harms that disproportionately affect racialized communities elsewhere were not addressed.

Thus far, we have emphasized aspects of the discourse that we see as problematic or downright frightening coming from a Canadian public institution. However, this is not how the proposal was presented by Thunder Bay. In fact, each of the proposed interventions was framed as an attempt to enhance inclusion of Indigenous youth. Indeed, the results of consultative conversations with sixteen youth residing in the city were used to situate the proposal in its inclusionary ends. Through questions such as "what are your ideas to improve and enhance community safety through technology and data?" the consultative process and the Smart Cities Challenge itself were framed from the top down to produce techno-solutionist approaches to inclusion (City of Thunder Bay, 2018, p. 14). Whether technology was even necessary was not a topic of discussion. The expansion of communication infrastructure was celebrated as a way to foster "connectedness to culture" and "pro-social" opportunities and wellness resources (City of Thunder Bay, 2018, pp. 9, 11). This implicit and often patronizing digital rights discourse emphasized the many (genuine) virtues and conveniences of internet access, while invasive surveillance explicitly targeting Indigenous residents of Thunder Bay was pitched as somehow intractable from the benefits of free or affordable access to telecommunication services.

By separating and labelling these distinct and contradictory discourses of technological emancipation and discipline, it becomes clear that attempting to manipulate already marginalized Indigenous youth by tightening police control through invasive surveillance would be unlikely to achieve inclusive ends and actually worsen relationships already fraught with centuries of violence. However, the logics of platformization and anticipation work to de-emphasize this tension. The ambiguity and mutability of platforms enables such contradictory ends to coexist – at least rhetorically.

Asking "who benefits from this ambivalence?" clearly renders the embeddedness of platformization and anticipation within the container logic of privatization. Police tighten control over urban residents while private vendors deepen public dependence on their services and technical tools to the end of maximizing profits. Whereas core stakeholders present a story about inclusion and free wi-fi, the consultative input from residents becomes market research used in attempts to convince them that ubiquitous surveillance improves their lives. One can extend this insight beyond Thunder Bay through the case of social media monitoring. It is Facebook that profits as racialized activists use the platform to organize for justice while the RCMP uses it as a tool for mass surveillance and social control. The specific social, political, and moral implications of this platformized power and resistance are largely irrelevant to Facebook as it algorithmically optimizes user newsfeeds to capture attention and commoditize it (Couldry & Mejias, 2019). It is thus the profit motive of platforms that accommodates and encourages the contradictions of platformization and anticipation. The consequent intensification of surveillance and the erosion of accountability deepen racial injustices to the end of maximizing private profits and institutional control.

Conclusion

The discursive logics of platformization and anticipatory governance are entangled with the concurrent privatization of cities and their services. These relationships necessarily and intractably infect any possible imagined public interest. The techno-solutionist and managerial approaches to urban governance we have described treat residents (especially those in marginalized communities) as problems to solve and risks to manage through accumulation and analysis of data that they produce. The use of non-disclosure agreements and intellectual property law protects private interests at the expense of civil liberties and racial justice. Neither the corporate smart city nor its police force serves the interests of residents. In this chapter, we have built upon existing insights into private influence in criminal justice by reflecting on the relationship between the proliferation of networked, privately procured technologies and ongoing racial discrimination in Canadian policing. The research ties together recent empirical findings regarding the use of platforms and predictive technologies by police to contribute to discussions about the interrelation of technology, race, and private influence in Canadian criminal justice. Our theoretical and empirical findings also stand to inform future international comparative discussions of privatization and private influence in criminal justice.

We have shown how Canadian police are at once subsumed by and exemplary of increasingly corporatized logics of urban management. Policing practices are evolving in tandem with the discursive logics of privatization, platformization, and anticipation, thereby amplifying and obfuscating racial discrimination in Canadian criminal justice. These trends facilitate the erosion of accountability, delegate discrimination to automated systems, and distract from the tensions emergent from private influence in policing. We began by defining the corporate smart city, detailing how privatization, platformization, and anticipation interact with prevalent racial discrimination in Canadian policing. We then discussed how platformization and anticipation extend the processual logics of privatization in Canadian policing, with the effects of evading accountability, intensifying racialized surveillance, and automating the injustices faced by racialized communities in Canada. We concluded with a content analysis of Thunder Bay's application to the pan-Canadian Smart Cities Challenge, in which the nested discursive logics that we discussed were deployed in attempts to justify the installation of pervasive surveillance equipment and to elide the tensions that emerge from the convergence of public and private domains in criminal justice.

Expanding private influence through deployment of specialized technological tools in Canadian policing is exacerbating pre-existing racial discrimination. This chapter has surfaced some of the understudied contexts in which this occurs, but ultimately there is a need for significantly more empirical research and rigorous accountability regarding deployments of data-driven technology in Canadian policing. This task becomes more difficult as proprietary control of data renders already obfuscated racially disaggregated statistics even more difficult to access. Despite this non-transparency, the purported objectivity of data-driven and automated tools is used to justify additional barriers to police accountability. Without humouring the techno-determinist narratives that support these trends, it is fair to expect that efforts to develop and adopt the technologies discussed herein will continue. In this light, it is time for Canadian activists, policy makers, academics, and members of the public to have more informed and robust conversations regarding the intersection of technology and racial discrimination in Canadian criminal justice.

References

Aguilar, B. (2020, March 1). OPP admit using controversial facial recognition software Clearview AI. *CP24.* https://www.cp24.com/news/opp-admit-using-controversial-facial-recognition-software-clearview-ai-1.4834032

Ahmed, M. (2018, May 11). Aided by Palantir, the LAPD uses predictive policing to monitor specific people and neighborhoods. *The Intercept.* https://theintercept.com/2018/05/11/predictive-policing-surveillance-los-angeles/

Angwin, J., & Larson, J. (2016, December 30). Bias in criminal risk scores is mathematically inevitable, researchers say. *ProPublica.* https://www.propublica.org/article/bias-in-criminal-risk-scores-is-mathematically-inevitable-researchers-say

Ayling, J., Grabosky, P. N., & Shearing, C. D. (2009). *Lengthening the arm of the law: Enhancing police resources in the twenty-first century.* Cambridge University Press.

Babu, A., & Nevill-Manning, C. (2016, February). Sidewalk Labs: Reimagining the city as a digital platform. [Video]. *YouTube.* https://www.youtube.com/watch?v=bPu8HvD7d9U

boyd, d., & Crawford, K. (2012). Critical questions for big data. *Information, Communication and Society, 15*(5), 662–679.

Braga, M. (2017, May 12). A secretive Silicon Valley tech giant set up shop in Canada. But what does it do? *CBC News.* https://www.cbc.ca/news/technology/palantir-silicon-valley-technology-giant-data-canada-1.4111163

Brayne, S. (2017). Big data surveillance: The case of policing. *American Sociological Review, 82*(5), 977–1008.

Brodeur, J. P. (2010). *The policing web.* Oxford University Press.

Broeders, D., Schrijvers, E., van der Sloot, B., van Brakel, R., de Hoog, J., & Hirsch Ballin, E. (2017). Big data and security policies: Towards a framework for regulating the phases of analytics and use of big data. *Computer Law and Security Review, 33*(3), 309–323.

Brooks, A. (2016). *Digital evidence management and analysis in the cloud.* IDC Consulting.

Brownlee, J., Hurl, C., & Walby, K. (Eds.). (2018). *Corporatizing Canada: Making business out of public service.* Between the Lines.

Byfield, N. P. (2019). Race science and surveillance: Police as the new race scientists. *Social Identities, 25*(1), 91–106.

Calgary Police Service selects Axon as vendor for body worn cameras. (2018, July 11). *Blue Line.* https://www.blueline.ca/calgary-police-service-selects-axon-as-vendor-for-body-worn-cameras-5589/

Carney, B. (2019, March 25). "Project Wide Awake": How the RCMP watches you on social media. *The Tyee.* https://thetyee.ca/News/2019/03/25/Project-Wide-Awake/

CBC. (2020, January 21). The end of anonymity? Facial recognition app used by police raises serious concerns, say privacy advocates. *The Current,* CBC Radio. https://www.cbc.ca/radio/thecurrent/the-current-for-jan-21–2020-1.5434328/the-end-of-anonymity-facial-recognition-app-used-by-police-raises-serious-concerns-say-privacy-advocates-1.5435278

Cities. (n.d.). *ShotSpotter.* https://www.shotspotter.com/cities/

City of Thunder Bay. (2018). *Details of the city's phase one application.* https://www.thunderbay.ca/en/city-hall/resources/Documents/Grants-Incentives-and-Funding-Programs/Smart-Cities-Challenge-Application.pdf

Coleman, R. R. M., & Brunton, D. W. (2016). "You might not know her, but you know her brother": Surveillance technology, respectability policing, and the murder of Janese Talton Jackson. *Souls, 18*(2–4), 408–420.

Couldry, N., & Mejias, U. A. (2019). Data colonialism: Rethinking big data's relation to the contemporary subject. *Television and New Media, 20*(4), 336–349.

Craig, S. (2016, November 13). RCMP tracked 89 Indigenous activists considered "threats" for participating in protests. *National Post.* https://nationalpost.com/news/canada/rcmp-tracked-89-indigenous-activists-considered-threats-for-participating-in-protests

Crump, C. (2016). Surveillance policy making by procurement. *Washington Law Review, 91*(4), 1595–1662.

D'Alessio, S. J., Eitle, D., & Stolzenberg, L. (2005). The impact of serious crime, racial threat, and economic inequality on private police size. *Social Science Research, 34*(2), 267–282.

Dhillon, J. (2017). *Prairie rising: Indigenous youth, decolonization, and the politics of intervention.* University of Toronto Press.

Edmonton Police Service. (n.d.). Operations and intelligence command centre. Retrieved January 1, 2021, from https://www.edmontonpolice.ca/CommunityPolicing/OperationalServices/PoliceCommunications/OICC/

Egbert, S. (2019). Predictive policing and the platformization of police work. *Surveillance and Society, 17*(1–2), 83–88.

Ferguson, A. (2017). Policing predictive policing. *Washington University Law Review, 94*(5), 1109–1189.

Gandy, O. H., & Nemorin, S. (2019). Toward a political economy of nudge: Smart city variations. *Information, Communication and Society, 22*(14), 2112–2126.

Gillespie, T. (2010). The politics of "platforms." *New Media and Society, 12*(3), 347–364.

Gold, H. (2015, July 17). ShotSpotter: Gunshot detection system raises privacy concerns on campuses. *The Guardian.* https://www.theguardian.com/law/2015/jul/17/shotspotter-gunshot-detection-schools-campuses-privacy

Gray, J. (2019, February 13). Toronto police end ShotSpotter project over legal concerns. *Globe and Mail.* https://www.theglobeandmail.com/canada/toronto/article-toronto-police-end-shotspotter-project-over-legal-concerns/

Guidotti, R., Monreale, A., Ruggieri, S., Turini, F., Giannotti, F., & Pedreschi, D. (2018). A survey of methods for explaining black box models. *ACM Computing Surveys (CSUR), 51*(5), 1–42.

Hajer, M. (2015). On being smart about cities: Seven considerations for a new urban planning and design. In A. Allen, A. Lampis, & M. Swilling (Eds.), *Untamed urbanisms* (pp. 50–64). Routledge.

Hannah-Moffat, K. (2019). Algorithmic risk governance: Big data analytics, race and information activism in criminal justice debates. *Theoretical Criminology, 23*(4), 453–470.

Harcourt, B. E. (2015). Risk as a proxy for race: The dangers of risk assessment. *Federal Sentencing Reporter, 27*(4), 237–243.

Hucklesby, A., & Lister, S. (Eds.). (2017). *The private sector and criminal justice.* Palgrave Macmillan.

IBM: Edmonton Police Service. (2018, October 9). *IBM.* https://www.ibm.com/case-studies/edmonton-police-service-hybrid-cloud-integration-crime

Infrastructure Canada. (2018a, March 26). *$5 million prize category winner – Town of Bridgewater, Nova Scotia.* https://www.infrastructure.gc.ca/cities-villes/winners-gagnants/5m-bridgewater-eng.html

Infrastructure Canada. (2018b, March 26). *$10 million prize category winner – City of Guelph and Wellington County, Ontario.* https://www.infrastructure.gc.ca/cities-villes/winners-gagnants/10m-guelph-wellington-eng.html

Infrastructure Canada. (2018c, March 26). *$10 million prize category winner – Nunavut Communities, Nunavut.* https://www.infrastructure.gc.ca/cities-villes/winners-gagnants/10m-nunavut-eng.html

Infrastructure Canada. (2018d, March 26). *$50 million prize category winner – City of Montréal, Quebec.* https://www.infrastructure.gc.ca/cities-villes/winners-gagnants/50m-montreal-eng.html

Infrastructure Canada. (2018e, September 6). *Participating communities.* https://www.infrastructure.gc.ca/sc-vi/map-applications.php

Janus, A. (2019, February 14). Toronto police scrap plans to acquire controversial gunshot-detection system. *CBC News.* https://www.cbc.ca/news/canada/toronto/toronto-police-scrap-plans-to-acquire-controversial-gunshot-detection-system-1.5019110

Joh, E. E. (2017a). Feeding the machine: Policing, crime data, and algorithms symposium: Big data, national security, and the Fourth Amendment. *William and Mary Bill of Rights Journal, 2,* 287–302.

Joh, E. E. (2017b). The undue influence of surveillance technology companies on policing (SSRN Scholarly Paper No. ID 2924620). *SSRN.* https://papers.ssrn.com/abstract=2924620

Joh, E. E. (2019). Policing the smart city. *International Journal of Law in Context, 15*(2), 177–182.

Kerrison, E. M., Cobbina, J., & Bender, K. (2018). Stop-gaps, lip service, and the perceived futility of body-worn police officer cameras in Baltimore City. *Journal of Ethnic and Cultural Diversity in Social Work, 27*(3), 271–288.

Kitchin, R. (2014a). *The data revolution: Big data, open data, data infrastructures and their consequences.* SAGE.

Kitchin, R. (2014b). The real-time city? Big data and smart urbanism. *GeoJournal, 79*(1), 1–14.

Kitchin, R., Lauriault, T. P., & McArdle, G. (2015). Smart cities and the politics of urban data. In S. Marvin, A. Luque-Ayala, & C. McFarlane (Eds.), *Smart urbanism: Utopian vision or false dawn?* (pp. 16–33). Routledge.

Koops, B.-J., Newell, B., & Škorvánek, I. (2019). Location tracking by police: The regulation of "tireless and absolute surveillance." *UC Irvine Law Review, 9*(3), 635–698.

LeBeuf, M.-E. (2011). *The role of the Royal Canadian Mounted Police during the Indian residential school system*. Royal Canadian Mounted Police. http://resource.library.utoronto.ca/eir/EIRdetail.cfm?Resources__ID=1577043

Lee-Shanok, P. (2019, May 30). Privacy advocates sound warning on Toronto police use of facial recognition technology. *CBC News*. https://www.cbc.ca/news/canada/toronto/privacy-civil-rights-concern-about-toronto-police-use-of-facial-recognition-1.5156581

Livesey, B. (2017, May 5). Spies in our midst: RCMP and CSIS snoop on green activists. *National Observer*. https://www.nationalobserver.com/2017/05/05/news/spies-our-midst-rcmp-and-csis-snoop-green-activists

Lorinc, J. (2017, November 6). LORINC: Let's talk about Sidewalk Labs' $50 million investment. *SpacingToronto*. http://spacing.ca/toronto/2017/11/06/lorinc-lets-talk-about-sidewalk-labs-50-million-investment/

Louis, E. S., Saulnier, A., & Walby, K. (2019). Police use of body-worn cameras: Challenges of visibility, procedural justice, and legitimacy. *Surveillance and Society*, 17(3–4), 305–321.

Lyon, D. (2001). *Surveillance society: Monitoring everyday life*. McGraw-Hill Education.

Madden, M., Gilman, M., Levy, K., & Marwick, A. (2017). Privacy, poverty, and big data: A matrix of vulnerabilities for poor Americans. *Washington University Law Review*, 95(1), 53–125.

Makuch, B. (2017, August 30). Canadian police tracked a Black Lives Matter vigil in Vancouver. *Vice*. https://www.vice.com/en_ca/article/8xmk8a/canadian-police-tracked-a-black-lives-matter-vigil-in-vancouver

Manojlovic, D. (2018). *Vancouver Police Department to the Vancouver Police Board* (No. 1809C01). Vancouver Police Department.

March, H. (2018). The Smart City and other ICT-led techno-imaginaries: Any room for dialogue with Degrowth? *Journal of Cleaner Production*, 197, 1694–1703. https://doi.org/10.1016/j.jclepro.2016.09.154

Marcoux, J., & Nicholson, K. (2018, April 5). Deadly force: Fatal encounters with police in Canada: 2000–2017. *CBC News*. https://newsinteractives.cbc.ca/longform-custom/deadly-force

Marquis, G. (2016). *The vigilant eye: Policing Canada from 1867 to 9/11*. Fernwood.

Mayhew, S. (2014, November 4). Calgary police select NEC's facial recognition technology. *Biometric Update*. https://www.biometricupdate.com/201411/calgary-police-select-necs-facial-recognition-technology

Maynard, R. (2017). *Policing Black lives: State violence in Canada from slavery to the present*. Fernwood.

McNeilly, G. (2018). *Broken trust: Indigenous people and the Thunder Bay Police Service*. Office of the Independent Police Review Director.

Meuse, M. (2017, July 23). Vancouver police now using machine learning to prevent property crime. *CBC News*. https://www.cbc.ca/news/canada/british-columbia/vancouver-predictive-policing-1.4217111

Millar, P., & Owusu-Bempah, A. (2011). Whitewashing criminal justice in Canada: Preventing research through data suppression. *Canadian Journal of Law and Society*, 26, 653–661.

Morozov, E. (2013). *To save everything, click here: Technology, solutionism, and the urge to fix problems that don't exist*. Allen Lane.

Morozov, E., & Bria, F. (2018, January 22). *Rethinking the smart city: Democratizing urban technology. Rosa Luxemburg Stiftung*. http://www.rosalux-nyc.org/rethinking-the-smart-city/

Munn, N. (2017, February 13). "Predictive policing" is coming to Canada's capital, and privacy advocates are worried. *Vice*. https://www.vice.com/en_us/article/jpaew3/ottawa-police-strategic-operations-centre-canada-surveillance

National Inquiry into Missing and Murdered Indigenous Women and Girls. (2019). *Reclaiming power and place: The final report of the National Inquiry into Missing and Murdered Indigenous Women and Girls*. https://www.mmiwg-ffada.ca/final-report/

Ngo, H. V., Neote, K., Cala, C., Antonio, M., & Hickey, J. (2018). The experience of ethno-cultural members with racial profiling. *Journal of Ethnic and Cultural Diversity in Social Work, 27*(3), 253–270.

Noble, S. U. (2018). *Algorithms of oppression: How search engines reinforce racism*. New York University Press.

Office of the Privacy Commissioner of Canada. (2021, February 3). *News release: Clearview AI's unlawful practices represented mass surveillance of Canadians, commissioners say*. https://www.priv.gc.ca/en/opc-news/news-and-announcements/2021/nr-c_210203/

Ontario Human Rights Commission. (2018). *A collective impact: Interim report on the inquiry into racial profiling and racial discrimination of Black persons by the Toronto Police Service*. http://ohrc.on.ca/en/public-interest-inquiry-racial-profiling-and-discrimination-toronto-police-service/collective-impact-interim-report-inquiry-racial-profiling-and-racial-discrimination-black

Ottawa Police Service. (2018, November 30). Service initiative. https://ottawapolice.icrt-ops1.esolg.ca/en/annual-report-2017/service-initiative.aspx

Owusu-Bempah, A., Luscombe, A., & Finlay, B. M. (2019). Unequal justice: Race and cannabis arrests in the post-legal landscape. In A. Potter & D. Weinstock (Eds.), *High time: The legalization and regulation of cannabis in Canada* (pp. 114–131). McGill-Queen's University Press.

Parsons, C. A., & Israel, T. (2016). *Gone opaque? An analysis of hypothetical IMSI catcher overuse in Canada* (SSRN Scholarly Paper No. ID 2901522). *SSRN*. https://papers.ssrn.com/abstract=2901522

Pearson, H. (2019, August 14). All front-line Calgary police officers now wearing body cameras. *Global News*. https://globalnews.ca/news/5766999/calgary-police-body-worn-cameras-permanent/

Plantin, J.-C., Lagoze, C., Edwards, P. N., & Sandvig, C. (2018). Infrastructure studies meet platform studies in the age of Google and Facebook. *New Media and Society, 20*(1), 293–310.

Raji, I. D., & Buolamwini, J. (2019). Actionable auditing: Investigating the impact of publicly naming biased performance results of commercial AI products. In *Proceedings of the 2019 AAAI/ACM Conference on AI, Ethics, and Society – AIES 19* (pp. 429–435).

Rankin, J., & Winsa, P. (2012, March 9). Known to police: Toronto police stop and document black and brown people far more than whites. *Toronto Star.* https://www.thestar.com/news/insight/2012/03/09/known_to_police_toronto_police_stop_and_document_black_and_brown_people_far_more_than_whites.html

Richardson, R., Schultz, J., & Crawford, K. (2019). Dirty data, bad predictions: How civil rights violations impact police data, predictive policing systems, and justice (SSRN Scholarly Paper No. ID 3333423). *SSRN.* https://papers.ssrn.com/abstract=3333423

Roberts, D. (2000, February 18). RCMP to probe alleged police link to native freezing deaths. *Globe and Mail.* https://www.theglobeandmail.com/news/national/rcmp-to-probe-alleged-police-link-to-native-freezing-deaths/article4160406/

Robertson, K., Khoo, C., & Song, Y. (2020). *To surveil and predict: A human rights analysis of algorithmic policing in Canada. The Citizen Lab.* https://citizenlab.ca/2020/09/to-surveil-and-predict-a-human-rights-analysis-of-algorithmic-policing-in-canada/

Roth, A., & McIntyre, C. (2020, May 7). *Breaking down Sidewalk Labs' decision to abandon its Toronto smart-city project. The Logic.* https://thelogic.co/news/special-report/breaking-down-sidewalk-labs-decision-to-abandon-its-toronto-smart-city-project/

Royal Canadian Mounted Police. (2017, April 18). *Terrorism and violent extremism awareness guide. Royal Canadian Mounted Police.* http://www.rcmp-grc.gc.ca/en/terrorism-and-violent-extremism-awareness-guide

Royal Canadian Mounted Police. (2018, April 16). *Royal Canadian Mounted Police 2018–2019 departmental plan. Royal Canadian Mounted Police.* http://www.rcmp-grc.gc.ca/en/royal-canadian-mounted-police-2018–19-departmental-plan

Sadowski, J., & Pasquale, F. (2015). The spectrum of control: A social theory of the smart city. *First Monday, 20*(7). https://doi.org/10.5210/fm.v20i7.5903

Scola, N. (2018, July–August). Google is building a city of the future in Toronto. Would anyone want to live there? *POLITICO Magazine.* https://politi.co/2ICaQGW

Sohal, J. (2018, January). January's app of the month: GeoDASH. *ESRI.* https://resources.esri.ca/news-and-updates/january-s-app-of-the-month-geodash

Starr, P. (1988). The meaning of privatization. *Yale Law and Policy Review, 6*(1), 6–41.

Talaga, T. (2017). *Seven fallen feathers: Racism, death, and hard truths in a northern city.* House of Anansi Press.

Toronto Police Services Board. (2019, May 30). *Public meeting agenda.* http://www.tpsb.ca/images/agendas/PUBLIC_AGENDA_May30.pdf

Tunney, C. (2020, March 4). RCMP denied using facial recognition technology – then said it had been using it for months. *CBC News.* https://www.cbc.ca/news/politics/clearview-ai-rcmp-facial-recognition-1.5482266

Ullrich, P. (2019). Data and obstacle: Police (non)visibility in research on protest policing. *Surveillance and Society, 17*(3–4), 405–421.

Urkosky, B. (2016, March 20). ACTION – black out for justice – TODAY. *Calaméo.* https://en.calameo.com/read/0055742873013001ba3bf

White, A. (2014). Post-crisis policing and public-private partnerships: The case of Lincolnshire police and G4S. *The British Journal of Criminology, 54*(6), 1002–1022.

Wortley, S. (2019). *Halifax, Nova Scotia: Street checks report.* Nova Scotia Human Rights Commission.

Wortley, S., & Owusu-Bempah, A. (2009). Unequal before the law: Immigrant and racial minority perceptions of the Canadian criminal justice system. *Journal of International Migration and Integration, 10*(4), 447–473.

Wortley, S., & Owusu-Bempah, A. (2011). The usual suspects: Police stop and search practices in Canada. *Policing and Society, 21*(4), 395–407.

Zedner, L. (2006). Liquid security: Managing the market for crime control. *Criminology and Criminal Justice, 6*(3), 267–288.

Zuboff, S. (2019). *The age of surveillance capitalism: The fight for a human future at the new frontier of power.* Profile Books.

5

Platforms and Privatizing Lines

Business Improvement Areas, Municipal Apps, and the Marketization of Public Service

DEBRA MACKINNON

Cities and the private sector have rolled out a range of market- and tech-based "solutions" to replace and augment forms of urban governance, policing, and service delivery. Referred to as new public management or entrepreneurial urbanism, business improvement areas (BIAs)[1] and their evolving practices exemplify the confluence of these variegated corporate models. Now fixtures on the urban landscape, with over 400 in Canada, BIAs and their memberships have become "front-line workers" left to navigate systemic urban problems such as affordable housing, informal settlements, cuts to social services, and more recently the opioid crisis. Not in the business of solving these problems – it is not their job, and they cannot – BIAs have focused on the performance of "clean and safe" areas for consumption.

To address property crime, cleanliness, and disorder, BIAs have adopted a range of initiatives – from "brandscape" beautification and target hardening to ambassadors, clean teams, and private security programs. The identification and removal of refuse and risk are matters of concern for BIAs, and ensuring clean and safe passage becomes a baseline for all other improvements in the area (Lippert, 2010, 2012). However, like policing BIAs, carrying out clean and safe mandates requires a web of public and private actors oriented toward a common goal (Brodeur, 2010; Sleiman & Lippert, 2010). Both contributing to and affected by forms of splintering urbanism (Graham & Marvin, 2001) and administrative fragmentation[2]

(Bénit-Gbaffou, 2008), BIAs have found innovative ways of navigating the privatization of infrastructure and the resulting fragmented services to draw attention to *matters of concern* in their areas. Reflecting the economic logics of new public management, monitoring, quantifying, and reporting have become a critical means of translating BIA concerns into *matters of fact*.[3] These data-driven practices not only further corporatization, since business metrics (e.g., "return on investment" and "key performance indicators") are used to evaluate city services, but also further integrate BIAs into city services and networks.

In this chapter, I focus on an empirical case of corporatization, BIA private policing, and city service delivery. Specifically, I examine how five Vancouver BIAs have used VanConnect – a citizen-to-government (C2G) application – to navigate the splintered streetscape. Initially conceptualized as a form of citizen engagement and a city tool for automating 311 calls for service, BIAs have become the second largest user group of VanConnect. Given the increased interest in smart cities and data-driven initiatives (see Duncan & Barreto, this volume), this chapter updates discussions of BIA roles and responsibilities and analyzes the impacts of private influences in the allocation of public resources and services. Rather than presenting a straightforward case of entrepreneurialism, privatization, or responsibilization, I trace the complex assemblage of public and private actors necessary for carrying out "clean and safe" projects, providing rich nuances to ongoing discussions of corporatization (Brownlee et al., 2018). I ask: Who do BIAs work for, and what type of work are they doing? As 311 apps and smart city initiatives are becoming more common, I highlight data produced by these organizations and their resulting knowledge politics – how the city, and its needs, come to be understood through the BIA gaze. Rather than remunicipalize services, I argue, the use of VanConnect and resulting BIA knowledge claims reinforce the directing, diverting, and districting of services into these privately managed areas.

To advance discussions of BIA governance, I bring together concepts from geography, sociology, and criminology to explore the intersections of splintering urbanism, policing, and privatization. I begin the chapter with an overview of BIAs, drawing from discussions of premium network spaces and corporatization to conceptualize them as actors concerned with the creation and management of value. Although BIAs predate neo-liberalism (see Frieden & Sagalyn, 1989; Valverde, 2012, 2016), they continue to be interesting sites for analyzing privatization, market forces, and innovative practices. I offer a short background on changing BIA roles and responsibilities to contextualize my case and methods. In particular, I unpack changing BIA clean and safe policing practices and adoption of the VanConnect application by BIAs. After providing a brief summary of the app's features and uses, I explain the integration of VanConnect into existing BIA practices by analyzing discourses of "delegation" and "supplementation." I challenge normative understandings of BIAs as entrepreneurial agents of "self-help" by dwelling on the work of public agencies in carrying out clean and safe projects, specifically how BIA work is captured by the city and vice versa. I contend that the use of VanConnect not only further integrates BIAs into the web of city governance and increases their legitimacy but also forwards BIA matters of concern. I conclude the chapter by reflecting on the corporatization of VanConnect – as an effective albeit unintended tool – for directing, diverting, and districting premium spaces.

Splintering, Corporatizing, and Policing Main Street

BIAs have been discussed as both responses to and outcomes of urban sprawl and hollowing, the proliferation of commercial environments, the decreasing powers of local governments, and the shift to public-private partnership models (Hoyt & Gopal-Agge, 2007). Highly mobile and contingent on local conditions, BIAs can be understood as privately governed but publicly sanctioned geographic areas that implement private taxation to extend municipal services (Hoyt & Gopal-Agge, 2007; McCann & Ward, 2012). Although the extension of services varies by jurisdiction, broadly BIA mandates seek to maintain and improve the economic vitality of the area (Bookman & Woolford, 2013; Hannigan, 1999). Simultaneously enabling and privatizing forms of regulation and control, combined with other entrepreneurial initiatives (e.g., condominium development, downtown retail centres, highway systems, telecommunication infrastructure, surveillance partnerships, etc.), BIAs facilitate, create, and redevelop cities into literal and metaphorical fortified enclaves and enclosures – *cities within cities* (Brenner et al., 2010; Caldeira, 2000; Frieden & Sagalyn, 1989). For Graham and Marvin (2001), BIAs reflect the splintering streetscape – a product of the unbundling of infrastructure and the instating of bypass strategies – resulting in the emergence of *premium networked spaces*. As they note, these malls without walls "amount to the splintering of a carefully selected system of traditional streets from the wider metropolitan fabric" (p. 261).

Similar to the capture of public agencies by industry, to some degree BIAs reflect the broader process of neo-liberalization and growing corporate power (Joh, 2004). To varying degrees, BIAs exhibit elements of corporatization detailed by Brownlee et al. (2018), including arm's-length administration, expanding managerial control through business logics, and public-private integration. Exemplifying practices of contracting out, load-shedding, and commodification, marketization and policing coexist and combine through the governance of urban life and "the little urban things" (Lippert, 2014).

This process is clearly seen through the expansion of BIA crime control and clean and safe initiatives (Huey et al., 2005; Mopas, 2005; Sleiman & Lippert, 2010). Attempting to maintain safety and security in these areas, BIAs have become integral actors "responsible" for establishing and maintaining order in cities – in other words, policing. Agents and forms of private policing, BIAs are accountable primarily to their stakeholders: that is, the owners of private properties and their interests (Reeve, 2004; Stenning, 2000). Similar to studies of private policing, BIAs exemplify this fusion "or perhaps growing confusion" between the roles of public and private police (Stenning, 2000, p. 328; see also Brodeur, 2010). However, like other aspects of these quasi-state or networked forms of governance (Morçöl & Wolf, 2010), their roles, responsibilities, and jurisdictions have repeatedly been called into question.

Shifting Roles and Responsibilities of BIAs: Supplementary Policing

One of the last major North American cities to adopt BIAs, Vancouver experimented with this urban governance model in the 1990s (Mackinnon 2019a). This occurred alongside Vancouver's positioning for global city status and two decades of urban "redevelopment" and "regeneration" (Blomley, 2004; Ley & Dobson, 2008; Smith, 1996). From the 1980s onward, epitomized by the World Exposition on Transportation and Communication in 1986 and the Winter Olympics in 2010, Vancouver saw the intensification of market-driven gentrification through mass condoization funded by public-private partnerships (Ley, 1981; Ley & Dobson, 2008). These partnerships and mega-events helped not only to solidify new forms of urban governance (e.g., condoization, large-scale oversight committees, and development conglomerates) but also to justify increased policing and the adoption of surveillance technologies (Boyle & Haggerty, 2011; Mackinnon, 2019b; Molnar, 2015). As noted by a City of Vancouver official, broken windows policing was integral in this shift from industrial to retail and residential development, and sanitization efforts were built into BIA and community policing mandates from the outset (Mackinnon, 2019a).

In Vancouver, the production of clean and safe areas, specifically "move-along" practices carried out by BIA ambassadors, has been a repeated point of contention. An exercise in both public and private policing, these exclusionary practices target people sleeping rough, panhandling, vending, or engaging in "anti-social behaviour," directing them to leave both private and public spaces. In 2008, the Vancouver Area Network of Drug Users filed a complaint with the BC Human Rights Tribunal against the Downtown Vancouver Business Improvement Association (DVBIA). The case concerned the move-along practices targeting Indigenous people with physical and mental health disabilities from outside a business and park in the area (Burgmann, 2015). In 2010, the case was dismissed by the BC Human Rights Tribunal; it was then submitted to the BC Supreme Court in 2012. In 2015, the court found the DVBIA's practice in violation of the BC Human Rights Code. The DVBIA proceeded to appeal this verdict at the BC Court of Appeal in 2018, overturning the lower court's ruling.

This chapter draws from research on two projects concerning Vancouver BIA policing in the post-tribunal context. Seeking to update foundational studies in Vancouver BIA policing, this work explored shifting practices and partnerships, specifically focusing on BIA data-driven initiatives (including use of the VanConnect app) in five downtown Vancouver BIAs: Robson Street, Downtown Vancouver, Hastings Crossing, Strathcona, and Hastings North (see Figure 5.1). This chapter draws from twenty interviews with BIA staff and city officials, five work shadows with private security guards and clean teams, participant observations in the areas, and news media documents and city and BIA materials from 2010 onward.

In the aftermath of the Human Rights Tribunal case, the city has clarified the scope of BIA clean and safe practices:

> I know our council strongly believes that policing should be done by police, but there are other things that communities can do, supplementary things. The intent is not to replace police. [BIAs] are not enforcement; they know their bounds. They are eyes and ears. They are recording data. They are tracking hotspots. They are cleaning. They are referral agencies. They are calling police when they see something that needs police support. They're doing a range of things that deal with safety and security issues without being police, and that's an issue.

To this City of Vancouver BIA program coordinator, it was not policing if it was not carried out by police. As Stenning (2000) suggested, moving past

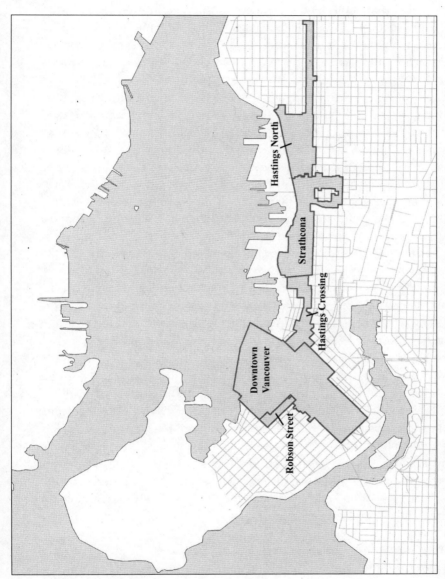

FIGURE 5.1 Vancouver BIA field sites in the city's downtown core. | Courtesy of author.

the conventional mindset of policing as the responsibility and activity of the state and its public police forces remains a challenge. For the coordinator, rather than focus on the practices or their implications, the classification of actions as "policing" depends on the legitimacy of the actors. Although not called policing, central policing practices, such as data collection, hotspot tracking, and referrals, were cast as "supplementary" things that BIAs can do.

As commonly stated throughout the BIA community, rather than privatizing or "taking over," the BIAs generally conceived of their supplementary actions as aligned with or helping the city. On good terms with the city, all noted the common goal of a "perfect," "cleaner," or "safer" city. As groups of collective actions, BIAs have been cast as successful, independent economic actors and exemplars of "self-help" (Brooks & Strange, 2011). Once again troubling roles, legitimacy is bound up with an ethic of responsibility and enterprise. "Volunteering to be taxed," BIAs frame their activities in the area as "good business" and delegate themselves as the most capable stewards. Although most BIAs were resolved to helping out, others suggested that the level of city services that they received was insufficient. For instance, one executive director, after detailing the BIA's services, programs, and events, suggested that the city was downloading its responsibilities. Potentially exhibiting responsibilization (Garland, 1996; Rose, 2000) or governing at a distance (Rose, 1990), the role of public services (albeit in some cases not enough) troubles this vein of theorizing.

BIAs' clean and safe initiatives and security models appear to be private endeavours; however, as Sleiman and Lippert (2010) argued, they are actually "anchored" by public services and/or funds. This anchoring highlights not only increasing corporatized service delivery (Brownlee et al., 2018) but also, as explored in the following case of VanConnect, the role of public agencies in seemingly private ventures. The following case offers an overview of the app and BIA uses, the implications of BIA user groups, and the resulting integration and extension of the BIA gaze into the city's technological and physical infrastructure.

A Tool for the Job: Uses and Users of VanConnect

Launched in 2015, the VanConnect app was designed as a digital complement to the city's 311 non-emergency call line and generates data for the city's internal dashboard. As part of Vancouver's digital strategy, alongside other e-government initiatives (e.g., city wi-fi, C2G apps), the city hopes that its dashboard and the resulting data will help to "develop insight" and

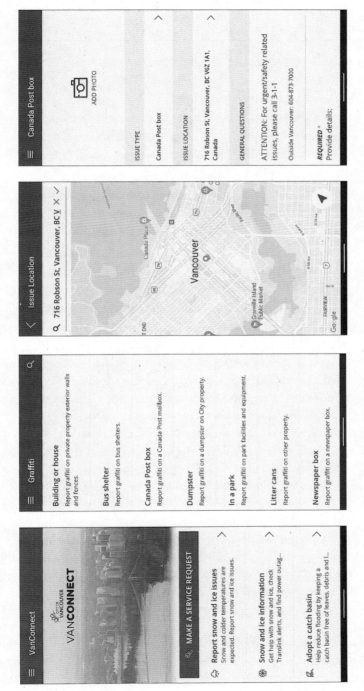

FIGURE 5.2 VanConnect app submission process for a graffiti service request. | Courtesy of VanConnect app and author.

FIGURE 5.3
Top ten VanConnect service requests.

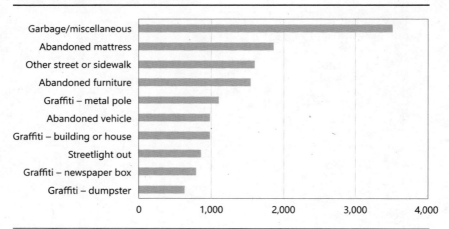

Courtesy of City of Vancouver, 2016.

better "inform decision making and governance." The app, similar to other 311 and C2G technologies, such as "See Click Fix" or "Fix My Street," offers a range of services, including service requests, push notifications (e.g., updates, news, and emergency info), city directories, maps of amenities, notices of events, and more.[4] However, the main use-case is the service request feature. Citizens (defined through the app as users with accounts) are encouraged to log specific public maintenance issues (see Figure 5.2).

Once submitted and received, service requests are directed to the agency responsible for the asset, and the citizen-user is given real-time status updates and notified when the request has been completed. The app is primarily used to report garbage and graffiti problems (see Figure 5.3).

While "citizens," the intended users of the app, account for 44 percent of calls for service, in 2016 BIAs were the second largest user group, accounting for 36 percent of calls for service, and their use continues to increase (see Figure 5.4).[5] Considered "customer-users," according to the director of digital platforms, VanConnect updated and real-timed accountability relations between the city and BIAs. This classification as a user group by the city demonstrates the integration and privileging of the business community.

BIAs' use of the app was also beneficial to the city. With clear BIA-based use-case and a substantial pool of daily active users, the city was able to demonstrate the return on investment (ROI). Furthermore, BIAs served as

FIGURE 5.4
Breakdown of all service requests by users.

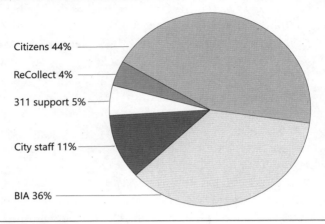

Courtesy of City of Vancouver, 2016.

advocates for the digital solution and in many cases brought other users onboard (e.g., businesses and other BIAs). Without the formal legal powers or "tools" of public agencies, BIAs' use of this app presents matters of fact as measures of loss, risk, and disorder (Stenning, 2000). Invoking logics similar to those of austerity urbanism, BIAs can be seen as capitalizing and corporatizing a public smart city tool.

Delegated Cleaning: BIA Uses
As explained by the BIA program coordinator, VanConnect and its precursor 311 were built into many BIA programs in order to access city services and fulfil clean and safe mandates:

> The VanConnect app has been very well received. It used to be, you had to call 311 and log on … Some of the BIA's main activity in safety and security, graffiti removal, and garbage cleanup isn't necessary running the program itself. It started by calling through 311 and getting the city to place order[s] on properties which don't remove graffiti and to create these databases of them and keep sending them in, and to complain about garbage in the alleys, and to complain about this, that, and the other thing. Then, with the VanConnect app, it's so much easier to be able to log that stuff, and the city likes it too, because it's a lot easier to track the data on what is coming in, and [it's] very, very well received.

The Vancouver BIA program coordinator, tempering critiques of downloading and responsibilization, stressed that city services should be an element of BIA programs. They reaffirmed the city as the "anchor" for programming. Although the app's developers envisioned citizen users as use-cases, the director of digital platforms had some understanding of how BIA staff were using the app for service delivery:

> For example, property use inspectors, sorry, street use inspectors? They would typically walk, I guess, they patrol or drive. I don't know how they get around. They might see somebody inappropriately using a sidewalk or a street. I don't know exactly what, let's say they have a patio where they shouldn't or whatever it is. They'll report that on a piece of paper. Bring it back to their desk. Put it into an Excel spreadsheet. Send it off to the relevant group that should be taking care of ticketing. It's really disjointed ... They now use VanConnect for service requests. They can go snap a picture of whatever the infraction is, along with details about it. It's all geolocated and stored in one location for them. And they can go on to the next, so it's cut down on some of the pieces of paper and work.

In this hypothetical example, similar to many advertisements for the app,[6] calls for service were framed as disjointed and unclear, and VanConnect was presented as a means of simplifying and automating the "call" process. Having it "all in one place" was a time-saving and cost-effective tool for patrolling the public and private realm (or navigating the splintered streetscape). However, BIA use of the app was not limited to "inspectors" since each BIA had incorporated VanConnect into its security plans, community safety and policing initiatives, ambassador programs, and daily commutes for some staff members.

Although partially constrained by the app's capabilities, the five studied BIAs, as well as many of the twenty-two BIAs in Vancouver, made use of VanConnect – though through different programs, to various degrees, and for different purposes. Within a spectrum of frequent to moderate users, one BIA had extensively integrated VanConnect into its long-standing community policing programs. According to the executive director, logging every overflowing garbage bin and every discarded needle kept the area clean and safe. Another executive director explained VanConnect's integration into program operations, referring to a "well-worn hierarchy" for reporting matters to the city (through VanConnect), the private graffiti removal company, and other agencies. This executive director, versed in the fragmentation of services, explained the various in-house, contracted, and city-based constituents (i.e., "security agencies") assembled as part of the clean and safe team. In detailing the activities of the team, the executive director also characterized the various threats to the public realm that they dealt with: graffiti, debris, needle collection. Framing the work of the patrollers as getting ready for business hours, the executive director noted that their practices centred on the clean and safe passage of businesses and their clients. And their use of the city tool helped them to further their own mandates of economic revitalization.

Supplementing VanConnect: Working with or for the City?
All of the BIAs welcomed and applauded the city-led and -operated innovative initiative. VanConnect enabled them not only to direct services to their areas but also to incorporate sophisticated smart technology into their daily practices – without having to build or maintain the system. However, many BIA staff members noted the limitations of VanConnect for their organizational purposes. During patrols with ambassadors and clean teams, all of them mentioned that they carried two or more devices (e.g., work phone, personal phone, tablet, and/or radio) and noted the specific purpose of each. For example, some used a work phone for VanConnect, a tablet for a proprietary platform, a radio for internal communication, and a cellphone for emergency and 311 calls (e.g., for services not supported by VanConnect). Some staff even commented on wanting to streamline the process but admitted that "it just makes sense, that's how these agencies and city services work," referring to the splintering streetscape and their deviced workarounds. VanConnect and the other tools served as a "bypass strategy," networking particular constituents with public and private service delivery. BIAs as "premium spaces" and the products of bypass strategies (re)perform entailed practices, reinforcing a vicious cycle of splintering (Graham & Marvin, 2001).

While some BIA staff members had workarounds, drawing connections between the limitations of the app and the aforementioned uses, others suggested features that they would like to see built into the app as well as effective channels for incorporating user feedback. For example, one community safety manager asked "how much are they working with the people that are using it? We don't get any input. We've been through them once and talked with them, but there should be constant feedback. They should be looking at the businesses to drive the app. Then the public will get more use from the data; you'll see the reports come in." To some BIA staff, their use of and advocacy for the app meant that they could have a greater say in its future or at least in its functionality. A common point of contention among them was that their actions seemed to be complementary rather than adversarial. For example, some BIAs saw utility in being able to log encampments, register street-related activities, send push notifications during emergencies, and suggest locations for new assets. However, VanConnect did not support the logging of people or "street-related activities." The director of digital platforms, specifically referencing the logging of encampments and the need for value-sensitive design, explained that these activities were far from the jurisdiction or ability of the app.

However, the city – recognizing the work and influence of BIAs – responded to their requests for input with a standard process and decision tree for fielding suggestions. Features that would improve service requests, decrease workflow, and promote straight-through processing were seen as suitable for addition. To the city, "improvement" included the addition of features that were ends in themselves, did not create additional communication or work, and were aligned with city mandates. However, in some cases, the city was open to changing service delivery practices, especially if doing so meant keeping key user groups engaged and using the app. To make VanConnect a viable digital solution (e.g., to ensure the ROI, reduce costs, and expand users), the city acknowledged the role of BIAs in the process.

Although city services anchored BIA programs, BIAs treated as a key user group for the app's success complicated the anchor and steward position. VanConnect is a public app and service, yet this process demonstrates a clear commitment to taking care of business as well as the provisioning of private channels to the city. Like other "we-government" initiatives, its affordances and limitations (re)produce struggles over (knowledge) politics in the splintered streetscape (Baykurt, 2011).

Partially in response to these affordances and limitations, all of the BIAs went beyond the reporting features of VanConnect. Rather than outmode previous BIA surveillance, the app became another layer of practice. From spreadsheets to proprietary platforms all of the BIAs engaged in additional and supplementary data collection (see also Murakami Wood & Mackinnon, 2019). To BIAs, producing their own records and keeping track of interactions with the city were important for maintaining accountability, transparency (to stakeholders), and service delivery. A director of operations explained, we also track it internally because not everything is recorded by the city. We have a self-directed app that we developed, and every time we see something that's happened – like a light has gone out, or a banner is torn, or something needs to be replaced – we report it as well for our own records and also to audit how quickly things are being addressed by the city and what they are.

The director of operations explained that "not everything is recorded by the city," demonstrating a disconnect between the BIA and city *matters of concern*. "Everything" also reflects a level of *administrative fragmentation* since the city was not necessarily concerned with private or potentially "personal issues" of the BIAs. This supplementary reporting, though initially a means of demonstrating the ROI to their members and stakeholders, also made visible and quantified BIA work. For example, one BIA kept meticulous records of the 1,378 hours of micro cleaning, or 1,200 garbage bags and 1,600 needles that were disposed of by their clean team (DVBIA, 2019). In other words, although not counted in VanConnect, by recording and reporting their activities outside the app, the BIAs extend their gaze beyond the concerns inscribed in the app – reinforcing a *politics of visibility* (Crang & Graham, 2007). All BIA staff, when explaining their range of programs, stressed that they wanted to let the city know about the clean and safe issues on *their streets:*

> Our ambassadors, our clean team, if they're picking up needles, they're still going to put it into the [VanConnect] app and our app and say that they picked them up. Just so we have an idea of how big the situation is. There's no point [in our team] going around and cleaning it all up and having everyone think it's hunky-dory, when it's not.

The community safety manager noted the effects of reporting. Although the desired remedy was not always achieved, they stressed the need for persistence:

> It's the follow-up as well ... When you look at the list of the reports that [the city is] working on, they're quite far behind. They're overwhelmed, they brought in the system, and not everything is being focused on. I would love to know – not that you would ever know an accurate figure or what's out there – but we know what's being reported. And if people actually start

using it, then we're aware of it a bit more. That's why we report so much. We're encouraging people to use these apps or call it in, whatever it is.

The community safety manager noted how multiple issues (e.g., austerity, backlogs, unanswered calls for service) increased frustration with both the system and the dark figure of "crime" or "asset-related issues." Once again engaged in (but also enacted because of) a permanent critique of the government, a BIA's reporting practices reaffirmed this laggard governance framework (Barns, 2012). Despite overburdening the current system, it was argued, reporting not only gave the city a more comprehensive picture as rendered by the BIAs but also helped it to plan accordingly for further service delivery and infrastructure. To the BIAs, making their work, as well as the problems in the area, visible also made their perceived remedies more compelling. For instance, rather than holding the city to account, or engaging in double-entry bookkeeping, these supplementary and evidenced practices hailed particular responses prefigured by *relations of visibility* (Espeland & Lom, 2015). One operations manager, when explaining roles and responsibilities, unpacked this relation of visibility:

> The Community Policing Centres (CPC) in our area are doing work similar to what our ambassadors are doing right now – picking up and identifying needles, identifying graffiti. Our ambassadors are doing that already. What we've been trying to do, make work with the CPC, is to say, "Hey, can we just handle the needles and the graffiti, and we'll send you the data? In exchange, that frees you up to go and talk to our members" … It's better coming from the CPC and VPD. We're still negotiating that. We're in a good position, and we're asking them to come and do more patrols in our area. It's tough, but we know spending more time on the streets helps us both. They're trying to allocate, but their resources are very tight.

In saying that, the operations manager drew together the argument detailed above: the manager noted an overlap in roles and responsibilities, was cognizant of similar matters of concern, and used the data to broker resources. Worried about responsibilization or *externalization* of costs, quantification and reporting have become core practices of clean and safe initiatives. To BIA staff, reporting – rather than being an end to a particular incidence– was a means of securing a better budget allocation. Through these app-based practices of self-help or self-serving, access or bypass was secured through the reporting of supplementary work. These practices of securitization not only fortify spaces (Lippert & Walby, 2013) but also strengthen the claims that BIAs can make and their position or role in urban governance, in terms of both accessing resources and making claims about the areas.

Right-Sizing the City: The Marketization of 311

To the city, the data sourced from BIAs, as well as from citizens, were critical not only for the success of VanConnect, as mentioned, but also for fuelling the internal city dashboard. Housed in the Digital Platforms office at City Hall, the dashboard and interface present real-time service-level agreements (SLAs) of various departments. To the city manager, the dashboard served as a top-down tool, bringing visually fragmented service delivery under the purview of the city. These calls for service "letting the city know" highlighted the functioning and performance of internal and contracted service delivery. Remediated through the dashboard, VanConnect data became a "high-level" "snapshot" of city functioning – based upon a narrow range of benchmarks and key performance indicators (KPIs).

These market logics, common in "smart city" and "urban (big) data" discussions, reinforce technocratic and market-driven solutionism for determining city needs. Through the marketization of 311, Vancouver attempted to "right-size the city" – that is, let logics of supply and demand "play out." While attempting to make the city less reactionary, by anticipating future needs or right-sizing the city, VanConnect accelerated expectations and demonstrated the current, or reasonable, limitations of the tool. Although outsourcing and automating, as well as claiming to "democratize" reporting, the city still had a limited number of workers to respond to public realm issues. Budgets and allocations served to temper the "production and dissemination of technological fantasies" (Crang & Graham, 2007, p. 791). The director of digital platforms explained the city's response to the increase in reporting and expectations:

> We've had some challenges internally in terms of changes with management, certain departments saying they don't want to take on another channel or additional workload. They're like "We're already busy enough." So you get that kind of push back. We're trying to change the conversation to say, "Listen, just because a resident tells you something, that a streetlight is out or there's a dead animal on the road or whatever it is, doesn't mean it takes priority over every single other piece of work that you have to do." But it is work that is in our city, and we need to know about it in order to right-size our fleet, to right-size our staff, to right-size our budgets.

Not only enabling particular forms of oversight and accountability, the reorganization – read as marketization – of 311 also resulted in the redirecting of service and potentially the reprioritizing of service. Reports, many from businesses and BIAs, consisted of translated dashboard data transformed into KPIs or SLAs – the delivery of which was imperative to demonstrating the ROI of VanConnect. Transforming calls and reports into evidence-based data, this approach to city governance is posited to ensure rational, logical, and impartial decisions (Kitchin, 2014). This sense of impartiality through data gives city managers not only an empirical defence (Haque, 2012) but also an air of accountability. Although the next steps are focused on increasing users and functionality, the director of digital platforms noted the power of additional data combinations:

> I think that's directly where the opportunity is. That it's taking the data that we're getting from VanConnect and combining [them] with other data sets. We've started to do that on the dashboard side. We can use this in the decision-making process around where to allocate limited resources. That's the other kind of driver that's come out of it, the data that the app has generated. Our conversations are better, a bit more intelligent, using data to deliver a better service.

While partially tempering expectations of big data urbanism, the director invoked other data discourses, specifically the sense that "more data is better." In agreement, the city manager saw "more data" as a better means of allocating resources and promoting evidence-based discussions. Arguably, these are laudable aims. The co-option of VanConnect by BIAs demonstrates the role of private interest in diverting and directing governance. Like the BIA itself, data collection is already centred on premium spaces, which reinforce particular ways of seeing the city. These accounts not only directed both day-to-day service delivery but also provided benchmarks for right-sizing the city. However, rather than fix, democratically bundle, or lessen splintering, the collection of VanConnect data furthers bypass strategies.

Advocacy and Access: A Tale of Two Bins

Beyond ensuring SLAs and producing a track record of city performance, BIA staff explained how they used their data to improve conversations with the city. As stated by one executive director, "our data lets me know what's going on and better advocate for my area." While data collection was key to city decisions, the BIAs also used their records to advocate for their areas. For instance, another executive director explained that they used these records to draw attention to ongoing matters of concern, such as "the lack of garbage bins in an area, lighting issues, worn-out crosswalks in need of repainting, traffic flow and areas that would benefit from pedestrian-activated lights, ... dumping spots, [and] challenges with city property."

The various forms of data collection enabled BIAs not only to direct service delivery but also to secure public realm planning and long-term improvement. Beyond advocating for service, these accounts demonstrated the quality of assets and in some cases were used to justify a greater quantity of resources and assets. For example, in recounting their clean and safe practices, all BIA staff discussed garbage and garbage bins – "I'm constantly reporting garbage and garbage cans," one said. A point of exasperation, most offered anecdotes of repeated calls for service complicated by a lack of bins and illegal dumping. While critical of broken windows policing and gentrification, one executive director explained how public realm issues were perpetuated by city perceptions:

> We have more people that put litter on the ground down here. That means more resources and more attention should go towards that kind of thing. In reality, we're getting the same amount as the rest of the city. That continued stigma is never going to go away unless you dedicate the resources to it. It's really frustrating for me. I've been trying to get a trash can on this block. In two years, nothing's happened. Then I see new trash cans in other parts of the city, and that really bugs me ... I'm asking for one trash can, and I see like a dozen new ones on this other street alone. I don't want to point fingers or anything, but there is that stigma, and there is that sense of "Oh, well, it's dirty already anyway, what can you do?" ... If we were to try to put a trash can out ourselves, it's like "Did you get a permit for that?" It's hard, it gets so frustrating.

Despite engaging in reporting activities and advocacy, the executive director called attention to particular delivery and diverting practices. For the executive director, it seemed that the city was far more interested in improving other areas that appeared to be more straightforward to fix. Similar to the BIAs, the city was also interested in doable problems. And, as recounted in this case, problems became more doable through the networking of actors and corporatized bypass structures. Although BIAs are often in premium spaces, not all are, nor are all *premium networked spaces* equal. As explained by the city BIA program coordinator, there was a sense in the city that areas without BIAs would be at a "competitive disadvantage." BIAs are themselves assets and subject to valuation by a host of actors, including the city.

Just a couple of blocks down the street, one operations manager told a very different story of garbage bins:

> We're tracking quite a lot of information so that we can see if we are meeting our goals or figure out where we need to redirect resources. It really helps us figure out what attention the city needs. For example, it might help us determine whether or not additional garbage cans may need to be installed somewhere. On occasion, we may ask certain questions like, "Hey, we got an extra fifty garbage cans. Where would you like best to put them?" So we need to use our cleaning data with our pedestrian data to figure out where the best locations are ... We try to cover quite a lot of data on the idea that, when we get asked, we can figure it out.

Based upon this tale of two bins, or the juxtaposition of anecdotes alone, it would be far too simple to suggest that Vancouver plays favourites or is not concerned about perceptions. However, elements of the accumulated advantage are seen in the privileging of the BIA data economy – BIAs with larger budgets are often able to advocate for further resources. In this case, those able to allocate staff to populate the city dashboard, and representing key revenue-generating areas, were often rewarded.

Discussion: Directing, Diverting, and Districting

Better enabled by app-based practices (among others), BIAs have found innovative means, loopholes, and technologies for navigating the splintering streetscape and carrying out their clean and safe mandates. This splintered streetscape, as argued by Graham and Marvin (2001), is one that BIAs have had a causal hand in establishing and maintaining. Through the unbundling of infrastructure, the creation of bypass routes, and the rebundling process, BIAs have become a compelling model for creating and maintaining premium networked spaces (Graham & Marvin, 2001; Ward, 2003). However, now an expectation, the proliferation of BIAs in urban centres calls into question what is premium, since arguably not all premium spaces are equal. Not wholly isomorphic and exacerbating splintering, BIAs are also located on and have to navigate these uneven geographies. To varying degrees, BIAs are often the ones left to rebundle the remaining pieces of infrastructure and public services.

Outwardly presenting a semblance of *institutional thickness* – that is, the alignment of governmental, corporate, and social enterprise mandates and activities (Amin & Thrift, 1994) – BIAs and these related apps, I contend, have created or contributed to a fragmentation of urban governance. These apps have enabled practices of directing, diverting, and districting by empowering BIAs to navigate their splintered streetscapes better, incentivizing the vicious cycle of splintering and more administrative fragmentation. Although BIAs capitalize on elements of thickness (e.g., maintaining institutional presence, fostering high levels of interaction, adopting a clear and purposeful mandate, and creating mutual awareness of a common goal), their practices concentrate in particular nodes and areas. Smart technologies have enabled BIAs to help themselves: *diverting resources, directing city futures, and enforcing districting practices*, albeit partially (see Murakami Wood & Mackinnon, 2019). Although appearing to facilitate institutional thickness by aligning actors toward a common corporate goal, the thickness produced through these self-serving practices is uneven – for some premium spaces are better positioned than others, resulting in uneven delivery.

Although the adoption of VanConnect required no capital outlay for the technology, it still required staff and resources to adopt it or build it into existing programs. As noted by city staff and most of the executive directors (regardless of their BIAs), those with more person power and resources were better able to fuel the app and made more use of it. By securing public funds, BIAs furthered this practice through load-shedding and upstreaming responsibilities. Despite having subsidized clean teams and beautification projects, by defining their own roles and Rolodexes, the BIAs solidified the city's responsibilities for basic maintenance. As firmly stated by all city officials, maintenance is the responsibility of the city. Although the city remains officially responsible for how service is deployed, where and why services get delivered is more partial than impartial.

Data, visuals, and other narratives shared among members, stakeholders, officials, and the public further stabilized these knowledge and ontological claims. Through their work, BIAs engaged in a "politics of seeing and being seen" (Koskela, 2003, p. 295). Seen as matters of fact, these visual devices directed attention to BIAs' matters of concern and enabled the directing of future resources. Being construed as the most capable stewards, and possessing "the data," enabled them to advocate for greater services and assets in their areas. Not a universal BIA-city experience, the recognition by some BIAs that "now the city comes to us" exemplifies their directing power. "More premium" here is understood in terms of a BIA's ability to maintain levels of ontological security, furthered through these economic and spatial practices of fragmentation. Cognizant of the zero sum interurban competition, by stabilizing fashion and hype as "innovation," this image serves to advance resources and service delivery (Harvey, 1989).

BIAs, already products of districting themselves, with the use of apps and supplementary data, further advance spatial fragmentation. By bringing issues "back" under the purview of the city – back in the sense of being compiled through the city dashboard – VanConnect partially redistricts the city or remunicipalizes city services. However, this use emphasizes the private influences and marketization of city services. These directing practices of BIAs further spatial boundaries between areas of the city (e.g., between commercial areas as well as between more residential and industrial areas). Able to profit from administrative fragmentation, the success of these BIAs and their continued splintering practices highlight perverse incentivization. Presented as making the crisis of urban governance more manageable, these solutions further problems of fragmentation. In other words, this digital divide further fuels and reinforces spatial divides and districts.

BIAs have created a new role in the management of public and private realms as well as the liminal spaces between them – the particularly fragmented and supposedly broken municipal services. These practices of diverting, directing, and districting are nothing new, for these claims about degovernmentalization are the same as those that initially established BIAs and premium spaces. The adoption of smart technologies by BIAs is another isomorphic practice, extending their ontological politics and security. With the help of the city, BIAs have positioned themselves as another layer of governance. Not necessarily the privatization of services, their integration demonstrates the increasing role of private and corporate actors in city governance (see Duncan & Barreto, this volume). Similar to critiques launched at policy makers for myopic views and limited understanding of private police (see Stenning, 2000), this case highlights the corporatization of public services by private groups. Challenging lay notions of responsibilization and self-help, BIAs' directing, diverting, and districting of services could not be done without public services. With this acknowledgment of the city's role in these partial privatizing processes, more accountability and equity are needed to ensure the just dispersal of resources. As we continue to see more 311 apps and data-driven policing services, more attention needs to be paid to the creation of the data and the knowledge politics, spatial boundaries, and ordering practices that they reify.

Notes

1. The acronym BIA is more commonly used in Canada; however, it is synonymous with terms used in other jurisdictions. These terms include "business association," "business improvement district," "business improvement zone," "business revitalization zone," "community improvement district," "commercial district management authorities," "neighbourhood improvement districts," "public improvement district," "self-supported municipal improvement district," "special services area," and "special improvement district."
2. Bénit-Gbaffou (2008, p. 1934) defines fragmentation as the "de-solidarization of the city no longer functioning as a system but more and more as uncoordinated 'fragments' drifting apart."
3. For an expanded discussion, see Mackinnon (2019a, 2020, 2021).
4. The VanConnect app, though managed in house, is based upon Lagan Technologies, and the city pays licensing and support fees. Lagan Technologies is part of KANA Software, a private company (with North American headquarters in California), and provides customer relationship management tools for governments.
5. I speculate that BIA calls for service comprise more than 36 percent. First, these statistics are from 2016, and the success of larger BIAs has served to enrol other BIAs (see below). Second, and harder to account for, many BIA staff (e.g., non-ambassadors/clean team members) stated during interviews that they would use their personal phones/accounts to log requests. Although clean team members and ambassadors shared devices and accounts (making BIA activity easier to determine), executive directors and other staff who submitted requests on their personal accounts during their commutes or visits to members would not be counted by the city as "BIA activity."
6. See https://vancouver.ca/vanconnect.aspx.

References

Amin, A., & Thrift, N. (1994). *Globalization, institutions, and regional development in Europe.* Oxford University Press.

Barns, S. (2012). Retrieving the spatial imaginary of real-time cities. *Design Philosophy Papers, 10*(2), 147–156.

Baykurt, B. (2011). Redefining citizenship and civic engagement: Political values embodied in FixMyStreet.com. *AoIR Selected Papers of Internet Research, 1,* 1–18.

Bénit-Gbaffou, C. (2008). Unbundled security services and urban fragmentation in post-apartheid Johannesburg. *Geoforum, 39*(6), 1933–1950.

Blomley, N. K. (2004). *Unsettling the city: Urban land and the politics of property.* Routledge.

Bookman, S., & Woolford, A. (2013). Policing (by) the urban brand: Defining order in Winnipeg's Exchange District. *Social and Cultural Geography, 14*(3), 300–317.

Boyle, P., & Haggerty, K. D. (2011). Civil cities and urban governance: Regulating disorder for the Vancouver Winter Olympics. *Urban Studies, 48*(15), 3185–3201.

Brenner, N., Peck, J., & Theodore, N. (2010). Variegated neoliberalization: Geographies, modalities, pathways. *Global Networks, 10*(2), 182–222.

Brodeur, J. P. (2010). *The policing web*. Oxford University Press.

Brooks, L., & Strange, W. C. (2011). The micro-empirics of collective action: The case of business improvement districts. *Journal of Public Economics, 95*(11–12), 1358–1372.

Brownlee, J., Hurl, C., & Walby, K. (Eds.). (2018). *Corporatizing Canada: Making business out of public service*. Between the Lines.

Burgmann, T. (2015, April 11). Downtown Vancouver ambassadors discriminated against homeless. *CBC News*. http://www.cbc.ca/news/canada/british-columbia/downtown-vancouver-ambassadors-discriminated-against-homeless-1.3029392

Caldeira, T. (2000). *City of walls: Crime, segregation and citizenship in Sao Paulo*. University of California Press.

City of Vancouver. (2016). VanConnect update [PowerPoint file].

Crang, M., & Graham, S. (2007). Sentient cities, ambient intelligence and the politics of urban space. *Information, Communication and Society, 10*(6), 789–817.

DVBIA. (2019). What we do: Downtown clean team. *Downtown Vancouver*. https://www.dtvan.ca/what-we-do/clean-safe/clean-team/

Espeland, W., & Lom, S. (2015). Noting numbers: How quantification changes what we see and what we don't. In M. Kornberger, L. Justesen, A. K. Madsen, & J. Mouritsen (Eds.), *Making things valuable* (pp. 18–37). Oxford University Press.

Frieden, B. J., & Sagalyn, L. B. (1989). *Downtown Inc.: How America rebuilds cities*. MIT Press.

Garland, D. (1996). The limits of the sovereign state: Strategies of crime control in contemporary society. *British Journal of Criminology, 36*(4), 445–471.

Graham, S., & Marvin, S. (2001). *Splintering urbanism: Networked infrastructures, technological motilities and the urban condition*. Routledge.

Hannigan, J. (1999). *Fantasy city: Pleasure and profit in the postmodern metropolis*. Routledge.

Haque, U. (2012). What is a city that it would be "smart"? *Volume #34: City in a Box*. ISSUU. https://issuu.com/archis/docs/volume-34-preview

Harvey, D. (1989). From managerialism to entrepreneurialism: The transformation in urban governance in late capitalism. *Geografiska Annaler. Series B, Human Geography, 71*(1), 3–17.

Hoyt, L., & Gopal-Agge, D. (2007). The business improvement district model: A balance review of contemporary debates. *Geography Compass, 1*(4), 946–958.

Huey, L., Ericson, R., & Haggerty, K. (2005). Policing fantasy city. In D. Cooley (Ed.), *Re-imagining policing in Canada* (pp. 140–208). University of Toronto Press.

Joh, E. E. (2004). The paradox of private policing. *Journal of Criminal Law and Criminology, 95*(1), 49–132.

Kitchin, R. (2014). The real-time city? Big data and smart urbanism. *GeoJournal, 79*(1), 1–14.

Koskela, H. (2003). "Cam Era" – The contemporary urban panopticon. *Surveillance and Society, 1*(3), 292–313.

Ley, D. (1981). Inner-city revitalization in Canada: A Vancouver case study. *The Canadian Geographer, 25*(2), 124–148.

Ley, D., & Dobson, C. (2008). Are there limits to gentrification? The contexts of impeded gentrification in Vancouver. *Urban Studies, 45*(12), 2471–2498.

Lippert, R. K. (2010). Mundane and mutant devices of power: Business improvement districts and sanctuaries. *European Journal of Cultural Studies, 13*(4), 477–494.

Lippert, R. K. (2012). "Clean and safe" passage: Business improvement districts, urban security modes, and knowledge brokers. *European Urban and Regional Studies, 19*(2), 167–180.

Lippert, R. K. (2014). Neo-liberalism, police, and the governance of little urban things. *Foucault Studies, 18*, 49–65.

Lippert, R. K., & Walby, K. (Eds.). (2013). *Policing cities: Urban securitization and regulation in a 21st century world.* Routledge.

Mackinnon, D. (2019a). *Mundane surveillance: Tracking mobile applications and urban accounting in Canadian business improvement areas* [Unpublished PhD dissertation]. Queen's University.

Mackinnon, D. (2019b). Piecing it together, studying public private partnerships: Freedom of information as oligoptic technologies. In K. Walby & A. Luscombe (Eds.), *Freedom of information and social science research design* (pp. 123–137). Routledge.

Mackinnon, D. (2020). Activated alleyways: Mobilising clean and safe dwelling in Business Improvement Areas. In L. Anders & A. Zhang (Eds.), *Transforming Cities Through Temporary Urbanism* (pp. 155–169). Springer.

Mackinnon, D. (2021). Policing by another name and entity: BIAs, delegation, and public and private technologies. *Criminological Encounters, 4*(1), 206–211. doi: 10.26395/CE21040116

McCann, E., & Ward, K. (2012). Assembling urbanism: Following policies and "studying through" the sites and situations of policy-making. *Environment and Planning A, 44*(1), 42–51.

Molnar, A. (2015). The geo-historical legacies of urban security governance and the Vancouver 2010 Olympics. *The Geographical Journal, 181*(3), 235–241.

Mopas, M. (2005). Policing in Vancouver's Downtown Eastside: A case study. In D. Cooley (Ed.), *Re-imagining policing in Canada* (pp. 92–139). University of Toronto Press.

Morçöl, G., & Wolf, J. F. (2010). Understanding business improvement districts: A new governance framework. *Public Administration Review, 70*(6), 906–913.

Murakami Wood, D., & Mackinnon, D. (2019). Partial platforms and oligoptic surveillance in the smart city. *Surveillance and Society, 17*(1–2), 176–182.

Reeve, A. (2004). Town centre management: Developing a research agenda in an emerging field. *Urban Design International, 9*(3), 133–150.

Rose, N. (1990). *Governing the soul: The shaping of the private self.* Routledge.

Rose, N. (2000). Government and control. *British Journal of Criminology, 40*(2), 321–339.

Sleiman, M., & Lippert, R. K. (2010). Downtown ambassadors, police relations and "clean and safe" security. *Policing and Society, 20*(3), 316–335.

Smith, N. (1996). *The new urban frontier: Gentrification and the revanchist city.* Psychology Press.

Stenning, P. C. (2000). Powers and accountability of private police. *European Journal on Criminal Policy and Research, 8*(3), 325–352.

Valverde, M. (2012). *Everyday law on the street: City governance in an age of diversity.* University of Chicago Press.

Valverde, M. (2016). Ad hoc governance: Public authorities and North American local infrastructure in historical perspective. In M. Brady & R. K. Lippert (Eds.), *Governing practices: Neoliberalism, governmentality and the ethnographic imaginary* (pp. 199–217). University of Toronto Press.

Ward, K. (2003). Entrepreneurial urbanism, state restructuring and civilizing "New" East Manchester. *Area, 35*(2), 116–127.

PART 3

Private Influences and Privatization in Courts, Prisons, and Jails

6

Private Risk Assessment Instruments and Artificial Intelligence in Canada's Criminal Justice System

NICHOLAS POPE and REBECCA JAREMKO BROMWICH

Introduction
The single biggest lesson to be gleaned from recent technological advances is that algorithmic logics and rationales, in terms of how they are constructed and implemented, need to be subjected to closer scrutiny. Data privacy and cybersecurity have been noted increasingly as concerns. Indeed, after some 29 million Facebook users were victims of data breaches in 2018, as highlighted by the Cambridge Analytica scandal, and 13.4 million files were leaked from law offices in the Paradise Papers leak, personal privacy and machine learning were brought to the forefront of the public dialogue. However, where legal technologies are concerned, data security is not even the biggest problem. Rather, the larger threat posed to the integrity of legal institutions is the construction of categories in code and the reliance of artificial intelligence (AI) on those categories. Mechanistic and rigid modes of organizing data threaten fundamentally to undermine the case-by-case, nuanced decision making foundational to the common law tradition.

Criminal justice is an area where the stakes are high, and mistakes can be costly, in terms of both economics and human lives. For instance, a wrongful conviction can lead to costly litigation and have terrible ethical implications. Furthermore, as discussed in the introduction to this volume, corporatization and commercialization are encroaching increasingly on the criminal law sphere. Because of these contextual factors, adopting for decision-making purposes AI that was often developed in the private sector, and relies on the deployment of risk assessment instruments, which predict an individual's risk of reoffending based upon empirical data rather than a person's intuition, is seen as an efficient and objective addition to an overburdened criminal justice system. Criminologists and other social scientists largely have accepted that an objective, evidence-based approach is the best way to make criminal justice decisions (Lowenkamp et al., 2012, pp. 12–13). With technological advances in machine learning, risk assessment instruments are becoming increasingly accurate and widely used in a variety of government institutions (Kehl et al., 2017, p. 2). Although some of these instruments are created by government and non-profit organizations, there has been unprecedented private sector involvement in designing and marketing risk assessment instruments and providing services to governments (Tonry, 2014, p. 167). It is these privately designed instruments that we seek to examine critically in this chapter.

Conceptually, this chapter provides an overview and description of emergent and highly technical risk assessment tools and focuses explicitly on their implications for the administration of justice (see also Kohm, this volume). Empirically, this chapter looks at which instruments are in use and in which jurisdictions and contexts, and we consider critically the level of private development and ownership of these tools. We then interrogate worrisome policy implications of the use of these instruments, stressing that important dimensions of the humanistic, case-by-case, common law tradition are threatened potentially by the incursion of mechanistic risk assessment into the criminal justice process.

Canada is recognized as a "major player" in the worldwide development of risk assessment instruments (Luther & Mela, 2006, p. 413). However, the US criminal justice system uses privately developed risk assessment instruments at more decision points than Canada. Because of this, and the larger scale of the US criminal justice system, courts and academics have written more about their legal implications. Comparatively, the literature related to the legal restrictions on their use in Canada is scarce.

We will attempt to lay a groundwork for the discussion of private risk assessment instruments in the Canadian context. We start by providing background on what risk assessment instruments are and how they work. We then outline the more developed jurisprudence in the United States. Finally, we explore relevant cases and laws in Canada in terms of how they apply to the use of private risk assessment instruments and how they compare with or contrast to practices in the US criminal justice system. We focus on two of the most important issues surrounding risk assessment instruments: transparency and accuracy.

We conclude that Canada is likely to have greater restrictions than the United States on the use of private risk assessment instruments, ensuring greater transparency and accuracy. With respect to transparency, we show how Canadian courts, unlike American courts, require disclosure of the scoring algorithms of any risk assessments being considered, even if they are non-determinative or in possession of a third party. With respect to accuracy and bias, we conclude that Canada's judicial system offers stronger legal protections than those in the United States in two ways. First, Canadian law requires that instruments be validated in order to be used in corrections decisions. Second, in Canada, if it can be demonstrated that an instrument results in an unjustified disproportionate impact on a certain racialized or ethnic group, then its use will be deemed unconstitutional, whereas in the United States this is much less likely.

Based upon our comparative analysis, we argue that Canada is better equipped than the United States to preserve individuals' rights while embracing predictive risk instruments. However, we urge continued vigilance and caution; any uncritical acceptance of risk assessment tools in the criminal justice system itself poses risks to the liberty interests of Canadians as well as to the humanistic, case-by-case dimensions of the common law tradition. We argue that the question of whether proprietary considerations can preclude disclosure of the internal workings of risk assessment instruments must be resolved in favour of greater transparency. Moreover, for complex instruments that use machine-learning technologies, developers must provide easy-to-understand explanations of the factors weighted in relation to how defendants are conceived and understood within the algorithm's code. Finally, policy makers must engage in a robust discussion on what constitutes a non-discriminatory distribution of errors when one group of people has a higher rate of recidivism than another.

Risk Assessment Instruments

Various risk assessment instruments have been developed over the past few decades. These instruments can range from simple hand-scored tests to complex software that uses machine learning. To understand their implications for our justice system and how the law will apply to them, we must first understand where they are used and how they work. In this section, we outline where risk assessment instruments are used in the criminal justice system, explain the basics of how machine-learning risk assessment instruments work, and describe the two most popular private instruments used in North America.

Uses in the Criminal Justice System

Risk assessment instruments are used in three general areas in Canada and the United States: corrections, pretrial, and sentencing. Risk assessments were initially used in the corrections system to make decisions related to parole eligibility, inmate security classification, prison rehabilitation programs, supervised releases, and the imposition of release conditions (Hamilton, 2014, p. 234). Canada was a leader in this area, but California and other states have also adopted these instruments. These tools often use static factors to assess risk and dynamic factors to target areas for treatment (Kehl et al., 2017, p. 10). More recently, risk assessments have been used in pretrial contexts such as bail hearings and diversion (Hamilton, 2014, pp. 234–235). These tools generally focus solely on static risk factors to predict recidivism or flight risk and do not address dynamic factors such as the rehabilitative needs of offenders. One such tool, the Public Safety Assessment, is used in twenty-nine American jurisdictions, including the entire states of Arizona, Kentucky, and New Jersey (Kehl et al., 2017, p. 10). Certain US jurisdictions have even started to use risk assessment instruments in sentencing. Five states now *require* the use of risk assessments in sentencing, whereas others allow but do not require it (Kehl et al., 2017, p. 16). After an offender has been convicted in one of these jurisdictions, an officer of the court prepares a pre-sentencing report for the judge, which, in the first states where it is mandatory, includes the scores from a risk assessment. The judge is free to use this information as she or he sees fit (Kehl et al., 2017, p. 15). In Canada, the use of risk assessments in sentencing is much more limited; usually, they are used only in the sentencing process if a dangerous offender application is made, and generally they are presented as one part of the expert opinion of a psychologist (John Howard Society of Alberta, 2000, p. 5).

How Risk Assessment Instruments Work

How risk assessments produce scores varies greatly from simple, hand-scored instruments to tools built with complex, machine-learning software. The following discussion provides an overview of these different kinds of instruments and how they work. An example of a simple, hand-scored instrument is the Security Reclassification Scale used by Corrections Canada. The official filling out the assessment must answer several questions about the inmate, and a numerical value is assigned to each response. For example, one question asks how many serious disciplinary offences the inmate has committed in custody. An answer of none corresponds to 0.5; one, 1.0; two, 1.5; and three or more, 2.0. The assessor adds up the numerical values for each answer, and the resulting total is the inmate's score (*May v Ferndale Institution*, 2005, paras. 135–136).

At the other end of the spectrum are instruments that use machine learning. The most common machine-learning model used for risk assessment algorithms is called a random forest. A random forest is created by training hundreds of smaller machine-learning models called decision trees, each on a slightly different subset of a data set. Using different data to train each tree means that they are all different and might reach different decisions. This is done to prevent overfitting, which happens when a machine-learning algorithm configures itself too closely to the contours of the training data, so it accurately classifies the training data but is less accurate with the new data. Each tree essentially gets one vote, and the classification with the most votes is the output classification of the random forest (Maini & Sabri, 2017, p. 54).

Random forests have two useful features for criminal justice risk assessments. First, it is possible to measure the relative power of individual predictor variables. For instance, if a random forest model is fed data from people who have experienced trauma and people who are living in poverty, it might be able to yield insight into whether the trauma or the socioeconomic deprivation is a stronger predictor of criminality than experiencing victimization. Second, random forests allow designers to specify cost ratios for different types of variables (Barnes & Hyatt, 2012, p. 8). All risk assessments make mistakes, but not all mistakes are equally bad, and random forests allow the programmers to make those kinds of judgments. For example, classifying someone as low risk when that person is actually high risk (*underclassification*) could result in the person being freed and committing a crime. Criminal justice system decision makers might judge this worse than classifying a low-risk offender as high risk (*overclassification*), resulting in that person's incarceration. To avoid classification errors, programmers can increase the cost ratio for underclassification so that, though the algorithm might make the same number of mistakes, it will make more overclassifications than underclassifications.

Examples of Instruments: COMPAS and LSI-R

To provide a more concrete understanding of risk assessment instruments, below we describe two of the most popular private risk assessment instruments used in Canada and the United States: the Correctional Offender

Management Profiling for Alternative Sanctions (COMPAS) and the Level of Service Inventory – Revised (LSI-R). These tools were developed chiefly using traditional statistical methods. What machine learning does to bolster those methods is leverage the capacity to do vastly more calculations and compare much larger data sets than is feasible for human researchers.

COMPAS is a web-based tool for assessing recidivism risk developed in 1998 by the private company Northpointe. It is used in many jurisdictions throughout the United States (Northpointe, 2012, pp. 1–2). It was initially created to assist probation, parole, and bail decisions but has since expanded to use in sentencing (*State v Loomis*, 2016). COMPAS can output forty-one different scales that are either risk assessment or needs scales (Northpointe, 2012, p. 2). The three risk assessment scales are pretrial, general, and violent recidivism (*State v Loomis*, 2016, para. 14). The output is a number from 1 to 10 that predicts by decile the likelihood of reoffending compared with others in the norm group. There are currently eight norm groups: a male and female group for each of prison/parole, jail, probation, and composite. Northpointe adjusts norm groups to reflect the population of the state in which the user is located as well as by gender and other demographic data (Freeman, 2016, p. 81). The comparative sample against which data are assessed for the current version of the algorithm comes from 30,000 COMPAS assessments conducted between January 2004 and November 2005 in prison, parole, jail, and probation sites across the United States (Northpointe, 2012, p. 2). The variables used to create the assessments come from a 137-question survey and public criminal records (Freeman, 2016, p. 80). The variables cover five main areas: criminal involvement, relationship/lifestyles, personality/attitudes, family, and social exclusion (Electronic Privacy Information Center, n.d., Background section, para. 2). Northpointe does not disclose how the risk scores are determined or how the factors are weighed because it considers COMPAS a proprietary instrument and a trade secret (*State v Loomis*, 2016, para. 51).

LSI-R was developed by the Canadian company Multi-Health Systems and, as of 2010, used in nine Canadian provinces, twenty-three American states, and several other countries throughout the world (Casey et al., 2014, p. A-31). The data sample on which it relies to make comparisons consisted of 19,481 American inmates, 4,240 American community offenders, and 2,370 Canadian inmates (Multi-Health Systems, 2017, p. 3). It was developed for use in rehabilitation efforts and has been adapted for use in sentencing in several jurisdictions, including California and Washington (Kehl et al., 2017, p. 11).

LSI-R bases its assessment on the answers from a fifty-four-question survey, with questions in ten areas: criminal history, leisure/recreation, education/employment, companions, financial, alcohol/drug problems, family/marital, emotional/personal, accommodation, and attitudes/orientation (Multi-Health Systems, 2017, p. 3). Each question is scored as either a yes (1) or a no (0), and the sum is the total score (Casey et al., 2014, p. A-32). That score is then used to classify individuals into one of three risk levels: minimum, medium, or maximum. Although test developers suggest certain score ranges for these levels, they recommend that jurisdictions determine the ranges appropriate for their contexts (Casey et al., 2014, p. A-33). The risk assessment instruments discussed above, and others like them, are increasingly in widespread use, particularly in the United States. We discuss the legal uses of these instruments below.

US Jurisprudence

As mentioned above, risk assessment instruments have been used in more contexts in the United States than in Canada. Consequently, American courts have considered their legality more specifically than have Canadian courts. For this reason, we will start our legal analysis with a discussion of US jurisprudence before turning to Canada. American courts generally have been accepting of private risk assessment instruments despite recognizing their downsides. We will discuss two leading cases in which US courts have permitted the use of private instruments in sentencing and then consider the instruments' legality under the Equal Protection clause of the US Constitution.

Malenchik v State

In *Malenchik v State*, a 2010 case before the Indiana Supreme Court, the court held that a sentencing judge may consider risk assessment scores as long as they are used only to supplement other evidence that independently supports the sentence, not to replace the judge's evaluation (p. 568). On appeal, the Supreme Court considered whether, and in what manner, a sentencing judge may consider the results from LSI-R and similar assessment tools. The defendant argued that they should not be considered because they preclude individualized assessment, lack scientific reliability, are discriminatory, and are inconsistent with reformation as a goal of Indiana's penal code. He also argued that his right to counsel was violated because the scoring sheets were not provided to his counsel prior to the sentencing hearing.

The Supreme Court disagreed with the defendant on each of these issues. The court held that the use of instruments such as LSI-R does not undercut the court's responsibility to craft an individualized sentence. Rather, the instruments enhance a sentencing judge's evaluation (*Malenchik v State*, 2010, p. 573). The court held that LSI-R is sufficiently reliable to warrant consideration of the scores along with other information. It also stated that it was not discriminatory for the risk assessments to use the factors that they did because those factors were already required by statute to be presented for judicial consideration (p. 574). The court held that the use of risk assessments is consistent with the goal of reformation because they provide more research-based information to help the sentencing judge craft a sentence with maximum potential for reformation (p. 575). Finally, the court rejected the defendant's claim of a violation of the right to counsel because the defendant had access to the Pre-Sentence Investigative (PSI) report before sentencing and could challenge the results outlined in the report (p. 575). Thus, the risk assessment instrument was permitted to bolster and support the discretion of judges, not to supplant it.

State v Loomis

In 2016, the Supreme Court of Wisconsin came to a similar conclusion regarding the use of COMPAS in sentencing in *State v Loomis*. Despite the secret and proprietary nature of COMPAS, the court allowed sentencing judges to consider it as long as it is non-determinative and the PSI report includes certain cautions. In this case, the sentencing judge ordered a PSI report, which included a COMPAS risk assessment (para. 12). The defendant's risk scores indicated a high risk for recidivism (para. 16). The PSI report also included a caution that COMPAS scores should not be used to determine the severity of a sentence or whether a defendant should be imprisoned (para. 17). The judge referenced the COMPAS scores along with other factors in ruling out probation (para. 19) and sentencing the defendant to seventeen and a half years in prison (para. 22).

The defendant appealed his sentence to the Court of Appeal and subsequently the Supreme Court. The Supreme Court considered whether the use of COMPAS at sentencing violates a defendant's right to due process on any of three grounds: (1) it violates the defendant's right to be sentenced on accurate information; (2) it violates the defendant's right to an individualized sentence; and (3) it improperly uses gendered assessments in sentencing.

Regarding the first issue, the defendant claimed that the proprietary nature of COMPAS prevented him from ensuring that he was sentenced on accurate information (*State v Loomis*, 2016, para. 46). COMPAS does not disclose how risk scores are determined or how factors are weighted. The defendant therefore could not challenge the scientific validity of the instrument or verify the accuracy of his score (para. 52). The Supreme Court acknowledged the concerns about accuracy and bias, and it brought up the issue that COMPAS had not been renormed to ensure accuracy for Wisconsin's specific population (paras. 59–64). However, it determined that these concerns were not sufficient to constitute a violation of due process. The defendant had the opportunity to verify the accuracy of the inputs (the questions that he answered and his criminal record), and he had full access to the output scores on the PSI report. The ability to challenge the inputs and outputs fulfilled his right to be sentenced on accurate information, even if he did not have access to the internal algorithm (paras. 55–56).

To address concerns about accuracy, the Supreme Court held that PSI reports with COMPAS scores must provide the following cautions: (1) the proprietary nature of COMPAS has been invoked to prevent disclosure of information related to how factors are weighed or how risk scores are determined; (2) the risk assessments compare defendants to a national sample, but no cross-validation study for a Wisconsin population has yet been completed; (3) some studies of COMPAS risk assessment scores have raised questions about whether they disproportionately classify minority offenders as having higher risks of recidivism; and (4) risk assessment tools must be constantly monitored and renormed for accuracy because of changing populations and subpopulations (*State v Loomis*, 2016, para. 66).

Regarding the second issue, the defendant claimed that the use of COMPAS scores violated his right to an individualized sentence because it amounted to sentencing based upon group data, not upon his unique charges and character (*State v Loomis*, 2016, para. 67). The Supreme Court rejected this argument, saying that, if the COMPAS scores were the determinative factor, then there would be concerns about due process, but the COMPAS scores along with other factors give the sentencing judge as much information as possible to arrive at an individualized sentence (para. 72). To ensure this approach, the court required that PSI reports using COMPAS scores include a fifth caution: that COMPAS scores are able to identify groups of high-risk offenders only, not a particular high-risk individual, because they are based upon group data (para. 74).

Regarding the third issue, the defendant claimed that COMPAS's use of gender as a factor violates the right not to be sentenced on the basis of gender (*State v Loomis*, 2016, para. 75). Because of the proprietary nature of COMPAS, neither party knew exactly how COMPAS considers gender. The state claimed that COMPAS does the same analysis for men and women but then compares each offender to a normative group of the same gender, necessary for statistical accuracy. The defendant claimed that COMPAS considers gender as a criminogenic factor, but he objected to the use of gender for either purpose regardless (paras. 76–77).

The Supreme Court rejected the defendant's argument on two grounds. First, it agreed with the state that any risk assessment that does not consider gender will be less accurate. Therefore, since including gender promotes accuracy, it serves the interests of institutions and defendants rather than a discriminatory purpose, so it does not violate rights of due process (*State v Loomis*, 2016, para. 83). Second, the court held that the defendant had not met his burden of proving that the sentencing judge had relied on gender as a factor, because it was unknown what influence gender had on the COMPAS score, and the sentencing judge had mentioned multiple factors other than the COMPAS score in his decision (para. 85).

In summary, the Wisconsin Supreme Court acknowledged that there were serious issues regarding accuracy and bias and that it was impossible to know exactly how COMPAS reached its final score. However, the court decided that these concerns could be addressed by cautioning sentencing judges so that they know about the concerns and by requiring that a COMPAS score alone should not determine a sentence. Not surprisingly, there has been a great deal of criticism of the *Loomis* decision among American legal scholars. The main criticism is that cautioning sentencing judges about the myriad issues in using COMPAS does not resolve the issues. Katherine Freeman (2016, p. 97) has argued that, by allowing COMPAS scores in PSI reports as long as they come with warnings, the court placed its faith in sentencing judges' ability to refrain from being swayed too heavily by COMPAS results. Studies have shown that people are susceptible to "automation bias": that is, they trust computer-generated assessments even when faced with evidence of the systems' inaccuracies. For example, in one study, as Freeman notes, participants followed a robot during a fire drill even though it clearly led them away from marked exits and broke down (p. 98). Many experts warn that, even if decision makers are told to apply their own judgment and use algorithms only as decision supports, they can begin to abdicate their responsibility (Bird, 2018; Oswald et al., 2018, pp. 232, 240).

Thus, permitting the use of risk assessment instruments in the legal context can pose risks for the fairness and transparency of the administration of justice not mitigated by the cautionary guidance set forth in the case law.

Potential Equal Protection Challenges

Scholars have also raised the possibility of arguments made under the Equal Protection clause of the US Constitution having more success at reining in the use of private risk assessment instruments such as COMPAS because they employ certain protected factors as inputs. Under the Equal Protection clause, laws or policies that classify people using certain factors can be subject to three different tiers of analysis: rational basis review, heightened review, and strict scrutiny (Hamilton, 2014, p. 242).

Instruments using variables other than gender, race, or citizenship would be subject to a rational basis review and permissible as long as the use of the instrument serves a legitimate public purpose and the classifications drawn are reasonable in light of that purpose (Hamilton, 2014, p. 242, citing *McLaughlin v Florida*, 1964, para. 191). Courts consistently have accepted public safety, prison security, and rehabilitation as legitimate goals in criminal justice circumstances (Hamilton, 2014, p. 244). Regarding whether risk assessment instruments, and the factors that they use, are rationally related to the purposes, the 2013 case *People v Osman* is instructive. A defendant was scored on Static-99, a sexual recidivism instrument. One of the variables used is whether a person has cohabited with an intimate partner; a negative response contributes to a higher risk score. The defendant challenged the use of this tool under the Equal Protection clause, and the court held that, since studies had shown that cohabitation experience predicted sexual recidivism, using it as a factor was rationally related to the legitimate purpose (Hamilton, 2014, p. 246, citing *People v Osman*, 2013, para. 15). Thus, it is very likely that risk assessment instruments will survive an Equal Protection challenge if race and gender are not used as factors.

When gender is used as a factor, heightened review will apply, which requires the use of the factor to be related substantially to a sufficiently important governmental interest for it to be permissible (Hamilton, 2014, p. 243, citing *Miss Univ for Women v Hogan*, 1982, p. 724). Legal scholars have differing opinions on whether the use of gender could survive this analysis (Hamilton, 2014, p. 250). The key would be for officials to offer studies that show sufficiently strong correlations between gender and the behaviour that they are trying to predict (Hamilton, 2014, p. 254). If race or citizenship is used as a factor, then strict scrutiny would apply, requiring the policy to be tailored narrowly to achieve a compelling governmental purpose and use the least restrictive means (Hamilton, 2014, p. 243, citing *Perry Educ Ass'n v Perry Local Educators' Ass'n*, 1983). Many scholars say that instruments using these factors would fail this strict scrutiny (Hamilton, 2014, p. 257). This point is mostly moot since none of the currently popular risk assessment instruments explicitly uses either factor (Hamilton, 2014, p. 257).

Despite risk assessment instruments not explicitly including race, many other socio-economic factors, such as education or employment, can act as proxies for race, causing the results of the assessments to classify racialized persons disproportionately as higher risk (Hamilton, 2014, p. 261). These factors would be subject only to a rational basis review, and the disproportionate impact based upon race would not be subject to review since the US Supreme Court has held that laws and policies are not unconstitutional solely because of a racially disproportionate impact (Hamilton, 2014, p. 262, citing *Washington v Davis*, 1976, p. 239). The "settled rule" is that Equal Protection "guarantees equal laws, not equal results" (Hamilton, 2014, p. 262, citing *Pers Adm'r of Mass v Feeney*, 1979, p. 273).

The foregoing shows that courts have conceded that it is necessary to be cautious about allowing the use of risk assessment instruments to supplant the judgment of people appointed to decision-making roles. Nonetheless, the cautionary guidance provided by this case law might not be enough to prevent the de facto abdication of decision making in light of the ease of deferring to an instrument's findings.

Canadian Law

Canadian courts have not dealt with the use of private risk assessments such as COMPAS as directly as have American courts. However, there are cases in corrections and sentencing that shed some light on the approach that we argue Canadian courts are likely to take. In the following section, we reflect on what we believe this approach would look like. Based upon existing jurisprudence, Canadian courts likely would require that private risk assessment instruments be more transparent and provide confirmation of accuracy and lack of bias. At the same time, the law leaves room for proprietary considerations to trump transparency, something that we stress must not be permitted.

Transparency Obligations

Canadian courts have dealt at length with disclosure requirements for the use of risk assessment instruments to classify the security levels of inmates. The leading case in this area is *May v Ferndale Institution* (2005). In contrast to the American approach, the Supreme Court of Canada held that, even if risk assessment scores are non-determinative, the government has the duty to disclose the scoring matrix, or internal algorithm, of the risk assessment, not merely the inputs and outputs.

In this case, five inmates were serving life sentences for murder or manslaughter in a minimum-security prison (*May*, 2005, para. 4). After a former inmate in another province committed a sensational crime, Correctional Services Canada (CSC) reviewed the security classifications of all inmates serving life sentences in minimum-security prisons who had not completed their violent offender programming. CSC used the Security Reclassification Scale (SRS), a computer application–based risk assessment, to assess all five inmates. It assessed them as medium security and subsequently transferred them to medium-security prisons (paras. 5–6).

The Standard Operating Procedures on the Security Classification of Offenders stated that SRS scores are subject to variation in only two situations: (1) when the score is within 5 percent of the cut-off for another level and (2) when a caseworker believes it necessary to override the results, includes a detailed justification of the decision, and a supervisor approves the decision (*May*, 2005, paras. 113–115). The inmates applied for *habeas corpus* on the ground that their right to procedural fairness was breached by CSC's failure to disclose the scoring matrix for the SRS, and the case eventually made its way to the Supreme Court. The inmates argued that, by not disclosing the scoring matrix, CSC violated the disclosure requirements in the Charter of Rights and Freedoms, as recognized in *R v Stinchcombe* (1991), and the duty of procedural fairness that applies to administrative decisions. The court rejected the charter argument, saying that the *Stinchcombe* duty to disclose all relevant information is applicable only in the context of criminal proceedings in which innocence is at stake, not in post-conviction administrative decisions (para. 91).

However, the Supreme Court agreed that CSC violated the duty of procedural fairness. The court stated that the duty of procedural fairness is reflected in, and bolstered by, the disclosure requirements in section 27(1) of the Corrections and Conditional Release Act ([CCRA,] 1992); (*May*, 2005, para. 94). Section 27(1) requires that CSC give the inmate, at a reasonable period before the decision is to be made, "all the information to be considered in the taking of the decision or a summary of that information." The court held that the duty of disclosure for transfer decisions is thus substantial and extensive (para. 100).

CSC made two arguments, similar to the arguments raised in the American cases, in its attempt not to disclose the scoring matrix. The first was that the scoring matrix was not available, and the second was that the SRS score was not determinative. With regard to the unavailability of the scoring matrix, the Supreme Court found that the matrix was not truly unavailable; it was merely CSC's practice not to produce it (*May*, 2005, para. 110). Therefore, the matrix should be disclosed (para. 112). Four years later the Saskatchewan Court of Appeal expanded on this issue when it held that, when a third-party contract psychologist conducts the assessment and has possession of the files, CSC still has the obligation to disclose the matrix. The Court of Appeal interpreted section 27(1) to include all information directly relevant to understanding the psychologist's report and "under CSC's power and control or obtainable by CSC on a timely basis and with reasonable effort" (*R v Bishop*, 2009, para. 16). The Court of Appeal explicitly left open the possibility that some information in possession of a third party might not have to be disclosed, for example if there were proprietary or contractual considerations preventing CSC from obtaining the material or disclosing it to the inmate (para. 19).

CSC's second argument in *May* (2005) was that the matrix did not have to be disclosed because the SRS score was not determinative. Officers had discretion if the score was within 5 percent of a cut-off value, and if not they could use an override. However, the Supreme Court found that the procedure for an override confirmed rather than invalidated the presumptive nature of the SRS. The Standard Operating Procedures stated that, for officers to override the score, they must include a detailed analysis justifying it under three headings: institutional adjustment, escape risk, and risk to public safety (para. 114). The override must then be approved by a supervisor or in some cases the assistant commissioner (para. 115). Therefore, the court could not accept CSC's argument that the SRS is only a preliminary assessment tool because the SRS presumptively classifies inmates and constitutes an important aspect of the classification process (para. 116).

Although in *May* (2005) the override function was not actually used on any of the inmates, nor was any score varied because of being within 5 percent of a cut-off (para. 115), later decisions affirmed the disclosure requirement even when scores were varied. In *Khela v Mission Institution* (2014), an inmate who had undergone an SRS assessment was transferred to a higher-security prison after CSC overrode the security classification. The Supreme Court held that, for the score to be overridden, it would have to have been "considered" within the meaning of section 27(1); therefore, the scoring matrix must be disclosed (para. 97). In *Cliff v Kent Institution* (2016), a similar situation occurred, but the inmate was classified at a level higher than his score suggested because he was within the 5 percent discretionary range. The BC Supreme Court considered this "virtually indistinguishable from *Khela*" and held that the SRS matrix needed to be disclosed (paras. 25, 35–36).

Although these cases involve corrections security classification decisions rather than sentencing, as in *Loomis* (2016), it is unlikely that courts would impose a less onerous disclosure requirement on criminal sentencing decisions than administrative decisions in the corrections context. The applicable *Stinchcombe* (1991, para. 21) standard for disclosure is that all "relevant information" must be disclosed, more expansive than the *May* (2005, para. 92) standard of disclosing all "information considered."

In sum, Canada appears to be headed in a different direction than the United States with regard to disclosure of the internal workings of risk assessment instruments. Canadian courts require disclosure of the scoring algorithms of any risk assessments considered, even if they are non-determinative and in the possession of a third party. The question remains, however, whether proprietary algorithms would be insulated from disclosure.

Concerns: Accuracy and Bias

The 2018 Supreme Court case *Ewert v Canada* gives a strong indication that Canada will require more assurance of accuracy and lack of bias from private risk assessment instruments than is currently required in the United States. Although in *Loomis* (2016) the Wisconsin Supreme Court allowed sentencing judges to consider scores from non-validated instruments as long as the pre-sentencing reports cautioned that the instruments were not validated, in *Ewert* (2018, para. 67) the Supreme Court of Canada instructed the government to conduct research on possible bias in the instruments and either stop using them or modify them in some way if bias is found.

The plaintiff in *Ewert* (2018, paras. 8–9) was a Métis man serving a life sentence for murder and sexual assault. Throughout his time in prison, CSC relied on the results of five risk assessment instruments in making decisions about him. Ewert claimed that the tools were developed and tested predominantly on non-Indigenous populations and that there was no research confirming that they were accurate for Indigenous persons (para. 12). CSC had been aware of these concerns since 2000 but had not conducted any research to verify their accuracy on Indigenous persons (para. 17).

Ewert claimed that CSC violated three laws by not ensuring the accuracy of the instruments for Indigenous persons: (1) section 24(1) of the CCRA,

(2) section 7 of the Charter of Rights and Freedoms, and (3) section 15 of the charter. The Supreme Court agreed that there was a violation of section 24(1) of the CCRA but found no evidence proving either charter violation. Section 24(1) of the CCRA states that "[CSC] shall take all reasonable steps to ensure that any information about an offender that it uses is as accurate, up to date and complete as possible." CSC argued that this stipulation requires only that information be properly gathered and recorded and should not apply to ensuring the accuracy of the results of risk assessment instruments (*Ewert*, 2018, para. 42), which cannot be described as "accurate" or "inaccurate"; rather, they have different levels of predictive validity (para. 43). The court rejected CSC's argument, saying that section 24(1) applies to the results of the tools (para. 41), and the obligation to take "all reasonable steps" to ensure that information is "as accurate ... as possible" means that CSC must take steps to ensure that the test scores on which it relies "predict risks strongly rather than those that do so poorly" (para. 43).

Ewert bore the burden of proof, but he did not have to prove that CSC actually relied on inaccurate information. He merely had to prove that CSC failed to take all reasonable steps to ensure that it did not rely on inaccurate information (*Ewert*, 2018, para. 47). Ewert satisfied this burden by proving that CSC was aware of concerns about cultural bias; it had conducted research on some other instruments and stopped using them for Indigenous inmates, and other jurisdictions had conducted research on the validity of some of the impugned instruments. Despite this, CSC failed to conduct any research on those instruments, and the Supreme Court found that this violated section 24(1) (paras. 49–50). The court ruled that, if CSC wanted to continue to use the instruments, then at minimum it must conduct research on whether and to what extent they are subject to cross-cultural variance when applied to Indigenous offenders. Further action might be required depending on the outcome of the research: CSC might have to stop using the instruments or modify them in some way (para. 67).

Ewert's charter claims were not successful, but the Supreme Court laid out the test that future challenges would need to meet. Ewert argued that, under section 7, CSC's use of the instruments deprived him of personal liberty and security contrary to the principles of fundamental justice of arbitrariness and overbreadth (*Ewert*, 2018, para. 69). The court did not decide whether those interests were engaged and proceeded solely with an analysis of the principles of fundamental justice (para. 70). It stated that a law that bears no connection to its objective is arbitrary. A law that is rational in some cases but has no rational connection between its purpose and some of its impacts is overbroad (para. 71). The trial judge had found that, given the absence of evidence of accuracy for Indigenous offenders, the instruments were arbitrary with respect to Indigenous inmates and overbroad with respect to the entire inmate population (para. 72). However, the Supreme Court disagreed, holding that uncertainty about the extent to which the tests are accurate for Indigenous persons is not sufficient to establish that there is no rational connection between reliance on the tests and the relevant government objective (para. 73). Ewert needed to prove that the tests actually were less accurate for Indigenous than non-Indigenous persons, and he failed to meet this onus (para. 74).

Ewert failed on his section 15 argument for a similar reason. The criteria to establish a violation of section 15 are (1) that a policy creates a distinction based upon an enumerated or analogous ground and (2) that it has the effect of reinforcing, perpetuating, or exacerbating the claimant's historical position of disadvantage (*Kahkewistahaw First Nation v Taypotat*, 2015, paras. 19–21). Ewert claimed that CSC was using "reliable or true" information to make decisions about non-Indigenous persons but using "unreliable or false" information to make decisions about Indigenous persons and that this led to harsher treatment and prolonged incarceration of Indigenous inmates (*Ewert*, 2018, para. 77). Because Ewert established only a risk that the instruments were less accurate for Indigenous persons, not that they actually were, the Supreme Court held that there was not sufficient evidence to find a section 15 violation (para. 79).

If Ewert had proven that the instruments were less accurate for Indigenous persons, then the government would have had the opportunity to justify the sections 7 and 15 violations under section 1. To be justified, the use of the instruments must be for a pressing and substantial objective, and the means by which the objective is furthered must be proportionate. For the means to be proportionate, they must have (1) a rational connection to the objective, (2) a minimal impairment of the right, and (3) proportionality between the effects and the objective (*R v Oakes*, 1986, paras. 69–70). Although there might be a pressing and substantial objective of ensuring public safety and prison security, it is very unlikely that the government would succeed under section 1 because using less accurate instruments, rather than accurate instruments, would certainly not be minimally impairing unless the government could prove that there was no way to create a more accurate instrument for Indigenous persons. However, because all risk assessment instruments have some degree of error, a more difficult question could arise: How should errors be distributed? A controversy in the United States surrounding COMPAS exemplifies this dilemma.

In 2016, ProPublica examined the COMPAS risk scores for more than 7,000 people arrested in Broward County, Florida, in 2013 and 2014 and checked how many of them were charged with new offences in the next two years. ProPublica found that the algorithm made mistakes with Black and white defendants at roughly the same rate but in different ways. COMPAS labelled 45 percent of Black defendants who did not go on to reoffend as high risk, whereas it labelled only 23 percent of white defendants who did not go on to reoffend as high risk. In contrast, COMPAS labelled 48 percent of white defendants who did reoffend as low risk but made the same mistake on Black defendants only 28 percent of the time (Larson et al., 2016). Because of this and similar findings, ProPublica claimed that COMPAS was biased against Black people (Angwin et al., 2016).

Northpointe denied ProPublica's allegations, claiming that the scores are not biased because they mean the same thing regardless of the defendant's race. For example, 60 percent of white defendants classified in the seventh decile reoffended, and 61 percent of Black defendants with the same score reoffended. The similarity holds true for each of the ten risk levels. *The Washington Post* reanalyzed the data and pointed out that whether the scores were fair depends on how "fair" is defined. Northpointe and ProPublica used different measures of fairness, and it is impossible to satisfy both fairness criteria at the same time because the overall rate of recidivism for Black defendants is higher than for white defendants (Corbett-Davies et al., 2016). It is possible that this issue could arise in Canada, in which case Canadian courts would need to determine which way of distributing errors, if any, is permissible.

In the area of sentencing, Canadian courts generally have accepted the use of risk assessment instruments when their results are presented as part of the testimony of a qualified expert witness, such as a psychologist. The experts can administer the tests properly, use multiple instruments, weigh their results, inform the court of any limitations of each instrument as it applies to the particular case, and be cross-examined on their conclusions (see *R v Grayer*, 2007; *R v Taylor*, 2012).

Yet some judges have expressed concerns about using risk assessments in pre-sentencing reports (see *R v Epp*, 2005, para. 9). In one case, the sentencing judge was not willing to give any weight to three different risk assessment scores (ORAMS, Static-99, and Stable 2000) in a pre-sentencing report because he had many concerns, including that there was a lack of information on the training or qualifications of the probation officer who had administered the assessments, that only one of the three instruments had been validated, and that the risk assessments had taken into account information not contained in the facts before the court (*R v Hildebrandt*, 2005, para. 32). These cases suggest that the most appropriate way for judges to consider risk assessment results is when they are presented by qualified experts as one part of their testimonies, not when they are included merely as unexplained numbers in pre-sentencing reports.

In summary, Canada's laws related to accuracy and bias in risk assessment algorithms are much stronger than those in the United States in two ways. Although the US case law does enjoin, as discussed, decision makers to exercise caution and not to fetter their discretion to machines, the cautionary guidance in American case law is not as specific or detailed as that provided in Canada. Canadian law requires instruments to be validated in order to be used in corrections decisions; a written caution that the instrument has not been validated will not suffice. Also, in Canada, if studies find that an instrument results in an unjustified disproportionate impact on a certain race or ethnic group, it will be deemed unconstitutional, unlike in the United States, where discriminatory impacts from instruments that do not include race as an input variable would not be subject to strict scrutiny.

Critical Analysis of Canadian Law
Based upon the comparison of instruments and their uses, we argue that certain safeguards in Canadian law are likely to produce more equitable and just results than the American system and should be affirmed. However, there is still a cause for concern and a need for vigilance. The trend across sectors in Canada, as well as in the United States, is toward increased reliance on artificial intelligence, machine learning, and risk assessment in quantified calculations using automated tools. The common law tradition hinges on individualized, case-by-case decision making. It is important that unanswered questions in Canada's approach to risk assessment instruments be resolved in a way that most protects individuals' rights.

A clear advantage of Canadian jurisprudence is that it requires transparency and accuracy of risk assessment instruments regardless of whether other factors are determinative. This is in stark contrast to the American jurisprudence that ignores the reality of automation bias and assumes that a written caution will alleviate all concerns. Although so far the case law has addressed only the transparency requirement in relation to corrections decisions, it is both logical and imperative that this standard be extended to the pretrial and pre-sentencing contexts since they involve decisions that can have an even greater impact on an individual's freedom.

The question that *R v Bishop* (2009) left unanswered of whether contractual or proprietary considerations might stand in the way of disclosure needs to be resolved in favour of transparency. The government should not be able to shield itself from disclosure by off-loading responsibility to a third party and signing a contract that limits disclosure. Criminal justice decisions need robust safeguards because of the liberty interest at stake. If a private company is not willing to disclose the internal algorithms, then the government should turn to another provider willing to do so or itself fund the development of an instrument. Twenty-nine jurisdictions in the United States have demonstrated that this is feasible through their use of the Public Safety Assessment to assist with pretrial detention decisions (Kehl et al., 2017, p. 10). The developer of that assessment, a non-profit foundation, makes all factors and scoring matrices publicly available (Laura and John Arnold Foundation, n.d., pp. 3–4).

An additional complication arising from the use of machine learning in risk assessments is that the internal algorithm can be so complicated that it is unintelligible to humans. Thus, simply disclosing the algorithm might not be enough to allow an individual to understand the decision. In these cases, we propose that two elements be provided to give meaningful disclosure. First, the code itself should be disclosed to defence counsel so that experts can run tests to see what results would stem from small changes to the defendant's input data, such as changing the age or gender. Second, the developer should disclose in plain language the weight of each factor in the final outcome. Because many of the newest risk assessment algorithms use a random forest model, this sort of information can be obtained from the system. If another machine-learning model is used, then a similar human-readable explanation of the results should be provided to the highest extent possible given technological constraints. If no human-readable explanation is possible, then that model should not be used.

Conclusion

Private risk assessment instruments are used in many areas of the criminal justice system, and their use will probably increase as our society becomes more and more reliant on technology. Artificial intelligence is likely to be deployed in an increasingly wide range of circumstances to make decisions based upon large quantities of data tabulated by these instruments. Canadian lawyers and the public alike need to pay close attention to how data are organized by these risk assessment instruments and how those data are used by artificial intelligence to make decisions, or the results could be catastrophic to the continuation of the common law tradition. We are entering a moment when legal tech, analytics, and artificial intelligence are increasingly central to the practice of law and the administration of justice, just as serious concerns are being raised about the dangers of these emergent technologies (see also Duncan & Barreto, this volume). The platforms enabling risk assessment algorithms to work are constructed, often by private, for-profit companies, without scrutiny, through a labyrinthine matrix of details, where the operation of languages of code, and the manipulation of algorithms, mix with the discourses of formal law. Additionally, to protect the common law tradition, in the present and in the future, new levels of scrutiny should be involved in how legal tech platforms organize, and make sense of, data.

Although Canada appears to have stricter laws regulating their use than the United States, there are still key legal uncertainties that call out for public, legal, and judicial vigilance to prevent overuse of and overreach by these instruments. It is unclear at present whether requirements for transparency will preclude proprietary algorithms or whether proprietary algorithms will limit transparency. It is also not clear which imperfect instrument is less biased: the one that has the same error rate at each risk level for racialized groups and non-racialized groups or the one that overclassifies racialized groups at the same rate as non-racialized groups. Government policy makers, academics, and judges will soon need to address these questions and other questions about how to assess, evaluate, and effectively and justly use private risk assessment tools while maintaining fundamental foundations of the common law tradition. It is crucial to ensure that Canada proceeds with a nuanced and fair approach to the increasing use of private risk assessment instruments in its criminal justice system.

References

Angwin, J., Larson, J., Mattu, S., & Kirchner, L. (2016, May 23). Machine bias. *ProPublica*. https://www.propublica.org/article/machine-bias-risk-assessments-in-criminal-sentencing

Barnes, G., & Hyatt, J. (2012). *Classifying adult probationers by forecasting future offending*. National Institute of Justice, US Department of Justice.

Bird, E. (2018, July 25). Witness panel 2. In *Technology and the Law Policy Commission – Algorithms in the justice system public evidence session 1*. Law Society of England and Wales. https://www.lawsociety.org.uk/policy-campaigns/articles/public-policy-technology-and-law-commission/

Canadian Charter of Rights and Freedoms, Part 1 of the *Constitution Act, 1982*, being Schedule B to the *Canada Act 1982* (UK) 1982, c 11.

Casey, P. M., Elek, J. K., Warren, R. K., Cheesman, F., Kleiman, M., & Ostrom, B. (2014). *Offender risk and needs assessment instruments: A primer for courts*. National Center for State Courts. https://www.ncsc.org/~/media/microsites/files/csi/bja%20rna%20final%20report_combined%20files%208-22-14.ashx

Cliff v Kent Institution, 2016 BCSC 1525.

Corbett-Davies, S., Pierson, E., Feller, A., & Goel, S. (2016, October 17). A computer program used for bail and sentencing decisions was labeled biased against blacks. It's actually not that clear. *The Washington Post*. https://www.washingtonpost.com/news/monkey-cage/wp/2016/10/17/can-an-algorithm-be-racist-our-analysis-is-more-cautious-than-propublicas/?utm_term=.2b1043dc6b5b

Corrections and Conditional Release Act, SC 1992, c 20.

Electronic Privacy Information Center. (n.d.). Algorithms in the criminal justice system. https://epic.org/algorithmic-transparency/crim-justice/

Ewert v Canada, 2018 SCC 30, 423 DLR (4th) 577.

Freeman, K. (2016). Algorithmic injustice: How the Wisconsin Supreme Court failed to protect due process rights in State v. Loomis. *North Carolina Journal of Law and Technology*, *18*, 75–106. http://ncjolt.org/wp-content/uploads/2016/12/Freeman_Final.pdf

Hamilton, M. (2014). Risk-needs assessment: Constitutional and ethical challenges. *American Criminal Law Review*, *52*, 231–291.

John Howard Society of Alberta. (2000). Offender risk assessment. https://johnhoward.ab.ca/pub/pdf/C21.pdf

Kahkewistahaw First Nation v Taypotat, 2015 SCC 30, [2015] 2 SCR 548.

Kehl, D., Guo, P., & Kesseler, S. (2017). Algorithms in the criminal justice system: Assessing the use of risk assessments in sentencing. *Responsive Communities Initiative, Berkman Klein Center for Internet and Society, Harvard Law School*. https://dash.harvard.edu/bitstream/handle/1/33746041/2017-07_responsivecommunities_2.pdf

Khela v Mission Institution, 2014 SCC 24, [2014] 1 SCR 502.

Larson, J., Mattu, S., Kirchner, L., & Angwin, J. (2016, May 23). How we analyzed the COMPAS recidivism algorithm. *ProPublica*. https://www.propublica.org/article/how-we-analyzed-the-compas-recidivism-algorithm

Laura and John Arnold Foundation. (n.d.). Public safety assessment: Risk factors and formula. http://craftmediabucket.s3.amazonaws.com/uploads/PDFs/PSA-Risk-Factors-and-Formula.pdf

Lowenkamp, C. T., Holsinger, A. M., Robinson, C. R., & Cullen, F. T. (2012, December). When a person isn't a data point: Making evidence-based practice work. *Federal Probation*, *76*(3), 11–21. https://www.uscourts.gov/sites/default/files/76_3_2_0.pdf

Luther, G., & Mela, M. (2006). The top ten issues in law and psychiatry. *Saskatchewan Law Review, 69*, 401–440.
Maini, V., & Sabri, S. (2017). *Machine learning for humans.* https://www.dropbox.com/s/e38nil1dnl7481q/machine_learning.pdf
Malenchik v State, 928 NE 2d 564 (Ind 2010).
May v Ferndale Institution, 2005 SCC 82, [2005] 3 SCR 809.
McLaughlin v Florida, 379 US 184 (1964).
Miss Univ for Women v Hogan, 458 US 718 (1982).
Multi-Health Systems. (2017). LS brochure 2017. *ISSUU.* https://issuu.com/mhs-assessments/docs/ls-cmi.lsi-r.brochure_insequence
Northpointe. (2012). *Practitioners' guide to COMPAS.* http://www.northpointeinc.com/files/technical_documents/FieldGuide2_081412.pdf
Oswald, M., Grace, J., Urwin, S., & Barnes, G. C. (2018). Algorithmic risk assessment policing models: Lessons from the Durham HART model and "experimental" proportionality. *Information and Communications Technology Law, 27*(2), 223–250.
People v Osman, No H037818 2013 Cal App Unpub Lexis 2487 (Cal Ct App Apr 8, 2013).
Perry Educ Ass'n v Perry Local Educators' Ass'n, 460 US 37 (1983).
Pers Adm'r of Mass v Feeney, 442 US 256 (1979).
R v Bishop, 2009 SKCA 117, 337 Sask R 243.
R v Epp, 2005 SKPC 71 at para 63.
R v Grayer, 2007 ONCA 13, [2007] ONCA 13.
R v Hildebrandt, 2005 SKPC 35, [2005] SJ No 491.
R v Oakes, [1986] 1 SCR 103, 26 DLR (4th) 200.
R v Stinchcombe, [1991] 3 SCR 326, [1991] SCJ No 83.
R v Taylor, 2012 ONSC 1025, [2012] OJ No 1564.
State v Loomis, 881 NW 2d 749 (Wis 2016).
Tonry, M. (2014). Legal and ethical issues in the prediction of recidivism. *Federal Sentencing Report, 26*, 167–176.
Washington v Davis, 426 US 229 (1976).

7

The Implications of Food Privatization in Jails

A Case Study of the Ottawa-Carleton Detention Centre

KAITLIN MacKENZIE

Introduction

In this chapter, we explore the food system in a provincial jail in Ontario, Canada, through the lens of criminal justice privatization (Dolovich, 2005; Feeley, 2002; Lundahl et al., 2009; Moore et al., 2013; Parenti, 2013) and from socio-cultural perspectives on prison culture and food (de Graaf & Kilty, 2016; Godderis, 2006a, 2006b; Murguía, 2015). Given the extent to which food implicates individual and collective prisoner experiences in myriad symbolic and embodied ways (de Graaf & Kilty, 2016; Godderis, 2006a, 2006b; Murguía, 2015; Smoyer & Lopes, 2017), we suggest that it can serve as an illustrative case through which to study the social consequences of criminal justice privatization.

Although undertheorized, the individual and collective social effects of privatization in correctional contexts have not escaped public attention; news media coverage of the perils of correctional food systems is illustrative (e.g., Benjoe, 2016; Burgmann, 2008; CBC, 2016; Collins, 2016; Fraser, 2016; Graney, 2015). More broadly, researchers have commented on the tension between the competing logics of corrections and profit, illustrating how a prisoner's quality of life and human rights can be affected negatively when competing corporate priorities take precedence. As noted by Gran and Henry (2007), processes of privatization within corrections can relocate the social responsibility for punishment, rehabilitation, and public safety to private interests with little to no public accountability (see also Zyfi & Macklin, this volume). Competing concerns, such as those about quality-of-life indicators and human rights, can stand in tension with profit motives.

We begin our analysis by highlighting the importance of food in correctional contexts. As we note, the cultural and social significance of food in society has been well theorized by cultural studies researchers (Holtzman, 2006; Lupton, 1994; Valentine, 1999). Such authors have established that eating practices are not merely driven by biological needs but are also tied to, and hence reveal, socio-cultural norms and meanings (Barthes, 1975; Simmel, 1997). Within carceral contexts, food is likewise the site of varied meanings, carrying vast practical and symbolic importance (de Graaf & Kilty, 2016; Godderis, 2006a, 2006b; Murguía, 2015). Thus, the implications of correctional food models, insofar as they shape food and eating circumstances, are potentially wide-reaching and salient in subjective experiences of incarceration (Smoyer & Lopes, 2017).

We then turn to our case study of a privatized food system in Ontario, tracing its political roots and economic underpinnings and outlining its basic operational model. Flowing from a neo-conservative paradigm that involved both government downsizing and "no frills" corrections (McElligott, 2007; Moore & Hannah-Moffat, 2002), the "cook-chill" model promised cost savings and enhanced efficiency by bringing provincial food services into the private realm. We consider how the purported benefits of this model were quickly contradicted, however, by claims of inefficiency, waste, and ballooning costs, as revealed in documents such as government audit reports (Office of the Auditor General of Ontario, 2000, 2008). This case study effectively illustrates an instance of load-shedding in Canada, in which private actors are contracted (Newburn, 2001) to provide services in certain areas of public operations, without being given full ownership (Luscombe et al., this volume).

Finally, we turn to the social effects of food services. We draw from accounts of thirty-three individuals who spent time in an Ontario jail to provide further evidence that food consumption can become a site of "concrete" and "symbolic" punishment (Sexton, 2015; Smoyer & Lopes, 2017). At the embodied level, the institutional diet implicates the body in the experience of punishment, while, at the symbolic level, it serves as a "status degradation ceremony" (Garfinkel, 1956, p. 420), communicating to prisoners an impaired human status. At the collective level, we consider how food becomes implicated in prisoner culture, allowing prisoners to enact social meanings through food practices in ways that both aggravate and ameliorate the "pains of imprisonment" (Sykes, 1958). We conclude by discussing the social issues that arise when correctional operations are inadvertently shaped by the practices of for-profit agencies before briefly discussing the benefits of alternative food systems.

The Meaning of Food in Prison

Sociological research has demonstrated the significant role that food plays within the context of the prison, as it does beyond prison walls (Brisman, 2008; de Graaf & Kilty, 2016; Johnson et al., 2018; Jones, 2017; Murguía, 2015, 2018; Smoyer, 2014, 2015a, 2015b; Smoyer & Lopes, 2017; Ugelvik, 2011; Vanhouche, 2015). Food is often implicitly woven into everyday life and, whether realized or not, plays a significant cultural and symbolic role in the lives of all individuals (de Graaf & Kilty, 2016). Indeed, rather than simply serving as a means to avoid starvation and bodily degradation, food involves a ritual and performance tied to particular socio-cultural meanings (de Graaf & Kilty, 2016; Godderis, 2006a; Lupton, 1994; Tisdale, 2000; Ugelvik, 2011; Visser, 1991). Throughout one's lifetime, food plays a role in shaping one's identity, whether it is connected to certain foods eaten throughout childhood, to repetition of foods, or to rituals built upon certain types of foods (Brisman, 2008; Godderis, 2006a).

A growing body of research sheds light on the meaning of food within the context of penal settings. Key to this research is understanding the paradoxical role of food in the prison as a site of both power and resistance. On the one hand, insofar as prisoners lack control over all aspects of food experiences – for example, how food is managed, prepared, served, and eaten – food becomes the site of power and control. In this sense, it can become the source of concrete and symbolic pain (Sexton, 2015; Smoyer & Lopes, 2017), thus becoming implicated in the "pains of imprisonment" (Sykes, 1958). On the other hand, within certain settings, food becomes an opportunity to exercise choice and agency and to enact social meanings (de Graaf & Kilty, 2016; Godderis, 2006a; Ugelvik, 2011).

As Sexton (2015, p. 121) states, concrete punishments tend to hinge on "the presence or absence of concrete, material things." In other words, concrete punishments involve tangible items (or the absence thereof) and can involve an embodied component. In the case of food, researchers have noted that prisoners often describe the food served as disgusting, inedible, and rotten (de Graaf & Kilty, 2016; Jones, 2017; Smoyer & Lopes, 2017), meaning that prison food becomes a component of punishment (Jones, 2017). In addition to being served poor food, prisoners in certain contexts might lack choice in what they consume or how it is prepared (de Graaf,

2013; Godderis, 2006a; Ugelvik, 2011), thereby preventing them from exerting preference or taste in food-related experiences.

The embodied effects of prison food illustrate Foucault's (1975) notion of "marks to the body" inflicted by the penal institution. Indeed, physical changes to the body caused by prison food (Johnson et al., 2018) are illustrative of the continued effects of imprisonment. In her study of incarcerated women, Smith (2002, p. 203) noted that women described how food affected their bodies negatively, causing problems such as "weight gain and loss, constipation, diarrhea and vomiting." Similarly, in the Canadian context, de Graaf and Kilty (2016) found that female prisoners perceived a lack of control over their bodies; this was exemplified at the Ottawa-Carleton Detention Centre by a high-fat and high-carbohydrate diet, which resulted in women gaining weight.

Of course, such embodied or concrete punishments can also be experienced at the symbolic level, communicating subjective meanings and affecting prisoners' self-identities (Sexton, 2015; Smoyer & Lopes, 2017). Weight changes caused by prison fare can alter one's identity perception, often negatively affecting how one sees oneself (de Graaf & Kilty, 2016; Ugelvik, 2011). De Graff and Kilty (2016) note that weight gain caused by prison food, combined with lack of physical exercise, functions as a "status degradation ceremony," negatively affecting the prisoner's sense of self and serving as a physical reminder of one's incarcerated status.

Symbolic pains can also be experienced in and through the meanings communicated by way of food and eating practices. As noted, food and eating rituals have specific socio-cultural meanings (de Graaf & Kilty, 2016; Godderis, 2006a; Lupton, 1994; Tisdale, 2000; Ugelvik, 2011; Visser, 1991). Thus, how food is cooked, prepared, and presented communicates certain social meanings (Holtzman, 2006; Lupton, 1994). In the prison context, prisoners might lack control over all aspects of eating, including, most notably, the nature and quantity of food, but also the rituals around it, including when and how one eats, thereby constraining one's social relationship with food and eating (Brisman, 2008; Godderis, 2006a). Eating conditions that disrupt cultural customs pertaining to food, such as inadequate or the absence of utensils (which can result in eating with one's hands), can precipitate a sense of dehumanization among prisoners (de Graaf & Kilty, 2016; Jones, 2017; Smoyer & Lopes, 2017).

Researchers studying prison food experiences have also noted important gendered, racial, and ethnic implications (de Graaf & Kilty, 2016; Smoyer, 2014, 2015a; Smoyer & Lopes, 2017). Importantly, the conditions of imprisonment, such as food systems, are not experienced in a universal fashion; rather, they are mediated by factors at the subjective level (Jones, 2017; Sexton, 2015). Researchers have emphasized, for example, that loss of control over the food preparation process can be a gendered punishment insofar as women have experienced food through broader gendered norms (e.g., cooking meals for the family; see Smoyer & Lopes, 2017). Weight gain caused by prison fare can also be experienced in relation to dominant sociocultural meanings of feminine beauty (de Graaf & Kilty, 2016). Cultural and ethnic factors can also shape one's experiences of food. For example, lacking control over food options and modes of preparation, prisoners might not have access to culturally/ethnically appropriate dishes (Godderis, 2006b). How gender and ethnicity interplay with prisoners' experience of food is indicative of the subjective nature of punishment (Sexton, 2015); in other words, similar conditions, such as food provisions, can be experienced differently by distinct groups and individuals (Jones, 2017). Jones (2017, p. 79) posits that, though punishment implies the treatment of someone in "an unfair or harsh way," there is an additional layer of punishment that can arise depending on how an act is interpreted.

Food as the Site of Meaning and Resistance among Prisoners
Although researchers have noted how food becomes the site of power and control in the context of the prison, they have also emphasized how it becomes the site of resistance (de Graaf & Kilty, 2016; Godderis, 2006b; Ugelvik, 2011). As Godderis (2006b, p. 259) explains, resistance includes "a variety of methods and techniques that prisoners use to confront the daily pressures of their confinement." She notes that acts of resistance can occur at both micro and macro levels, individually and collectively. The goal of acts of resistance, no matter the size, is often to attain a sense of power and autonomy (de Graaf & Kilty, 2016; Smoyer, 2015b).

On a larger scale, hunger strikes are a common non-violent mechanism of using food, or the lack thereof, to contest institutional power (Brisman, 2008; Jones, 2017). More subtle forms of resistance might not explicitly contest institutional power but seek to imbue counterpunitive meaning in carceral objects and spaces and, in effect, reduce the pains of imprisonment (Godderis, 2006b; Ugelvik, 2011). As Brisman (2008) notes, such activities can be "legitimate," such as recognized ethnic-based food groups, which involve the preparation and consumption of culturally appropriate meals. Other forms of food-based resistance can be "illegitimate" insofar as they are against institutional rules. For example, Ugelvik (2011, p. 57) notes that food modification is a form of resistance that enables prisoners to "position themselves as autonomous subjects." Food trading, selling, and hoarding can also enable prisoners to regain some control over when, where, and what they decide to eat (Brisman, 2008; Smoyer, 2015b).

In some settings, such as lower-security prisons, food, including its preparation and consumption, can become the source of positive meaning among prisoners. In contrasting the food systems in a women's provincial jail and a women's federal prison, de Graaf and Kilty (2016, p. 30) noted that women in the federal system, living in minimum- and medium-security institutions, have more freedom to make dietary decisions on a day-to-day basis, "which showed a positive effect on their relational experiences with food while incarcerated." In fact, having the ability to prepare one's own food, to an extent, can provide a sense of autonomy and improve how food is experienced in an environment in which power and decision-making abilities are severely constrained (de Graaf & Kilty, 2016; Jones, 2017; Vanhouche, 2015). When prisoners find ways to prepare their own food, researchers suggest, it is a calming experience, providing pleasure, joy, and autonomy, compared with prisoners served pre-made meals (Vanhouche, 2015).

Insofar as meal preparation and eating are tied to cultural influences, food rituals can also become a way to enact or connect with social identity (Brisman, 2008). For example, Godderis (2006b) found that, in response to the perceived lack of culturally appropriate meal options, prisoners organized ethnic-based food groups, in which once a month either individually or collectively they would prepare and eat their own cultural foods. Such food groups allow prisoners to reconnect with their ethnic identities, if only on a monthly basis. In such groups, as Godderis noted, prisoners can exert some degree of autonomy over food rituals: groups "allowed individuals to access foods that were not normally available on the inside, to prepare the food as they desired and to have the opportunity for a social meal outside of the regular dining area" (p. 262).

In summary, research shows that food carries great practical and symbolic importance in penal settings. In some ways, food experiences can become implicated in the experience of punishment. At a physical level, poor food and insufficient quantities can have embodied effects, such as hunger, gastrointestinal issues, and weight gain (Johnson et al., 2018; Smith, 2002). At a symbolic level, poor-quality food and the conditions of eating can communicate a set of social meanings that prisoners relate to their depreciated status as prisoners (de Graaf & Kilty, 2016; Jones, 2017; Smoyer & Lopes, 2017). At the same time, however, prisoners can imbue food and eating practices with their own meanings, with varied implications for the pains of imprisonment and prisoner dynamics.

Thus, though the circumstances surrounding food are mediated by prisoner culture, the institutional parameters of food provisions shape what is possible in prisoners' experiences of food. How food is managed, produced, and served, therefore, can have implications not only for individual prisoners but also for the social climate within the penal space. Understanding how food systems interact with prisoners' social worlds, as well as the forms of resistance in response to such systems, can be an important step in crafting and promoting policy changes intended to improve the quality of life within carceral spaces (Burkhardt, 2019). With this in mind, we now turn to the cook-chill method, a privatized food system currently in place at the provincial level in Ontario, before considering the implications of this system for prisoners' individual and collective experiences with food at the Ottawa-Carleton Detention Centre and the larger implications of privatizing elements of the correctional system.

Food in Ontario Corrections

As a point of departure for our analysis, it is first necessary to situate Ontario's correctional system within a national landscape. Canada's correctional system is two-tiered; federal institutions are run by a national agency, Correctional Service Canada, and have jurisdiction over those who have been sentenced to a custodial term of two years or more, whereas provincial and territorial institutions are run by their respective provincial and territorial governments and have jurisdiction over those serving less than two-year sentences as well as those remanded to custody to await court proceedings (Correctional Service Canada, 2019). Federalism thus enables considerable variation in correctional systems, with provincial and territorial systems operating somewhat autonomously from national correctional philosophies of the day. This trend was well exemplified in the 1990s in Ontario under the neo-conservative rule of Mike Harris, who explicitly challenged the "Club Fed" model embraced by the federal government (Ralph et al., 1997).

Changes to the provincial correctional system in Ontario were part of a broader neo-conservative agenda dubbed the "common-sense revolution." In addition to embracing principles such as efficiency, privatization, and austerity, the movement promoted a "no-frills" correctional system designed to be harsh and punitive (McElligott, 2007; Moore & Hannah-Moffat, 2002). This punitive sentiment was explicit in political speech; for example, the corrections minister at the time stated that "this is not the federal equivalent of the penal system. We want jails to be places where people don't want to go and don't want to stay ... We're very much focused on a no-frills facility" (quoted in Harris, 2000). Moving toward this model involved, among other things, the systematic removal of perceived "frills" from provincial jails, such as programming, facilities, and amenities such as televisions, and a greater reliance on cell confinement (McElligott, 2007; Moore & Hannah-Moffat, 2002).

The nature of prison food was also affected by shifts during this period, specifically by the privatization of food services. To be sure, prison food has a long-established history of poor quality, and this was true in the Ontario context, evidenced by news coverage of prisoner-led food protests ("Detention Centre," 1997; "Inmates," 1998). In the new model, however, responsibility for food in correctional institutions was moved to the private realm, reducing public accountability while introducing the logic of profit. Rather than having on-site kitchens where prisoners themselves could take part in the process of food production, a cook-chill model relocated food production off site to a centralized production centre at Maplehurst Correctional Centre in Milton, Ontario. There, food is mass-produced by employees (including prisoners) and then frozen, shipped to institutional sites, reheated, and served (Office of the Auditor General of Ontario, 2008). According to the Ontario Ministry of the Solicitor General (2018), the food provided must adhere to *Eating Well with Canada's Food Guide*. A multinational corporation called Compass Group (2019), which claims to be a leading food service company, runs the production centre at the jail, which provides meals for prisoners around the province. By transferring responsibility to the private sector and utilizing this style of mass production, this model promised efficiency and cost savings for the government (Buitenhuis, 2013). As defined by Luscombe et al. (this volume), this model involves one of the most prominent aspects of privatization, a load-shedding approach that incorporates the private company Compass Group into the public sphere of provincial corrections. Whereas Newburn (2001) points to the commodification of policing as a hybrid public-private model, this case study demonstrates how this model has also seeped into the commodification of food in correctional spaces.

The costs associated with running the centralized production site were quickly identified as exceeding expectations. The Office of the Auditor General of Ontario reported in 2000 that the original budget of $5 million had increased to $9.5 million and that, rather than providing for the food needs of ten institutions, it would provide only for six. Similarly, the costs of retrofitting and equipping institutions to meet the needs of the new model had been estimated at less than $100,000 but proved to be much greater at $3.9 million. The auditor general also noted problems in the areas of cost savings, productivity, meeting food needs, and unmet deliveries, which required external purchasing.

Eight years later the Office of the Auditor General of Ontario (2008) noted that the cook-chill model provided food for about 46 percent of provincial prisoners and that, as of 2009, the cost of the private contract, commencing in 2002, would reach $54.8 million. The auditor general questioned whether the efficiency and cost saving promised had been effectively measured, noting that the minister "had not completed an assessment of whether the cost savings originally anticipated were achieved in food costs, staffing, and kitchen equipment" (p. 87). The office continued to point to issues of inefficiency; for example, in visits to select sites, the auditor general found a problem of excess meals (i.e., prepared meals that left the kitchen, went unserved, but could not be returned because of health and safety reasons) that lacked explanation. It was clear that the original claims of cost effectiveness and efficiency promised by the privatization of food services were reasonably being called into question. Indeed, one of the auditor general's recommendations was to "perform a cost-benefit analysis of the current outsourcing of ... 'cook-chill'" (p. 87).

Perhaps just as importantly, questions have also arisen about the quality of food under the cook-chill model. For example, in its 2015 public report, the Community Advisory Board for the Ottawa-Carleton Detention Centre noted that institutional staff reported receiving spoiled food shipments and that prisoners and advocates reported food that was "soggy, spoiled or unpalatable" (Porter et al., 2015). The board also estimated that 65–90 percent of the food was not eaten. In its following annual report, the board noted that these concerns had not been resolved: "The quality of the cook-chill food, including taste, nutritional value, and freshness, continues to be a consistent concern expressed by inmates" (Porter et al., 2017). The board recommended that the province's Ministry of Community Safety and Correctional Services (MCSCS) review the cook-chill model "to determine how best to improve or replace it as soon as possible so as to ensure that inmates are served at minimum ... palatable, unspoiled and nutritious meals that they will generally consume on a regular basis" (Porter et al., 2015).

In 2016, a Task Force for the Ottawa-Carleton Detention Centre (OCDC) was initiated by Minister of Community Safety and Correctional Services

Yasir Naqvi. The Task Force was established to address ongoing issues at the jail and comprised various community organizations, government officials, union members, staff, the superintendent, and other professionals (Ontario Ministry of Safety and Correctional Services, 2016). Following careful review, the Task Force identified an action plan consisting of forty-two recommendations to be implemented in the jail in the short, medium, and long term. One item on the list of recommendations published by the Task Force addressed the poor quality of the food within the jail: "MCSCS should re-evaluate its food delivery system options including dietary requirements, quality of food items purchased and costs" (Ontario Ministry of Safety and Correctional Services, 2016).

Three follow-up progress reports were subsequently published, addressing each recommendation. The third OCDC Task Force progress report indicated that "work is continuing on the formalization of a continuous quality improvement process for the Cook Chill Program" (Ontario Ministry of Safety and Correctional Services, 2017). Despite the history of dissatisfaction with this method of food preparation, and media reports of hunger protests by prisoners (Day, 2015; Seymour, 2015, 2016), the cook-chill method remains in place in Ontario and more widely across Canada. In the following section, we elaborate on the social consequences of this model by drawing from the narratives of former prisoners in the Ottawa-Carleton Detention Centre. Highlighting individual and collective social experiences of food, prisoners' accounts illuminate the tension that can emerge between profit and human rights in the context of criminal justice privatization.

Case Study: Food Experiences at the Ottawa-Carleton Detention Centre

Recognizing that punishment can extend beyond what is formally recognized as such, Sexton (2015) puts forth a conceptualization of punishment that includes what is experienced as punishment by prisoners, regardless of whether it is formally intended or recognized as such in law. This conceptualization of punishment allows for consideration of the "informal" pains associated with imprisonment that are not, legally, part and parcel of one's formal sentence. It therefore also allows room to consider how private influences can play a role in shaping punishment in its articulated forms, albeit in ways that can be indirect or unrecognized.

Poor-quality food and negative food experiences are exemplary here; such issues are not written in the official punishment narrative (i.e., as represented in law), but nonetheless they have profound implications for one's experience of punishment and can be shaped by the practices of service providers that operate outside the government. Food is particularly illustrative because of both its symbolic and its practical meanings (Smoyer & Lopes, 2017). As discussed, within the prison environment, food serves multiple symbolic meanings, operating simultaneously as the site of power (e.g., through lack of choice and poor quality) and resistance (e.g., through its use as a currency and source of identity expression). It also operates, however, as a concrete punishment experienced in and through the body. Furthermore, as recurring components of daily routines, the symbolic and concrete meanings associated with food are heavily embedded in the carceral experience; it is therefore not surprising that food often carries great meaning and importance in the narratives of prisoners.

It is against this backdrop that we explore subjective experiences of punishment in the context of an Ontario jail, the Ottawa-Carleton Detention Centre, focusing on how food and eating practices become the site of punishment. The local jail in Canada's capital city of Ottawa has been in the media spotlight consistently over the years as a result of poor conditions; key problems include overcrowding, violence, frequent lockdowns, inadequate health care, unsanitary living conditions, and poor food (Cockburn, 2009; Hurley, 2010; O'Neill, 2004; "Ottawa's Jail," 2004; Pilieci, 2017; Porter et al., 2015, 2017). Over 60 percent of OCDC prisoners are on remand (Lofaro, 2016), meaning that they have yet to be tried and/or sentenced and are instead awaiting their day in court. Thus, despite their legal status of "presumed innocent," those detained at OCDC face exceedingly harsh conditions.

Data on prisoners' experiences are drawn from interviews conducted with thirty-three former prisoners in 2015 and 2016 using a narrative-style interviewing approach (Spector-Mersel, 2010). Information about the research study was advertised at several public locations (e.g., community centres and social service agencies); interested persons contacted the researcher to schedule an interview. Participants selected the time and place for an interview and were compensated for their time. In terms of demographic breakdown of the sample, sixteen participants were women, seventeen were men, and twenty-six of thirty-three were white, and the ages ranged from early twenties to mid-fifties. The narrative-style interviewing approach involved asking the former prisoners to share their stories of incarceration, encouraging them to speak about events and circumstances that they viewed as important. Specifically, interviews commenced with a single question ("Can you tell me about your experience of incarceration?"), with prompts and follow-up questions used when appropriate. The interviewing approach enabled the organic emergence of themes, allowing the interviewer to gain an understanding of the themes that held salience from the perspectives of prisoners. It was in this context that the importance of food in their experiences was revealed, evidenced by the time and emphasis given to the topic.

Here we focus on both the concrete and the symbolic meanings (Smoyer & Lopes, 2017) that prisoners associated with food, analyzing how such meanings came to be implicated in the experience of punishment. At the concrete level, we note the following themes: poor quality, insufficient quantity, extended times between meals, lack of accommodation, and health costs, such as weight changes and gastrointestinal issues. At the symbolic level, we describe the dehumanization that occurs when individuals are deprived of nutritious food and perceive the food and eating conditions to be unfit for people.

Food Quality and Quantity at OCDC

The two most prominent themes among interviewees pertained to food quality and quantity. When it came to quality, the food was described almost exclusively in negative terms, such as "garbage," "disgusting," "crap," "horrible," "awful," and "terrible." Jones (2017, p. 79) states that "neglecting or disregarding the quality or condition of food ... is also insidious" and certainly an added punishment of incarceration. Prisoners commented that, in addition to the poor taste, the food sometimes contained foreign objects, was mouldy, past the expiration date, or not properly cooked. Interestingly, some prisoners were aware of the process of production and linked problems with food quality to this process. One prisoner noted that

> there's no nutrients now because they have ovens now that steam them, that they're all cooked, they're [frozen], and then they're shipped down from [Milton] or something and then brought in in packages, and then they put them in these ovens, and they're heated up so hot, so it kills all the vitamins and nutrients that's in the food, because, you know, being flash-froze, and then reheated real hot, it kills the nutrients in the food. So, basically, you're just getting calories to keep yourself alive in there.

Of perhaps equal concern was the insufficient quantity of meals. Prisoners are served three meals a day, and as noted by the institution's Community Advisory Board (Porter et al., 2015) the last meal is served between 4:00 p.m.

and 5:30 p.m., without further provisions. Because of small portions, the extended time between supper and the following day's breakfast, and/or refusal to eat food because of its poor quality, prisoners felt like they were "starving" if they did not have canteen funds: "They're boxed portions, right, you know what I mean, they just give you enough to survive. Anything else after that you pay for. They don't give you any snacks. You know, there are people with dietary issues, right? Even with dietary issues, they give them next to nothing." Indeed, those with special dietary needs, whether because of medical concerns, ethical/cultural beliefs, or allergies, can find it nearly impossible to obtain adequate options. One woman spoke of the "constant struggle" that she experienced trying to access adequate vegetarian meals. She noted that at times she was given crackers and peanut butter in place of meaningful options because of the lack of alternatives. Those with allergies likewise noted difficulty accessing adequate alternatives and were often served meals that contained ingredients to which they were allergic. Issues with accommodation also have been noted by the Community Advisory Board in its reports (Porter et al., 2017). The board noted that some ethnic-based food accommodations are available, such as kosher meals (noted as provided by a different contractor and of higher quality), but also indicated a continued lack of accommodation for Indigenous dietary needs: "Efforts to meet the cultural needs of Aboriginal inmates with respect to access to traditional foods on a daily basis and for ceremonial purposes must be prioritized" (Porter et al., 2016).

The lack of choice available to prisoners as a result of the food production system serves to alienate them from the process of preparing and consuming food; they have little to no say about what they eat, when, or how much. De Graaf and Kilty, who studied the food experiences of incarcerated women in Ontario, including at the Ottawa-Carleton Detention Centre, argue that this food system "contributes to the breaking down of the self by disrupting one's sense of autonomy and control over the body" (2016, p. 31). In this context, one's experience with food, including the inability to express agency, make choices, or determine the parameters around eating, becomes a key embodied pain of imprisonment.

Prisoners' accounts, however, also show the importance of the symbolic implications of this food system, which prisoners felt communicated to them that they were undeserving of adequate or decent food. A sense of dehumanization shaped discussions on eating, evidenced by frequent references to how the food – in taste and delivery – was fit for animals. One prisoner shared that "the meals are disgusting. It's like you're eating out of a dog dish." This echoes de Graaf and Kilty's interviews with prisoners in the same detention centre; one woman stated that "the food is like dog food" (2016, p. 32).

The conditions of eating, which can relate more to the institutional policies than the process of food production, compounded the sense of dehumanization while eating. Such conditions included time limits on mealtimes (forcing individuals to eat quickly), a lack of proper utensils (at times requiring one to eat with one's hands), and unhealthy environments (e.g., inside cells close to the communal toilet). Symbolically, then, food serves as a "status degradation ceremony" (de Graaf & Kilty, 2016, p. 31; Garfinkel, 1956, p. 420), communicating to prisoners their impaired human status.

Food and Prisoner Culture

As other authors have noted, food tends to have varied meanings in penal settings, where it is simultaneously the site of power and control. Food also provides opportunities to prisoners to carve out social meanings. Among prisoners, food can become embedded in their culture, operating, for example, as a currency/unit of exchange, a source of group identity, or an expression of social solidarity (Brisman, 2008; de Graaf & Kilty, 2016; Smoyer, 2015b; Ugelvik, 2011). Although the ways in which food and eating are implicated in individual and collective food experiences are shaped by an array of factors, prevailing food systems, combined with the organizational management of eating practices, can shape the social possibilities of food experiences. In our case study, food was discussed most often as having a divisive effect on prisoner culture, becoming the site of fights, thefts, and tensions, particularly given that food was perceived to be of insufficient quantity and quality.

For example, some male prisoners in the dormitory units explained that food was wheeled in on carts, leaving it to be distributed by prisoners. This distribution, however, was prone to asymmetries, with prisoners who were informally "in charge" (because of their social status and/or level of physical capacity) potentially controlling who ate and how much. This asymmetrical distribution was said to be particularly evident in the case of more appetizing foods, such as fruit or dessert. Furthermore, some inmates perceived meal distribution as fused with racial politics; more specifically, some white men thought that racialized prisoners tended to express more in-group solidarity relative to white prisoners. Illustrating this perception, one man explained that power in his unit was wielded by Black prisoners, and this translated into racial disparities in food provisions: "There was maybe ...

thirty Blacks and maybe ten whites. And so the Blacks, they'd give them the food carts, they were in the range because there were so many of them, they were taking people's food, they were not giving, they were taking their desserts, they were taking their oranges, their bananas."

Here we can see how the food system in place, specifically the quality and quantity of meals, can shape the carceral environment, yet existing dynamics among prisoners (e.g., perceived racial tensions) also mediate the social implications. In addition to the effects of hunger on discipline and mood (Porter et al., 2017), food — perceived to be in short supply and seldom of good quality — can pit prisoners against each other. Yet they did refer to incidents in which food was used in mutually beneficial ways (e.g., trading) and as a means to express solidarity (e.g., in acts of giving). One prisoner recalled mastering the art of food trading, by which he continuously purchased canteen items to trade for healthier food options, such as fresh fruit, from other prisoners' meals. Food items could also be used as a form of currency; another man noted that he would do cleaning in exchange for desserts. Indeed, men described "wheeling and dealing" with food items as common; such activities allowed them to work together with limited resources to achieve improved individual outcomes. As de Graaf and Kilty (2016, p. 41) note, trading is a means by which prisoners "collaboratively enable greater autonomy over dietary choice and control over the pre-set menus."

For women, food did not appear to have a divisive effect since they were less likely to have ingrained social hierarchies and more likely to have social connections. In this context, food was sometimes used in ways that promoted solidarity. One woman recalled that, because she lacked canteen funds, other women would share food items with her. "Everybody gave me everything, 'cause they like to see me eat." Another woman, who had surgery while incarcerated, recalled how women gifted her with canteen items to express their support. De Graaf and Kilty (2016, p. 38) also discussed the role of food sharing among women at the OCDC. They found that "participants recounted that exhibiting an ethic of care through mutually sharing food helped to generate a sense of togetherness that made incarceration more manageable for all."

We are not suggesting that the food system in place is fully deterministic of prisoners' social realities of food, but nonetheless it shapes the social possibilities for food and eating. The social implications of this system are varied, likely shaped by the different dynamics within units and ranges, where power struggles, racial tensions, and in-group sentiments can mediate group food experiences. Within prisoner culture, food thus appears to reflect and reproduce social norms and meanings, not only operating as a symbol of broader social themes but also creating particular opportunities for social interactions. Thus, while operating as a site of embodied and symbolic punishment, food also becomes a means through which social meanings are actively created by prisoners themselves.

Implications and Conclusions

Ontario corrections continue to be shaped by the neo-conservative "no frills" legacy fully embraced by the provincial government in the 1990s (Moore et al., 2013), which continues through practices such as public-private partnerships in corrections. Although privatization is often heralded as a cost-saving endeavour in penal institutions (MacDonald, 1992; Thomas, 1997), actual outcomes often stray from such promises (Feeley, 2002; Lundahl et al., 2009; Vanhouche, 2015). Furthermore, critics note that privatization of the justice system is problematic, arguing that public entities should not incorporate for-profit contractors in the administration of justice (DiIulio, 1988; Schwartz & Nurge, 2004). The profit-driven essence of privatization, particularly within the realm of criminal justice, runs the risk of creating a demand for services, infrastructure, or technologies where it is not necessarily needed (McMahon, 1998), leading to an overall expansion of social controls (Feeley, 2002). Insofar as profit motives underpin operational processes, competing priorities, including quality of life and human rights, are at risk (Parenti, 2013). According to Dolovich (2005, p. 438), for penal policies and their associated practices to be considered legitimate, they must adhere to two principles – "the humanity principle, which obliges the state to avoid imposing punishments that are gratuitously inhumane; and the parsimony principle, which obliges the state to avoid imposing punishments of incarceration that are gratuitously long." The privatized food system at the OCDC does not adhere to Dolovich's humanity principle, as illustrated in this case study, in addition to other works on the same institution (de Graaf & Kilty, 2016).

Indeed, the situation at the Ottawa jail illustrates the tension that emerges when competing mandates of profit and corrections meet. Prisoners' personal accounts and institutional review bodies (Ontario Ministry of Safety and Correctional Services, 2016, 2017; Porter et al., 2015, 2017) suggest that food serves as a concrete punishment to the body, through inadequate quality and quantity, while symbolically punishing the mind through an additional "status degradation ceremony" (Garfinkel, 1956, p. 420), which makes the prisoners feel undeserving of decent food. Although the social rituals and customs for food are varied, the nature of the food system, at least for men, appears to aggravate tensions embedded in the social environment.

In contrast to the private cook-chill model are localized systems that enable prisoner involvement in food activities, including selecting groceries, cooking and preparing meals, and engaging in dining rituals and practices. Such models are reported to have positive outcomes for prisoners (de Graaf & Kilty, 2016; Godderis, 2006b; Vanhouche, 2015). For example, Vanhouche (2015) outlines the benefits for prisoners who have the opportunity to prepare their meals from scratch in an on-site kitchen and compares their attitudes toward a privatized food system, in which ready-made meals are frozen and supplied to prisons by a private company. As Vanhouche notes, prisoners believe that, compared with prepared frozen meals, the food that they prepare in a kitchen is healthier and provides "a way to escape the boredom of prison life" (p. 52). Kitchen positions can offer marketable skills to employees, in line with the provincial government's aim to "provide practical skills in a real-life environment to assist inmates to prepare for return to the community" (Ministry of the Solicitor General, 2020).

Likewise, others have noted that being provided with the opportunity to prepare meals in an on-site kitchen allows for a higher degree of control over one's food intake and can allow prisoners to feel a sense of comfort and autonomy in an institution largely devoid of such freedoms (de Graaf & Kilty, 2016; Godderis, 2006b). Allowing prisoners to use on-site kitchens can also provide the opportunity for culturally sensitive food preparation and a reconnection with ethnic traditions. Godderis (2006b) explored prisoners' ethnic identity groups that prepared culturally appropriate meals and enjoyed them outside the regularly prescribed eating areas on a monthly basis, giving the prisoners a sense of identity, autonomy, pleasure, and agency since they were not confined to the prescribed food and eating area of their day-to-day lives. However, prisoners could benefit from hosting such activities more frequently than once every month (Jones, 2017).

The practical and symbolic benefits of localized food systems that draw prisoners into food-related practices are in competition with the cost-saving arguments made by proponents of private models generally and cook-chill models specifically despite excessive costs (Office of the Auditor General of Ontario, 2000). Furthermore, the cook-chill method, and other forms of privatization within the criminal justice system, fall in line with the "no frills" ideology that has shaped corrections in Ontario despite the resulting consequences for prisoners' welfare (Moore et al., 2013). According to

Burkhardt (2019), effecting policy changes within the criminal justice system ought to involve paying closer attention to resistance: that is, to listen to those who contest the current food system in place and use food as a site of resistance (de Graaf & Kilty, 2016; Godderis, 2006b; Ugelvik, 2011). In Ontario institutions, which in many cases continue to suffer from inadequate programming and an overreliance on cell confinement (Ontario Ministry of Safety and Correctional Services, 2016), prisoner-involved food systems can provide opportunities not only to enhance food quality but also to give prisoners kitchen skills, allowing them to be productive and assert some form of agency in otherwise restrictive environments. Indeed, such a model can be beneficial to prisoners and staff alike, improving overall moods and benefiting prisoners physically with healthier food options while allowing individuals to establish positive social meanings with the processes of food production and consumption.

This chapter contributes to research on the social effects of criminal justice privatization through a case study of food and eating practices in the context of a private cook-chill model. Food in correctional institutions can have an array of individual and social consequences given both the symbolic meanings and the practical implications of food consumption (Smoyer & Lopes, 2017). The importance of food in prisoner culture and individual routines renders food systems an area of key concern among those assessing the social consequences of criminal justice privatization; indeed, food experiences can shed light on the concrete and daily effects of private influences on the subjective nature of punishment.

References

Barthes, R. (1975). Toward a psychosociology of contemporary food consumption. In E. Foster & R. Forster (Eds.), *European diet from pre-industrial to modern times* (pp. 20–27). Harper and Row.

Benjoe, K. (2016, January 8). Inmates again refusing trays to protest food quality at Regina jail. *Leader-Post* [Regina]. https://leaderpost.com/news/local-news/inmates-again-refusing-trays-to-protest-food-quality-at-regina-jail

Brisman, A. (2008). Fair fare: Food as contested terrain in US prisons and jails. *Georgetown Journal on Poverty Law and Policy*, 15(1), 49–93.

Buitenhuis, A. J. (2013). *Public-private partnerships and prison expansion in Ontario: Shifts in governance 1995 to 2012* [Unpublished MA thesis]. University of Toronto. https://tspace.library.utoronto.ca/bitstream/1807/42694/6/Buitenhuis_Amy_J_201311_MA_thesis.pdf

Burgmann, T. (2008, November 24). Jail food may have been tainted officials say. *The Globe and Mail*. https://www.theglobeandmail.com/news/national/jail-food-may-have-been-tainted-officials-say/article17975087/

Burkhardt, B. (2019). Contesting market rationality: Discursive struggles over prison privatization. *Punishment and Society, 21*(2), 162–186.

CBC. (2016, January 7). Premier Brad Wall not waffling on jail food comments. *CBC News*. https://www.cbc.ca/news/canada/saskatchewan/inmates-refusing-food-at-regina-correctional-centre-1.3393366

Cockburn, N. (2009, November 20). Poor jail conditions, court delays affect us all. *The Ottawa Citizen*, C3.

Collins, C. (2016, February 25). The cost of privatized food in public institutions. *Rabble*. http://rabble.ca/news/2016/02/cost-privatized-food-public-institutions

Compass Group Canada. (2019). https://www.compass-canada.com/

Correctional Service Canada. (2019). Frequently asked questions. https://www.csc-scc.gc.ca/media-room/009-0002-eng.shtml

Day, M. (2015, December 3). OCDC goes into lockdown, hunger strike continues. *The Ottawa Sun*. https://ottawasun.com/2015/12/03/ocdc-goes-into-lockdown-hunger-strike-continues/wcm/bbf10ad7-6d6d-4ab0-8d77-408d111e3268

de Graaf, K. (2013). *Disciplining women/disciplining bodies: Exploring how women negotiate health and bodily aesthetic in the carceral context* [Unpublished PhD dissertation]. University of Ottawa.

de Graaf, K., & Kilty, J. M. (2016). You are what you eat: Exploring the relationship between women, food, and incarceration. *Punishment and Society, 18*(1), 27–46.

Detention centre inmates protest over quality of food. (1997, March 15). *The Ottawa Citizen*, C2.

DiIulio, J. (1988). What's wrong with private prison? *Public Interest, 29*, 66–83.

Dolovich, S. (2005). State punishment and private prisons. *Duke Law Journal, 55*(3), 437–546.

Feeley, M. (2002). Entrepreneurs of punishment: The legacy of privatization. *Punishment and Society, 4*(3), 321–344.

Foucault, M. (1975). *Discipline & punish: The birth of the prison*. Éditions Gallimard.

Fraser, D. C. (2016, February 11). Complaints about food in jail went way up after private contractor took over. *Leader-Post* [Regina]. https://leaderpost.com/news/saskatchewan/complaints-about-food-in-jail-went-way-up-after-private-contractor-took-over

Garfinkel, H. (1956). Conditions of successful degradation ceremonies. *American Journal of Sociology, 61*(5), 420–424.

Godderis, R. (2006a). Food for thought: An analysis of power and identity in prison food narratives. *Berkeley Journal of Sociology, 50*, 61–75.

Godderis, R. (2006b). Dining in: The symbolic power of food in prison. *The Howard Journal of Criminal Justice, 45*(3), 255–267.

Gran, B., & Henry, W. (2007). Holding private prisons accountable: A socio-legal analysis of "contracting out" prisons. *Social Justice, 34*(3–4), 173–174.

Graney, E. (2015, August 8). New Saskatchewan jail food provider subject of past complaints. *Leader-Post* [Regina]. https://leaderpost.com/news/local-news/new-saskatchewan-jail-food-provider-subject-of-past-complaints

Harris, M. (2000, November 19). Tough law to create "no-frills" jails: Ontario challenges federal laws to produce a system "no one will want to call home." *The Ottawa Citizen*, A1.

Holtzman, J. D. (2006). Food and memory. *Annual Review of Anthropology, 35*, 361–378.

Hurley, M. (2010, November 27). Somali inmates say guards beat them, rules were followed in dealing with "disruptive" men, authorities say. *The Ottawa Citizen*, D1.

Inmates begin detention centre hunger strike: Prisoners angry at "inedible," bug-ridden food. (1998, March 7). *The Ottawa Citizen*, E2.

Johnson, C., Chaput, J. P., Rioux, F., Diasparra, M., Richard, C., & Dubois, L. (2018). An exploration of reported food intake among inmates who gained body weight during incarceration in Canadian federal penitentiaries. *PloS One, 13*(12), 1–17.

Jones, M. O. (2017). Eating behind bars: On punishment, resistance, policy, and applied folkloristics. *Journal of American Folklore, 130*(515), 72–108.

Lofaro, J. (2016, April 25). "It's a nightmare for them": Mothers of inmates in Ottawa jail to host public forum. *Ottawa Metro*.

Lundahl, B. W., Kunz, C., Brownell, C., Harris, N., & Van Vleet, R. (2009). Prison privatization: A meta-analysis of cost and quality of confinement indicators. *Research on Social Work Practice, 19*(4), 383–394.

Lupton, D. (1994). Food, memory and meaning: The symbolic and social nature of food events. *The Sociological Review, 42*(4), 664–685.

MacDonald, D. (1992). Private penal institutions. In M. Tonry (Ed.), *Crime and justice: A review of research* (pp. 132–158). University of Chicago Press.

McElligott, G. (2007). Negotiating a coercive turn: Work discipline and prison reform in Ontario. *Capital and Class, 31*(1), 31–53.

McMahon, M. (1998). Control as enterprise: Some recent trends in privatization and criminal justice. In S. Easton (Ed.), *Privatizing correctional institutions* (pp. 109–128). The Fraser Institute.

Ministry of the Solicitor General. (2018). *Inmate information guide for adult institutions*. Ontario Ministry of the Solicitor General. https://www.mcscs.jus.gov.on.ca/english/corr_serv/PoliciesandGuidelines/CS_Inmate_guide.html#P215_28865

Ministry of the Solicitor General. (2020). Offender programs and services. *Ontario Ministry of the Solicitor General*. https://www.mcscs.jus.gov.on.ca/english/corr_serv/OffenderProgramsServices/offender_programs.html

Moore, D., & Hannah-Moffat, K. (2002). Correctional renewal without the frills: The politics of "get tough" punishment in Ontario. In J. Hermer & J. Mosher (Eds.), *Disorderly people: Law and the politics of exclusion in Ontario* (pp. 105–121). Fernwood.

Moore, D., Leclerc Burton, K., & Hannah-Moffat, K. (2013). "Get tough" efficiency: Human rights, correctional restructuring, and prison privatization in Ontario, Canada. In A. Friedman & C. Parenti (Eds.), *Capitalist punishment: Prison privatization and human rights* (pp. 152–161). SCB Distributors.

Murguía, S. J. (2015). The politics of food behind bars. In H. L. Davis, K. Pilgrim, & M. Sinha (Eds.), *The ecopolitics of consumption: The food trade* (pp. 89–100). Rowman and Littlefield.

Murguía, S. J. (2018). *Food as a mechanism of control and resistance in jails and prisons: Diets of disrepute.* Rowman and Littlefield.

Newburn, T. (2001). The commodification of policing: Security networks in the late modern city. *Urban Studies, 38*(5–6), 829–848.

Office of the Auditor General of Ontario. (2000). *Special report on accountability and value for money.* http://www.auditor.on.ca/en/content/annualreports/arreports/en00vfm/304en00vfm.pdf

Office of the Auditor General of Ontario. (2008). *2008 annual report of the Office of the Auditor General of Ontario.*

O'Neill, J. (2004, October 30). Corrections ministry, jail system go on trial. *The Ottawa Citizen,* E1.

Ontario Ministry of Safety and Correctional Services. (2016). *Ottawa-Carleton Detention Centre Task Force action plan.* https://www.mcscs.jus.gov.on.ca/english/Corrections/OttawaCarletonDetentionCentreTaskForce/OCDCTaskForceActionPlan.html

Ontario Ministry of Safety and Correctional Services. (2017). *Ottawa-Carleton Detention Centre Task Force recommendations: Progress report #3. Ontario Ministry of Safety and Correctional Services.* https://www.mcscs.jus.gov.on.ca/english/Corrections/OttawaCarletonDetentionCentreTaskForce/OCDCTaskForceProgressReport3.html

Ottawa's jail is a disgrace. (2004, November 2). *The Ottawa Citizen,* C4.

Parenti, C. (2013). Privatized problems: For-profit incarceration in trouble. In A. Friedman & C. Parenti (Eds.), *Capitalist punishment: Prison privatization and human rights* (pp. 152–161). SCB Distributors.

Pilieci, V. (2017, February 25). Lockdown at Ottawa jail for "security reasons" leads to court delays. *The Ottawa Citizen,* A3.

Porter, M., Anderson, J., Dunbar, J., & Jesseman, R. (2015). *Community Advisory Board annual report. Ontario Ministry of Safety and Correctional Services.* http://www.mcscs.jus.gov.on.ca/english/corr_serv/CABs/OCDC/CAB_OCDC.html

Porter, M., Anderson, J., Dunbar, J., & Jesseman, R. (2017). *Community Advisory Board annual report. Ontario Ministry of Community Safety and Correctional Services.* http://www.mcscs.jus.gov.on.ca/english/Corrections/CommunityAdvisoryBoards/OttawaCarletonDetentionCentre/CABReport2016OttawaCarletonDetentionCentre.html

Porter, M., Anderson, J., Dunbar, J., Jesseman, R., & Boudreau, G. (2016). *Community Advisory Board annual report. Ontario Ministry of Safety and Correctional Services.* https://www.mcscs.jus.gov.on.ca/english/Corrections/CommunityAdvisoryBoards/OttawaCarletonDetentionCentre/OCDC2015CABReport.html

Ralph, D. S., Régimbald, A., & St-Amand, N. (1997). *Open for business, closed to people: Mike Harris's Ontario.* Fernwood.

Schwartz, M. D., & Nurge, D. M. (2004). Capitalist punishment: Ethics and private prisons. *Critical Criminology, 12*(2), 133–156.

Sexton, J. S. (2015). Toward a prison theology of California's ecclesia incarcerate. *Theology, 118*(2), 83–91.

Seymour, A. (2015, December 9). Inmates win "minor changes," drop food protest at Ottawa jail. *The Ottawa Citizen.* https://ottawacitizen.com/news/local-news/inmates-win-minor-changes-drop-food-protest-at-ottawa-jail

Seymour, A. (2016, April 11). Inmates stage "hunger strike" over Ottawa jail conditions. *The Ottawa Citizen.* https://ottawacitizen.com/news/local-news/inmates-stage-hunger-strike-over-ottawa-jail-conditions

Simmel, G. (1997). The sociology of the meal. In D. Frisby & M. Featherstone (Eds.), *Simmel on culture: Selected writings* (pp. 29–31). SAGE.

Smith, C. (2002). Punishment and pleasure: Women, food and the imprisoned body. *The Sociological Review, 50*(2), 197–214.

Smoyer, A. B. (2014). Feeding relationships: Foodways and social networks in a women's prison. *Affilia, 30*(1), 26–39.

Smoyer, A. B. (2015a). "It's the black girls that have the most": Foodways narratives and the construction of race in a women's prison. *Food and Foodways, 23*(4), 273–285.

Smoyer, A. B. (2015b). Making fatty girl cakes: Food and resistance in a women's prison. *The Prison Journal, 96*(2), 191–209.

Smoyer, A. B., & Lopes, G. (2017). Hungry on the inside: Prison food as concrete and symbolic punishment in a women's prison. *Punishment and Society, 19*(2), 240–255.

Spector-Mersel, G. (2010). Narrative research: Time for a paradigm. *Narrative Inquiry, 20*(1), 204–224.

Sykes, G. M. (1958). *The society of captives: A study of a maximum security prison.* Princeton University Press.

Thomas, C. W. (1997). Comparing the cost and performance of public and private prisons in Arizona, Florida. Center for Studies in Criminology and Law, University of Florida.

Tisdale, S. (2000). *The best thing I ever tasted: The secret of food.* Riverhead Books.

Ugelvik, T. (2011). The hidden food: Mealtime resistance and identity work in a Norwegian prison. *Punishment and Society, 13*(1), 47–63.

Valentine, G. (1999). Eating in: Home, consumption and identity. *The Sociological Review, 47*(3), 491–524.

Vanhouche, A. S. (2015). Acceptance or refusal of convenience food in present-day prison. *Appetite, 94,* 47–53.

8

Shape Shifting

The Penal Voluntary Sector and the Governance of Domestic Violence

RASHMEE SINGH

Introduction

Analyses of privatization in the criminal justice system typically centre on the triad of police, prison, and security. This body of scholarship has generated significant insights into practices of outsourcing, load-shedding, and degovernmentalization, as well as the state and non-state relations formed in their administration, though Canadian research on these topics is still burgeoning (Luscombe et al., this volume). The predominant focus on these three criminal justice institutions and the roles that they perform in managing public disorder, however, has resulted in the neglect of forms of crime that do not fit this mould. The term "privatization" also exerts a discursive effect on the range of non-state entities considered in analyses of criminal justice partnerships. Evocative of market logics, what often comes to mind are scenarios of offloading fuelled by government rationales that non-state entities can fulfill traditional criminal justice responsibilities more efficiently, at lower costs, or in ways that generate profits. Largely excluded from consideration in this framing are non-profit, voluntary, and charitable organizations despite their long-standing partnerships with the criminal justice system (see also Kohm, this volume). Drawing attention to these oversights is important given the central questions driving this collection of work and the range of phenomena that it seeks to understand. Specifically, which recent shifts in the government have created the needs, opportunities, or pressures for the increased privatization of criminal justice? Additionally, how is the involvement of private and non-state entities influencing and reshaping the policing, prosecution, and punishment of crime?

To address these questions and shift analyses of privatization in different directions, in this chapter I examine the role and influence of voluntary organizations and grassroots feminist agencies in the governance of domestic violence in Toronto. I focus specifically on the confluence of political rationalities and interests that enabled their incorporation into official responses to domestic violence, which ultimately materialized in the establishment of the city's specialized domestic violence plea courts in the late 1990s. The plea courts are notable for their reliance on a roster of eleven voluntary organizations to deliver provincially accredited and standardized Partner Abuse Response (PAR) programs for court-mandated, domestic violence offenders. Based upon the Duluth, Minnesota, model of domestic violence intervention, which advocates for feminist agencies to partner with police and courts in a watchdog role, the plea court initiative positions voluntary organizations as leading figures in their alliances with the criminal justice system.

Drawing from ethnographic observation of the specialized court process and interviews with PAR counsellors and advocates conducted intermittently over an eighteen-year period, I reveal alternative conceptualizations of outsourcing and responsibilization between voluntary organizations and the criminal justice system and narrow in on the forces driving these partnerships that have yet to be captured in existing analyses of privatization. In so doing, I argue that, in contrast to existing theorizations of criminal justice partnerships involving voluntary organizations, which conceptualize non-state entities as losing, or at risk of losing, their autonomy, original mandates, and political influence, Toronto's field of domestic violence governance reveals that power disparities are not always fixed, nor are directives unilaterally determined by state agendas. Rather, depending on the degree to which voluntary and criminal justice interests resonate within partnerships, voluntary organizations can maintain their mandates and significantly shape official responses to crime, often in ways that extend well beyond the original scope of their responsibilities. I contextualize this analysis in relation to two distinct, yet overlapping, fields of scholarship: the literature on the penal voluntary sector (PVS) and a growing body of contemporary work on governing practices in neo-liberalism, which emphasizes ethnography as a central method for examining the formation and effects of alliances between state and non-state entities (Brady & Lippert, 2016). A key endeavour in both fields is the production of empirical research on criminal justice partnerships that nuances understandings of their formation and effects.

I begin with a review of the PVS scholarship, focusing on the insights and debates currently informing the literature. I then detail the methodology, which emphasizes the examination of penal partnerships not as fixed entities but as assemblages. Following a brief discussion of the origins of Toronto's specialized domestic violence courts, I narrow in on three specific moments in the government–criminal justice–community relations that represent significant power shifts between state and non-state actors. Each of these historical moments illuminates the fluidity of the criminal justice–community partnership and the various ways in which state power intervenes and retreats over time.

The Penal Voluntary Sector

Recent scholarship on the penal voluntary sector provides the most relevant insights for analyzing Toronto's specialized court response to domestic violence, given its exclusive focus on the role of non-profit and philanthropic organizations within the criminal justice system, as well as its interest in examining the conditions that have led to the formation of the sector. As is the case in the broader criminal justice literature on privatization, PVS scholars cite marketization and neo-liberalism as key forces in the contemporary development and proliferation of PVS regimes. Although they note that collaborations between the voluntary sector and the criminal justice system are nothing new (Hucklesby & Corcoran, 2016; Mills et al., 2011; Tomczak, 2017), several assert that what differentiates past and present collaborations is their shift from a "nice to have" service to a "core provider" of criminal justice responsibilities (Hucklesby & Corcoran, 2016, p. 14; Maguire, 2012; Maguire et al., 2019). Relating these changes to parallel transformations in government policy, PVS scholars based in the United Kingdom draw attention to state rhetoric invoking a mixed economy of service provision and the growing use of market logics in social service delivery. In the same way that non-state entities have become enlisted to administer social welfare and other forms of public aid traditionally distributed through government bureaucracies, a "third sector" is observable in criminal justice in which responsibilities for offender management and rehabilitation are becoming contracted out increasingly to voluntary and social service organizations (Corcoran, 2011; Maguire, 2012). PVS scholars largely attribute the embrace of these practices to broader neo-liberal logics and associated practices of devolution, though debates in this literature also question the degree to which these forces can explain the expansion of this sector (Maguire, 2012; Tomczak 2014, 2017).

Along with seeking to explain the forces driving the contemporary expansion of the "third sector" in criminal justice, PVS scholars focus on how these developments are reshaping the mandates and habits of the non-profit agencies involved in these collaborations. A key concern raised in this literature is the potentially depoliticizing impact of these alliances on social justice and advocacy organizations (Armstrong, 2002; Corcoran, 2009; Kendall & Knapp, 1995; Maguire, 2012; Mills et al., 2011). Scholars refer in particular to the processes of "mission creep" (Poole, 2007) and "penal drift" (Maguire et al., 2019). Whereas the former relates to instances in which voluntary organizations gradually deviate from their founding philosophical principles once they ally with the criminal justice system, the latter refers to the practices and logics that they are forced to adopt once they agree to deliver programs to offenders mandated to attend their services through the criminal justice system (see Mulone, this volume). Empirical examinations of penal voluntary organizations additionally draw attention to the impact of managerial logics on service delivery and the multiple ways in which funding contingencies require agencies to adopt evaluation criteria that rely on a reduction in recidivism as the ultimate indicator of success (Armstrong, 2002; Corcoran, 2009; Maguire, 2012; Mills et al., 2011). Scholars caution that these criteria could lead to a denial of services to the individuals who might require them the most; once success is defined as crime reduction and funding is contingent on reducing recidivism, agencies will have few choices but to recruit the clientele most likely to guarantee their program's success.

These realities have generated broader concerns about whether non-profit agencies are becoming puppets of the criminal justice system and agents of penal expansionism (Tomczak & Thompson, 2019). Whether the criminal justice system's growing reliance on voluntary organizations constitutes a form of net widening is another recurring theme in this literature. The few existing empirical studies of what non-profit-based service providers do in their day-to-day work both confirm and complicate the notion that the penal voluntary sector operates as "an insidious means of netting more people into the formal criminal justice system" (Armstrong, 2002, p. 354). Armstrong's (2002) seminal research on the development of a Massachusetts-based decarceration initiative for juvenile offenders in the 1970s reveals how community-based residential facilities reproduce rather than replace carceral power through "cloning the penal institution" (p. 354). Goddard (2012) and Singh (2012) find that, though community-based actors given the responsibility of offender supervision and reform do adopt the risk management logics typical of criminal justice entities, these orientations coexist with welfarist approaches that aim to alter the conditions that contribute to crime in the first place. Maguire et al.'s (2019) recent analysis of over 200 penal voluntary organizations (PVOs) in the United Kingdom verifies that, though agencies do experience penal drift, many also engage in concerted efforts to resist criminal justice logics and practices, a heterogeneity also reflected in Kaufman's (2015) analysis of re-entry services operating in the United States. Tomczak and Thompson (2019) add nuance to understandings of net widening, classifying the work of voluntary organizations as supportive of social integration but in ways that continue to expand the net of carceral control.

My analysis of Toronto's specialized domestic plea courts addresses the key conceptual debates raised in PVS scholarship in relation to penal drift, mission creep, and depoliticization of voluntary organizations once they partner with the criminal justice system and offers a temporal dimension to these discussions. Examinations of the multiple governing networks between state and non-state actors at various points in time reveal that few aspects of these relations, including the interests and investments of key actors, are static. Accordingly, concerns about penal voluntary organizations "losing themselves" or becoming penal clones are better understood as formations that emerge at certain moments rather than as total organizational reconfigurations. An analysis of the conditions that led to the emergence of the domestic violence plea courts and the formation of the penal voluntary sector also reveals that marketization and neo-liberalism (as they have been discussed so far) exerted far less of an influence than pro-criminalization liberal feminist logics that emphasized the systemic treatment of domestic violence "just like any other crime" (Gruber, 2020; Martin & Mosher, 1995). Legal reforms to domestic violence policies throughout the United States and Canada over the past four decades illuminate the central role of the battered women's movement (BWM) in enabling "community" – both in its abstract and in its material form – to emerge as a key terrain of governance (Garner & Maxwell, 2008; Pence, 1983). Although neo-liberalism undoubtedly provides an important analytical context for understanding the resonance of feminist reform and conservative government interests, this coalition had more to do with agreement about "tough on crime" approaches to crime control than with the general adoption of devolution as a governing practice.

Penal Partnerships as Assemblages

This analysis draws from nearly two decades of ongoing ethnographic research on Toronto's domestic violence courts and the agencies that partner with them to deliver court-mandated PAR counselling to abusers who have pled guilty to domestic violence offences. As a former PAR coordinator for the Coalition against Violence (CAV),[1] the grassroots feminist organization that once partnered with the criminal justice system and the Ontario Ministry of the Attorney General (MAG) to implement and administer the city's specialized plea courts in the late 1990s, my analysis of the courts' penal voluntary sector is informed by my two years of professional involvement in co-managing the roster of eleven organizations operating as accredited PAR program providers. During that time, I also participated in training crown prosecutors, public defenders, and law enforcement personnel for their roles in the courts and worked with them on a weekly basis. My PAR coordinator responsibilities additionally entailed working in all five plea courts throughout the city to enrol defendants in PAR programs. Although I left the organization in 2002, I continued to work in the domestic violence courts in a different capacity before beginning my doctoral program in 2004. I returned to the courts intermittently between 2007 and 2013 for ethnographic observation as an academic researcher and returned to research them in 2020. My continued involvement in these networks has allowed me to remain in the know about the vagaries of the domestic violence courts, the partnerships that fuel their administration, the fate of the CAV, and the changes to funding and governance structures of the PAR agencies over the years.

My position as an "insider" in this field in multiple capacities allowed me to observe the intricacies of the relations among the CAV, PAR providers, provincial government funders, and criminal justice officials and how they transformed over time. Between 1997 and 2015, the CAV operated as the key mediator between the Ministry of the Attorney General and the roster of PAR providers, acting simultaneously as an advocate for the community-based organizations involved in the process and as a "watchdog" in relation to the government and the courts. Unity among grassroots partners was a key principle informing CAV management of the roster of agencies. To ensure that the non-state players remained a united front, the organization convened monthly meetings with representatives from each agency to address ongoing problems and concerns in the courts. My attendance at these meetings allowed me to acquire behind-the-scenes insights into the conflicts that emerged among PAR providers, the Ministry of the Attorney General, and criminal justice officials and the solutions developed to address obstacles. Additionally, my presence in the domestic violence plea courts allowed me to observe first hand how criminal justice and community partnerships unfolded in the prosecution process. The monthly

PAR meetings and the courts were important sites for understanding the intricacies of penal voluntary partnerships, the power struggles that emerged between the PAR providers and the courts, and the various strategies put in place to resolve the conflicts.

Although my professional involvement at the CAV was limited to two years, returning to the courts as an academic researcher enabled me to examine them with a different set of eyes and interests. My previous knowledge and experience helped me to make sense of my data and sensitized me to changes that emerged both in the prosecution process and in the relationships among the key players. Although I was no longer privy to the conversations that transpired at the monthly PAR meetings, through interviews with PAR providers and members of the CAV, most of whom were my former colleagues, I was able to derive an understanding of what I had missed. I was surprised to see that very little had changed from when I was at the organization, particularly in relation to the complaints that PAR providers raised about their working relationships with the provincial government and criminal justice system. The three issues that repeatedly occupied PAR meeting agendas over the course of my two years at the CAV continued to surface: funding constraints, victim safety, and concerns that both the police and the courts were too lackadaisical in their handling of cases. The recurrence and persistence of these problems are not surprising given that they reflect – perhaps more than any other complaint about PVS relations – the power struggles that ensue in criminal justice partnerships.

In interpreting and integrating the data that I gathered in my professional experiences with the findings that I acquired through more traditional academic research methods, I draw from the insights of Brady and Lippert (2016) and others who emphasize methodological approaches that analyze governing regimes as assemblages. Lippert and Pyykkönen (2012) define the assemblage as a "contingent and creative ensemble of distinctive material and social elements that can include knowledges, ways of seeing and calculating, human capacities, mundane and grand devices, kinds of authorities, spatialities, and governmentalities ... that converge and which seek a specified outcome among those who govern" (cited in Brady & Lippert, 2016, p. 15). Along with enabling the capture of a diverse array of heterogeneous processes, an important aspect of this process is the emphasis on how assemblages are modified over time. Rabinow (2009) highlights the importance of considering temporal dimensions and the need for researchers to generate theoretical claims about governing regimes with the realization that they are typically experimental and short lived, even though they are often developed in response to long-standing social problems. Finally, approaching an analysis of governing relations as assemblages guards against reductionist theorizations that assume a singular origin or source in their formation. Brady and Lippert (2016) illuminate the potential of this approach to advance scholarship that nuances the use of neo-liberalism as an analytical category, an important endeavour given that it is now ubiquitous as an explanation of virtually all contemporary regulatory projects (see also Collier, 2012; Rose et al., 2006).

Examining the penal voluntary partnerships that comprise Toronto's field of domestic violence governance as an assemblage allows for the observation of social and political forces, as well as contingent factors, that so far have not been captured in the existing PVS scholarship explicating the proliferation of criminal justice partnerships in recent decades. In nuancing the use of neo-liberalism as an analytical construct, as well as concepts such as mission creep and penal cloning, the discussion additionally points to processes other than governing trends in devolution that enabled this penal partnership to form. Finally, examining the study of governing relations as an assemblage rather than a static set of actors and interests inherently disrupts any pre-fixed imaginary of penal partnerships as relations in which non-state entities forever operate as passive and downtrodden puppets of penal power. Although power differentials do exist, this analysis illuminates the agency and autonomy that voluntary organizations exert in their criminal justice partnerships and how state power shifts in response. The remaining discussion illustrates this shape shifting as well as the various political rationalities, knowledges, and contingent factors that influenced the development of the courts and the involvement of voluntary organizations in their administration.

The Origins of Toronto's Domestic Violence Plea Courts

Toronto's specialized domestic violence court process is based upon a framework of governance that first emerged in the early 1980s in Duluth, Minnesota. Known as the Duluth Abuse Intervention Project (DAIP) and more generally as the coordinated community response approach, the initiative was developed by renowned feminist activist and social worker Ellen Pence and is currently one of the most widely practised models of domestic violence intervention in North America (Allen et al., 2010). The DAIP is notable for its incorporation of and reliance on an array of non-state actors in criminal justice collaborations. Educators and social workers help to operate PAR programs for abusers, and advocates play central roles in facilitating information sharing between relevant stakeholders and, most importantly, ensuring that police and courts do not drop charges or neglect cases. Although the formal involvement of advocates, concerned citizens, and social workers in responses to domestic violence is a long-standing practice (Garner & Maxwell, 2008; Quinn, 2008), what distinguishes Pence's model from previous ones is the degree of influence that non–criminal justice entities exert in these collaborations. In the past, the rationale for including non-state actors, particularly social workers, in official responses stemmed from the idea that their expertise was required to supplement police and court responses. This is still the case in Pence's approach. However, instead of primarily designating community players as supplemental experts in partnerships, the DAIP additionally underscores their involvement as watchdogs over their criminal justice counterparts. The emphasis on systemic accountability is reflective of the second wave, liberal, and radical feminist logics that predominated at the time. These perspectives defined and equated justice and safety for abused women with criminal convictions, harsh punishments, and heightened surveillance of abusers.

The notion of incorporating feminist advocates into official criminal justice responses to domestic violence for the purpose of policing the police and the courts gained traction as the BWM became a dominant force in penal reform throughout the 1980s (Bumiller, 2008; Gruber, 2020). Advocating in a context of criminal justice neglect of domestic violence incidents, liberal and radical feminist reformers were unequivocal in their support for tough on crime interventions that would enhance the policing and punishment of domestic violence offenders. This "zero tolerance" approach was manifested most explicitly in Canada through the adoption of mandatory charging and aggressive prosecution policies in jurisdictions in the 1980s (Hilton, 1988; Martin & Mosher, 1995). It is in this broader context that Pence's envisioning of community involvement – and its relationship with criminal justice officials – must be understood. The purpose of "community" in the coordinated community response approach is to enforce criminal justice compliance with zero tolerance strategies of criminalization (Garner & Maxwell, 2008), an objective that Pence emphasized given the BWM's ongoing concerns that "lawmakers, police officers, judges, prosecutors, probation officers, and social workers consistently failed to use their institutional powers to protect women from further abuse or to sanction men for their violence" (Shepard & Pence, 1999, p. 8).

Toronto's specialized domestic violence courts derive directly from Pence's DAIP model. Her framework was first introduced in Toronto's anti-violence sector by service providers and advocates interested in developing an intersectoral response to domestic violence that would focus on bridging gaps in the health and social services sector and ensuring that cases involving abused women did not slip through the cracks. Organizers focused on creating policies and procedures to enable communication and information sharing among shelters, hospitals, and a variety of anti-violence services. The project ultimately expanded to include the criminal justice system in 1992 with the encouragement of Pence, at the time (serendipitously) pursuing a doctorate in sociology from the University of Toronto (Singh, 2012b). By the late 1990s, the organization focused its advocacy efforts on collaborating with the Ministry of the Attorney General, law enforcement personnel, prosecutors, and community organizations to develop the infrastructure for Toronto's specialized courts.

In keeping with Pence's DAIP approach, the CAV positioned itself as the overseer of the plea courts and the roster of voluntary organizations enlisted to provide PAR programs to defendants found guilty through the specialized domestic violence courts. Along with ensuring that criminal justice officials, particularly crown attorneys and police, operated in accordance with mandatory charging and prosecution strategies, the CAV created a process of accreditation for the voluntary agencies interested in becoming PAR providers. To gain acceptance, agencies were required to adopt the Duluth model of domestic violence counselling (CAV, 1998). This model, known for its incorporation of the "Power and Control Wheel," is a tool that Pence designed to educate abusers and to assist them with connecting their abusive behaviour to broader patriarchal forces (Pence & Paymar, 1993). The approach represented an explicit repudiation of the notion that domestic violence is the result of the actions and behaviour of a few mentally ill or angry men. In lieu of a therapeutic approach, the Duluth model emphasizes socio-educational group counselling. The Ministry of the Attorney General gave the CAV free rein to design the standardization process and recruit service providers to assess their appropriateness for PAR provision, which essentially entailed ensuring that agencies adopted a feminist understanding of domestic violence. Multiple agencies were required to deliver programming given the size and diversity of Toronto's demographics.

The Resonance of Domestic Violence Reform
The success of the CAV in developing its criminal justice partnership and positioning itself as the overseer was largely the result of its reform efforts

resonating with the broader political logics that prevailed at the time. Concerns raised by crown attorneys in relation to domestic violence case backlogs also contributed to an appetite for reform. The coalition initiated its reform efforts at a time when law enforcement and Ontario provincial courts became subject to intense criticism following two high-profile domestic homicide cases in the mid-1990s. The homicides happened to coincide with an award-winning *Toronto Star* series that investigated the prosecution of 133 incidents of domestic violence in 1995 (Singh, 2012b). As a consequence of this public scrutiny, MAG officials, prosecutors, and Toronto police were receptive to engaging with CAV reformers and experimenting with different legal responses to domestic violence. The coordinated community response framework, which emphasized the criminal justice system's higher compliance with mandatory charging and prosecution strategies, coincided well with the Conservative government's general "law and order" approach to crime control.

The coalition's promotion of a specialized domestic violence plea court, designed to expedite the prosecution of domestic violence cases and create incentives for defendants to plead guilty to their charges, was another feature of the coalition's reform plans that appealed to crown prosecutors and MAG officials. Specialized domestic violence plea courts would allow prosecutors to resolve their cases more quickly and efficiently by streamlining their administration. Whereas in regular courts, cases appeared in bail courts and then remained unresolved for months until prosecutors were assigned to them, in the specialized prosecution process all domestic violence cases would be funnelled immediately from a bail court into a plea court and then assigned to a dedicated domestic violence crown attorney. Once in the plea court, defendants had the option to plead guilty immediately to their charges or contest them and move their cases to a domestic violence trial court. The specialized plea court offered prosecutors a novel solution to the frustrations that they were encountering as a result of "recanting witnesses,"[2] many of whom either resisted pursuing charges from the beginning or experienced a change of heart after months of waiting to testify. The initiative allowed victims who wished to resume their relationships with their partners to do so more quickly through the removal of a "no contact" bail condition, which remains in effect in all domestic violence cases until they are resolved either by trial or by guilty plea. Given that the general time frame for case resolution through the traditional courts could be months or even a year, crown attorneys found the prospects of expedited resolutions extremely alluring. The revamping of administrative procedures, which emphasized interventions such as a dedicated courtroom and a specialized domestic violence prosecutor, ensured that cases did not get lost in the system and backlogged in bureaucracy.

A final factor facilitating the coalition's reform agenda was the intense focus on police accountability in the wake of Jane Doe's successful civil lawsuit against the Toronto Police Service. Doe sued the police for failing to warn women about a serial rapist in her neighbourhood despite their full knowledge of a pattern of attacks and the likelihood of their attribution to a single assailant. Although the incident occurred in the mid-1980s, the legal battle over police accountability lasted fifteen years, casting the issue of gender discrimination and insensitivity into the forefront of public concern (Ceric, 2001). During this time, CAV advocates found the police particularly amenable to reforming their policies in relation to gender-based violence. In 1991, the chief of police initiated the department's review of investigative and training interventions and worked in conjunction with the coalition to create the department's new policy. CAV organizers described the relationship as "harmonious," with the police chief meeting regularly with the agency's survivor-led Accountability Committee to review drafts and assist with the development of the department's new policies. The discourse of police accountability surfaced as the rationale for the department's creation of specialized domestic violence units (CAV, 1998).

Shifting CAV Responsibilities in the Plea Court Assemblage

This broader climate of reform and the desire for changes in the prosecution of domestic violence cases carved out a unique space for the CAV as both a watchdog and an administrative penal voluntary organization. In its role as an advocacy agency, which the coalition adopted as its primary identity, staff performed as the feminist pressure group that Pence envisioned in her framework. As the umbrella organization in charge of overseeing the PAR roster, liaising between crown prosecutors and PAR providers, and enrolling domestic violence offenders into counselling programs directly from the plea courts, the coalition performed in a more secretarial and administrative capacity in relation to the criminal justice system.

Interestingly, though the CAV was undoubtedly successful in accomplishing its criminal justice reform objectives through its formal advocacy role, it exerted the most influence on the courts through its administrative responsibilities and functions. The most influential figures to emerge in this regard were the PAR coordinators. The impact that the coordinators exerted in their roles had little to do with any specific expertise in or analysis of domestic violence, though these positions required a stance supportive of criminal justice involvement. Rather, their influence evolved largely from the fact that they were the only "routine players" (Galanter, 1974) in the early intervention court network as it evolved over the years. When the court first began, the PAR coordinator's responsibilities were limited to reviewing program options with offenders who wished to plead guilty, filling out the appropriate forms, answering questions about the PAR programs, and assisting defendants with their program selections based upon language and geographic needs. The PAR coordinators also had to ensure that prosecutors and defence attorneys possessed the requisite completion reports to proceed with sentencing and that they received the necessary enrolment and contact information to anticipate the arrival of court defendants for their programs.

Over time, however, the PAR coordinators transformed from form fillers to quasi-legal figures whose responsibilities included advising defendants of their legal options, screening them for their appropriateness in the plea court, explaining the consequences of guilty pleas, discussing sentencing options, and drafting bail conditions. These were not activities that CAV administrative workers should have undertaken in the courts. However, as crown attorneys and duty counsels rotated out of the specialized domestic violence prosecution process, the PAR coordinators emerged as the only figures with the requisite institutional and working knowledge of the plea courts. This led the legal professionals in the assemblage to trust the coordinators with their responsibilities. Eventually, as a series of obstacles emerged in the courts, including the temporary departure of duty counsel because of funding cuts, the PAR coordinator emerged as one of the most significant figures in the prosecution process, operating as a hybrid of public defender and crown prosecutor (Singh, 2017).

As a quasi-legal administrative figure who absorbed over time the responsibilities of defence counsel and crown prosecutor, the PAR coordinator was able to operate as the watchdog that Pence and the DAIP never could have envisioned. Although PVS scholars would question this transformation of the PAR coordinator into a penal clone, the change aligned with, rather than diminished, the CAV mandate to ensure criminal justice accountability in domestic violence cases. This development, however, was not inevitable, nor was it permanent. What extended the organization's influence on case prosecutions were the administrative needs of crown prosecutors, who were struggling to fulfill and maintain their responsibilities in the plea court network because of high caseloads, time constraints, and the suspended involvement of duty counsel.

PAR coordinators continued to perform a more enhanced, quasi-legal role in the plea courts for a number of years until 2015, when the CAV officially ended its collaboration with the Ministry of the Attorney General and the organizations delivering the PAR programs. By that time, the original founder and director of the coalition had left, and the agency had been under new management for five years. In its public announcement of the decision to leave the partnership, the agency cited the provincial government's decision to reduce the length of the PAR programs from sixteen to twelve weeks as well as concerns that the Liberal government was not taking the complaints raised in relation to victim safety in the courts seriously. Also notable was the direct reference to the administrative responsibilities of the PAR coordinator in the courts, which new directors (accurately) conceptualized as exploitative. Whereas previously this involvement was seen as an opportunity to keep watch over the courts, its meaning shifted as the coalition underwent its own changes.

PAR Providers and the Plea Court Boycott
Under the auspices of the CAV, the PAR agencies also exerted an extraordinary influence on the prosecution of cases in the plea courts, particularly in relation to ensuring that crown attorneys did not deviate from their original agreements to mandate only those offenders who agreed to plead guilty to the PAR programs. PAR providers had a vested interest in this arrangement, asserting that the failure of crown attorneys to comply with the court's initial vision would diminish their leverage and ability to hold offenders accountable during counselling sessions. Some also emphasized the symbolic effects of guilty pleas and criminal convictions and the need for punitive sanctions to relay the message that domestic violence is an intolerable criminal offence. The coalition and PAR providers were attentive to the guilty plea issue given the potential of crown attorneys to permit defendants to attend counselling via a peace bond if they were resistant to pleading guilty. As a result, the coalition advocated for, and crown prosecutors agreed to, sending only defendants with guilty pleas to PAR programs and to sentence them to one of two non-custodial sentences upon their successful completion of a program: a conditional discharge, a temporary

finding of guilt that can be removed from one's record after a period of two years, or a suspended sentence, a lifelong criminal conviction. Both sentences typically carry a period of probation from six to eighteen months. Since the courts were reserved for first-time offenders with no previous criminal convictions or histories, CAV advocates, PAR providers, and crown prosecutors viewed these sentences as proportionate to the crimes. Although differences would ultimately arise among PAR providers over the adherence to zero tolerance and tough on crime philosophies (Singh, 2012a), PAR providers, under CAV direction, were largely unified in their stance toward the insistence on guilty pleas.

A variety of contingent factors, however, ultimately threatened this consensus between prosecutors and PAR providers. According to CAV staff, the most disruptive were 9/11 and the securitization of American borders following the terrorist attacks. The response to heightened security shifted how border officials interpreted conditional discharges. Despite the fact these sentences technically were not criminal records in Canadian criminal law, American border guards no longer recognized them as fleeting findings of guilt. As a consequence, individuals with conditional discharges on their records were unable to enter the United States for work or personal reasons. These restrictions and their effects on those who required entry to the country for professional reasons raised concerns about the severity and the proportionality of the sentence. This shift in the meaning and implication of conditional discharges ultimately generated significant due process concerns in the early plea courts as defence attorneys became reluctant to advise their clients to plead guilty, particularly in cases in which victims did not wish to proceed with charges, typically the majority of them (Dawson & Dinovitzer, 2001). In response, crown prosecutors reneged on their original agreements governing the plea deals and began to offer defendants peace bonds on the condition that they completed their sixteen-week PAR counselling programs successfully. From the prosecutor's perspective, this change in procedure was necessary to ensure the successful resolution of cases in the courts.

Although the CAV and PAR providers understood this rationale, for counsellors the decision proved to be extremely disruptive. PAR providers expressed concerns that the "peace bond guys" did not admit their culpability once they arrived at their group counselling sessions, a prerequisite to their involvement in PAR programs. Their denial caused a ripple effect among other defendants in the educational groups. In addition, participants who were promised peace bonds and the withdrawal of their charges upon the successful completion of their programs were reluctant to reveal any information in groups for fear that it would jeopardize their deals. In response, all eleven PAR agencies, under the guidance of the coalition, decided to launch what they referred to as the "PAR Freeze." In so doing, the PAR agencies refused to accept referrals from all of the provincial plea courts, effectively shutting them down for nearly two months. The boycott ended when the Ministry of the Attorney General intervened to provide a solution to the conflict that would appease PAR providers but also address the concerns of prosecutors, effectively mediating their conflicting interests.

Conclusion

The origin story of Toronto's specialized domestic violence court process and the formation of the penal voluntary sector in the governance of domestic violence offenders illuminates a very different criminal justice and community-based partnership than the alliances examined so far in the PVS scholarship and the privatization literature more generally. In contrast to the typical story of neo-liberal devolution, in which voluntary agencies are absorbed into the criminal justice system and operate as passive partners to law enforcement agencies and the courts, both the CAV and the PAR providers performed a central role in directing the prosecution of cases through the specialized plea courts and in defining the terms of participation for all of the players involved in the partnership. The roots of this penal voluntary partnership have little to do with broader neo-liberal trends that position non–criminal justice entities as more efficient and cost-effective mechanisms for carrying out criminal justice responsibilities. Rather, they emerge from feminist logics that remain suspicious of the capacities of police and courts to govern domestic violence cases in ways that ensure offender accountability and victim safety.

This fundamental distinction draws attention to how voluntary organizations consciously inserted themselves into this alliance in both an advocacy and an administrative capacity. Along with developing the infrastructure for the specialized domestic violence court process, the coalition defined the terms of accreditation for PAR providers and in so doing constituted what the reform of domestic violence offenders would entail. The institutionalization of the Duluth curriculum, which conceptualized domestic abuse as a structural form of violence rooted in patriarchy, also signalled the coalition's success in ensuring that "the social" was not lost in criminal justice responses to domestic abuse. Retention of the social in this governing regime further distinguishes it from typical neo-liberal interventions, which individualize the sources of crime and reduce explanations of its occurrence to bad choices and poor self-control (Garland, 2001; Rose, 1996). However, the emphasis on zero tolerance approaches and meaningful punishments for the objectives of both general and specific deterrence illuminates the resonance of the CAV approach with broader neo-liberal trends in crime control adopted by the Conservative Ontario government at the time. This alignment, along with several contingent factors in the mid- to late 1990s, which generated significant public concern and scrutiny about the failures of police and courts to respond effectively to violence against women, enabled the coalition to implement its criminal justice reforms.

The advent of the CAV and its role in developing Toronto's penal voluntary sector in criminal justice responses to domestic violence also illuminate alternative conceptualizations of responsibilization that have yet to be captured in the existing literature on criminal justice and community partnerships. The coalition, as well as a number of PAR organizations, conceptualized their role as systemic watchdogs. As has been illustrated, fulfilling this objective entailed exerting pressures on prosecutors to ensure their compliance with the agreed upon sentencing recommendations and screening procedures for cases in the domestic violence courts. Although the boycott launched by PAR providers ultimately materialized for more practical than ideological interests, the event revealed how they and the coalition used their power to steer prosecutors back into the original design of the domestic violence plea courts. The success of the PAR boycott also reveals the degree to which these organizations now operate as an essential component of the criminal justice system, rather than "nice to have" services.

There is no way to predict the social, political, administrative, and contingent factors that will continue to materialize in this assemblage and how they will affect the penal voluntary sector and the governance of domestic violence more generally. The multiple reconfigurations of the CAV and its ultimate removal from the assemblage were contingent on events that occurred spontaneously over time and likely could not have been predicted. Although further research is required to determine the specific forces that generated the departure of the coalition from the courts, which occurred under a Liberal Ontario government, the more direct role now performed by the Ontario Ministry of the Attorney General in the governance of the PAR providers and courts underscores how penal partnerships remain in constant flux. This reality signals the need to use caution when theorizing the formation and effects of privatization and voluntary sector involvement in the criminal justice system.

Notes

1 All names are pseudonyms.
2 The "problem" of the "recanting witness" was an inevitable consequence of mandatory arrest and prosecution policies, which essentially prevented victims of domestic violence from dropping charges and forced them to participate during trials if cases could not be resolved via guilty pleas (Landau, 2000; Martin & Mosher, 1995).

References

Allen, N. E., Javdani, S., Anderson, C. J., Rana, S., Newman, D., Todd, N., Lehrner, A., Walden, A., Larsen, S., & Davis, S. (2010). *Coordinating the criminal justice response to intimate partner violence: The effectiveness of councils in producing systems change.* US Department of Justice.

Armstrong, S. (2002). Punishing not-for-profit: Implications of non-profit privatization in juvenile punishment. *Punishment and Society, 4*(3), 345–368.

Brady, M., & Lippert, R. (2016). Introduction. In M. Brady & R. Lippert (Eds.), *Governing practices: Neoliberalism, governmentality, and the ethnographic imaginary* (pp. 3–34). University of Toronto Press.

Bumiller, K. (2008). *In an abusive state: How neoliberalism appropriated the feminist movement against sexual violence.* Duke University Press.

Ceric, I. (2001). Organizing for accountability: Community legal clinics and police complaints. *Journal of Law and Social Policy, 16*(9), 241–259.

Coalition against Violence. (1998). *Best practice guidelines: A compilation of guidelines for responding to woman abuse across various sectors* [Unpublished document].

Collier, S. J. (2012). Neoliberalism as big Leviathan, or ... ? A response to Wacquant and Hilgers. *Social Anthropology, 20*(2), 186–195.

Corcoran, M. (2009). Bringing the penal voluntary sector to market. *Criminal Justice Matters, 77*(1), 32–33.

Corcoran, M. (2011). Dilemmas of institutionalization in the penal voluntary sector. *Critical Social Policy, 31*(1), 30–52.

Dawson, M., & Dinovitzer, R. (2001). Victim cooperation and the prosecution of domestic violence in a specialized court. *Justice Quarterly, 18*(3), 593–622.

Galanter, M. (1974). Why the "haves" come out ahead: Speculations on the limits of legal change. *Law and Society Review, 9*(1), 95–160.

Garland, D. (2001). *The culture of control: Crime and social order in a contemporary society.* University of Chicago Press.

Garner, J. H., & Maxwell, C. D. (2008). Coordinated community responses to intimate partner violence in the 20th and 21st centuries. *Criminology and Public Policy, 7*(4), 525–535.

Goddard, T. (2012). Post-welfarist risk managers? Risk, crime prevention and the responsibilization of community-based organizations. *Theoretical Criminology, 16*(3), 347–363.

Gruber, A. (2020). *The feminist war on crime: The unexpected role of women's liberation in mass incarceration.* University of California Press.

Hilton, N. Z. (1988). One in ten: The struggle and disempowerment of the battered women's movement. *Canadian Journal of Family and the Law, 7*, 313–336.

Hucklesby, A., & Corcoran, M. (Eds.). (2016). *The voluntary sector and criminal justice*. Springer.

Kaufman, N. (2015). Prisoner incorporation: The work of the state and nongovernmental organizations. *Theoretical Criminology, 19*(4), 1–20.

Kendall, J., & Knapp, M. (1995). A loose and baggy monster. In J. D. Smith, C. Rochester, & R. Hedley (Eds.), *An introduction to the voluntary sector* (pp. 66–95). Routledge.

Landau, T. C. (2000). Women's experiences with mandatory charging for wife assault in Ontario, Canada: A case against the prosecution. *International Review of Victimology, 7*(1–3), 141–157.

Lippert, R., & Pyykkönen, M. (2012). Introduction: Immigration, governmentality, and integration assemblages. *Nordic Journal of Migration Research, 2*(1), 1–4.

Maguire, M. (2012). Big society, the voluntary sector and the marketisation of criminal justice. *Criminology and Criminal Justice, 12*(5), 483–494.

Maguire, M., Williams, K., & Corcoran, M. (2019). "Penal drift" and the voluntary sector. *The Howard Journal of Crime and Justice, 58*(3), 430–449.

Martin, D. L., & Mosher, J. (1995). Unkept promises: Experiences of immigrant women with the neo-criminalization of wife abuse. *Canadian Journal of Women and the Law, 8*, 3–44.

Mills, A., Meek, R., & Gojkovic, D. (2011). Exploring the relationship between the voluntary sector and the state in criminal justice. *Voluntary Sector Review, 2*(2), 193–211.

Pence, E. (1983). The Duluth Domestic Abuse Intervention Project. *Hamline Law Review, 6*, 247–275.

Pence, E., & Paymar, M. (1993). *Education groups for men who batter: The Duluth model*. Springer.

Poole, L. (2007). Working in the non-profit welfare sector: Contract culture, partnership, compacts and the "shadow state." In G. Mooney & A. Law (Eds.), *New labour/hard labour? Restructuring and resistance inside the welfare industry* (pp. 233–261). Policy Press.

Quinn, M. C. (2008). Anna Moscowitz Kross and the home term part: A second look at the nation's first criminal domestic violence court. *Akron Law Review, 41*, 733–762.

Rabinow, P. (2009). *Anthropos today: Reflections on modern equipment*. Princeton University Press.

Rose, N. (1996). The death of the "social"? Refiguring the territory of government. *Economy and Society, 26*(4), 327–346.

Rose, N., O'Malley, P., & Valverde, M. (2006). Governmentality. *Annual Review of Law and Social Science, 2*, 83–104.

Shepard, M. F., & Pence, E. L. (Eds.). (1999). *Coordinating community responses to domestic violence: Lessons from Duluth and beyond* (Vol. 12). SAGE.

Singh, R. (2012a). When punishment and philanthropy mix: Voluntary organizations and the governance of the domestic violence offender. *Theoretical Criminology, 16*(3), 269–287.

Singh, R. (2012b). *Grassroots governance: Domestic violence and criminal justice partnerships in an immigrant city* [Unpublished PhD dissertation].
Singh, R. (2017). "Please check the appropriate box": Documents and the governance of domestic violence. *Law and Social Inquiry, 42*(2), 509–542.
Tomczak, P. (2014). The penal voluntary sector in England and Wales: Beyond neoliberalism? *Criminology and Criminal Justice, 14*(4), 470–486.
Tomczak, P. (2017). *The penal voluntary sector.* Routledge.
Tomczak, P., & Thompson, D. (2019). Inclusionary control? Theorizing the effects of penal voluntary organizations' work. *Theoretical Criminology, 23*(1), 4–24.

PART 4

Private Actors in National Security and Border Control

9
Evidence of High Policing Pluralization in Canada

ALEX LUSCOMBE

Introduction

In the United States, it is widely regarded that the field of national security intelligence, or "high policing" (Brodeur, 1983), is no longer the sole domain of the state. The lion's share of the annual intelligence budget in the United States goes not to major public players such as the National Security Agency (NSA), the Central Intelligence Agency, or the Federal Bureau of Investigation but to their contractors. The extent of private involvement in high policing in the country became especially apparent in the wake of the controversy surrounding the documents leaked by Edward Snowden in 2013. Snowden, an intelligence contractor working for Booz Allen Hamilton, stole millions of classified records from the NSA and worked with journalists to analyze and periodically disclose them to the public. His revelations made headlines worldwide, forever changing the public's perception of what, exactly, high policing agencies such as the NSA do in the name of "national security" (Bauman et al., 2014).

As a corollary to Snowden's actions, American intelligence professionals began to voice concerns about how easy it was for Snowden to steal the classified documents from the NSA's internal system. Much emphasis was placed on his trustworthiness, a concern that would spiral eventually into a larger debate about the trustworthiness of private intelligence contractors in general. Given differences in the hiring practices, training styles, and motivations of private contractors, can they really be trusted with access to the highest level of state secrets? Whereas public sector intelligence agents were characterized as selfless, loyal, and patriotic (and therefore better at keeping secrets), their private intelligence counterparts were depicted as the opposite: selfish, disloyal, and unpatriotic.

Although there is much to be learned from the controversies surrounding Snowden's revelations, the emphasis on issues of "outsourcing" and "privatization" that has emerged as a result contains some crucial limitations. The one that I wish to engage with in this chapter pertains specifically to the matter of generalizability. An extensive literature has emerged documenting the rise of America's "industrial-espionage complex" (Keefe, 2010). We have, however, little sense of how these trends documented in the context of the United States may or may not generalize to other countries like Canada. In "low policing" scholarship on private security, regional and national variations are often overlooked (Singh & Light, 2019). The same is true, I argue, of high policing scholarship. By being too quick to generalize findings from a single country, especially one as seemingly anomalous in so many ways as the United States (Doob & Webster, 2006; Jouet, 2017), we risk overlooking and undertheorizing many factors that can constrain and/or enable the spread of private actors in the sector of the criminal justice system that we are studying (Singh & Light, 2019).

In this chapter, I examine empirically questions about the degree to which high policing pluralization is unfolding in the Canadian context. The word *pluralization* in this context, adopted from policing studies, refers to the increasing involvement of private actors in high policing operations (Loader, 2000). To what extent has Canada's high policing apparatus been affected by trends toward policing pluralization documented in countries such as the United States (e.g., Keefe, 2010; Shearing & Stenning, 1983)? The high level of official secrecy surrounding all matters of national security and intelligence makes outside scholarly research difficult but not impossible (Luscombe & Walby, 2015). Research on high policing – like any top secret agency or program – requires the industrious triangulation of many different sources in the hope of arriving at some more complete, but still partial, answer than the one started with (Walters & Luscombe, 2019), what anthropologist of nuclear secrecy Hugh Gusterson (1997) called "polymorphous engagement."

In search of evidence of pluralization in Canada's high policing apparatus, I looked to four places: procurement arrangements, accountability mechanisms, public controversies, and events and publications of the non-profit sector.[1] Each of these sources offers a partial look at issues of high policing pluralization in Canada. In my analysis, I focus on the activities of Canada's three foremost high policing agencies: the Canadian Security Intelligence Service (CSIS), Communications Security Establishment Canada (CSEC), and the Royal Canadian Mounted Police (RCMP). My findings suggest a more ambivalent state of affairs than much of the existing literature, based almost exclusively upon developments in the United States, might have us believe. In some respects, Canada's high policing apparatus seems to be pluralizing in much the same ways as its Five Eyes partner to the south; in other respects, we see differences in the spread of pluralization that invite the need for additional research.

This chapter has three parts. First, I provide an overview of the key concepts and literatures with which I engage. To conceptualize issues of national security pluralization, I rely primarily on Brodeur's (1983, 2010) theory of high and low policing and related interventions in high policing pluralization (Chesterman, 2008; Hoogenboom, 2006; Keefe, 2010; O'Reilly, 2015; O'Reilly & Ellison, 2005). Second, I take stock of existing evidence of pluralization guided by my investigations of high policing in the four thematic areas noted above – procurement, accountability, public controversy, and the non-profit sector. In the discussion and conclusion, I reflect on the broader significance of these findings and their implications for literature on high and low policing and pluralization.

High Policing Pluralization

High Policing Defined

This chapter focuses on issues of pluralization of national security intelligence in Canada, conceptualized as high policing. The term high policing comes from Brodeur (1983), who, in an influential essay, drew a distinction between high and low policing in criminology. Simply put, *low policing* was meant to demarcate those "ordinary" and visible forms of policing that Brodeur loosely defined as "forceful reaction[s] to *conspicuous* signs of disorder, whether or not of a criminal nature" (p. 512). An example is a uniformed beat officer who makes an arrest for drug use or some other street-level offence. *High policing*, in contrast, is political policing. Rather than simply react to visible signs of disorder, high policing "reaches out for potential threats in a systemic attempt to preserve the distribution of power in a given society" (p. 513). CSIS and CSEC are quintessential examples of high policing agencies in Canada. Although Brodeur never explicitly developed a theory of low policing, a shortcoming that he later acknowledged (2007, p. 26), he did set out to identify the durable characteristics of high policing and where possible distinguished low from high policing along these various axes. In his first monograph on high and low policing, Brodeur (1983) identified four essential features of political police. Later, in his book *The Policing Web*, Brodeur (2010) extended the list of features to nine.

First, high policing is "absorbent policing": it seeks to control the population by collecting, storing, and analyzing information to generate intelligence. Second, high policing tends toward the conflation of legislative, judicial, and executive powers. Unlike low policing, it is not "uniquely bound to enforce the law and regulations as they are made by an independent legislator" (Brodeur, 1983, p. 513). Third, the goal of high policing is to preserve the status quo. National security and the protection of the political regime are the raison d'être of high policing. Fourth, high policing involves extensive use of informants to generate information. Fifth, in high policing crimes, the state is the intended victim. Sixth, high policing can involve the use of criminals to help carry out its goals. Seventh, high policing is deeply secretive. Eighth, high policing is premised on the regular and unchecked use of deception. And ninth, high policing involves the use of extralegal strategies.

Of course, many of these features are not exclusive to high policing. Low-level drug busts, for example, frequently rely on the use of undercover agents and paid informants (Loftus & Goold, 2012). And, given the recent emphasis on "intelligence-led policing" in low policing contexts (Burcher & Whelan, 2019), one could hardly argue that the collection and storage of information are unique to high policing. It is thus best conceived as a label used to denote a particular set of discourses and practices. In Brodeur's view, a given policing activity can be labelled high only if it "displays several of the features" noted above, since to classify "all police 'knowledge work' into high policing results in inflating the concept to the point where it loses all heuristic value" (2010, p. 224). Canada's domestic intelligence and signals intelligence agencies, CSIS and CSEC, are labelled high policing organizations only to the extent that their discourses and practices conform to particular characteristics noted above (Brodeur & Leman-Langlois, 2006). It could be argued that the RCMP is primarily a low policing organization, but the branches that deal with issues of intelligence and national security are certainly high policing ones from this perspective.

High Policing Pluralization

In recent years, debates about high policing theory in criminology have turned toward one of the more significant developments in the larger criminal justice system, namely *pluralization* (Chesterman, 2008; Hoogenboom, 2006; Keefe, 2010; O'Reilly, 2015; O'Reilly & Ellison, 2005). Writing about the United States, Keefe (2010, p. 297) suggests that by 2008 "the relationship between U.S. intelligence and the private sector had grown so symbiotic that it was often impossible to disentangle the two." As Hoogenboom (2006, p. 380) concludes his influential piece on the subject, "the intelligence landscape is changing fundamentally," and the emergence of new private and hybrid actors – what he calls "grey intelligence" – is a driving force of this change. To the extent that the state wishes to retain a high level of ownership and control of "the business of espionage," the kind of wholesale privatization that one finds in the American prison system, for example, has not occurred. The more accurate word to use in this context is *outsourcing*, which many scholars have suggested should be distinguished from outright privatization (Fitzgibbon & Lea, 2018; White, 2015). At a more general level, the increasing involvement of private actors in high policing can also be referred to as *pluralization*, a word that usefully captures this change without making any assumption about the extent to which responsibility for state functions has been put into private hands. With very little known about how private actors might be involved in and influencing high policing in Canada, I use the term pluralization.

Until more recently, high policing theory, as initially developed by Brodeur (1983), failed to acknowledge the extent to which high policing functions are, and in some countries always have been, fulfilled by private actors (see O'Reilly & Ellison, 2005). The United States is one country where private actors have long had a hand in the world of high policing (Chesterman, 2008; Churchill, 2004; Shorrock, 2008). Today the role of private and hybrid actors in high policing is expanding rapidly, albeit to varying degrees in different parts of the world. In response to these changes, several scholars have sought to think through the potential implications of pluralization for traditional high policing structures (Keefe, 2010) and for the various features of high policing theorized by Brodeur (O'Reilly & Ellison, 2005). Although some commentators have defended high policing pluralization (Hansen, 2014), most have raised concerns about it by pointing to a variety of potential pathologies detailed below. These pathologies pertain to issues of private versus public interests, flaws in the contracting process, and a lack of transparency/accountability in pluralized high policing arrangements.

Pathologies of High Policing Pluralization

The importation of private entities into high policing introduces a number of "organizational pathologies" (Sheptycki, 2004) to the field. Here I make note of three. First, there are concerns about the interests and loyalties of private high policing agents. It is regularly suggested that the interests of private actors can, but do not necessarily, align with those of the state for which they are working. Private agents are characterized as motivated by profit and loyal to their employers rather than the "higher order" interests of the state (Hansen, 2014, pp. 65–67). Whereas the state seeks to protect its citizens and base of power, private contractors are more likely to have profitability as their principal motivation. Regardless of why an employee chooses to work for a private high policing agency, "the fact remains that these firms are market-driven, for-profit entities ... [They] must ultimately answer to their shareholders and to the bottom line, and as such, there is a subtle but fundamental misalignment between their priorities and incentives" and those of the state agency for which they are working (Keefe, 2010, p. 297). Whereas public high policing agencies can have only one client (i.e., the state that calls them into existence), private high policing agencies can have multiple clients (Brodeur, 2010; O'Reilly, 2015, p. 289), creating potential conflicts of interest. In the wake of two of the biggest intelligence leaks in American history – the Stratfor hacking incident, a case involving a dump of nearly 5 million classified records via Wikileaks stolen from Stratfor's computer network in 2011, and the revelations of Booz Allen Hamilton contractor Edward Snowden in 2013 about the global spying activities of the National Security Agency – these concerns about the presumed motivations and loyalties of private versus public high policing officials have become a central point of debate (Bean, 2015; Hansen, 2014).

Second, organizational pathologies have been identified with the high policing procurement and contracting process (Chesterman, 2008; Keefe, 2010; Shorrock, 2008). It has been suggested that private contractors, despite having identical qualifications and training, are often paid far more than their public counterparts for the same work. As Keefe (2010, pp. 303–304) finds in the American context, "intelligence agencies pay approximately $125,000 [US] a year for each government employee, and $207,000 for contract workers performing similar services." Many intelligence contracts in the United States are awarded through non-competitive bidding arrangements, which ultimately deprive "the government of the ability to shop around for the most feasible project proposal or the most attractive price" (Keefe, 2010, pp. 300–1). Other issues have been raised – although again they might be specific to the American context – with the lack of accountability in the intelligence contracting process. In the American intelligence field, high policing companies are regularly awarded "cost plus" contracts, meaning that they can go over budget if necessary, and when they fail to produce the anticipated results (which often they do, especially in the area of technological innovation) they are "seldom punished" (Keefe, 2010, p. 301). Because intelligence contracts are classified, their details in the United States are either limited in public databases or excluded from publication altogether, only furthering the deficit of accountability (Crampton et al., 2014, p. 209).

Third, there are concerns about the lack of transparency and accountability in public-private high policing configurations (Chesterman, 2008; Hoogenboom, 2006; van Buuren, 2014). Private high policing agencies are not subject to nearly the same degree of transparency and accountability as their government counterparts. As a result, private high policing agents, in some countries at least, are regularly contracted to carry out work that public agents cannot legally or morally justify themselves (Hoogenboom, 2006, p. 377). This increases the overall unlawfulness or extralegality of a country's high policing apparatus. Marx (1987) conceptualizes this use of private agents as the "hydraulic principle": the more constrained public high policing agencies are (e.g., by oversight requirements), the more likely they are to outsource tasks to unhindered private actors (see also Jamieson & McEvoy, 2005). The most frequently cited example of this principle is America's use of rendition, strategically facilitated through the use of private aircraft companies to transport prisoners (Chesterman, 2008, p. 1061). More egregiously, private high policing agencies were also contracted by the Central Intelligence Agency to carry out "enhanced interrogations" (involving torture) at the controversial US-run Abu Ghraib prison (Chesterman, 2008, p. 1063). By relocating intelligence functions beyond the reach of traditional oversight and accountability mechanisms, private entities make high policing operations more secretive, removing ever-greater amounts of information from the public record. Next I turn specifically to the question of high policing pluralization in Canada. Although these pathologies are indeed troubling, the vast majority of supporting evidence comes from the United States. I lay out the analytical plan and reasons for the current study of high policing procurement, accountability, and controversy and the role of the non-profit sector in resisting or promoting the spread of pluralization in Canada (for more on the role of the non-profit sector in criminal justice, see Singh, Kohm, both this volume).

Reasons for the Current Study

In studies of Western high policing agencies, the working consensus appears to be that private actors are playing an increasingly central role in our intelligence communities. As Hoogenboom (2006, p. 373) writes, "next to formal state intelligence one increasingly finds private, more informal intelligence." Countries with smaller intelligence communities, however, such as Canada, have not been explicitly considered in this debate. The vast majority of studies of high policing pluralization have focused on developments in the United States, which for a variety of reasons, not least of which includes differences in history and size of intelligence community, might not be representative of those in Canada. To date, existing literature on matters of high policing in Canada has focused primarily on public agencies with only minimal consideration of private actors (Brodeur, 1983; Leman-Langlois, 2018; Monaghan & Walby, 2012a, 2012b; Walby & Anaïs, 2012; Whitaker et al., 2012).

Indeed, the growth of private intelligence contractors appears to be much more pronounced in the United States than in any other country in the world (O'Reilly & Ellison, 2005, p. 695). Throughout Washington, DC, private intelligence contractors have become so pervasive that Shorrock (2008, p. 34) characterizes them as a "virtual shadow government." Shorrock estimated that 70 percent of the US intelligence budget is now spent on private intelligence contractors, awarding $400 billion worth of contracts in 2007 alone (p. 34). These private intelligence contractors are involved in a wide array of high policing activities in the United States, from the more computer-oriented and technical end of the spectrum (e.g., data mining and analysis) to the more coercive and extralegal end (e.g., coercive interrogation, rendition).

The degree to which these characteristics of US high policing generalize to Canada has not been tested or explored empirically. High policing structures in Canada are very different from those south of the border. Canada's high policing agencies have unique histories, mandates, and legal powers, and the intelligence community in Canada is significantly smaller in terms of budget, staffing, and number of agencies (Whitaker et al., 2012). Differences in culture and politics between the United States and Canada offer potential additional sources of variation that affect high policing in the two countries. Below, focusing on the themes of procurement, accountability, public controversy, and the non-profit sector, I take stock of available evidence of high policing pluralization in Canada.

High Policing Pluralization in Canada

Procurement Arrangements

In assessing the extent to which high policing in Canada has pluralized, an obvious place to start is government procurement. Unfortunately, the lack of transparency and accountability in high policing procurement in Canada severely limits any insight into this process that one might be able to gain. In Canada, the general stance of the federal government seems to be that procurement, like other aspects of high policing, ought to be as secretive as possible. This secrecy-first orientation toward high policing procurement was made clear in 2006 when Prime Minister Stephen Harper committed to creating a new procurement ombudsman position under the Federal Accountability Act tasked with reviewing and investigating complaints about federal contracts, all the while excluding the Senate, the House of Commons, and CSIS from its remit. Whereas the exemption of the former two was justified on the ground that they had "special legal status," the exemption of CSIS was justified on the ground that "knowledge of their procurement could compromise their operations" (Naumetz, 2008). The deeply secretive nature of high policing procurement makes it exceptionally difficult to gain insight into the particulars of the government's contracts with private entities.

CSIS and CSEC do not publicly disclose the names of companies from which they procure goods and services. The RCMP does not disclose the names of companies with which it deals on matters related to national security. The federal government's online contract portal contains no information on national security contracts. As a CSIS procurement official explained in a public hearing, CSIS procurement information "isn't available anywhere online, because we don't publicly share any information about our business" (House of Commons, 2017). Lists of vendors and private partners associated with CSIS are maintained on a classified "in-house" database accessible only to those on a need-to-know basis with the necessary security clearance. High policing procurements made by CSEC and the RCMP are accessible on the same basis.

The procurement activities of high policing agents in Canada are excluded from disclosure, competition, and other formal rules by way of national security exceptions (NSEs). Whereas all transactions conducted by CSIS and CSEC are protected by default by these exceptions, the RCMP must opt to apply them given its hybrid structure and mandate (i.e., not everything that it procures is related to high policing). When an NSE is invoked by the federal government, the procuring department is allowed to circumvent normal rules mandating competitive bidding and exclude itself from one or more international trade agreements. It can secretly pick preferred bidders for a high policing good or service. Federal high policing agencies that procure goods and services under NSEs also do not have to justify publicly any of their actions, including the decision to invoke an NSE.

In 2017, in response to a series of controversies surrounding NSEs in Canada, several MPs called for a review of the process (Crawford, 2017a). Although limited, the review did provide some valuable insight into how high policing agencies in Canada conceive of and justify the NSE process. As Karen Robertson, a CSIS procurement official, explained to the MPs, "we invoke [an] NSE on every transaction, so there's no discretion applied" (House of Commons, 2017). Robertson cited two reasons for doing so. First, an NSE conceals knowledge of private relationships and privately procured equipment from its targets, which if made aware of "the equipment we procure and our technological capabilities ... could defeat or counter our investigative efforts" (House of Commons, 2017). The same logic, Robertson suggested, could explain why every transaction needs to be granted an NSE, no matter how ostensibly benign the actual good or service procured. As Robertson went on to explain,

> knowledge of CSIS' procurement needs, even of seemingly innocuous contracts, may enable hostile actors to better understand our existing capabilities and resources. This is due to the potential mosaic effect of aggregating publicly released information about our procurement requirements, costs, and practices. As such, protecting how CSIS purchases goods and services matters just as much as protecting what we procure. Revealing any link to CSIS in a public tender may reveal our operational techniques, jeopardize our operations, and endanger employee safety. It could also risk the reputation and safety of those entities that supply us with goods and services. (House of Commons, 2017)

National security exceptions, it is claimed, protect both CSIS and the private companies with which it works from outside scrutiny. Especially noteworthy in this passage is the mention of *reputation*, implying that NSEs are not just about safety and security but also about the protection of private business interests. Second, Robertson made claims about the importance of secrecy in ensuring flexibility. NSEs give CSIS greater "flexibility to define the requirements for a particular contract or vendor in light of our operational considerations and awareness of the threat environment" (House of Commons, 2017). By linking security with flexibility, the secretive and potentially non-competitive nature of high policing contracting appears to be justified.

There are two additional federal agencies in Canada responsible for high policing–related procurement: Shared Services Canada (SSC) and Public Services and Procurement Canada (PSPC). SSC and PSPC are similarly authorized to invoke national security exceptions. These two agencies are authorized to procure goods and services for the RCMP, CSIS, and CSEC in addition to those agencies' own in-house procurement capabilities. In 2012, Shared Services Canada received blanket approval, called an "omnibus NSE," to apply NSEs to the purchase of all "goods and services related to the Government of Canada's email, networks and telecommunications, and data centre infrastructure, systems and services."[2] Internal documents disclosed under the federal Access to Information Act reveal that SSC consulted with senior officials at CSIS, CSEC, PSPC, the Department of National Defence, the Treasury Board, and the Privy Council Office before requesting this omnibus NSE. Each of the consulted parties agreed, showing if nothing else just how ingrained the secrecy-first attitude is in Canada's high policing field.

When reading about national security exceptions on the federal government's webpages, one gets the impression that high policing agents and their clients are encouraged to use them. Indeed, to make NSEs easy to obtain, the government provides clients with a simple fill-in-the-blanks request letter template (Public Works and Government Services Canada, 2018). In the letter, a bidding party seeking to obtain an NSE needs to explain how the procurement relates to "Canada's 'national security interests' or, pursuant to Canada's international obligations, 'the maintenance of international peace and security'" (Public Works and Government Services Canada, 2012). From reading this template and the accompanying instructions, one does not get the impression that applying for an NSE is a difficult or arduous process.

There has been concern about the lack of transparency and accountability in Canada's high policing procurement process. Setting off the MPs' inquiry into national security exceptions noted above, the abuse of NSEs by the federal government briefly became the subject of media and political attention in Canada in 2017. After failing to win a large IT contract with Environment Canada, the California-based company HP (previously Hewlett-Packard) brought allegations against the procuring agency, Shared Services Canada, in the Canadian International Trade Tribunal (CITT) (Crawford, 2016). HP alleged that SSC had inappropriately invoked an NSE to disqualify it from bidding on the contract, valued at $430 million, later secretly awarded to IBM Canada. In March 2017, the tribunal issued its written determination, siding with HP (Crawford, 2017b). In response to SSC's argument that the tribunal did not have jurisdiction to review the use of NSEs, and that SSC did not have to provide a "plausible reason" for invoking an NSE, the CITT disagreed, concluding that "SSC, in effect, treats the NSE as a general license to void potential suppliers' right to seek review of government procurement actions" (*Hewlett-Packard (Canada) Co v Shared Services Canada*, 2017).

Despite the tribunal's decision in this case, little has been done to improve the transparency and accountability of the NSE process. In fact, the federal government has moved in the inverse direction. Legislative changes now make it impossible for bidding companies to challenge NSEs in the CITT (Chase & Fife, 2019). The Canadian government has amended the tribunal's governing regulations forcing the automatic "dismissal of a complaint in respect of which a national security exception ... has been properly invoked by the relevant government institution" (Government of Canada, 2019). In this context, "properly invoked" has nothing to do with articulating sufficient justification to the public, bidding companies, or other stakeholders. We are simply to assume that, when an NSE is invoked, the reasons provided are necessary and sufficient. What matters is that the correct federal authority has signed and approved the application prior to the day that the contract is awarded (Government of Canada, 2019).

Prior to these changes, there was no default provision forcing the CITT to dismiss a complaint based upon the mere presence of a national security exception. Now companies that seek to challenge an NSE-protected transaction in Canada have to resort to the courts, which will cost far more and, compared with a CITT hearing, create no obligation for the government to halt the contract during the proceeding (Chase & Fife, 2019). Perhaps until there is a major court challenge, the NSE process, like much of high policing, will remain secretive. Despite calls for greater transparency and accountability in high policing procurement, little has been done to resolve the matter. The government has done very little to inform the public about how procurement works in the context of national security exceptions. Even basic public statistics on how many times NSEs are invoked are nowhere to be found. The independent accountability units for CSIS, CSEC, and the RCMP, which I turn to next, have also not once acknowledged the issues that could stem from this high level of secrecy and lack of accountability in procurement activities.

Accountability Mechanisms
CSIS is overseen by the Security Intelligence Review Committee (SIRC), CSEC by the Office of the Communications Security Establishment Commissioner (OCSEC), and the RCMP by the Civilian Review and Complaints Commission (CRCC). These three federal agencies regularly conduct reviews of and publish annual reports and other commentaries on the activities of CSIS, CSEC, and the RCMP. I was only able to find material related to high policing pluralization in several of the annual reports from SIRC and OCSEC. I also looked at the results of performance audits carried out by the Office of the Auditor General of Canada (OAGC) since there is a chance that they could probe matters of high policing in Canada under the Auditor General Act. I identified two OAGC reports relevant to high policing pluralization. Ultimately, these reports reveal little. Still, they are worth showcasing, if only to demonstrate that a crucial issue that we might expect to be discussed by accountability agents is in fact hardly acknowledged at all.

The Security Intelligence Review Committee first commented on increasing cooperation between CSIS and private entities (outside SIRC's jurisdictional powers) in 2003. In its report that year, the committee noted that CSIS had "reorganized its operational structure and began to deploy resources in *novel ways*" (Security Intelligence Review Committee, 2003, p. viii; emphasis added). The committee cited two sample initiatives: the Chemical, Biological, Radiological-Nuclear Research Technology Initiative, a multi-year public-private partnership initiative aimed at advancing Canada's preparedness for consequential chemical, biological, or radiological-nuclear events, and the RCMP's Integrated National Enforcement Teams, a regionally based network policing initiative involving a mix of state and private actors (Royal Canadian Mounted Police, 2014). CSIS, the committee went on to explain in its report, was in the process of intensifying its interagency cooperation, "both with old partners in new ways and with entirely new entities" (Security Intelligence Review Committee, 2003, p. viii). As a course of action, SIRC stated that the best it could do in this emergent context was to keep a vigilant watch. As CSIS "expands its operational relationships with organizations not subject to the Committee's review, the

Committee will remain alert to the compliance issues this and other such novel arrangements might raise" (SIRC, 2003, p. ix). Exactly how SIRC was to do this was left unclear.

Cooperation between CSIS and private actors, referred to as "nontraditional partners," was again highlighted by SIRC in its annual report in 2011: "Traditionally, CSIS's relationships were with domestic and foreign partners in the public sector, such as domestic police services, other Canadian government departments and agencies, or governments or institutions of foreign states. Today, the Service is also reaching out to nontraditional partners, such as the private sector" (p. 13). Unfortunately, the committee had little to say about the nature of budding relations between CSIS and the private sector, referring only tersely to public-private information-sharing arrangements and the potential "investigative value" (Security Intelligence Review Committee, 2015, p. 15) that public-private partnerships can bring to high policing. SIRC also noted actions taken to give more private sector employees security clearances to "allow for more meaningful exchanges on issues relating to national security threats" (2015, p. 15). It was recommended that CSIS articulate to its regional offices a "service-wide strategy on managing its relations with the private sector," a recommendation that CSIS reported it met in the form of a directional statement from upper management (Security Intelligence Review Committee, 2012, p. 10).

Turning to the annual reports of OCSEC, the office that oversees the activities of CSEC, one finds even less meaningful insight into the extent of pluralization. The vast majority of these annual reports deal with the issue of CSEC's interception of private communications, a concern that became especially prominent in the wake of Snowden's revelations in 2013 (Leman-Langlois, 2018). Indeed, the only CSEC initiative relevant to high policing pluralization discussed was the Information Technology Security (ITS) program, which had a mandate "to protect government communications and communications systems"; as the office reflected on this program, "to respond to a significantly expanded client base and greater demand for its services, the ITS program has actively sought cooperative partnerships and alliances with government and private sector organizations" (Office of the Communications Security Establishment Commissioner, 2003, p. 8). Again, this was not a very informative revelation.

Finally, I identified two performance audits conducted by the OAGC of "security in contracting" in 2007 and 2013. As noted in the 2007 report, the government frequently contracts with private sector individuals and organizations who can provide expertise or economies of scale not found in government. Such contracting helps the government to deliver its programs and services effectively and efficiently and to meet its objectives. In many cases, the federal government has to entrust protected or classified information and assets to a contractor so that the contracted work can be completed.

The goal of the 2007 audit and 2013 follow-up review was to assess the extent to which contracting federal agencies – including CSIS, CSEC, and the RCMP – were abiding by the correct policies and procedures in protecting the "sensitive information and assets entrusted to industry" in these arrangements (Office of the Auditor General of Canada, 2007). In the 2013 report, the OAGC reviewed eighty-six private sector contracts held by CSIS, sixty by CSEC, and forty-two by the RCMP, though unfortunately it did not state what percentage of total contracts these numbers made up. The nature of the contracts was also not described anywhere in the 2007 and 2013 reports. One thing the OAGC did make clear in its audit reports, however, is that these agencies are failing to safeguard information sufficiently in these public-private relationships. Identifying a number of "serious weaknesses" in its 2007 audit, in its 2013 report the OAGC found that little had changed five years down the road: "Overall, progress has been unsatisfactory in implementing the commitments made in response to our 2007 recommendations." Beyond what is disclosed in these reports, one finds very little additional detail about the nature and extent of high policing pluralization in the context of accountability. The relatively safe and seemingly co-opted nature of high policing accountability mechanisms keeps them from advancing a narrative that could be construed as too hostile or adversarial (see Brodeur, 1983; Leman-Langlois, 2018). Their modus operandi seems to be to direct attention away from potential controversy rather than toward it. Still, the occasional high policing controversy does arise in the public sphere, as I discuss next.

Public Controversies

As Best and Walters (2013) argue, public controversies present researchers with a valuable window into and means of studying issues of national security secrecy. In the United States, investigative journalists have done a great deal of the leg work necessary to bring to light the extent of high policing pluralization (see, e.g., Shorrock, 2008). In my searches of news articles, blogs, and other online sources for high policing pluralization controversies in Canada, I found only one notable case. The controversial incident concerned a public-private partnership in the building of CSEC's new headquarters in Ottawa in 2011.

Construction of the new facility, valued at $1.2 billion (Weston, 2013), started in 2011 and was completed in 2015. Controversy broke out in January 2011 when CSEC announced that it would be outsourcing ninety-one jobs at the agency to Plenary Group, the company responsible for designing, financing, and building the facility. Plenary Group is a private Australian consortium specializing in the financing, development, and management of public infrastructure through public-private partnerships. At the time of writing, Plenary Group claimed to have a portfolio of forty-seven public-private partnership projects valued at over $33 billion in the United States, Canada, and Australia (Plenary Group, 2019). The jobs were to include security guards, IT support staff, and various other facilities-management positions, jobs that Plenary Group would be responsible for staffing for thirty years (Freeze, 2011). According to the Union of National Defence Employees (UNDE, 2011a), the component of the Public Service Alliance of Canada that represents employees of CSEC, this public-private partnership arrangement, in which a private company designs, finances, builds, and maintains a government facility, was the first of its kind in Canada.

With the announcement to outsource ninety-one jobs to Plenary Group, the UNDE launched an extensive anti-outsourcing campaign. Although ultimately the campaign was unsuccessful, it nonetheless offers an illuminating glimpse of issues of high policing pluralization in Canada. The campaign consisted of a now-defunct website (www.securityforsale.ca) to which Canadians were directed by paid advertisements on Google (Freeze, 2011).[3] The UNDE purchased Google AdWords to target the ad to anyone who searched the names of the political figures supporting CSEC's decision. It purchased newspaper and radio ads. It also ran an internal campaign that consisted of handing out lanyards to CSEC employees branded with "an unlocked lock emblazoned with a Canadian maple leaf" (UNDE, 2011a).

In a briefing note made available on the campaign website, the UNDE (2011a) articulated six reasons that it was opposed to the outsourcing of ninety-one jobs at CSEC. First, it expressed concerns about cost. Citing the private construction of a military facility in North Bay, Ontario, as a "cautionary case," the UNDE highlighted the unanticipated costs that can come from outsourcing work to private companies. Second, the UNDE pointed to the heightened potential for foreign influence when work is outsourced to non–public sector employees. Here the emphasis was on the assumed motivations, trustworthiness, and loyalties of private sector employees, depicted as being profit motivated, less trustworthy, and loyal to their employer rather than the state. As the UNDE briefing note puts it, "a private contractor has overall profit as the base-motivation for completing the required work; it can be assumed the hiring procedures will be less stringent and the loyalty of the individuals being hired will be to their private employer and not the Government of Canada. They will not swear a public service oath." Because of these assumed attributes of private sector employees, the UNDE suggested that they would be at greater risk of being compromised, rendering Canada's national security more susceptible to foreign influence. Third, outsourcing the jobs would place the whole of the CSEC infrastructure, a complex interconnected system, at greater risk. Even though the ninety-one jobs could be perceived as low level, the work of these employees in fact would be crucial to CSEC's higher-level operations. Work such as pulling cables through walls, moving offices, and managing parking might seem to be trivial but is vital in "ensuring that core systems of CSE are maintained, operating at peak efficiency, and most importantly, secure." Fourth, the UNDE made arguments about impacts on worker productivity. Different security clearances for these outsourced employees would mean that, each time they accessed a secure area to do work, everything would need to be covered up, systems powered down, and work temporarily ceased. This was already the case, the UNDE argued, for outsourced cleaning crews and would be no different for the ninety-one "maintenance" jobs. Fifth, it was suggested that, by allowing these private employees to take public sector jobs, CSEC could be at risk of losing access to foreign intelligence from Five Eyes and other intelligence partners who become concerned about CSEC based upon the "perceived or real security breaches" that private contractors amplify and create. And sixth, the UNDE underscored that private employees would have "unfettered access" to a number of secure areas within the CSEC headquarters and that tracking their activities in these areas would be difficult. As the UNDE put it, "overall the culture of CSE relies on an understanding that all within the facility have undergone the same rigorous security screening. Unlike the majority of CSE workers, contractors would not undergo psychological evaluations or polygraph tests." The implication, of course, is that private contractors, apparently less trustworthy, could be up to no good in a secure area of the building, and CSEC would not learn about this until it was too late.

Of these six reasons, the most strongly emphasized and most prominent in the UNDE's engagement with the media and in its public ads was the concern about security. On the securityforsale.ca webpage, the UNDE posted a video of an anonymous CSEC employee, filmed in silhouette, who argued that the outsourcing of the ninety-one positions put Canada's national security at stake. As the silhouetted employee says at one point in the video, "where are our assurances that these people will have the same loyalties?" The first question on the FAQ section of securityforsale.ca was "why does this website exist?" The answer was to "prevent potentially debilitating flaws" in CSEC's plan to build a new headquarters, notably the outsourcing of the ninety-one jobs to private contractors. As the UNDE went on to reason, one does not see headlines about the lack of terrorist attacks, because CSEC cannot take credit for its successes. It requires secrecy to protect its methods, sources, and know-how. Letting private contractors into CSEC risks undermining this essential secrecy: "Canada's national security workers are concerned about precisely this problem [of leaks] when non-public services staff are permitted inside the most secure facility in Ottawa" (UNDE, 2011b).

Such concerns are by no means unique to the Canadian context. Since the Snowden revelations, animosity toward private contractors, perceived as inherently less trustworthy, has become a recurring theme in discussions about the sanctity of high policing operations in both the United States and Canada. Such concerns have pushed some outside commentators, including non-profit organizations tied to the high policing field, to pursue efforts at (re)legitimating the place of private actors in national security. In Canada, the absence of a major institution such as the Intelligence and National Security Alliance, a non-profit organization dedicated to defending high policing pluralization in the United States, has played a significant part in enabling claims such as those of the UNDE to go unchallenged. I discuss next this absence of a strong pro-pluralization non-profit organization in Canada.

The Non-Profit Sector

In the United States, one non-profit organization in particular plays a massive role in catalyzing public-private relations in high policing. This is the Intelligence and National Security Alliance (INSA), founded in 1979. Its core mission is to provide "a nonpartisan forum for collaboration among the public, private, and academic sectors of the intelligence and national security communities that bring together committed experts in and out of government to identify, develop, and promote practical and creative solutions to national security problems" (INSA, 2019). It boasts more than 160 corporate partners on its website that it seeks to bring into contact with the extensive high policing community in the United States through annual conferences and ad hoc networking and training events (some of which require security clearance). The alliance also regularly puts out op-eds and publications on matters relevant to high policing pluralization. My research confirms that, as of yet, Canada does not have an institutional equivalent of INSA. After attending its annual conference in 2018, I can also say that Canadian high policing agencies do not appear to have much, if any, involvement with INSA.[4]

Nevertheless, there has been some engagement from the non-profit sector on matters of high policing pluralization in Canada, in particular from the Conference Board of Canada (CBoC). The CBoC is a non-profit think tank that conducts research and hosts meetings and conferences on a range of issues related to economics, industry performance, and public policy. Similar to INSA, it aims to operate at the intersection of the "private, public and social realms" (CBoC, 2019). In 2013, the CBoC was awarded a grant by Public Safety Canada to investigate why the private sector did not more fully participate in Canadian high policing efforts. Ultimately, the CBoC was in favour of high policing pluralization. As Hoganson (2014, p. 13), the author of its report argued, the private sector should be viewed not only as a resource in the fight against terrorism but also as a "catalyst for new approaches by providing new insights and access to technological innovations for combatting terrorism." The private sector, Hoganson stressed, excels at research and development, and, even though many of the technologies that it creates are not designed specifically for high policing, they could be adapted easily for this function: "New developments (e.g., surveillance technology, biometric techniques, explosives detection equipment, sophisticated computer security measures, interoperable communication systems) can be leveraged to improve public sector counter-terrorism efforts, and thus can contribute to the process of enhancing security and preventing terrorist attacks" (p. 19). The major strength of the private sector to act as a catalyst in this way is its ability "rapidly and constantly [to] adapt to an evolving security environment" (p. 19), in contrast to the public sector, viewed as slow moving and static.

Discussion and Conclusion

In this chapter, I have examined issues of high policing pluralization in Canada. In search of evidence of pluralization, I have looked to four likely places: procurement arrangements, accountability mechanisms, public controversies, and the non-profit sector. From each of these four focal areas, we have learned something about the role of private actors in high policing, though not nearly enough to make a rigorous assessment of the degree to which pluralization is reshaping high policing in Canada. From the available evidence, effectively kept thin because of the high level of secrecy in high policing programs in Canada, we also do not get a sense of how pluralization might be occurring and learn little about what the actual public-private arrangements look like in practice. Private entities play a role in Canada's high policing apparatus, but what role exactly remains a mystery. To conclude this chapter, I reflect on four of the broader implications of my findings for literature on high policing pluralization and point to some avenues for future research.

First, the role of private actors in high policing in Canada appears to be exceptionally secretive, especially regarding procurement. Extensive secrecy surrounding procurement and contracting expenditures in Canada acts as a major barrier to assessing the extent to which private actors are involved in the provision of national security, even at a high level of generality. In the United States, similar declines in government openness have been documented (Crampton et al., 2014, p. 209), though in general the procurement system appears to be more open. The lack of a strong investigative journalism tradition in Canada, especially regarding issues of national security, adds to the overall lack of visibility of public-private arrangements in high policing. In the United States, the most insightful analysis, in the only major book-length project on the subject, comes from Tim Shorrock (2008), an investigative journalist. The deep digging and investigative work that he conducted for *Spies for Hire* are the source of much of the existing evidence base for high policing pluralization in the United States. As Brodeur (1983, p. 510) theorized in his first major intervention on high policing, Canada's news media play a central role in upholding the more "secretive aspects of high policing" through their limited engagement and penchant for sensationalism. At least in relation to high policing pluralization, this negative characterization of news media appears to be less true in the United States than in Canada, where investigative journalism is much rarer. More research is needed on the secrecy of high policing pluralization in Canada, particularly in comparison with that of the United States. We need more critical discussion on the justifications for this secrecy and whether transparency would have the kind of damaging effect on national security that high policing professionals say it would. At the moment, the pluralization of high policing in Canada may very well be pushing forward, albeit with little to no democratic debate or consensus in outside publics.

Second, the lack of engagement from federal accountability agencies with issues of high policing pluralization is troubling. SIRC and OCSEC, the accountability agencies of CSIS and CSEC, respectively, have explicitly acknowledged the increasing role of private entities in these agencies' operations. Yet both accountability bodies seem to be reluctant (perhaps unable) to scrutinize these arrangements, let alone call them into question. The few lines that have appeared in their annual reports are far from sufficient. If pluralization, as SIRC claims, is one of the major changes affecting the organization of high policing in Canada, then we should expect to see more commentary on it, particularly given the many implications of pluralization for people's rights, privacy, and trust in the legitimacy of government. Private entities are also, as SIRC points out, outside its jurisdiction. The same is true of OCSEC and the CRCC; they do not have jurisdiction over the private entities with which CSEC and the RCMP cooperate. This is a chief concern about potentially detrimental impacts on the state of high policing accountability in Canada that these agencies ought to do more to address publicly.

Third, public controversy surrounding CSEC's public-private construction and facility maintenance contract points to a potentially significant source of variation in the pluralization of Canadian and American high policing. The central claims maker in the construction controversy was the public sector union, the Public Service Alliance of Canada. In Canada, two of its three major high policing agencies, CSIS and CSEC, are represented by this union. In the United States, in contrast, its three major intelligence agencies – the Federal Bureau of Investigation, Central Intelligence Agency, and National Security Agency – are denied collective bargaining rights under the Federal Service Labor-Management Relations Statute (Slater, 2003, p. 306). If the actions of the Public Service Alliance of Canada in relation to the outsourcing of ninety-one jobs at CSEC are indicative of larger trends, then unionization might be acting as a constraint in the expansion of pluralization efforts in high policing in Canada. Although the ninety-one jobs were still outsourced, the backlash and publicity were indeed significant and in this respect might continue to play a role in shaping future efforts to pluralize high policing in Canada. The comparative role of unions in high policing pluralization deserves greater attention in the literature. This might be a vital source of difference both internationally, as between Canada and the United States, and institutionally, in light of the fact that the RCMP only recently acquired the right to union representation (CBC News, 2019).

And fourth, the absence of a non-profit sector association such as the Intelligence and National Security Alliance in Canada, I suggest, is another valuable point of difference worth exploring in future research on high policing pluralization. The report from the Conference Board of Canada is indicative of a private sector that is interested in "the business of national security" but only in the early stages of organizing compared with its private sector counterparts in the United States. INSA has become a major player in the push for pluralization in the American high policing field through its conferences, training sessions, research publications, op-eds, and regular news media interventions. In Canada, a powerful, catalyzing agent such as INSA has not yet materialized but might in the years to come.

Notes

1 As a fifth, I also scoured national security budgets but to no avail. The detailed breakdowns of Canada's high policing budgets, like those of most countries, are classified.
2 ATI Request A2017-00205, Shared Services Canada.
3 The partial contents of the website, including the briefing note discussed below, are available via the Internet Archive's Wayback Machine, https://web.archive.org/web/20110310010246/http://securityforsale.ca/.
4 It is not unusual for Canadian policing agencies to become involved in American-based professional associations when no equivalent is available in Canada (see, e.g., discussions in Sanders & Condon, 2017). This does not appear, however, to be the case with INSA, for reasons that I will not explore here.

References

Bauman, Z., Bigo, D., Esteves, P., Guild, E., Jabri, V., Lyon, D., & Walker, R. B. (2014). After Snowden: Rethinking the impact of surveillance. *International Political Sociology, 8*(2), 121–144.

Bean, H. (2015). Privatizing intelligence. In R. Abrahamsen & A. Leander (Eds.), *Routledge handbook of private security studies* (pp. 79–88). Routledge.

Best, J., & Walters, W. (2013). Translating the sociology of translation. *International Political Sociology, 7*(3), 345–349.

Brodeur, J.-P. (1983). High policing and low policing: Remarks about the policing of political activities. *Social Problems, 30*(5), 507–520.

Brodeur, J.-P. (2007). High and low policing in post-9/11 times. *Policing: A Journal of Policy and Practice, 1*(1), 25–37.

Brodeur, J.-P. (2010). *The policing web.* Oxford University Press.

Brodeur, J.-P., & Leman-Langlois, S. (2006). Surveillance fiction or higher policing. In K. Haggerty & R. Ericson (Eds.), *The new politics of surveillance and visibility* (pp. 171–198). University of Toronto Press.

Burcher, M., & Whelan, C. (2019). Intelligence-led policing in practice: Reflections from intelligence analysts. *Police Quarterly, 22*(2), 139–160.

CBC News. (2019). National Police Foundation wins right to represent Mounties in collective bargaining. https://www.cbc.ca/news/politics/national-police-federation-union-rcmp-mounties-1.5210796

Chase, S., & Fife, R. (2019, June 24). Ottawa makes it harder for bidders to challenge national security exceptions. *The Globe and Mail.* https://www.theglobeandmail.com/politics/article-procurement-rules-rewritten-to-give-ottawa-power-to-invoke-national/

Chesterman, S. (2008). "We can't spy ... if we can't buy!" The privatization of intelligence and the limits of outsourcing inherently governmental functions. *European Journal of International Law, 19*(5), 1055–1074.

Churchill, W. (2004). From the Pinkertons to the PATRIOT Act: The trajectory of political policing in the United States 1870 to the present. *CR: The New Centennial Review, 4*(1), 1–72.

Conference Board of Canada (CBoC). (2019). About us. https://www.conferenceboard.ca/about-cboc/default.aspx

Crampton, J. W., Roberts, S. M., & Poorthuis, A. (2014). The new political economy of geographical intelligence. *Annals of the Association of American Geographers, 104*(1), 196–214.

Crawford, A. (2016, December 12). Trade tribunal looking into weather supercomputer contract. *CBC News.* https://www.cbc.ca/news/politics/supercomputer-trade-tribunal-security-shared-services-1.3886265

Crawford, A. (2017a, February 23). MPs investigate use of national security exceptions in federal procurement. *CBC News.* https://www.cbc.ca/news/politics/national-security-exceptions-contracts-procurement-1.3996229

Crawford, A. (2017b, April 21). Trade tribunal slams federal government on use of national security exceptions. *CBC News.* https://www.cbc.ca/news/politics/shared-services-canada-citt-procurement-trade-1.4078478

Doob, A. N., & Webster, C. M. (2006). Countering punitiveness: Understanding stability in Canada's imprisonment rate. *Law and Society Review, 40*(2), 325–368.

Fitzgibbon, W., & Lea, J. (2018). Privatization and coercion: The question of legitimacy. *Theoretical Criminology, 22*(4), 545–562.

Freeze, C. (2011, May 3). Union accuses senior Tories of selling out national security. *The Globe and Mail.* https://www.theglobeandmail.com/news/politics/ottawa-notebook/union-accuses-senior-tories-of-selling-out-national-security/article610862/

Government of Canada. (2019). *Canadian International Trade Tribunal Procurement Inquiry Regulations.* SOR/93–602.

Gusterson, H. (1997). Studying up revisited. *PoLAR: Political and Legal Anthropology Review, 20*(1), 114–119.

Hansen, M. (2014). Intelligence contracting: On the motivations, interests, and capabilities of core personnel contractors in the US intelligence community. *Intelligence and National Security, 29*(1), 58–81.

Hewlett-Packard (Canada) Co v Shared Services Canada. (2017, March 20). Canadian International Trade Tribunal.

Hoganson, C. (2014). *Bridging the gaps: Voices from the private sector on counter-terrorism*. Conference Board of Canada. https://www.conferenceboard.ca/(X(1)S(soo1rmftpp120x1pt4quyx11))/e-Library/abstract.aspx?did=6112

Hoogenboom, B. (2006). Grey intelligence. *Crime, Law and Social Change, 45*(4), 373–381.

House of Commons. (2017). *Standing Committee on Government Operations and Estimates*. Parliament of Canada. https://www.ourcommons.ca/DocumentViewer/en/42-1/OGGO/meeting-73/evidence

Intelligence and National Security Alliance (INSA). (2019). Who we are. https://www.insaonline.org/about/

Jamieson, R., & McEvoy, K. (2005). State crime by proxy and juridical othering. *British Journal of Criminology, 45*(4), 504–527.

Jouet, M. (2017). *Exceptional America*. University of California Press.

Keefe, P. R. (2010). Privatized spying: The emerging intelligence industry. In L. Johnson (Ed.), *The Oxford handbook of national security intelligence* (pp. 296–309). Oxford University Press.

Leman-Langlois, S. (2018). State mass spying as illegalism. *Critical Criminology, 26*(4), 545–561.

Loader, I. (2000). Plural policing and democratic governance. *Social and Legal Studies, 9*(3), 323–345.

Loftus, B., & Goold, B. (2012). Covert surveillance and the invisibilities of policing. *Criminology and Criminal Justice, 12*(3), 275–288.

Luscombe, A., & Walby, K. (2015). High policing and access to information. *Police Practice and Research, 16*(6), 485–498.

Marx, G. T. (1987). The interweaving of public and private police undercover work. In C. D. Shearing & P. C. Stenning (Eds.), *Private policing* (pp. 172–193). SAGE.

Monaghan, J., & Walby, K. (2012a). Making up "terror identities": Security intelligence, Canada's Integrated Threat Assessment Centre and social movement suppression. *Policing and Society, 22*(2), 133–151.

Monaghan, J., & Walby, K. (2012b). "They attacked the city": Security intelligence, the sociology of protest policing and the anarchist threat at the 2010 Toronto G20 summit. *Current Sociology, 60*(5), 653–671.

Naumetz, T. (2008, May 19). Parliament, CSIS exempt from contracts scrutiny. *Toronto Star*. https://www.thestar.com/news/canada/2008/05/19/parliament_csis_exempt_from_contracts_scrutiny.html

Office of the Auditor General of Canada (OAGC). (2007). *2007 October report of the Auditor General of Canada*. http://www.oag-bvg.gc.ca/internet/English/parl_oag_200710_01_e_23825.html

Office of the Auditor General of Canada (OAGC). (2013). *2013 spring report of the Auditor General of Canada.* http://www.oag-bvg.gc.ca/internet/English/parl_oag_201304_02_e_38187.html

Office of the Communications Security Establishment Commissioner (OCSEC). (2003). *2002–2003 annual report.* https://www.ocsec-bccst.gc.ca/s21/s46/s8/eng/2002-2003-annual-report

O'Reilly, C. (2015). The pluralization of high policing: Convergence and divergence at the public-private interface. *British Journal of Criminology, 55*(4), 688–710.

O'Reilly, C., & Ellison, G. (2005). "Eye spy private high": Re-conceptualizing high policing theory. *British Journal of Criminology, 46*(4), 641–660.

Plenary Group. (2019). About. https://plenarygroup.com/about

Public Works and Government Services Canada (PWGSC). (2012). 3.105. National security exceptions. https://buyandsell.gc.ca/policy-and-guidelines/supply-manual/section/3/105

Public Works and Government Services Canada (PWGSC). (2018). 3.7. Annex: National security exception request letter: Template. https://buyandsell.gc.ca/policy-and-guidelines/supply-manual/section/3/105

Royal Canadian Mounted Police (RCMP). (2014). Integrated national security enforcement teams. http://www.rcmp-grc.gc.ca/secur/insets-eisn-eng.htm

Sanders, C., & Condon, C. (2017). Crime analysis and cognitive effects: The practice of policing through flows of data. *Global Crime, 18*(3), 237–255.

Security Intelligence Review Committee (SIRC). (2003). *Annual report 2002–2003.* http://www.sirc-csars.gc.ca/anrran/2002-2003/index-eng.html

Security Intelligence Review Committee (SIRC). (2011). *SIRC annual report 2010–2011: Checks and balances.* http://www.sirc-csars.gc.ca/anrran/2010-2011/index-eng.html

Security Intelligence Review Committee (SIRC). (2012). *SIRC annual report 2011–2012: Meeting the challenge.* http://www.sirc-csars.gc.ca/anrran/2011-2012/index-eng.html

Security Intelligence Review Committee (SIRC). (2015). *SIRC annual report 2014–2015: Broader horizons: Preparing the groundwork for change in security intelligence review.* http://www.sirc-csars.gc.ca/anrran/2014-2015/index-eng.html

Shearing, C. D., & Stenning, P. C. (1983). Private security: Implications for social control. *Social Problems, 30*(5), 493–506.

Sheptycki, J. (2004). Organizational pathologies in police intelligence systems: Some contributions to the lexicon of intelligence-led policing. *European Journal of Criminology, 1*(3), 307–332.

Shorrock, T. (2008). *Spies for hire: The secret world of intelligence outsourcing.* Simon and Schuster.

Singh, A.-M., & Light, M. (2019). Constraints on the growth of private policing: A comparative international analysis. *Theoretical Criminology, 23*(3), 295–314.

Slater, J. (2003). Homeland security vs. workers' rights: What the federal government should learn from history and experience, and why. *University of Pennsylvania Journal of Labor and Employment Law, 6,* 295–356.

Union of National Defence Employees (UNDE). (2011a). External briefing note: Prepared for stakeholders in the CSE Long Term Accommodation Project. https://web.archive.org/web/20110310010246/http://securityforsale.ca/UNDE-External-Briefing-Note.pdf

Union of National Defence Employees (UNDE). (2011b). FAQ. https://web.archive.org/web/20110118021613/http://securityforsale.ca/faq/

van Buuren, J. (2014). From oversight to undersight: The internationalization of intelligence. *Security and Human Rights, 24*(3–4), 239–252.

Walby, K., & Anaïs, S. (2012). Communications Security Establishment Canada (CSEC), structures of secrecy, and ministerial authorization after September 11. *Canadian Journal of Law and Society, 27*(3), 365–380.

Walters, W., & Luscombe, A. (2019). Postsecrecy and place: Secrecy research amidst the ruins of an atomic weapons research facility. In M. de Goede, E. Bosma, & P. Pallister-Wilkins (Eds.), *Secrecy and methods in security research: A guide to qualitative fieldwork* (pp. 63–78). Routledge.

Weston, G. (2013, October 8). Inside Canada's top-secret billion-dollar spy palace. *CBC News*. https://www.cbc.ca/news/politics/inside-canada-s-top-secret-billion-dollar-spy-palace-1.1930322

Whitaker, R., Kealey, G. S., & Parnaby, A. (2012). *Secret service: Political policing in Canada from the Fenians to Fortress America*. University of Toronto Press.

White, A. (2015). The politics of police "privatization": A multiple streams approach. *Criminology and Criminal Justice, 15*(3), 283–299.

10

The Creeping Privatization of Immigration Detention in Canada

JONA ZYFI and AUDREY MACKLIN

Introduction

In recent decades, the immigration detention landscape has undergone sweeping transformations. Almost every state in the Global North has adopted an immigration detention policy and employs an array of facilities to warehouse immigration detainees. Some states, acting alone or through the European Union, promote and finance immigration detention facilities in the Global South, hoping to contain northward-bound migrants and asylum seekers. Increasingly, under the guise of national security, the Global North is strengthening and expanding immigration policies and practices to deprive asylum seekers and migrants of their human rights and liberties. Described by scholars as both a practice and a policy, detention can occur extraterritorially (as a form of interdiction), at the border, inside the border, or as a prelude to deportation (Arbel, 2016; Brouwer & Kumin, 2003; Nakache, 2011; Pratt, 2005; Rygiel, 2008; Silverman & Massa, 2012; Silverman & Nethery, 2015; United Nations General Assembly, 2017). Immigration detention often partakes of practices and spaces of incarceration and criminalization. But it also performs a function distinctive to migration control: that is, to continue and extend the project of separating the foreigner from the citizen. Thus, immigration detention also serves to maintain the narrative that sovereignty and the authority of the nation-state to control borders, both physical and social, remain intact.

This exclusionary impulse, underwritten by a particular vision of sovereignty, chafes against a range of domestic and international legal and human rights commitments. As underscored by an extensive body of international literature, this tension highlights a number of conceptual and legal issues. Perhaps the most salient is the asymmetry between the entitlement to seek asylum, enshrined in 1948 in the United Nations Universal Declaration of Human Rights, and a state's right to control who can enter and remain within its territory (Atak & Crépeau, 2013; Bloom, 2015; Brouwer & Kumin, 2003; Goodwin-Gill, 1986; Lahav, 2010; Lethbridge, 2017; Nakache, 2011; Silverman & Massa, 2012; Silverman & Nethery, 2015; Rodenhauser, 2014; United Nations General Assembly, 2017). Another anomalous dynamic is also at work here: even as the decision about whom to admit and whom to exclude is presented as a quintessentially public function, the state simultaneously delegates authority over certain immigration functions to private actors in the service of extending its power and asserting more control over migrants with less accountability. This creeping privatization of the apparatus of migration control is at once paradoxical and a predictable expansion of the privatization of government functions (Macklin, 2003; Rygiel, 2008).

In the sphere of asylum and refugee protection, states have long recruited private actors in the service of interdiction and deflection to prevent refugees from reaching their territories to claim protection. These private actors include airlines and maritime carriers, which face sanctions for boarding "improperly documented" travellers, and private contractors tasked with visa management (Bloom, 2013, 2015; United Nations General Assembly, 2017). Private security/paramilitary organizations also facilitate removals and deportations to states too dangerous for immigration officers to escort deportees or where they have no diplomatic presence.

Asylum seekers who manage to run the gauntlet and reach the border face an increasing likelihood of detention in some countries despite its demonstrated ineffectiveness in controlling migration movements and deportations (Ackerman & Furman, 2013; Atak & Crépeau, 2013; Brouwer & Kumin, 2003; Dench & Crépeau, 2003; Silverman & Molnar, 2016; Silverman & Nethery, 2015). Additionally, detention is used against migrants living inside the territory who face removal. Traditionally, the enforcement and management of immigration detention have been core functions of the state. However, states such as Australia, the United Kingdom, and the United States increasingly have utilized for-profit private actors to manage detention centres. In Canada, though explicit privatization in this sector has not been far reaching, the apprehension that the country will enrol in the "migration industrial complex" is not without merit (Doty & Wheatley, 2013; Fernandes, 2007; Flynn & Cannon, 2009; Golash-Boza, 2009; Trujillo-Pagan, 2014; United Nations General Assembly, 2017).

In this chapter, we focus on the encroachment of privatization into migration detention to explore how privatization articulates with practices of criminalization in Canadian immigration policy. This development is sandwiched between longer-standing practices of transferring responsibility (and liability) to private airline carriers for intercepting undocumented migrants on the way in and relying on private security firms and commercial airline carriers to undertake deportation orders on the way out. We address the use of private security firms to supervise and control detainees, the delegation of confinement from federal immigration detention centres to provincial jails, as well as the use of alternatives to detention through non-governmental organizations (NGOs) and private citizens who act as sureties in the community. The former aligns with trends toward privatization and the use of public-private partnerships with security firms (see Luscombe, this volume; Mulone, this volume). The latter is not a true instance of privatization, insofar as provincial jails used to detain migrants are public institutions, but we argue that it is part of an internal reconfiguration of the government's role in migrant detention. We note that the motive and mode of these intergovernmental arrangements are similar to contractual agreements between public and private entities. Additionally, these arrangements operationalize the literal resort to the criminalization of detention by permitting the confinement of migrants in penal institutions designed to punish people convicted of criminal offences. Some scholars note that privatization does not lead necessarily to deregulation but a tilt toward criminalization as a preferred form of regulation (Macklin, 2003). Beyond this, publicly funded programs enrol private citizens as sureties or bondspersons for detainees in the community, and these individuals assume the responsibility of monitoring and surveilling non-citizens released from detention on certain conditions.

Ultimately, we worry that the current socio-political climate regarding migrants and asylum seekers might accelerate the trend toward public-private partnerships and wholly privatized immigration detention centres. Documenting how current practices undermine transparency and public accountability regarding detention, to the detriment of the individuals detained, serves as both a warning and a caution about further privatization.

In the first part of this chapter, we provide a brief history of the criminalization of immigration detention and the rise of the immigration industrial complex. In the second part, we explore the influence of neo-liberal policies and increased reliance on a multiplicity of private entities to perform government tasks. In Canada, the privatization of immigration enforcement has occurred through carrier sanctions and the involvement of private security in detention. We briefly highlight carrier sanctions but focus on the involvement of private security in Canada's immigration detention regime. In the third part, we offer a detailed overview of the detention landscape in Canada, including the extensive use of carceral institutions. In the fourth part, we highlight alternatives to detention implemented as a response to the National Immigration Detention Framework. We conclude by raising the concern that trends of privatization and intergovernmental delegation undermine transparency, accountability, and human rights, in the name of efficiency and cost saving.

The Criminalization of Immigration Detention

The growing privatization of prison facilities over the past three decades, notably in the United States, United Kingdom, Australia, Germany, and South Africa, has been controversial and continues to affect the landscape of criminal justice policy. During the 1980s, the war on drugs generated overcrowding in prisons and skyrocketing costs. Rooted in free-market ideas, some turned for solutions to private entities that dangled the promise of efficiency, quality, and lower cost than public institutions (Enns & Ramirez, 2018; Shearing & Stenning, 1983; Vickers & Yarrow, 1991). Many scholars have exposed the privatization bonus as a chimera (Feeley, 2002; Pratt & Maahs, 1999) and expressed serious ethical concerns about private entities profiting from the incarceration of others (Doty & Wheatley, 2013; Enns & Ramirez, 2018; United Nations General Assembly, 2017).

There is little doubt that momentum driving the expansion of privatization in prisons also influenced the proliferation of similar trends in immigration detention. Indeed, declining crime rates and decarceration can incentivize the companies that profit from imprisonment to shift their energies to migrant detention. Post 9/11, fear-mongering rhetoric and xenophobia, especially against Muslim and racialized minorities, led to a rise in "crimmigration" policies. We mean by this term a blurring of immigration and criminal processes, categories, and technologies (Stumpf, 2006). They include the use of immigration law and policy to achieve ends traditionally reserved for the criminal justice system (e.g., punishment) as well as the deployment of criminal law and penal enforcement against migrants and forms of migration previously managed under administrative regimes.

With respect to detention, a 2017 memo from the Trump administration required the Department of Homeland Security to prepare to house roughly 80,000 immigration detainees each day (Kripa & Mueller, 2017). In 2018, over 60 percent of all detainees in the United States were held in private facilities, including hotels (Ellis & Hicken, 2019). The use of major hotel chains to house families and unaccompanied children taken into custody at the US border increased in 2020 as a response to the emergency border closure policies related to the COVID-19 pandemic (Dickerson, 2020). This practice has resulted in an unregulated shadow system of detention, weakened procedural protections, led to widespread human rights abuses, and expanded immigration detention facilities. These facilities, particularly those entirely privatized, are frequently run like private prisons and often considered "even more secretive and publicly unaccountable than public departments of corrections" (Gottschalk, 2016, p. 231; see also Penovic, 2014).

Deepa Fernandes labels the phenomenon of privatized securitization as the "immigration industrial complex." She describes how post-9/11 "big money is to be made as the government dramatically increases its reliance on the private sector to help carry out its war on terror" (cited in Stribley, 2017, para. 2). Based upon ideas developed in the context of military and penal institutions, the immigration industrial complex is understood as the convergence of public and private interests in the criminalization and enforcement of immigration (Doty & Wheatley, 2013; Fernandes, 2007; Flynn & Cannon, 2009; Golash-Boza, 2009; Hiemstra & Conlon, 2017). Several scholars suggest that insecurities that manifest in racism and xenophobia are responsible for the support of punitive policies and the reorganization and expansion of a system – including detention and deportation – used to keep minorities fragmented, frightened, and subordinate (Alexander, 2012; Enns & Ramirez, 2018; Sniderman et al., 2004). The shift toward privatized incarceration, both in prisons and in detention centres, can be viewed as another way that society "protects the nation" from those deemed undesirable and exploitable (Enns & Ramirez, 2018). As with the previous "complexes," "the creation of an undesirable other creates popular support for government spending to safeguard the nation" (Golash-Boza, 2009, p. 306). Not surprisingly, the United States operates the largest detention regime in the world and has played a central role in its global expansion, especially in the United Kingdom and Australia. The Australian model also makes use of offshore processing centres and detention camps in external territories and foreign states, such as Christmas Island and Papua New Guinea (Rygiel, 2008).

Both governments and corporations benefit enormously from the immigration industrial complex, the rhetoric of fear, and the discourse of *othering*, at the expense of the human rights of migrants and asylum seekers. Abetted by the expanding trend of governing through crime, privatization occurs at national, EU, and global levels in patent and tacit ways. Migration control functions traditionally considered as duties of the state are delegated to private actors (Bloom, 2015; Rygiel, 2008; United Nations General Assembly, 2017). States, including Canada, increasingly turn to private for-profit multinational corporations for the construction, management, and enforcement of immigration detention. In addition to outsourcing prison-like facilities to private companies, the US government in particular utilizes car-rental companies for transportation and deportation and major hotel chains to detain children and families, overseen by MVM, a private security company established by three former Secret Service agents (Dickerson, 2020). Furthermore, states contract private actors to process visa requests, provide security and surveillance technology, offer health and food services (see also MacKenzie, this volume), and assist with the deportation of foreign citizens to potentially dangerous countries. More implicitly, states frequently impose sanctions on airline carriers and bus companies that transport persons without proper documentation; they also develop multilateral agreements with international agencies, financial institutions, and third countries to manage migration flows, support deportations, and facilitate migrant labour pools (Bloom, 2015; CBC, 2019; Lethbridge, 2017).

Although states enjoy wide discretion over those allowed to enter and remain within their territories, international human rights norms and principles constrain practices of detention and deportation. The 1951 Refugee Convention, the 1967 Refugee Protocol, the 1967 International Covenant on Civil and Political Rights, and the 1989 Convention on the Rights of the Child are binding on the states that have ratified them, including Canada. In addition, there are several declarations and rules – such as the 1948 Universal Declaration of Human Rights and the 1988 Body of Principles for the Protection of All Persons under Any Form of Detention or Imprisonment – that while non-binding are considered to have persuasive force. In relation to detention, the crux in international human rights law is that immigration detention should be an exception, not the rule. When used, detention should be justified, its conditions should be humane, and the human rights of detainees should be upheld (Atak & Crépeau, 2013; Nakache, 2011; Silverman, 2014; United Nations Working Group on Arbitrary Detention, 2018). Moreover, in Canada, the Supreme Court decision in *Singh v Minister of*

Employment and Immigration (1985) affirmed that every asylum seeker or refugee on Canadian territory is entitled to claim protection under the Charter of Rights and Freedoms. The charter requires that the person in detention be informed of the reason for it, the right to legal representation, and the right to notify a representative of that person's government. However, unlike detention under criminal law, arrest and detention of foreign nationals can occur without a warrant (Canadian Border Services Agency [CBSA], 2018; Immigration Refugee Protection Act [IRPA], 2001; Nakache, 2011).

The Move toward Privatization in Canada

The increasing outsourcing of incarceration has been heavily influenced by neo-liberal policies. For our purposes here, the capacious term "neo-liberal" describes a set of practices that valorizes the market over the state in service delivery and promotes a vision of the independent, entrepreneurial, and self-sufficient citizen who neither expects nor requires the support of the state. These discourses and practices are driven partly by the wish to reduce costs and improve efficiencies (Arbogast, 2017; Bales, 2019; Feeley, 2002; Hucklesby & Lister, 2018). The rationale is that privatization of public services not only reduces public spending but also improves the quality of those services (Ackerman & Furman, 2013; Flynn & Bauder, 2015; Lacin, 2019; Menz, 2009, 2011; Pratt, 2005). However, the outcome is not necessarily less regulation, for "the state does not withdraw, instead enhancing its activities to serve big business" (Bales, 2019, para. 8). The government involves private actors in its operations – also referred to as load-shedding – without transferring ownership of its core functions (see Luscombe et al., this volume). Governing through crime is not incompatible with this model; indeed, as public programs and public support for impoverished, disadvantaged, and marginalized people diminish, they are replaced with punitive responses to the predictable consequences of vulnerability, neglect, and desperation. The involvement of private actors in the management and enforcement of immigration detention was preceded by their involvement in private prisons, policing, and other social care, fundamentally expanding the reach of government and social control. Thus, the immigration industrial complex is motivated not only by the desire to control migration and maintain power structures that render migrants docile and knowable but also by the resentment of racial and minority populations and the pursuit of profit (Bales, 2019; Enns & Ramirez, 2018; Feeley, 2002; Foucault, 1979, 2004; Rygiel, 2008).

Substantial responsibility related to a host of immigration functions has been transferred gradually to private actors through a hybrid operational model characterized by partnerships or P3s (public-private partnerships), thereby institutionalizing the role of private actors in delivering government services (Murphy, 2007; see Luscombe et al., this volume). Bloom (2015) highlights that a few large companies – such as VFS Global, Steria, WorldBridge, and Gerry's – are responsible for managing fingerprint databases such as EURODAC and some visa management systems in approximately three-quarters of states globally, though their involvement in decision-making processes varies. Once the physical and technical infrastructures are set up in one state, they can swiftly extend their services to other states with efficiency savings. Canada has not been immune to these trends, as made evident by the marked expansion of neo-liberal, market-based approaches to immigration and settlement. For example, Gerry's was conceived to process visa applications for Pakistani nationals in the United Kingdom but is now also responsible for processing Pakistani visas for Canada, France, India, Sweden, and the Netherlands, among other countries (Bloom, 2013, 2015). In 2013, Canada utilized private companies for the visa management of nationals from twenty-two different countries (Bloom, 2013). Flynn and Bauder (2015) point out that the provincial nominee programs and their implementation have increasingly involved private employers and higher-education institutions to assist with immigration selection and settlement. The dramatic increase in the proportion of economic migrants admitted to Canada as temporary foreign workers tied to specific employers, rather than as permanent residents, also reveals the tendency to view newcomers as potentially disposable factors of production in a marketplace, rather than as future citizens of a polity.

In Canada, two examples of the privatization of immigration enforcement stand out: carrier sanctions and the involvement of private actors in the detention and deportation of foreign nationals. Carrier sanctions primarily take the form of fines for airline and shipping companies that bring an undocumented migrant to a state's territory, unless that individual makes a successful refugee claim (Brouwer & Kumin, 2003; Galaski, 2018). In addition to a penalty of up to $3,200, carrier sanctions require airlines to cover all related medical and removal costs for undocumented migrants whom they have transported (Atak & Crépeau, 2013; Bloom, 2015; Brouwer & Kumin, 2003; Rodenhauser, 2014). Canada has made widespread use of such sanctions along with agreements to reduce administrative fees for demonstrated compliance. As of June 2019, the federal government has fifty-six of these agreements with commercial airlines (Keung, 2019). In 2018, a total of 1,860 passengers from Canada's top five source countries were prevented from travelling by airline carriers (Keung, 2019). This number has decreased noticeably since the introduction of the Electronic Travel Authorization program in 2015, which pre-screens visitors from visa-exempt countries. These policies erect less visible but more expansive barriers to entry. They also avoid the diplomatic tensions that accompany the imposition of visitor visas as a means of intercepting potential refugees (Arbel, 2016; Brouwer & Kumin, 2003; Macklin, 2013; Pratt, 2005).

Such sanctions work in tandem with visa regimes and offshore interdictions. To assist airline carriers with this task, the Canadian government currently deploys fifty-one immigration liaison officers abroad (Keung, 2019). However, since their role is confined to providing training and guidance to airline personnel, the latter make the final decision on whether a passenger will be allowed to board. Their role is to screen migrants and control flows of would-be asylum seekers before they reach a state's borders (Arbel, 2016; Atak & Crépeau, 2013; Bloom, 2015; Brouwer & Kumin, 2003). Thus, by pushing the border outward, functionally the responsibility to manage threats has been outsourced to airline personnel. However, unlike embassies, which can take months to make decisions on asylum claims, airline personnel – who do not possess the same expertise – make such decisions in a few minutes at best (Galaski, 2018). As Aiken (1999, p. 6) notes, "vast numbers of bona fide refugees are being caught up in the web of immigration control with devastating results." As private actors, airline officials are not bound by public law norms of fairness or accountability, and in any event their actions take place in other states, making recourse practically impossible.

As noted, states party to the 1951 Refugee Convention are obligated to abide by the *non-refoulement* principle in Article 33(1) of the convention. However, carrier sanctions and airport interdictions inhibit individuals from accessing procedures to seek protection, a prerequisite for the implementation of a state's *non-refoulement* obligation. Since the carrier is responsible for either preventing an undocumented migrant from reaching a state's territory or effectively removing the person, carrier sanctions pre-empt access to the protection of *non-refoulement*. Thus, by outsourcing control of the border, states, including Canada, evade their responsibilities for refugee protection.

Whereas Canada was a pioneer in deputizing private airlines and maritime carriers to interdict potential refugees, the United States, United Kingdom, and Australia surged ahead with contracting private security companies to build, own, and manage detention facilities. A handful of private corporations – namely, Serco, GEO Group, G4S, and Corbel Management Corporation – own and manage the vast majority of private prisons, in addition to offering policing services (Ackerman & Furman, 2013; Bloom, 2015; Doty & Wheatley, 2013; Flynn & Cannon, 2009; Lethbridge, 2017; Menz, 2009; Montgomery & Griffiths, 2015; Stribley, 2017). Indeed, the increasing competition for tenders has resulted in an overall trend toward lower expenditures, which, of course, is the point of the exercise. Coupled with poor training, the shift to a profit-centred model has resulted in a lack of access to fair asylum processes; inappropriate, inadequate, and insensitive service delivery, especially in relation to health care; substandard detention conditions and under-reporting of disturbances; the creation and exploitation of a captive labour force; and a blatant disregard for human rights (Bloom, 2015; Lethbridge, 2017; Penovic, 2014).

Recent scholarship and a report from the European Public Service Union highlight that mistreatment of detainees, deficient health care, unsafe living conditions, and violence have contributed to the deaths of detainees in countries throughout the European Union that rely on private companies for their detention management and deportation (Lacin, 2019; Lethbridge, 2017). Arbogast (2017) also documents overcrowding; detainees are forced to sleep and eat on the floor and have little access to health services. Some companies, such as G4S, confiscate mobile phones and charge detainees for telephone use, significantly impeding communication with families and legal representatives, ultimately hindering their ability to gather necessary documentation for their cases (Arbogast, 2017). Recent research also reveals how the privatized management of detention facilities can intensify violence against detainees, including sexual violence by paid staff (Arbogast, 2017; Lethbridge, 2017; Penovic, 2014).

The profit-seeking incentives to employ violence and to exploit detainees were revealed in Rodier's (2012) interviews with former G4S guards. They disclosed that they were "encouraged to use violence during deportation operations, under the threat of financial penalties" (p. 30). Although detainees are not legally authorized to work, they were frequently "hired" to perform operational tasks such as cooking and cleaning within the detention centres throughout Europe or to perform tasks such as assembling products for sale for the benefit of other organizations. Managing corporations can further reduce costs by paying detainees wages well below the legal minimums that they would be required to pay staff (Arbogast, 2017; Bales, 2019). It is beyond the scope of this chapter to address the agreements between EU member states and states of the Global South (especially Libya) whereby the latter detain migrants heading north. However, conditions in Libyan detention centres are notoriously cruel, inhuman, and degrading and include torture, abuse, killing, and forced labour (Bales, 2019; United Nations General Assembly, 2017).

In Canada, the role of private companies is still relatively limited. Companies are hired through competitive procurement processes to construct facilities, provide security, and manage most day-to-day operational services under the supervision of the Canadian Border Services Agency (CBSA). For example, LEC Engineering Contracting won the $23.1 million tender to construct the Surrey facility (Public Works and Government Services Canada [PWGSC], 2017b). Similarly, Lemay, a Montreal-based firm, won over $5 million in contracts for the Laval immigration holding centre (PWGSC, 2017a).

In the United Kingdom, Australia, and many other states, private security companies have been hired to fulfill policing functions at the border as well as regulatory functions by managing inland and offshore detention centres (Lacin, 2019; Montgomery & Griffiths, 2015). In Canada, the authority to detect, prevent, and detain unauthorized migrants and asylum seekers – with force if necessary – rests with the CBSA. Created in 2003, it is responsible for protecting the integrity of the immigration system and providing border services to support national security. Thus, partnerships with private companies are limited to the management of inland detention facilities under the instruction and guidance of CBSA officers. Canada has only three immigration detention facilities and otherwise makes widespread use of provincial jails to house immigration detainees. Although the CBSA has memorandums of understanding with British Columbia, Alberta, Ontario, and Quebec – and is in the process of negotiating them with other provinces – the conditions of detention for those housed in provincial jails are governed by the Ministry of Correctional Services Act and the policies and procedures of Correctional Services Canada (CBSA, 2021b). This means that, though in the vast majority of cases immigration detainees have not committed criminal offences, they are treated the same as inmates convicted of criminal offences and serving custodial sentences. Those held in detention centres are entirely in the hands of private security firms contracted to manage the facilities on behalf of the CBSA.

For example, the Garda Security Group Inc. was contracted to provide security for the Quebec region for 2019–21, costing a little over $18 million. In Toronto and Vancouver, the CBSA has repeatedly contracted G4S and Commissionaires, among other companies, to provide security, with the most recent 2019–20 G4S contract totalling $15.7 million (Poynter, 2012; PWGSC, 2019). Additionally, since 2003, Corbel Management Corporation has been contracted to manage the immigration holding facility in Toronto. In 2016, the CBSA renewed its contract with Corbel to manage the Toronto facility and support the transportation and relocation of detainees until 2028 for a total cost of $77.8 million (PWGSC, 2018). The Global Detention Project (2021) also reports that, since at least 2012, Serco has been lobbying the federal government on the subject of immigration detention services – or, as its website describes, "citizen services" (Serco, n.d.). *The Guardian* has also reported on a number of other private entities that thus far have been unsuccessful in lobbying the Canadian government for immigration detention and removal services. Finally, it is interesting to note that in 2012 Minister of Immigration and Citizenship Jason Kenney toured a number of Serco-run detention centres in Australia and tweeted that he "learned a lot" (Poynter, 2012).

Little has been written about public-private partnerships in Canadian immigration detention centres. With the exception of the Canadian Red Cross, NGOs as well as academics face challenges in gaining access to these facilities. The division of labour between the CBSA and private security in the daily operation of these facilities remains opaque. To this end, we interviewed Mac Scott, an immigration lawyer with Carranza Law LLP and an advocate for No One Is Illegal who works with immigration detainees and has been involved in several high-profile immigration cases. Scott informed us that immigration holding centres (IHCs) are run by the CBSA to the extent that their officers act as wardens, are responsible for all transfers between IHCs and jails, and conduct interviews with individuals released on bonds. However, all internal day-to-day operations are entirely conducted by licensed private security guards. They are also responsible for conducting background checks and collecting biometrics. Furthermore, CBSA liaison officers are available to provide on-site administrative assistance a few days a week, from 9 a.m. to 5 p.m., at provincial jails or on an as-needed basis.

A common criticism of private prisons and detention centres is the absence of meaningful oversight of and accountability for the use and abuse of power. However, in the case of migrant detention, there has never been any meaningful oversight and accountability of the CBSA, the public enforcement body responsible for immigration detention. It has been almost sixteen years since Justice O'Connor first recommended an independent review body for the CBSA in his Commission of Inquiry into the Actions of Canadian Officials in Relation to Maher Arar, yet despite the vast discretionary powers of the CBSA it continues to operate without genuine oversight. The CBSA, whose officers have been armed since 2007, is the sole federal law enforcement agency that has no dedicated, independent review body mandated to investigate complaints, initiate inquiries, or take disciplinary action. This is in stark contrast to every other significant police agency in Canada, which has some form of review or independent review body (Global Detention Project, 2018; Track & Paterson, 2017). At least sixteen people have died in CBSA custody since 2000 (Molnar & Silverman, 2017), but there is no formal mechanism that requires the CBSA to acknowledge publicly the deaths and no independent oversight body tasked with investigating the role of the CBSA in the events leading to the death of a detained individual.

Currently, if people wish to lodge a complaint against the CBSA, they must fill out an online feedback form with a 1,000-word limit to describe the incident or write to the CBSA Recourse Directorate. With the first option, once the complaint is received, the supervisor discusses it with the officer in question and might begin a review (Track & Paterson, 2017). The latter option is an internal complaint that goes directly to the CBSA president and does not have the ability to initiate a review. Information on what happens next is unavailable, symptomatic of the larger issues of transparency in this process. The 2015 Audit of Professional Standards at the CBSA also revealed that a variety of internal units within the Human Resources Branch and the Comptrollership Branch handle different aspects of CBSA conduct and standards (Track & Paterson, 2017). For example, when an allegation of wrongdoing is made, it is the responsibility of the senior officer for internal disclosure at the Office of Values and Ethics within HR, who also reports to the CBSA president, to determine whether an investigation is warranted. This office also oversees the policy on professional conduct and discipline. The Security and Professional Standards Directorate within Comptrollership oversees the education of officers on professional conduct and integrity, conducts preliminary analyses of misconduct, and performs administrative investigations when an allegation is made. The Liberal government promised to introduce oversight measures as part of its election campaign in 2015, but a legislative attempt in 2019 (Bill C-98) to grant the Public Complaints and Review Commission jurisdiction over the CBSA failed to make it through the parliamentary process (McSorley, 2019). In the absence of public accountability for CBSA misconduct, it follows that private contractors operate without meaningful accountability, least of all by the CBSA. In our interview with Scott, he stated that "there is no accountability mechanisms for these guys. Like the CBSA, you can complain about them, to them, or the person in charge, but little is ever done to hold them accountable. They are their own corporate entity."

The Canadian Red Cross and the United Nations High Commissioner for Refugees (UNHCR) have access to CBSA detention facilities but are not allowed to report any findings publicly (Global Detention Project, 2018; Track & Paterson, 2017). The new National Immigration Detention Framework emphasizes transparency as one of its four pillars. It contains the intention to publicize the Red Cross monitoring reports, but no transparency exists to date. Furthermore, there is no independent complaint and review mechanism within the Canadian government regarding CBSA policies and practices to ensure that it is upholding the rights of non-citizens with whom the agency interacts daily or to investigate negligence or wrongdoing by CBSA officers or private contractors when someone in their custody is harmed or dies. As the Jiménez Inquest concluded, "there is no independent, realistic method for immigrants to bring forward concerns or complaints" (Track & Paterson, 2017, p. 55). Processes within the CBSA are neither independent nor transparent. This lack of accountability understandably undermines public trust in the agency and sustains a culture of secrecy, particularly in relation to detention. Indeed, as the CBSA Code of Conduct emphasizes, when wrongdoing is suspected, the identities of officers are protected, ostensibly to shield them from reprisal (CBSA, 2018d). Even more poignant for the purposes of this chapter is the fact that CBSA contractors, including private security, are not subject to the Code of Conduct but simply asked that "they respect the spirit and intent of its requirements" (CBSA, 2018d).

The 2014 inquest into the death of Mexican national Lucía Vega Jiménez provided a rare insight into the day-to-day operations of these facilities and the degree of involvement of private security. In fact, when Jiménez died in CBSA custody, the CBSA suppressed disclosure to avoid public scrutiny and notified only the RCMP and BC coroner. However, the agency did prepare a media response in the event that the information was leaked (Track & Paterson, 2017). Jiménez was apprehended by transit authorities in Vancouver and held at the airport facility contracted to Genesis Security before being transferred to the high-risk section of the Alouette Correctional Centre for Women (Ball, 2014a; IHRP, 2018). She spent sixteen days at Alouette, where she met with a mental health screener and a nurse who determined that she needed further support and scheduled an appointment with the prison's mental health coordinator. Her record erroneously stated that she had already been released, and the appointment never took place. Shortly after, Jiménez was transferred back to the airport IHC to await deportation with no communication between the prison and the CBSA on her mental health condition. The next day she committed suicide while in detention (IHRP, 2018).

At the time, *The Tyee* reported that the CBSA employed 287 enforcement officers and 359 security guards throughout its three detention facilities (Ball, 2014b). The Vancouver airport IHC was staffed entirely by private security personnel (Ball, 2014b; IHRP, 2018). A spokesperson for the CBSA explained that private security companies are tasked with the "care and control of persons detained under IRPA at a CBSA immigration holding centre," "escorting detainees to and from the detention facilities," and "escorting and confirming their departure from Canada" (cited in Ball, 2014b, para. 4). This spokesperson also stressed that "other security duties may be performed as required by the CBSA" (cited in Ball, 2014b, para. 4). However, testimony from Genesis Security employees depicted less orderly and competent management of these facilities. Many emphasized that, in more than one instance, and contrary to the CBSA's four-guard requirement, not enough guards were on duty to fulfill their obligations. In fact, the inquest revealed that it was other female detainees who brought Jiménez to the attention of the guards by repeatedly knocking on the window of the control room. At that moment, the female guard was off-site conducting a detainee transfer, and another two guards were about to leave for a deportation transfer, leaving only one security guard on duty (Ball, 2014b; Carman, 2014). At the inquest, the guard left on duty admitted that he had falsified the room-check report because he was by himself and did not want to enter the rooms every thirty minutes as required (Carman, 2014; Track & Paterson, 2017).

The inquest lawyer also pointed out that, in addition to insufficient staff, private security guards hired to oversee and care for those in detention did not receive adequate or appropriate training and did not diligently perform room checks or supervision (Ball, 2014b). Although licensing requirements for security guards mandate training and a provincial examination, these and other requirements vary widely among the provinces. For example, all provinces require a criminal record check, but only a few request checks of the child abuse registry, correctional information, police records, previous licensing applications, mental health records, and English fluency. Except for Newfoundland and Labrador, and Quebec, which require sixty hours and seventy hours of in-class or online training, respectively, all other provinces and territories mandate only thirty-three and a half to forty hours of training for security guards. Passing grades for examination also differ. For example, British Columbia requires a 60 percent passing grade, and Alberta requires 80 percent, whereas other jurisdictions require 70 percent (Montgomery & Griffiths, 2015).

The guards employed by Genesis Security at the Vancouver airport facility testified that, to be hired at the detention centre, they were required to complete only four additional days of course work. It included a basic and an advanced security certificate and an introductory-level first aid certificate. The only training in relation to suicide prevention consisted of a printed package. Furthermore, security guards paid for their own training materials and bulletproof vests. Although CBSA agents require only a high school diploma, they are subject to comparatively more rigorous training, not only at the beginning of their careers but also as part of ongoing professional development. Following a strict screening process that includes a medical exam and psychological evaluation, all CBSA agents must complete month-long online training followed by four and a half months of in-residence training at the CBSA college in Rigaud, Quebec. The in-residence training includes a duty firearm course and a course on control defensive tactics in addition to courses on relevant policies, procedures, and legislation. The CBSA website also states that those in training are continually assessed both informally and formally and mandated to attend physical fitness sessions (CBSA, 2021a). Moreover, the in-residence training is followed by an on-the-job development phase as a trainee for one to one and a half years. Only upon completion of this on-the-job development can a trainee be appointed as a border services officer, and only after serving in this position for several years can one request an inland position (Ball, 2014; CBSA, 2021a). Apart from the qualitative and quantitative discrepancies in training requirements between private security guards and CBSA agents, the salary differential is also noteworthy. During the inquest, Genesis Security employees revealed that, after a probationary period of thirteen dollars per hour, security guards' wages would start at fifteen dollars per hour, or about $25,000 per year. Recent job postings on Indeed for security positions at the Surrey IHC offer a salary of $25,000 to $30,000 for twelve-hour shifts on a rotation work schedule of four days on, three days off. The ad also highlights that staff perks include "discounted movie tickets, gym memberships and much more!" (Indeed, n.d.). In comparison, the CBSA website promises that "as a trainee your annual salary will be $69,426 to $77,302" in addition to health and pension benefits (CBSA, 2021a). Once a trainee completes on-the-job development training, the salary increases up to $89,068.

Despite the paucity of academic research on privatized security in Canadian detention centres, extensive research in other states has exposed similar discrepancies in training and pay that lead to high staff turnover (Ackerman & Furman, 2013; Conlon & Hiemstra, 2014; Flynn & Cannon, 2009; Hiemstra & Conlon, 2017; Golash-Boza, 2009; Lacin, 2019). This was confirmed in our interview with Scott, who stated that "there are always different guards at the IHCs; there is a significant staff turnover. They are treated like crap by their employer, and the security guard union hasn't done the best job of representing them. Some of them take the job hoping that they can later transition and become a CBSA officer." He also highlighted that the security guards are often people of colour and from the same national or ethnic communities as the detainees whom they are tasked to supervise, which creates an odd power dynamic. Furthermore, research undertaken by the Global Detention Project on the privatization experiences of the United States, Australia, Germany, Italy, the United Kingdom, South Africa, and Sweden confirms that commercial relationships with government decision makers, and monopolization of the market by a few corporations, negatively affect the performance and quality of services in detention centres. And, unsurprisingly, the absence of accountability structures means that wrongdoing rarely is detected or holds few consequences (Flynn & Cannon, 2009; Lacin, 2019). Indeed, when Genesis Security's CEO was interviewed following the inquiry into the death of Jiménez, he stated that "nothing has changed" regarding the contract with the CBSA (Ball, 2014b).

Although accountability and transparency mechanisms arguably are eroded by privatizing tasks previously performed exclusively by government actors, this process also facilitates and legitimizes the power of private entities while diminishing the state's monopoly on coercive power and the deprivation of liberty (Feeley, 2002; Lacin, 2019; Montgomery &

Griffiths, 2015). The experience with private prisons indicates that the transfer of responsibility to private entities enables an expansion and a development of new forms of social control with little cost savings. Feeley (2002, p. 322) asserts that this entrepreneurial spirit, in essence, has "created vast numbers of government-franchised social control centres" that have increased the influence of private actors on immigration policy. Numerous scholars have argued that private entities consider the global migration crisis and the securitized reaction of states to protect their borders from undesirable migrants as a lucrative business opportunity and an invitation for the lowest bid (Arbogast, 2017; Bloom, 2015; Feeley, 2002; Lacin, 2019). These public-private partnerships do not denote an abandonment of migration control by the state (Ackerman & Furman, 2013; Menz, 2009, 2011; Rodenhauser, 2014). Rather, they "represent reinvented state forms of power and governance" (Lahav, 2010, p. 216). Pratt (2005) explains that detention is positioned precisely at the crossroads between sovereignty and the perpetuation of disciplinary power because, despite the coercive and prohibitive nature of sovereign practices, other actors, authorities, and technologies of exclusion also exist. Doty and Wheatley (2013) argue that, in the course of managing the migration crisis, state and private powers expand, and solutions become embedded in the immigration industrial complex, rendering long-term policy changes difficult.

Although states have delegated some of their sovereign coercive and performative powers to private actors by outsourcing border and immigration control functions, this shift has strengthened simultaneously the state's authority while diluting transparency and its human rights responsibilities (Arbogast, 2017; Bloom, 2015; Doty & Wheatley, 2013; Lacin, 2019). As exemplified by the inquiry into the death of Jiménez in Canada and many other similar cases, this outsourcing of public responsibilities to private actors via contracts presents challenges for investigation, prosecution, and redress for abuses and human rights violations. As Arbogast (2017, p. 61) underscores, "in the worst case scenario, particularly in cases of detainee deaths, the private company in question is expected to give up the contract." However, the contract is then awarded to another of the few companies offering services in this sector – none of which has a record free of human rights abuse allegations (Arbogast, 2017).

Although the state retains the formal obligation to protect human rights under domestic and international law (United Nations General Assembly, 2017), there is an emerging movement under the rubric of business and human rights to develop mechanisms by which private actors also bear obligations to protect human rights of migrants when undertaking migration-related state functions (Bloom, 2015). But the UN Guiding Principles on Business and Human Rights are neither mandatory nor enforceable against business entities. States retain the duty to protect against violations of human rights committed by state or non-state actors within their jurisdictions. Yet contractual agreements between the state and private security companies serve not only to augment state power but also to conceal human rights abuses and obscure the state's accountability and human rights responsibilities vis-à-vis the migrant. Such agreements also contribute to the criminalization of migration, the normalization of detention for profit, and the creation of powerful corporate interests invested in the expansion of the immigration industrial complex.

Detention of Migrants in Provincial Jails

The contractual allocation of public functions to the private sector tells only part of the Canadian story of immigration detention; the other part of the story unfolds with the delegation of confinement from federal immigration detention facilities to provincial penal institutions. Although not an instance of privatization, the arrangements share certain common features with it. First, the federal-provincial deals are profit-driven commercial arrangements managed through memorandums of understanding. Second, they are regulated through mechanisms that are not public or transparent.

To understand the extent of the private sector's involvement in the Canadian immigration detention space, it is important to situate detention in the larger immigration regime. The events of 9/11 did not initiate the securitization of migration (Macklin, 2001). For example, the arrival of four boats of Chinese nationals on the coast of British Columbia in 1999 spurred a number of legislative changes that expanded the powers of detention (CIC, 2002; Ibrahim, 2005). Of course, 9/11 did accelerate and aggrandize the role of securitization in discourse, policy, and implementation, but the 2001 Immigration and Refugee Protection Act was drafted before 9/11 and passed into legislation post-9/11 with no revision.

The twenty-first century ushered in more restrictive immigration and asylum policies, expanded enforcement, a greater proportion of migrants with temporary and precarious statuses, and intensified fortification of borders. Pratt (2005, p. 1) describes this compendium as the constitution of "immigration penality." Although immigration penality encompasses more than formal government institutions, detention and deportation are stripped of their character as mere "administrative" measures and emerge as punitive sanctions that play a key role in governing populations and creating citizens (Bosworth, 2017; Pratt, 2005; Silverman & Massa, 2012; Silverman & Nethery, 2015). Immigration penality – a variation of the concept of crimmigration – came to be governed by the crime-security nexus, heightened anxieties about terrorism, and vilification of asylum seekers (Bosworth, 2017; Pratt, 2005; Walters, 2002).

Some of the most draconian Canadian detention practices were pursued by the Conservative government of Stephen Harper in the wake of the boat arrivals of 492 Tamil asylum seekers off the coast of British Columbia in 2010. The government relentlessly pursued the detention of every passenger – including children – aboard the ships, even in the face of judicial release orders. In 2012, the Conservative government passed Protecting Canada's Immigration System Act (Bill C-31), which, *inter alia*, authorized a year's mandatory detention of designated "irregular arrivals" and five-year impediments to permanent resident status and family reunification for those recognized as refugees (Atak & Crépeau, 2013; Canadian Council for Refugees, 2013; IRPA, 2001; Zyfi & Atak, 2018). Although this "designated foreign national" regime was used only once by the Conservative government, it was not repealed by the successor Liberal government, even though it is almost certainly unconstitutional.

Detention Powers under IRPA

In Canada, the immigration detention system is governed through IRPA and its regulations. The detention regime applies not only to asylum seekers and failed refugee claimants but also to permanent residents and other migrants. Some await deportation, but some might pursue legal avenues to remain in Canada. Responsibility for the enforcement of "arrest, detention and removal" as well as "the establishment of policies respecting the enforcement" of the act (IRPA, 2001, s 4(2)) lies with the Minister of Public Safety and Emergency Preparedness – not the Immigration, Refugees and Citizenship Canada (IRCC) minister. Subsection 6(2) of IRPA delegates to the CBSA the authority to arrest and detain, among other discretionary powers (IRPA, 2001, s 6). Detention of foreign nationals can occur when reasonable grounds exist to believe one of the following: the foreign national is suspected of being a flight risk, or a danger to the public, their identity is not established, or detention is required to complete an examination (IRPA, 2001, s 55). A detainee can then be placed in an immigration holding centre or a provincial jail (CBSA, 2020c; IRCC, 2019). However, unlike the decision related to a detainee's placement, CBSA decisions to detain foreign nationals are subject to an initial review after forty-eight hours, seven days, and every thirty days thereafter by a member of the Immigration Division of the Immigration and Refugee Board (IRB), an independent administrative tribunal (IRB, 2018; NIDF, 2019). Within forty-eight hours of arrest, CBSA officers also have the power to release detainees prior to the first review of the Immigration Division if "the reasons for detention no longer exist" and can "impose any conditions ... that the officer considers necessary" (IRPA, 2001, s 56(1)).

CBSA officers also act as the minister's representatives in detention review hearings conducted by the Immigration Division of the Immigration and Refugee Board. Governed by several manuals and policy guidelines such as the Immigration Division Rules and the recently updated Guideline on Detention, these proceedings are quasi-judicial and adversarial. Adjudicators are required to consider the grounds for detention as well as several factors listed in the regulations before a decision on further detention or release is made. These factors include the reason for and length of time in detention, any element that can assist in determining the length of time that detention is likely to continue, any unexplained delay or lack of diligence, and any alternative to detention (IRPA, 2001, s 248). Unlike in the criminal justice system, adjudicators are required only to justify continued detention on a balance of probabilities and not bound by any legal or technical rules of evidence. This means that evidence introduced in the proceedings, which rely heavily on hearsay, is not tested in the same manner as in criminal courts and can sway a decision if deemed credible by the adjudicator (IRPA, 2001, s 173 (c) and (d)). This weakens procedural fairness particularly for long-term detainees less likely to be released and more likely to be held in carceral facilities.

Furthermore, as the Supreme Court decision in *Canada v Chhina* (2019, para. 57) emphasized, "the Immigration Division has no explicit power to examine harsh or illegal conditions," and the "responsibility for the location and conditions of detention rests with the CBSA or provincial correctional authorities." Officially, Canada has three IHCs, located in Toronto, Laval, and Surrey, all of which are categorized as medium security. The Toronto Immigration Holding Centre is a facility provided to the CBSA through a third-party service contract and was recently renovated to accommodate 183 beds. Correctional Services Canada owns the Laval centre, and the CBSA operates the 109-bed facility through a memorandum of understanding with Correctional Services. This IHC will be replaced by a new CBSA-owned facility next to Leclerc prison that was expected to be operational by 2021, but has yet to be completed. CBSA owns the Surrey facility, which replaced the Vancouver airport facility in March 2020 and can accommodate up to seventy detainees (CBSA, 2020a).

The CBSA detention manual explains that IHCs should always be the default facilities for detention if risk can be mitigated, and detention in provincial jails should be reserved for detainees who have served a criminal sentence and await deportation, those with criminal backgrounds, those deemed to be a danger to the public, or those whose high-risk behaviour cannot be managed within an IHC. In reality, nearly a third of detainees – including those without criminal records and suffering from mental health issues – have been placed consistently in correctional facilities since 2017 (CBSA, 2020b). Indeed, the vast majority of detainees are confined on grounds not related to public safety concerns. Since 2017, approximately 95 percent have been held because they were suspected to be flight risks, had unclear identities, were unlikely to show up for their hearing or removal proceedings, or for the purpose of completing routine examinations. Only about 5 percent of detainees are held because of public safety concerns. In most instances, the decision on where a detainee will be held is made solely based upon the risk assessment score assigned by a CBSA officer. Regardless of the outcome of the risk assessment, migrants located outside the geographical location serviced by an IHC are housed in a correctional facility (CBSA, 2020c). Data obtained through an access to information[1] request demonstrate that approximately 81 percent of detainees in provincial jails are held for the purpose of completing examinations, as flight risks, or to establish identities. In other words, they are not detained on grounds of public danger. The detention manual also explains that in isolated communities a detainee may be temporarily held at police stations or RCMP detachments until transferred to CBSA custody.

Despite a steady decrease in the overall number of persons in detention since 2012, the sudden spike in 2017–18 endured until the COVID-19 pandemic began. The CBSA attributed the increase to the removal of visa requirements for Mexican nationals in December 2016 and the steady irregular arrivals through the Canada-US border at Roxham Road in Quebec. Specifically, in 2017–18, CBSA statistics indicate, a total of 8,355 adults and 151 minors were detained compared with 6,268 and 162, respectively, for the previous year, reflecting an increase of one-third (CBSA, 2020b). For 2018–19 and 2019–20, the number of detainees continued to rise, with a total of

8,781 and 8,825 adults, respectively. In 2019, the CBSA began to count minors housed in detention with their parents or guardians, including those born in Canada, separately from those formally detained (CBSA, 2020b). Although the conditions of detention are the same for both groups, the former group is not subject to an order of detention, the rationale being that "housing" them is in the best interests of the child and the family unit. The vast majority of minors currently in detention are those "housed." For 2018–19, a total of 103 minors were "housed" in detention facilities, and 15 were formally detained. For 2019–20, 136 were housed and 2 detained (CBSA, 2020b). CBSA statistics show that the average length of detention decreased from 14.3 days in 2017–18, to 13.8 days in 2018–19, to 13.9 days in 2019–20. However, the statistics do not distinguish the average length of detention between those in IHCs and those in correctional facilities. Meanwhile, detention for twenty-four hours or less has doubled since 2016. An average of 47 percent of detainees are held for twenty-four hours or less (CBSA, 2020b).

In 2016, the minister of public safety and emergency preparedness instituted various reforms to reduce the number of long-term detainees, the reliance on provincial jails, and the detention of minors. In 2017, supported by a $138 million pledge, a new National Immigration Detention Framework was adopted to continue efforts to expand CBSA facilities and increase alternatives to detention (CBSA, 2020c). In spite of some notable improvements, key concerns about Canada's detention practices persist and have consistently been brought to attention by academics, civil society organizations, international bodies, and courts. The findings of the *Report of the 2017/2018 External Audit for Detention Reviews* (IRB, 2018) commissioned by the chair of the IRB confirmed many of the complaints. First, Canada is still among the few countries with indeterminate detention, including in relation to minors (IRPA, 2001). In comparison, the detention limit in France is thirty-two days, in Germany it is six months, and in Malta, the country with the longest limit in the European Union, it is eighteen months (Mainwaring & Silverman, 2017). In August 2017, the UN Committee on the Elimination of Racial Discrimination called on Canada to establish a legal time limit for immigration detention. As a result of the CBSA's new operational practices, which emphasize removal and potential release options, the number of detainees held for more than ninety-nine days has decreased by 48.3 percent over the past five years. Nevertheless, in 2019–20, 241 individuals were held in detention for longer than ninety-nine days (CBSA, 2020b). Most long-term detainees are held in Ontario jails.

One of Canada's longest-serving immigration detainees, Michael Mvogo, was detained for over nine years before being deported to Cameroon (Global Detention Project, 2021). Kashif Ali, a Ghanaian, was held for more than seven years in a maximum-security correctional facility because he lacked proof of citizenship and could not be deported (Global Detention Project, 2021; Kennedy, 2017b). More recently, Ebrahim Touré was released after more than five years in detention (Kennedy, 2017a). And the current longest-serving detainee has been held in a maximum-security jail for over six years (Silverman & Kaytaz, 2020). Indeed, more than two-thirds of those detained for longer than six months were held on grounds unrelated to public safety concerns. The external audit of 2018 highlighted that the lack of a clear limit to the length of detention can be attributed to shabby review proceedings by the Immigration Division and the CBSA's use of detention for unauthorized punitive purposes. Although the audit identified several areas of concern, it focused on breaches of procedural fairness and the failure of decisions to reflect adequately the submissions and evidence presented to adjudicators. It also made numerous recommendations and the overall finding that, "in a significant number of these hearings and decisions, there were notable discrepancies between the expectations articulated by the courts and the practice of the Immigration Division" (para. 5). The refusal of some adjudicators to comply with the law, as articulated by higher courts, amounts to a flouting of the rule of law.

Second, Canada is also among the few countries with anti-terrorism provisions that can and have been used to detain and deport individuals (Atak & Crépeau, 2013; Silverman, 2014). Third, Canada continues systematically to use maximum-security provincial jails to hold immigration detainees, including those suffering from mental health issues. Indeed, a detainee's mental health difficulties are sometimes used as an excuse to transfer an individual from an IHC to a jail (IHRP, 2015, 2018; Molnar & Silverman, 2017, 2018; Nakache, 2011; Silverman, 2014).

As previously stated, the decision to place a detainee in an IHC or a correctional facility depends largely on the risk assessment score assigned by a CBSA officer. Updated in February 2018, the National Risk Assessment for Detention (NRAD) form[2] is intended to ensure consistency in detention placement across the country. Replacing open-ended questions frequently left blank, the updated form introduces a point scale based upon nine factors, eight pertaining to risk and one to vulnerability (CBSA, 2016; Kennedy, 2017c, 2019; NIDF, 2019; Silverman & Kaytaz, 2020). The point scale of the new form was introduced partly as a response to the recommendations of the internal audit of immigration enforcement (CBSA, 2016). The audit highlighted a number of issues with how the CBSA was utilizing the NRAD form. Specifically, inaccurate or incomplete forms were common, there were long gaps in time between assessments, and in the majority of instances the form was missing from the detainee's file (CBSA, 2016). The new form was intended to be transparent and objective. However, the CBSA retains unfettered and unreviewable discretion in deciding where to place a detainee. A detainee has no means of contesting the decision; the Immigration Division regards this as beyond its jurisdiction, so detainees cannot raise it at their detention reviews.

The IRCC Operational Manual states that the nine risk and vulnerability factors allocate points, and the total score determines where a detainee will be held. Neither the manual nor any other publicly available document provides an explanation of the numerical points scale or stipulates how many points can be allocated for each factor. The NRAD form itself provides a breakdown for each category, albeit with no explanation of how risk is assessed. Silverman and Kaytaz (2020) argue that, by omitting a definition and justification of what it aims to assess, the form depends on one's past criminal background to predict future dangerousness, thereby reinforcing racialized and gendered assumptions of risk. Furthermore, the instructions at the top of the NRAD form indicate that "the risk factor points should be added whereas the vulnerability factor points must be subtracted." The risk factors are associated with the detention grounds under IRPA; however, the form is used when one is already detained (Silverman & Kaytaz, 2020). The form is used only to decide on the facility of detention, so its model presents a clear bias in favour of punitive conditions since eight of the nine factors pertain to risk. Silverman and Kaytaz (2020, p. 10) emphasize that this reflects a "constructed 'riskiness' and, by extension, who is worthy of protection by state actors."

The first two risk factors pertain to inadmissibility on grounds of security and organized criminality, respectively. If applicable, then each factor equates to six points. The third factor allots zero to three points based upon the number of years passed since the last known criminal offence or conviction. Closely related, the fourth and fifth factors assign points based upon the number of offences or convictions and the severity of the offences committed. Specifically, the fourth factor provides a spectrum of up to seven points for three or more offences or convictions involving threats or violent crimes. The fifth factor can lead to three points for an offence or conviction of a severely violent crime. Although the most recent updates to the

Detention Manual provide a list of examples of non-violent and violent crimes and the respective Criminal Code provisions, little detail is provided on how these crimes should be weighted in regard to the points value. The form itself simply lists examples of violent crimes for the fifth factor, such as murder, aggravated/sexual assault, assault with a weapon, torture, and genocide. The sixth factor relates to involvement in a major breach of the rules of an IHC during the past two years for a maximum of four points; the seventh factor provides four points if the detainee in question escaped or attempted to escape from legal custody in the past; and the eighth factor provides three points if the detainee has an outstanding criminal warrant for arrest or is a fugitive from justice. Finally, the ninth factor is the only one related to vulnerability and does not accumulate points. If the person is deemed to be vulnerable, only two points are deducted from the overall score. A vulnerable person is defined as "a person for whom detention may cause a particular hardship" and includes expecting and nursing mothers, minors, victims of trafficking, and those suffering from a mental illness, disability, or severe medical condition (IRCC, 2019, p. 24). In assessing vulnerability, the CBSA officer is required to consider the available services in the facilities.

The ninth factor is a yes or no question; thus, even if more than one category of vulnerability is applicable, it can be "selected" only once. Although detention should be a last resort and alternatives considered whenever possible, the notion of vulnerability does not permeate the NRAD form and carries little weight compared with other factors. Interestingly, it is also the only factor requiring that specific details be elaborated if selected. Also, CBSA officers are advised that, even when vulnerability is identified, detention is not precluded if there are concerns about the safety and security of the public. Although additional information supporting the CBSA officer's decision can be recorded in the narrative section of the form, the final decision is based upon the sum of points from the nine risk and vulnerability factors. Zero to four points indicate that the detainee should be placed in an IHC, where available; five to nine points indicate that the detainee should be placed in an IHC or provincial correctional facility, though IHCs are preferred because risk can be mitigated; and ten or more points indicate that the detainee should be held in a provincial correctional facility (IRCC, 2019). A score of zero does not exempt one from detention; it simply labels the person as low risk (Silverman & Kaytaz, 2020). And, if the person is placed in a correctional facility, then the chances of release diminish significantly.

The NRAD form also requires the CBSA officer to inform the detainee of the designated detention facility and give the person the opportunity to provide further details for the risk and/or vulnerability factors prior to the final decision. This is also a dichotomous issue, and the form emphasizes that, though the CBSA "officer is not bound by those comments[,] they must be taken into consideration." The form also indicates that the decision of the CBSA officer needs to be reviewed and approved by a supervisor, manager, or higher regional authority. Once finalized, the form needs to be placed in the detainee's case file, and a copy must be provided directly to the detainee as well as the selected detention facility. A follow-up NRAD assessment must be conducted within sixty days if detention continues or sooner if there is an observed change in the detainee's risk level. In reality, this does not always happen. Communication with lawyers working in this field, including Scott, confirms that in most instances the NRAD form is used only for the initial placements of detainees. An informant suggested that even this use is not meaningful because CBSA officers do not conduct careful assessments and often engage in their own ad hoc analyses of detainees' dangerousness or vulnerability. Often detainees are not interviewed or given a chance to elaborate on details, as required by the form, they are seldom provided with a copy, and follow-up assessments do not occur, especially in provincial jails, where the responsibility to do so falls with the CBSA detainee liaison. These practices make it challenging to review the decision about where to hold a detainee and contribute to lengthier detentions in provincial jails. Scott dubbed it an arbitrary process with no connection to procedural fairness or justice.

In carrying out its enforcement mandate, the CBSA currently has bilateral agreements with British Columbia, Alberta, Ontario, and Quebec – where the majority of detainees are located – to house immigration detainees in correctional institutions (CBSA, 2020a). Although detainees outside these provinces are also held in correctional institutions, the CBSA does not clarify the agreements that it has in place with these provinces. We speculate that they are similar to the existing memorandums of understanding. These contracts closely resemble the public-private partnerships that the CBSA has with private security firms regarding IHCs. The CBSA pays the provinces a per diem rate to incarcerate detainees. Since this rate differs for each carceral facility, the 2015 agreement[3] with Ontario (the only one that we have viewed) states that the rate "shall be the average of the per diem rates for all of Ontario's Correctional Institutions." Furthermore, this memorandum of understanding revealed that the CBSA pays Ontario an additional amount equivalent to 20 percent of the per diem rate for each day that an immigration detainee is held. This premium is intended to cover administration and overhead costs related to the accommodation of detainees. In 2013, the cost of detention per detainee per day was $259, compared with $196 per day per inmate incarcerated in a provincial facility (IHRP, 2015, 2018). The most recent agreements were negotiated in 2018, and there is no publicly available information on the details of the conditions and related costs. However, in 2018–19, the average cost of incarcerating an inmate in a provincial jail increased to $259 per day (Malakieh, 2020), so we infer that the cost of housing an immigration detainee has increased proportionately.

In 2017–18, a total of 1,831 (20 percent) detainees were held in jails; in 2018–19, the number was 1,679 (16 percent); in 2019–20, it was 1,932 (19 percent) (CBSA, 2020b). In 2020, notably, many detainees in IHCs were released with conditions because of the COVID-19 pandemic. The number of persons detained under the custody of Correctional Services remains alarmingly high. Thus, provinces profit substantially from contracts with the CBSA to house immigration detainees. In fact, in 2013 alone, the CBSA paid the provinces over $26 million to detain migrants in provincial jails. Over 80 percent of the total was paid to Ontario, where most detainees are held (IHRP, 2018). In an interview with the International Human Rights Program, Reg Williams – a previous director of immigration enforcement at the CBSA – pointed out that it would be more cost effective for the CBSA to build more IHCs than to contract the provinces (IHRP, 2018). Thus, though provincial jails are public institutions, their relationships with the CBSA are governed by contract and mimic the contractual relationship that the CBSA has with wholly private actors.

Individuals in provincial jails are not only confined in more restrictive settings but also more likely to be detained for longer periods of time compared with those held in IHCs. CBSA data obtained through an access to information request revealed that for 2017–18 detainees in correctional institutions were incarcerated nearly six times longer. More than twice as many detainees in correctional institutions were held for over ninety-nine days. These figures include vulnerable individuals with mental health conditions and suicidal ideation. As noted earlier, CBSA policy encourages the transfer of detainees from IHCs to correctional facilities because of their medical issues or mental health conditions. The CBSA might justify the transfers as serving the best interests of the detainees because more specialized medical and psychosocial supports can be accessed, and specific cells are available if isolation is required (IHRP, 2018). However, research consistently demonstrates that mental health care and services in correctional facilities are inadequate, unavailable, and/or challenging for immigration detainees to access (IHRP, 2018). CBSA officers can also transfer detainees who exhibit uncooperative, aggressive, disruptive, or generally "unacceptable" behaviour (IHRP, 2018, p. 78). In these instances, mental health conditions are viewed through a lens of danger and translated into risk factors rather than vulnerability factors. As interviews conducted by the International Human Rights Program highlighted, these detainees are then considered a "flight risk and danger to the public, not so much as someone who would benefit from release," and "once this image is created it is a hard one to dislodge and gets reinforced over and over at detention reviews, thus making [the] prospect of release or consideration of alternatives to detention improbable" (2018, pp. 63–64). Although mental health conditions must be considered a vulnerability, and detention hearings should serve as reviews for ongoing detention, in actuality mental health impairment serves to facilitate indefinite detention. Indeed, many of those detained in maximum-security facilities for prolonged periods of time have been racialized men suffering from mental health conditions, including Michael Mvogo, Kashif Ali, Ricardo Scotland, Ebrahim Toure, and Tusif Ur Rehman Chhina. The IHRP (2018) highlighted that the most common conditions were PTSD, depression, schizophrenia, and/or bipolar disorder. The conditions in maximum-security facilities not only amplify existing mental health conditions but also frequently produce new ones. Scott informed us that detainees are sometimes transferred from a jail to an IHC to evade media and public scrutiny, as was the case with Mvogo. He was transferred from a jail to an IHC since his case was garnering notable public attention, and the CBSA could "better control and keep an eye on the situation at an IHC."

Since detainees in provincial jails are under provincial jurisdiction, different challenges arise regarding accountability for care, safety, and conditions of detention, for no single government department is clearly accountable. The agreements with the provinces do not relieve the CBSA of its legal responsibilities for immigration detainees held under IRPA. Yet, as stipulated in the 2015 agreement with Ontario, "the conditions of detention and the treatment and privileges of persons detained ... shall be specified by the Ministry of Correctional Services Act ... and the policy and procedures of the Ministry of Community Safety and Correctional Services, which are applicable to inmates confined in provincial correctional institutions" (s 2.17). And, as emphasized by the IHRP (2018), Correctional Services in Ontario maintain that they are fully responsible for the care of all persons in their custody, including their health, safety, and discipline. Williams explained in an interview with the IHRP that the CBSA lacks any authority or responsibility in provincial jails. The UNHCR made similar findings in a report in 2011, highlighting that, once detainees are transferred to provincial jails, the CBSA no longer exercises control over their treatment and lacks authority to intervene on their behalf (IHRP, 2015, 2018).

Although they are managed as if they are imprisoned as offenders convicted of criminal offences, immigration detainees are not subject to the same procedural safeguards. The inferior legal and human rights protections afforded to non-citizens are rationalized on the basis that it is administrative detention, not punishment. Nevertheless, the Canadian Red Cross – the only organization that has been allowed to enter detention facilities and to monitor and report on the conditions and treatment of detainees since 1990 – has stressed that the CBSA must ensure that all immigration detainees, regardless of where they are held, are provided with similar rights, services, and conditions. The UNHCR and the Red Cross have consistently highlighted the disparities between immigration holding centres and correctional facilities in Canada. Detainees in jails are required to wear the designated jumpsuits and subjected to regular strip searches and frequent lockdowns. At times, they are also placed in solitary confinement for prolonged periods. During 2019–20, 17 percent of detainees (174) held in Ontario jails spent time in solitary confinement, with 13 percent of them in segregation for more than fifteen consecutive days, the limit recommended by the United Nations (Human Rights Watch, 2021; Kennedy, 2017c, 2019; Nakache, 2011). International instruments have recognized solitary confinement as a form of cruel, inhumane, and degrading treatment.

Moreover, immigration detainees constitute a particularly vulnerable and traumatized population. Since 2000, at least sixteen people have died while in immigration detention in Canada (Kennedy, 2018; Molnar & Silverman, 2017). In addition, in its 2019 report, the Canadian Red Cross stressed that immigration detainees receive insufficient information regarding their rights and responsibilities; have limited access to amenities, legal services, and programs, especially in correctional facilities; face challenges in accessing medical services even though international law requires health care to be provided regardless of one's legal status; and encounter obstacles in maintaining contact with families because of the lack of access to phones, the internet, and visits. These conditions often exacerbate their struggles to obtain the documentation needed for their cases. Finally, the Red Cross emphasized that commingling in correctional facilities between immigration detainees and those convicted of crimes needs to be addressed immediately. In fact, correctional officers and staff are often either unaware that detainees have not been convicted of crimes or lack sufficient training regarding immigration detention. Thus, detainees are subject to the same rules and treatment as inmates. Affirmed by interviews with correctional staff and other experts working with immigration detainees, the IHRP (2018) reported that provincial jails struggle with their duties as the number of criminally convicted inmates increases. In turn, there are glaring "legal black holes" regarding immigration detainees confined in provincial jails since no government body is explicitly responsible (p. 17). A recent Ontario Superior Court decision dubbed the system "Kafkaesque" and "a closed circle of self-referential and circuitous logic from which there is no escape" (*Scotland v Canada*, 2017, para. 74). Nonetheless, despite persistent calls for change from local, national, and international civil society organizations, as well as the United Nations and Canadian courts, the government continues to subject migrants to indeterminate detention and routinely to confine them in correctional facilities.

In theory, immigration detention should be administrative, not punitive. This means that detention must be linked to the immigration-related purpose of removal, not to free-standing goals of punishing migrants, coercing them to "surrender" and leave, or even warehousing those considered dangerous. Unlike incarcerated individuals, immigration detainees have not committed crimes, or, if they have, then they have completed their sentences. The consistent use of provincial carceral facilities instantiates the criminalization of migrants materially, institutionally, and irrefutably. It is simply impossible to deny that immigration detention is punitive when migrants are incarcerated in jails and governed in the same manner as offenders convicted of criminal offences, with only two differences. First, offenders serve determinate sentences, after which they must be released; migrants in detention never know if or when they will be released or removed. Second, both provincial corrections and federal immigration authorities disavow accountability for misconduct and abuse of migrants detained in jails. The province denies jurisdiction over migrants because they are detained under the authority of a federal statute, while the federal government denies accountability because the conditions of confinement are governed by provincial law. Although the excuse for unaccountability is jurisdiction rather than privatization, the net effect is similar.

Community Alternatives to Migrant Detention

Another key pillar of the National Immigration Detention Framework is the CBSA duty to consider alternatives to detention before and during detention under IRPA. In addition to existing mechanisms of in-person reporting, monetary deposits, and guarantors (who must be citizens or permanent residents), the CBSA introduced new risk-based programs in 2018 aimed at facilitating release whenever suitable (CBSA, 2020c). The new measures include a Community Case Management and Supervision (CCMS) program, a national Voice Reporting program, and an Electronic Monitoring (EM) program. Thus, the multiplicity of actors in the field of detention goes beyond substate governments and private companies. It includes NGOs and private citizens who become enrolled in the system as sureties or bondspersons for detainees, thereby assuming the responsibility of monitoring and surveilling non-citizens released from detention on conditions. Here the motive is less about profit than about avoidance of financial loss.

The CCMS program comprises the John Howard Society of Canada, the Toronto Bail Program (TBP), and the Salvation Army and is intended for individuals who do not have a bondsperson or require community support. Each of these organizations has a contract with the CBSA to determine an appropriate plan of release to mitigate risk, provide services and supports to the detainee upon release in the community, as well as to assist with reporting requirements (CBSA, 2018a). Geared to medium- or high-risk detainees who require a comprehensive and rigorous plan of release, the CCMS is available in urban centres across Canada, except for the Toronto-based TBP (CBSA, 2018c). The TBP has become the only real alternative for migrants who have been in long-term detention or have mental health conditions because the CBSA mistrusts other bondspersons. This is an issue because the TBP budgetary contract with the CBSA limits the caseload to 300 clients at any given time, which in turn reduces one's chances of release if the TBP rejects an applicant or is simply at capacity (IHRP, 2018; Khaikin, 2020). According to the IHRP and the Canadian Council for Refugees, in such instances detainees are denied release even if non-TBP alternatives exist. This preference is based upon the assumption that the "TBP is geared towards helping people report to CBSA and removal, whereas criminal rehabilitation programs are not" (IHRP, 2018, p. 65). Furthermore, the cost to supervise a detainee in the community is roughly a quarter of the cost of incarceration (Silverman & Kaytaz, 2020). However, Scott emphasized that, though the TBP follows the directions of the CBSA, it does have some independence. He stated that "it's a bit of a mixed bag, but they do some good work." The TBP offers assistance regarding work permits and health care and devises constructive solutions to help people remain on release. As a response to the COVID-19 pandemic, the TBP has taken on more people, beyond the limit. Scott also informed us that the bail program will soon be expanded to other regions and provinces, though it will be managed and run directly by the CBSA.

The Voice Reporting program is geared to low- to medium-risk individuals and available at inland enforcement offices. It requires individuals to report regularly to the CBSA through an automated telephone system that utilizes voice biometrics to confirm their identities and records their locations when making the calls. Only compatible Canadian cellphone or landline providers may be used. When calling, individuals are prompted to repeat the same phrase used when recording their voice templates so that the system can determine a match (CBSA, 2018b). Although the CBSA claims that this is a convenient method of reporting, anecdotal evidence suggests the contrary. Representatives of an NGO in Toronto informed us that their clients face difficulties at times accessing the system, that they are often required to report at night, and that the geotagging used for location verification is not always accurate, which the CBSA sometimes misinterprets as a breach of conditions. Scott also explained that initially this program was limited to individuals who had been issued removal orders. It was expanded later to include everyone who lost her or his refugee claim. This expanded scope significantly increases the surveillance of migrants in the community with little to no data privacy or protection.

The EM program is a pilot confined to the Greater Toronto Area and operated through a memorandum of understanding with the Correctional Service of Canada, responsible for the management of the technology (CBSA, 2018c; Khaikin, 2020). It is built upon real-time location data and intended as an add-on condition for high-risk individuals. Enrolment consists of two steps: an ankle bracelet monitor on the individual and a radio frequency modem at his or her residence. The use of surveillance technologies was motivated by the opposition to long-term detention, yet such electronic shackles – characteristic of parole-style oversight programs for the rehabilitation of offenders – further enmesh migrants in Canada's carceral system. Indeed, since the EM pilot began in Toronto, requests to utilize surveillance technologies as part of release conditions, predominantly in Quebec, have increased, at the expense of less invasive and coercive options (Khaikin, 2020).

The biometric voice system was developed using technology supplied by Connex, an Ontario company, and the EM equipment and technology are provided by a Vancouver company called JEMTEC, which has been lobbying the Canadian government for electronic monitoring services since 2000. The data gathered through JEMTEC is not protected and is stored on the servers of a privately owned sister company of Securus Technologies, a Texas-based prison communications firm (Khaikin, 2020). The CCMS organizations also utilize subcontractors for service delivery who collect and store their own data on the clients whom they serve. This raises important questions about data privacy and transparency, making an independent review body even more necessary.

The involvement of these third-party private actors in managing and policing the most vulnerable migrants imports high-tech surveillance into alternatives to detention. Similar to the NRAD form, these tools restrict the liberty of non-citizens by assessing uncertainty, thereby legitimizing and normalizing assumptions of risk and the fear that non-citizens are a danger to the public or that they will disappear once released (IHRP, 2018; Silverman & Kaytaz, 2020).

Conclusion

Detention is costly, and private companies and provincial governments engaged in providing it view it as a potential revenue stream. With the world currently facing unprecedented numbers of asylum seekers, displaced persons, and undocumented migrants, detention practices are on the rise. Profits are to be made at every step of the process in locating, detaining, housing, surveilling, and deporting these individuals. The immigration industrial complex also stands to benefit from a host of products and services related to detention, including the design and construction of facilities, security vehicles, related surveillance equipment and technology, as well as goods and services within facilities (Doty & Wheatley, 2013; Fernandes, 2007; Flynn & Cannon, 2009; Golash-Boza, 2009; Hiemstra & Conlon, 2017). A number of scholars have argued that the blurring of national security and immigration has not only exacerbated enforcement but also has eroded the rule of law and human rights constraints on legislative policies and practices (Doty & Wheatley, 2013; Fernandes, 2007; Golash-Boza, 2009; Pratt, 2005). Corporations have a significant stake in the criminalization and securitization of immigration. Advocates, non-governmental and non-profit organizations, and even academics respond with arguments and campaigns to facilitate migration and to develop and strengthen the international human rights regime (Doty & Wheatley, 2013; Hiemstra & Conlon, 2017; Menz, 2013).

These relationships demonstrate a multi-faceted and nuanced understanding of power, authority, and state responsibility. Although the reliance on private actors is often understood as diminishing the reach of the state, according to Nyers (2009, p. 2), "the state is not so much 'waning away' as being radically recast under changing historical conditions." In fact, in the context of immigration detention, it is argued that encouraging "entrepreneurs to develop new forms of sanctioning ... [has] drawn the state ever more deeply into the management of social control" (Feeley, 2002, p. 322). Hence, serving the neo-liberal agenda has broadened the scope of state control and power to which migrants are subjected. Under the aegis of deterrence and security, this trend has diminished state responsibility for protecting the human rights of detainees, while enhancing the enforcement of detention, without actually relinquishing sovereignty. Detention regimes have been legitimized and fortified despite evidence of their failure to meet policy goals and their long-term harmful effects on an already highly vulnerable population.

The immigration industrial complex is characterized by an intricate relationship of power between the state and private actors. Although at present Canada does not have any entirely private immigration detention centres, it does make widespread use of private companies to manage immigration holding facilities and assist in deportations. It also heavily utilizes private carrier sanctions, thereby enhancing the effectiveness of interdiction practices, jeopardizing potential routes of asylum, and subverting the principle of *non-refoulement*. Canada's over-reliance on correctional institutions to house immigration detainees replicates the contractual relations of privatized arrangements. The obstacles to transparency and accountability arise not from the delegation of public functions to private actors but by gaming jurisdiction, such that federal authorities deny responsibility for how provincial jails treat immigration detainees, and provincial correctional authorities deny accountability for people detained in their jails under federal immigration legislation. These mechanisms of privatization and jurisdictional gaming have in common the effect of exacerbating rights violations under conditions that make non-citizens less visible and the state less accountable.

Notes

1 ATI Request A-2019–17569.
2 A redacted copy of the NRAD form was privately shared with us by a refugee lawyer for the purpose of writing this chapter, so we cannot provide a copy of it. However, the ENF 20 manual that broadly describes the form is publicly available.
3 It can be accessed at https://endimmigrationdetention.files.wordpress.com/2015/06/cbsa-signed-agreement.pdf.

References

Ackerman, A. R., & Furman, R. (2013). The criminalization of immigration and the privatization of the immigration detention: Implications for justice. *Contemporary Justice Review, 16*(2), 251–263.

Aiken, S. (1999). New directions for refugee determination and protection in Canada. *Refuge, 18*(1), 12–17.

Alexander, M. (2012). *The new Jim Crow: Mass incarceration in the age of colorblindness*. The New Press.

Arbel, E. (2016). Bordering the Constitution, constituting the border. *Osgoode Hall Law Journal, 53*(3), 824–852.

Arbogast, L. (2017). Migrant detention in the European Union: A thriving business. *Migreurop*. http://www.migreurop.org/IMG/pdf/migrant-detention-eu-en.pdf

Atak, I., & Crépeau, F. (2013). The securitization of asylum and human rights in Canada and the European Union. In S. J. Satvinder & C. Harvey (Eds.), *Contemporary issues in refugee law* (pp. 227–257). Edward Elgar.

Bales, K. (2019, September 30). The immigration industrial complex: A global perspective on "unfree labour" in immigration detention. *Futures of Work, 9*. https://futuresofwork.co.uk/2019/09/30/the-immigration-industrial-complex-a-global-perspective-on-unfree-labour-in-immigration-detention/

Ball, D. P. (2014a, September 30). Deceased deportee's accent led to border services arrest. *The Tyee*. https://thetyee.ca/News/2014/09/30/Vega-Jimenez-Arrested-Accent/

Ball, D. P. (2014b, October 7). Private security outnumber border services in big cities. *The Tyee*. https://thetyee.ca/News/2014/10/07/Private-Guards-Outnumber-Border-Services-Officers-Major-Cities/

Bloom, T. (2013). *Statelessness and the delegation of migration functions to private actors, policy report no. 02/04*. United Nations University Institute on Globalization, Culture and Mobility.

Bloom, T. (2015). The business of migration control: Delegating migration control functions to private actors. *Global Policy, 6*(2), 151–157.

Bosworth, M. (2017). Immigration detention and penal power: A criminological perspective. In M. J. Flynn & M. B. Flynn (Eds.), *Challenging immigration detention: Academics, activists and policy-makers* (pp. 52–66). Edward Elgar.

Brouwer, A., & Kumin, J. (2003). Interception and asylum: When migration control and human rights collide. *Refuge: Canada's Periodical on Refugees, 21*(4), 6–24.

Canada Border Services Agency (CBSA). (2016). Internal Audit and Program Evaluation Directorate: Audit of immigration enforcement. https://www.cbsa-asfc.gc.ca/agency-agence/reports-rapports/ae-ve/2016/ie-emi-eng.html

Canada Border Services Agency (CBSA). (2018a). Community case management and supervision. https://www.cbsa-asfc.gc.ca/security-securite/detent/ccms-gccs-eng.html

Canada Border Services Agency (CBSA). (2018b). Voice reporting. https://www.cbsa-asfc.gc.ca/security-securite/detent/vr-rv-eng.html

Canada Border Services Agency (CBSA). (2018c). Electronic monitoring. https://www.cbsa-asfc.gc.ca/security-securite/detent/em-se-eng.html

Canada Border Services Agency (CBSA). (2018d). Code of conduct. https://www.cbsa-asfc.gc.ca/agency-agence/reports-rapports/acc-resp/code-eng.html

Canada Border Services Agency (CBSA). (2020a). Immigration holding centres. https://www.cbsa-asfc.gc.ca/security-securite/ihc-csi-eng.html

Canada Border Services Agency (CBSA). (2020b). Annual detention, fiscal year 2019 to 2020. https://www.cbsa-asfc.gc.ca/security-securite/detent/stat-2019-2020-eng.html#02

Canada Border Services Agency (CBSA). (2020c). National Immigration Detention Framework. https://www.cbsa-asfc.gc.ca/security-securite/detent/nidf-cndi-eng.html

Canada Border Services Agency (CBSA). (2021a). Border services officers: Recruitment. https://www.cbsa-asfc.gc.ca/job-emploi/recruitment-recrutement/menu-eng.html

Canada Border Services Agency (CBSA). (2021b). CBSA management response and action plan to the Canadian Red Cross 2018 to 2019 and 2019 to 2020 annual reports. https://www.cbsa-asfc.gc.ca/agency-agence/reports-rapports/security-securite/arr-det/mrap-rdpa-eng.html

Canada (Public Safety and Emergency Preparedness) v Chhina, 2019 SCC 29, [2019] 2 SCR 467.

Canadian Council for Refugees. (2013, February 21). Overview of C-31 refugee determination process. http://ccrweb.ca/en/refugee-reform

Canadian Red Cross. (2019). *Immigration detention monitoring program annual monitoring activity report*. https://www.cbsa-asfc.gc.ca/security-securite/detent/impd-pscd-eng.pdf

Carman, T. (2014, October 2). Security guards falsified reports. *Pressreader.* https://www.pressreader.com/canada/the-province/20141002/282544426534916

CBC. (2019, March 20). New $1B border strategy will get tough on irregular asylum seekers. https://www.cbc.ca/news/politics/border-strategy-budget-money-1.5064169

Citizenship and Immigration Canada (CIC). (2002). *Lessons learned: 1999 marine arrivals in British Columbia. Final report.* http://www.cic.gc.ca/english/research/evaluation/marine.html#detention

Conlon, D., and Hiemstra, N. (2014). Examining the everyday micro-economies of migrant detention in the United States. *Geographica Helvetica, 69*, 335–344.

Dench, J., & Crépeau, F. (2003). Introduction: Interdiction at the expense of human rights: A long-term containment strategy. *Refuge: Canada's Periodical on Refugees, 21*(4), 2–5.

Dickerson, C. (2020, August 16). A private security company is detaining migrant children at hotels. *New York Times.* https://www.nytimes.com/2020/08/16/us/migrant-children-hotels-coronavirus.html

Doty, R. L., & Wheatley, E. S. (2013). Private detention and the immigration industrial complex. *International Political Sociology, 7*(4), 426–443.

Ellis, B., & Hicken, M. (2019, November 5). Major hotels break promises on allowing feds to detain immigrants in their rooms. *CNN.* https://www.cnn.com/2019/11/05/us/ice-hotels-immigrant-detention-invs/index.html

Enns, P., & Ramirez, M. (2018). Privatizing punishment: Testing theories of public support for private prison and immigration detention facilities. *Criminology, 56*(3), 546–573.

Feeley, M. J. (2002). Entrepreneurs of punishment: The legacy of privatization. *Punishment and Society, 4*(3), 321–344.

Fernandes, D. (2007). *Targeted: Homeland security and the business of immigration.* Seven Stories Press.

Flynn, E., & Bauder, H. (2015). The private sector, institutions of higher education, and immigrant settlement in Canada. *Revue de l'integration et de la migration internationale, 16*(3), 539–556.

Flynn, M., & Cannon, C. (2009). The privatization of immigration detention: Towards a global view. Global Detention Project Working Paper No. 1.

Foucault, M. (1979). *Discipline and punish: The birth of the prison.* Vintage/Random House.

Foucault, M. (2004). *Security, territory, population – Lectures at the Collège de France 1977–1978.* Palgrave Macmillan.

Galaski, J. (2018, December 10). Ever wondered why refugees don't take the plane? *Liberties.* https://www.liberties.eu/en/news/why-refugees-do-not-take-the-plane/16529

Global Detention Project. (2018). Canada immigration detention. https://www.globaldetentionproject.org/countries/americas/canada

Global Detention Project. (2021). *Country report. Immigration detention in Canada: Progressive reforms and missed opportunities.* https://www.globaldetentionproject.org/wp-content/uploads/2021/04/GDP-Immigration-Detention-in-Canada-2021.pdf

Golash-Boza, T. (2009). The immigration industrial complex: Why we enforce immigration policies destined to fail. *Sociology Compass, 3*(2), 295–309.

Goodwin-Gill, G. (1986). International law and the detention of refugees and asylum seekers. *International Migration Review, 20*(2), 193–219.

Gottschalk, M. (2016). *Caught: The prison state and the lockdown of American politics.* Princeton University Press.

Hiemstra, N., & Conlon, D. (2017). Beyond privatization: Bureaucratization and the spatialities of immigration detention expansion. *Territory, Politics, Governance, 5*(3), 252–268.

Hucklesby, A., & Lister, S. (Eds.). (2018). *The private sector and criminal justice*. Palgrave Macmillan.

Human Rights Watch. (2021, June 17). "I didn't feel like a human in there": Immigration detention in Canada and its impact on mental health. https://www.hrw.org/report/2021/06/17/i-didnt-feel-human-there/immigration-detention-canada-and-its-impact-mental#_ftn209

Ibrahim, M. (2005). Securitization of migration: A racial discourse. *International Migration, 43*, 163–187.

Immigration and Refugee Board of Canada (IRB). (2018). *Report of the 2017/2018 external audit (detention review)*. https://irb.gc.ca/en/transparency/reviews-audit-evaluations/Pages/ID-external-audit-1718.aspx

Immigration and Refugee Protection Act (IRPA), SC 2001, c 27. https://www.refworld.org/docid/4f0dc8f12.html

Immigration, Refugees and Citizenship Canada (IRCC). (2019). *Operational instructions and guidelines. ENF 20: Detention*. https://www.canada.ca/en/immigration-refugees-citizenship/corporate/publications-manuals/operational-bulletins-manuals.html

Indeed. (n.d.). CBSA immigration holding centre officers – Calling all law enforcement graduates! https://ca.indeed.com/jobs?q=Detentionandadvn=196737733431339andvjk=e5db89236741cf32

International Human Rights Program (IHRP). (2015). Arbitrary imprisonment and cruel treatment of migrants with mental health issues in Canada. https://tbinternet.ohchr.org/Treaties/CCPR/Shared%20Documents/CAN/INT_CCPR_CSS_CAN_20682_E.pdf

International Human Rights Program (IHRP). (2018). Rights violations associated with Canada's treatment of vulnerable persons in immigration detention. https://ihrp.law.utoronto.ca/utfl_file/count/media/Canada%20UPR%20Final.pdf

Kennedy, B. (2017a, March 17). Caged by Canada: Part 1. *The Toronto Star*. http://projects.thestar.com/caged-by-canada-immigration-detention/part-1/

Kennedy, B. (2017b, March 17). Caged by Canada: Part 2. *The Toronto Star*. http://projects.thestar.com/caged-by-canada-immigration-detention/part-2/

Kennedy, B. (2017c, April 12). Canada's immigration detainees being locked up based on dodgy risk assessments, *Star* finds. *The Toronto Star*. https://www.thestar.com/news/investigations/2017/04/12/canadas-immigration-detainees-being-locked-up-based-on-dodgy-risk-assessments-star-finds.html

Kennedy, B. (2018, December 19). Jail medical staff gave Teresa Gratton methadone doses way above guidelines, and this caused her death. *The Toronto Star*. https://www.thestar.com/news/investigations/2018/12/19/jail-medical-staff-gave-teresa-gratton-methadone-doses-way-above-guidelines-and-this-caused-her-death.html

Kennedy, B. (2019, January 24). Hundreds of nonviolent immigration detainees sent to max-security jails as part of "abhorrent" government program. *The Toronto Star*. https://www.thestar.com/news/investigations/2019/01/24/hundreds-of-nonviolent-immigration-detainees-sent-to-max-security-jails-as-part-of-abhorrent-government-program.html

Keung, N. (2019, July 17). Record number of Canada-bound visitors barred from flights on advice of Canada border agents. *The Toronto Star.* https://go-gale-com.myaccess.library.utoronto.ca/ps/i.do?p=CPIandu=utoronto_mainandid=GALE%7CA602253395andv=2.1andit=randsid=summon

Khaikin, L. (2020, June 29). Criminalizing the most vulnerable: Migrant surveillance in Canada. *Canadian Dimension.* https://canadiandimension.com/articles/view/criminalizing-the-most-vulnerable-migrant-surveillance-in-canada

Kripa, E., & Mueller, S. (2017, August 21). Growing private detention industry threatens immigrants' rights on the U.S.-Mexico border. *The Architect's Newspaper.* https://www.archpaper.com/2017/08/private-detention-industry-us-mexico-border/

Lacin, I. O. (2019). Rethinking sovereignty: The implications of the role of private security companies in the prevention and the regulation of unauthorized flows. *Cambridge Review of International Affairs, 33*(3), 330–346.

Lahav, G. (2010). Immigration and the state: The devolution and privatisation of immigration control in the EU. *Journal of Ethnic and Migration Studies, 24*(4), 675–694.

Lethbridge, J. (2017). Privatisation of migration and refugee services and other forms of state disengagement. *Public Services International Research Unit.* https://www.epsu.org/sites/default/files/article/files/PSI-EPSU%20Privatisation%20of%20Migration%20%26%20Refugee%20Services_EN.pdf

Macklin, A. (2001). Borderline security. In R. J. Daniels, P. Macklem, & K. Roach (Eds.), *The security of freedom: Essays on Canada's anti-terrorism bill* (pp. 383–404). University of Toronto Press.

Macklin, A. (2003). Multiculturalism meets privatisation: The case of faith-based arbitration. *International Journal of Law in Context, 9*(3), 343–365.

Macklin, A. (2013). A safe country to emulate? Canada and the European refugee. In H. Lambert, J. McAdam, & M. Fullerton (Eds.), *The global reach of European refugee law* (pp. 99–131). Cambridge University Press.

Mainwaring, C., & Silverman, S. J. (2017). Detention-as-spectacle. *International Political Sociology, 11*(1), 21–38.

Malakieh, J. (2020, December 21). Adult and youth correctional statistics in Canada 2018/2019. *Statistics Canada.* https://www150.statcan.gc.ca/n1/pub/85-002-x/2020001/article/00016-eng.htm

McSorley, T. (2019, September 5). Border guards without boundaries: Why CBSA needs a watchdog. *Behind the Numbers.* https://behindthenumbers.ca/2019/09/05/border-guards-without-boundaries-why-cbsa-needs-a-watchdog/

Menz, G. (2009). The neoliberalized state and migration control: The rise of private actors in the enforcement and design of migration policy. *Debatte: Journal of Contemporary Central and Eastern Europe, 17*(3), 315–332.

Menz, G. (2011). Neo-liberalism, privatization and the outsourcing of migration management: A five-country comparison. *Competition and Change, 15*(2), 116–135.

Menz, G. (2013). The neoliberalized state and the growth of the migration industry. In T. Gammeltoft-Hansen & N. Nyberg Sorensen (Eds.), *The migration industry and the commercialization of international migration* (pp. 108–127). Routledge.

Molnar, P., & Silverman, S. J. (2017, November 15). Migrants are dying in Canadian detention centres. The government needs to act. *Maclean's.* https://www.macleans.ca/opinion/migrants-are-dying-in-canadian-detention-centres-the-government-needs-to-act/

Molnar, P., & Silverman, S. J. (2018, July 5). Canada needs to get out of the immigration detention business. *CBC.* https://www.cbc.ca/news/opinion/immigration-detention-1.4733897

Montgomery, R., & Griffiths, C. T. (2015). The use of private security services for policing. *Public Safety Canada.* https://www.publicsafety.gc.ca/cnt/rsrcs/pblctns/archive-2015-r041/2015-r041-en.pdf

Murphy, C. (2007). "Securitizing" Canadian policing: A new policing paradigm for the post 9/11 security state? *The Canadian Journal of Sociology, 32*(4), 449–475.

Nakache, D. (2011). The human and financial cost of detention of asylum seekers in Canada. *United Nations High Commissioner for Refugees.* https://www.refworld.org/docid/4fafc44c2.html

Nyers, P. (2009). Introduction: Securitizations of citizenship. In P. Nyers (Ed.), *Securitizations of citizenship* (pp. 1–14). Routledge.

Penovic, T. (2014). Privatised immigration detention services: Challenges and opportunities for implementing human rights. *Law in Context: Socio-Legal Journal, 31,* 10–47.

Poynter, B. (2012, November 29). Private prison firms look to cash in on Canada asylum crackdown. *The Guardian.* https://www.theguardian.com/world/2012/nov/29/canada-asylum-seekers-private-prison-companies

Pratt, A. (2005). *Securing borders: Detention and deportation in Canada.* UBC Press.

Pratt, T. C., & Maahs, J. (1999). Are private prisons more cost-effective than public prisons? A meta-analysis of evaluation research studies. *Crime and Delinquency, 45*(3), 358–371.

Public Works and Government Services Canada (PWGSC). (2017a, August 10). Immigration holding centre A&E project (EZ944-171885/001/MTC). *Buyandsell.gc.ca.* https://buyandsell.gc.ca/procurement-data/award-notice/PW-MTC-560-14362-001

Public Works and Government Services Canada (PWGSC). (2017b, December 14). Immigration holding centre construction (EZ899-180351/001/PWY). *Buyandsell.gc.ca.* https://buyandsell.gc.ca/procurement-data/award-notice/PW-PWY-015-8079-001

Public Works and Government Services Canada (PWGSC). (2018, June 22). Corbel Management Corp (47636-187661/001/TOR-000). *Buyandsell.gc.ca.* https://buyandsell.gc.ca/procurement-data/contract-history/47636-187661-001-TOR

Public Works and Government Services Canada (PWGSC). (2019, February 23). G4S Secure Solutions (Canada) Ltd/G4S Solutions de sécurité (Canada) Ltd (47419-199331/001/TOR-000). *Buyandsell.gc.ca.* https://buyandsell.gc.ca/procurement-data/contract-history/47419-199331-001-TOR

Rodenhauser, T. (2014). Another brick in the wall: Carrier sanctions and the privatization of immigration control. *International Journal of Refugee Law, 26*(2), 223–247.

Rodier, C. (2012). *Xénophobie business. À quoi servent les contrôles migratoires?* La Découverte.

Rygiel, K. (2008). The securitized citizen. In E. F. Isin (Ed.), *Recasting the social in citizenship* (pp. 210–238). University of Toronto Press.

Scotland v Canada (Attorney General), 2017 ONSC 4850.

Serco. (n.d.). Citizen services. https://www.serco.com/sector-expertise/citizen-services

Shearing, C., & Stenning, P. (1983). Private security: Implications for social control. *Social Problems, 30*(5), 493–506.

Silverman, S. J. (2014). In the wake of irregular arrivals: Changes to the Canadian immigration detention system. *Refuge: Canada's Journal on Refugees, 30*(2), 27–34.

Silverman, S. J., & Kaytaz, E. S. (2020). Examining the "National Risk Assessment for Detention" process: An intersectional analysis of detaining "dangerousness" in Canada. *Journal of Ethnic and Migration Studies*, 1–17. https://doi.org/10.1080/1369183X.2020.1841613

Silverman, S. J., & Massa, E. (2012). Why immigration detention is unique. *Population, Space and Place, 18*(6), 677–686.

Silverman, S. J., & Molnar, P. (2016). Everyday injustice: Barriers to access to justice for immigration detainees in Canada. *Refugee Survey Quarterly, 35*(1), 109–127.

Silverman, S. J., & Nethery, A. (2015). Understanding immigration detention and its human impact. In S. J. Silverman & A. Nethery (Eds.), *Immigration detention: The migration of a policy and its human impact* (pp. 1–12). Routledge.

Singh v Minister of Employment and Immigration, [1985] 1 SCR 177.

Sniderman, P. M., Hagendoorn, L., & Prior, M. (2004). Predisposing factors and situational triggers: Exclusionary reactions to immigrant minorities. *American Political Science Review, 98*, 35–49.

Stribley, R. (2017, June 29). What is the "immigration industrial complex"? *HuffPost*. https://www.huffpost.com/entry/what-is-the-immigration-industrial-complex_b_5953b8cae4b0c85b96c65e2c

Stumpf, J. P. (2006). The crimmigration crisis: Immigrants, crime, and sovereign power. *American University Law Review, 56*(2), 367–419.

Track, L., & Paterson, J. (2017). *Oversight at the border: A model for independent accountability at the Canada Border Services Agency*. British Columbia Civil Liberties Association CanLIIDocs 199. http://canlii.ca/t/7d8

Trujillo-Pagan, N. (2014). Emphasizing the "complex" in the immigration industrial complex. *Critical Sociology, 40*(1), 29–46.

United Nations General Assembly (UNGA). (2017, August 4). Report of the working group on the use of mercenaries as a means of violating human rights and impeding the exercise of the right of peoples to self-determination, A/72/150. https://undocs.org/pdf?symbol=en/A/72/286

United Nations Working Group on Arbitrary Detention. (2018, February 7). Advance edited version: Revised deliberation no. 5 on deprivation of liberty of migrants. *Office of the High Commissioner for Human Rights*. https://www.ohchr.org/Documents/Issues/Detention/RevisedDeliberation_AdvanceEditedVersion.pdf

Vickers, J., & Yarrow, G. (1991). Economic perspective on privatization. *The Journal of Economic Perspectives, 5*, 111–132.

Walters, W. (2002). Deportation, expulsion, and the international police of aliens. *Citizenship Studies, 6*(3), 265–292.

Zyfi, J., & Atak, I. (2018). Playing with lives under the guise of fair play. *International Journal of Migration and Border Studies, 4*(4), 345–365.

Postscript

Privatization Cultures and the Racial Order: A Dispatch from the United States

TORIN MONAHAN

Consider the following two scenes. In the first, paramilitary "rapid deployment teams" descend on Portland, Oregon, in July 2020 during the height of the racial justice movement and early in the COVID-19 pandemic (Kanno-Youngs, 2020). Agents from various branches of the Department of Homeland Security (DHS) cruise around in unmarked minivans, chasing down and forcibly abducting protesters without telling them why they are being apprehended or held (Goldberg, 2020). It is unclear whether the heavily armed agents, decked out in camouflage fatigues without identifying insignia, are members of law enforcement or random right-wing militia members responding to President Trump's call to "dominate" protesters in so-called liberal cities (Olmos et al., 2020). Both the ambiguity and the abductions produce a sense of terror, a feeling of vulnerability to indiscriminate and unaccountable violence that is one of the hallmarks of totalitarian regimes (Los, 2003; Monahan & Murakami Wood, 2018). (Fortunately, they also engender a sense of collective outrage that has the effect of consolidating even more support for the racial justice movement.) The state agents in these exercises were functioning more like private security forces, intentionally masking their identities and representative agencies, while completely ignoring due process, to instill maximum fear with minimum accountability.

Now for the second scene. In February 2020, a young Black man, Ahmaud Arbery, is jogging around his suburban neighbourhood in southern Georgia.

As he passes a house, a white man in his front yard sees Arbery and yells to his son to come help him confront the jogger (Fausset, 2020b). The two men, Gregory and Travis McMichael, grab a shotgun and a handgun, jump into their pickup truck (adorned with a Confederate flag sticker), and take off after Arbery (McLaughlin, 2020). Another white neighbour, William Bryan, follows in his vehicle to assist the McMichaels and film the subsequent confrontation. The pursuers pull ahead of Arbery, who tries to run past them. Travis McMichael, with handgun "cover" from his father in the truck's bed, gets out of the vehicle with his shotgun and, after a brief tussle, shoots Arbery three times and then mutters a racial slur over his dying body (McLaughlin, 2020). According to a prosecutor on the case, the perpetrators of this modern-day lynching were simply making a citizen's arrest of a suspected burglar and practising self-defence in shooting Arbery (Fausset, 2020a). It turns out that the father, Gregory McMichael, was a former police officer who had also worked in the local district attorney's (DA's) office, so he was known to those investigating the case (Orecchio-Egresitz, 2020). The police and DA's office saw no reason to make any arrest. It was not until the video of the shooting was released, fuelling even more public outrage against anti-Black violence, that arrests were made, seventy-four days after the murder (Ellis, 2020). In this scene, private civilians were emboldened to act like police and share their professed monopoly on (racial) violence. The assailants mobilized the most elementary form of privatization, "the adoption of public functions by private entities or individuals" (Finegan, 2013, p. 92). Various citizen's arrest, stand-your-ground, and gun-rights laws in the United States support these policing actions by civilians, particularly, as the evidence shows, for the maintenance of white supremacy.

Although the emphasis of this edited volume is on formal arrangements for the privatization of – and private influence on – criminal justice and security institutions, informal, ad hoc, and provisional arrangements can shed light on the messy realities of privatization writ large. With the two scenes sketched above, we see how privatization dynamics flow between institutions and the public; they percolate through society and are readily appropriated for political, discriminatory, and violent ends. Police and security personnel seek various privileges of the private sector, including reduced accountability and circumvention of legal restrictions. Certain members of the public (or of private industry) seek police-like authority and in many cases are actively sought as "partners" in law enforcement. Both moves contribute to patterns of abuse and evasions of accountability. Seen from this perspective, privatization is not simply a form of outsourcing, as the contributions to this volume make clear, but is instead a pernicious cultural logic that affords both the erosion of democratic governance and the violent preservation of racial hierarchies.

Granted, blurred boundaries between public and private sectors are nothing new, especially not for the provision of policing. Whether with forms of citizen policing and neighbourhood-watch campaigns over the centuries (Reeves, 2017), or private security contractors acting as state-funded mercenaries or guardians of residential gated communities (Abrahamsen & Williams, 2011; Monahan, 2010), or DHS sites contracting out to private data brokers to obtain information that would be illegal for them to collect on their own (Monahan & Palmer, 2009; Monahan & Regan, 2012), the relaxing of public-private boundaries has a long history littered with cases of abuse. Nonetheless, it is important to question whether we have encountered a shift intensifying and normalizing such arrangements and, if so, what the consequences might be. Certainly, the combination of neoliberalism and racial capitalism animates such developments in ways that amplify economic precarity and racial conflict throughout societies. As Loïc Wacquant (2009, p. 6) writes of the US context, "the 'invisible hand' of the unskilled labor market, strengthened by the shift from welfare to workfare, finds its ideological extension and institutional complement in the 'iron fist' of the penal state." The growth of the racialized prison industrial complex is clearly one outcome of these trends, in which private prisons and outsourcing of costs to prisoners and their families (e.g., through electronic monitoring and probation schemes) further entrench conditions of poverty and abjection (Eisen, 2018; Monahan, 2017).

Alongside documentable structural shifts of this sort, what is further troubling are the modes of violence afforded by cultures of privatization, broadly construed. As with the two scenes described above, both official and civilian police actions are embraced in the service of protecting the racial order, of shoring up white supremacy, seen as being under attack. Rather than being exceptional, though, these positionalities permeate US society and can be witnessed in much more mundane practices, such as with white homeowners using Nextdoor and Ring surveillance networks to profile racial minorities (Bridges, 2021; Kurwa, 2019). Although privatization and private influence might not be the direct causes of such practices, nonetheless they enable and aggravate them by inviting biased interpretations of threat and eroding forms of accountability. The United States might be a limit case of these problematics, but surely similar articulations are present in other national contexts as well. These examples underscore the need to interrogate dynamics of privatization so that scholars can also find pathways to confront foundational and persistent inequalities in societies.

References

Abrahamsen, R., & Williams, M. C. (2011). *Security beyond the state: Private security in international politics.* Cambridge University Press.

Bridges, L. (2021). Infrastructural obfuscation: Unpacking the carceral logics of the Ring surveillant assemblage. *Information, Communication & Society, 24*(6), 830–849.

Eisen, L.-B. (2018). *Inside private prisons: An American dilemma in the age of mass incarceration.* Columbia University Press.

Ellis, N. T. (2020, May 7). Why it took more than 2 months for murder charges and arrests in the death of Ahmaud Arbery. *USA Today.* https://www.usatoday.com/story/news/2020/05/07/ahmaud-arbery-shooting-video-prosecutor-arrest-mcmichael/3089040001/

Fausset, R. (2020a, May 7). 2 suspects charged with murder in Ahmaud Arbery shooting. *New York Times.* https://www.nytimes.com/2020/05/07/us/ahmaud-arbery-shooting-arrest.html

Fausset, R. (2020b, December 17). What we know about the shooting death of Ahmaud Arbery. *New York Times.* https://www.nytimes.com/article/ahmaud-arbery-shooting-georgia.html

Finegan, S. (2013). Watching the watchers: The growing privatization of criminal law enforcement and the need for limits on neighborhood watch associations. *University of Massachusetts Law Review, 8,* 88–134.

Goldberg, M. (2020, July 20). Trump's occupation of American cities has begun. *New York Times.* https://www.nytimes.com/2020/07/20/opinion/portland-protests-trump.html

Kanno-Youngs, Z. (2020, July 17). Were the actions of federal agents in Portland legal? *New York Times.* https://www.nytimes.com/2020/07/17/us/politics/federal-agents-portland-arrests.html

Kurwa, R. (2019). Building the digitally gated community: The case of Nextdoor. *Surveillance & Society, 17*(1–2), 111–117.

Los, M. (2003). Technologies of total domination. *Surveillance & Society, 2*(1), 15–38.

McLaughlin, E. C. (2020, June 4). Ahmaud Arbery was hit with a truck before he died, and his killer allegedly used a racial slur, investigator testifies. *CNN.* https://www.cnn.com/2020/06/04/us/mcmichaels-hearing-ahmaud-arbery/index.html

Monahan, T. (2010). *Surveillance in the time of insecurity.* Rutgers University Press.

Monahan, T. (2017). Regulating belonging: Surveillance, inequality, and the cultural production of abjection. *Journal of Cultural Economy, 10*(2), 191–206.

Monahan, T., & Murakami Wood, D. (2018). State and authority. In T. Monahan & D. Murakami Wood (Eds.), *Surveillance studies: A reader* (pp. 63–66). Oxford University Press.

Monahan, T., & Palmer, N. A. (2009). The emerging politics of DHS fusion centers. *Security Dialogue, 40*(6), 617–636.

Monahan, T., & Regan, P. M. (2012). Zones of opacity: Data fusion in post-9/11 security organizations. *Canadian Journal of Law and Society, 27*(3), 301–317.

Olmos, S., Baker, M., & Kanno-Youngs, Z. (2020, July 21). Federal officers deployed in Portland didn't have proper training, D.H.S. memo said. *New York Times.* https://www.nytimes.com/2020/07/18/us/portland-protests.html

Orecchio-Egresitz, H. (2020, May 8). Gregory McMichael had a career in local law enforcement for over 30 years and faced suspension for a lapse in gun training. *Insider.* https://www.insider.com/this-is-what-we-know-about-gregory-and-travis-mcmichael-2020-5

Reeves, J. (2017). *Citizen spies: The long rise of America's surveillance society.* New York University Press.

Wacquant, L. (2009). *Punishing the poor: The neoliberal government of social insecurity.* Duke University Press.

Contributors

Daniella Barreto holds an MSc in population and public health studies from the University of British Columbia, where her research focuses on violence and marginalized populations living with HIV. She is the digital activism coordinator at Amnesty International Canada and a research assistant at UBC's Centre for Gender and Sexual Health Equity.

Rebecca Jaremko Bromwich is the manager of equity, diversity, and inclusion for the international law firm Gowling WLG in Canada and Russia. She formerly served as the director of the graduate diploma program in conflict resolution in the Department of Law and Legal Studies at Carleton University and remains an adjunct professor with that department. A practising lawyer since 2003, she also worked as a crown attorney with the Ministry of the Attorney General in Ottawa. Bromwich received her PhD in 2015 from Carleton University in the Department of Law and Legal Studies, the first graduate of that program. She also has an LL.M. and an LL.B., received from Queen's University in 2002 and 2001, respectively, and holds a graduate certificate in women's studies from the University of Cincinnati. She is a co-editor of Robson Hall Law School's criminal law and justice blog, robsoncrim.com.

Jamie Duncan is a PhD student at the University of Toronto's Centre for Criminology and Sociolegal Studies and a researcher at the University of

Winnipeg's Centre for Access to Information and Justice. He is also a junior fellow of Massey College. Jamie has written and spoken about the use of advanced technology in policing and border security, political communications in the criminal justice field, as well as issues of accountability in technology and data governance. His work has appeared in outlets such as *The British Journal of Criminology* and *The Globe and Mail*.

Steven Kohm is a professor of criminal justice at the University of Winnipeg. He is lead editor of *Screening Justice: Canadian Crime Films, Culture and Society* (2017, Fernwood) and co-editor of *The Annual Review of Interdisciplinary Justice Research*, published by the Centre for Interdisciplinary Justice Studies (CIJS). His research is published in a variety of interdisciplinary scholarly journals. His Social Sciences and Humanities Research Council of Canada (SSHRC)–funded work on Canadian crime film has been adapted as a documentary video series produced by Eagle Vision Productions, an award-winning Indigenous-owned film and TV production company located in Winnipeg, Canada: http://uwinnipeg.ca/frozen-justice.

Alex Luscombe is a PhD candidate in the Centre for Criminology and Sociolegal Studies at the University of Toronto. His research focuses on policing and social control, data justice and information politics, and computational social science. He has worked as an international consultant for the Organisation for Economic Co-operation and Development. He is co-editor of *Freedom of Information and Social Science Research Design* (Routledge, 2019). Since 2017, he has served on the editorial board of *Criminological Highlights*, a University of Toronto publication aimed at providing criminal justice practitioners with an accessible overview of cutting-edge criminological research.

Kaitlin MacKenzie completed her master's thesis research at Carleton University, exploring the collateral consequences of incarceration among families of prisoners. Her research areas of interest are the pains of imprisonment for prisoners and their families and the impacts of privatization on prisoners.

Debra Mackinnon is an assistant professor of criminology in the Interdisciplinary Studies Department at Lakehead University. Her research interests include surveillance, policing, governance and regulation, smart technologies, and qualitative methods. Her current work examines the intersection of private security, surveillance technologies, and public-private partnerships in North American business improvement areas and their potential to limit accountability, deepen systemic racism, and exacerbate unequal service delivery. She has published in the *Canadian Journal of Sociology* and *Surveillance and Society*.

Audrey Macklin is the director of the Centre for Criminology and Sociolegal Studies and a professor and the chair of human rights in the Faculty of Law at the University of Toronto. She teaches, researches, and writes on all aspects of migration and citizenship law. She became a Trudeau fellow in 2017.

Torin Monahan is a professor of communication at the University of North Carolina at Chapel Hill. His research focuses on institutional and cultural transformations with new technologies, with an emphasis on surveillance and security programs. He has published over fifty articles or book chapters and six books, including *Surveillance Studies: A Reader* (with David Murakami Wood) and *Surveillance in the Time of Insecurity*. His areas of expertise include science and technology studies, visual culture, surveillance studies, ethnography, urban studies, and contemporary social and cultural theory. Monahan is co-editor-in-chief of the leading academic journal on surveillance, *Surveillance and Society*, and the principal investigator in the NSF-funded Platform Mediation research project.

Massimiliano Mulone is an associate professor in the School of Criminology at the University of Montreal and a researcher in the International Center for Comparative Criminology. His main research investigates the commodification of security – how policing and security are being transformed progressively from collective to private goods – and its consequences for the governance of security. He is currently conducting research on racial profiling by police as well as studies on the control of police deviance.

Nicholas Pope is a human rights lawyer in Ottawa whose work as a student-at-law was supervised by Rebecca Bromwich. He graduated from the University of Calgary Faculty of Law. Prior to going to law school, he was involved with social justice and civil liberties work in Canada and abroad. Pope was a restorative justice intern with the Mennonite Central Committee and a summer law student with Freedom Now in Washington, DC, where he worked on issues related to the arbitrary detention of prisoners of conscience. He was also a legal researcher and an advocacy officer, working in Jerusalem, and a refugee resettlement officer in Alberta.

Derek Silva is an associate professor of criminology at King's University College. His primary research interests include the configuration and reconfiguration of discourses of "radicalization" and violent extremism, sport, punishment, and inequality. His work can be found in various peer-reviewed journals as well as in edited volumes such as *The Handbook of Social Control* (2018) and *The Cambridge Handbook of Social Problems* (2018). Silva is also a co-editor (with Mathieu Deflem) of Emerald's *Sociology of Crime, Law and Deviance* annual volume and a co-host of *The End of Sport* podcast.

Rashmee Singh is an associate professor in the Department of Sociology and Legal Studies at the University of Waterloo. Her work examines the governance of domestic violence and the roles of grassroots organizations and quasi-legal actors in the process of prosecution. Her current research project explores the role of penal voluntary sector assemblages in specialized prostitution and human trafficking courts throughout the United States. She has published articles in *Theoretical Criminology, Law & Social Inquiry, Social Politics,* and the *British Journal of Criminology*.

Erin Gibbs Van Brunschot is a professor of sociology and the director of the Centre for Military, Security and Strategic Studies at the University of Calgary. Her research has focused on "risk management" and the use of technology as a means to reduce the likelihood of crime. She has investigated the use of technology to manage high-risk offenders and, more recently, studied the technology-risk nexus in policing as well as jurisdictional issues regarding the provision of security.

Kevin Walby is an associate professor of criminal justice at the University of Winnipeg. He has authored or co-authored articles in a number of journals. He is the author of *Touching Encounters: Sex, Work, and Male-for-Male Internet Escorting* (University of Chicago Press, 2012) and a co-author of *Municipal Corporate Security in International Context* (Routledge, 2015). He has also co-edited a number of volumes, most recently *Freedom of Information and Social Science Research Design* (Routledge, 2019) and is a co-editor of the *Journal of Prisoners on Prisons*.

Adam White has been a senior lecturer in criminology at the Centre for Criminological Research, School of Law, University of Sheffield, since 2016. Before arriving in Sheffield, he was a lecturer and then a senior lecturer in public policy in the Department of Politics, University of York. He has also spent time as a visiting scholar at the University of Washington (Seattle) and a researcher for Gun Free South Africa (Cape Town) and Demos (London). His research focuses on three interconnected themes: the rise of the private security and private military industries in the postwar era; corresponding issues of governance, regulation, and legitimacy in the security and military sectors; and the changing nature of state-market relations. Over the past decade, White has published thirty journal articles and book chapters on the privatization of criminal justice and defence as well as one book, *The Politics of Private Security: Regulation, Reform and Re-Legitimation*.

Jona Zyfi is a PhD candidate at the Centre for Criminology and Sociolegal Studies at the University of Toronto and a junior fellow at Massey College. Her research focuses on technology in immigration and asylum processes, cross-border governance and policy, and the international protection regime. She also serves as the student director for the Canadian Association for Refugee and Forced Migration Studies.

Index

access to information, 14, 231, 268, 274, 296
accountability, 5, 14, 16, 17, 55, 67, 83, 100, 105, 109, 110, 111, 113–15, 117, 118, 134, 138, 142, 146, 176, 183, 206, 209, 210, 213, 222, 223, 225, 227–29, 231, 232, 233, 235, 240, 241, 248–50, 255, 259, 260, 263, 265, 275, 277, 281, 290–92, 296, 297
airlines, 248, 249, 252, 254, 255
airports, 255, 261, 262, 268
anti-terrorism provisions, 270
apps, 15, 108, 116, 127, 128, 130, 132–40, 142, 144–46
artificial intelligence, vi, 8, 107, 153, 171–73
assemblage, 56–59, 61, 64, 67, 68, 127, 200, 202, 204, 205, 209, 210, 214, 298
Auditor General, 177, 183, 184, 192, 233, 235
Australia, 12, 33, 37, 236, 248, 250, 251, 256–58, 263

borders, vi, 4, 9, 13, 16, 17, 212, 219, 228, 247, 248, 251, 253, 255, 257, 262, 264, 265, 268, 296, 299
Brodeur, J.P., 6, 9, 13, 31, 81, 102, 106, 126, 129, 221, 223, 224, 225, 226, 228, 235, 240,
Business Improvement Areas/Districts (BIAs), vi, 5, 15, 33, 55, 126–32, 134–46, 297

campus security (postsecondary), 14, 74–85, 87, 88, 91, 93
Canada, iii, iv, v, vi, viii, ix, 3–17, 33–35, 37, 38, 48, 49, 51–53, 55–59, 67–70, 76, 78, 80, 86, 87, 90, 99, 100, 104–12, 118, 126, 154–57, 159, 165, 167, 170, 171, 173, 176, 177, 182, 185, 202, 206, 221, 222–25, 227–33, 235, 236–42, 247, 248, 250, 252–57, 259, 261, 264, 266–70, 276–79, 281, 295–97
Canadian Border Services Agency (CBSA), 253, 257

Canadian Centre for Child Protection (C3P), 14, 49, 51, 69
Canadian Security Intelligence Service (CSIS), 11, 223
Charter of Rights and Freedoms, 65, 78, 83, 165, 168, 253
Child Find Manitoba, 14, 50, 51
city services, 127, 132, 135–38, 146
clean and safe (practices/mandates), 15, 126, 127, 128, 129, 130, 132, 136, 137, 139, 140, 143, 144
Coalition against Violence (CAV), 203, 204, 207–09, 211–14
commercialization, 6, 12, 33, 34, 39, 75, 153
commission of inquiry, 259
Communications Security Establishment (CSE), 223, 233, 234, 237, 238
community, 10, 14, 16, 29, 36, 49, 50, 55, 60, 66, 68, 75–78, 82, 83, 87, 88, 105, 107, 116, 129, 132, 134, 136, 137, 139, 140, 158, 184–86, 188, 192, 200–8, 213, 214, 228, 239, 249, 275, 278, 279
community policing, 29, 129, 136, 140
community safety, 36, 116, 136, 137, 139, 140, 184, 275
COMPAS, 157, 158, 160–64, 170
consumerism, 34
consumption, 16, 52, 126, 177, 180, 181, 193
corporate security, 31, 75, 76, 85, 87, 88, 92, 298
corporatization, 6, 11, 12, 15, 56, 62, 75, 84, 102, 127–29, 146, 153
crime, vii, 29, 30, 36–39, 51–54, 56–58, 60–62, 74, 77, 87, 91, 104, 106–10, 112, 114, 115, 126, 129, 140, 157, 165, 198, 199, 201, 202, 206, 208, 212, 214, 224, 250, 252, 253, 266, 271, 272, 277, 296, 298; prevention of, 60, 61

Criminal Code, 11, 52, 78, 86, 87, 272
criminal justice system, vi, vii, viii, 4–8, 13, 55, 58, 79, 86, 92, 115, 153–57, 172, 173, 192, 193, 198–204, 207, 209, 213, 214, 222, 225, 250, 267
criminalization, 202, 206, 247, 249, 250, 251, 265, 277, 280
"crimmigration," 250, 266
culture, 15, 39, 40, 48, 49, 58, 67, 74, 113, 114, 116, 176, 177, 182, 189, 191, 193, 228, 237, 260, 296, 297
cyberspace, 51, 52

data, 15, 31, 38, 42, 49, 100–4, 106–13, 116–18, 127, 130, 132, 135, 137, 138, 140–46, 153, 154, 157, 158, 161, 170, 172, 173, 186, 204, 228, 231, 268, 274, 279, 280, 292, 296
democracy, viii
detention, vi, 7, 16, 17, 172, 176, 179, 182–86, 188, 189, 247–81, 298
DiMaggio, P., 14, 28–31, 38, 42
discourse, 15, 32, 34, 35, 39, 101, 103, 109, 114, 116, 128, 142, 173, 209, 224, 252, 253, 265, 298
discrimination, 81, 90, 100, 101, 104, 105, 109, 110–12, 114, 115–18, 155, 159, 160, 162, 171, 209, 269, 291
domestic violence, vi, 16, 198–200, 202, 203, 205–11, 213–14, 298
dramatization, of security, 32
Dupont, B., 9, 27, 30–32, 34, 36, 37, 40

economics, 153, 239
e-government, 132
emergency systems and preparedness, 14, 38, 74, 115, 132, 134, 137, 251, 266, 269
Ericson, R., 3, 6, 10
ethnicity, 180
expertise, vii, 8, 29, 38–40, 79, 84, 85, 87, 112, 206, 210, 235, 255, 297

food, vi, 7, 16, 76, 100, 176–93, 252
foundations. *See* police foundations
freedom of information, 10, 296, 298

gender, viii, 100, 105, 158, 160, 162, 163, 172, 179, 180, 209, 271, 290, 295
government, 7–9, 11, 13–16, 51, 56, 61–65, 69, 84, 89, 90, 99, 100, 102, 103, 127, 132, 138, 140, 154, 165, 167, 169, 172, 173, 177, 182, 183, 185, 186, 191, 198, 200, 202, 203, 204, 211, 214, 226–32, 234–37, 239, 240, 241, 248, 250–55, 257, 258, 260, 263, 264, 266, 275, 277, 280
de Graaf, K., 176–81, 188–93

health care, 34, 40, 186, 256, 275, 276, 279
high policing, vi, 16, 17, 106, 221–42
Homeland Security, 251, 290
human rights, viii, 16, 105, 110, 112, 130, 176, 177, 185, 191, 247, 248, 250, 251, 252, 256, 264, 265, 274, 276, 280, 281, 297

images, v, 14, 48, 49–53, 55, 57–61, 63, 65–70, 107, 109, 111
immigration, vi, 17, 247–55, 257–61, 264–67, 269–78, 280, 281, 299
Immigration and Refugee Protection Act, 265
Indigenous peoples, 105, 112, 130
inequality, 6, 15, 17, 105, 113, 114, 298
insecurity, 297
insurance, 89
institutional isomorphism, v, 14, 27–29, 32, 38, 40–42
intelligence, vi, 5, 8, 10, 11, 15, 16, 31, 34, 57, 63, 106–8, 153, 171, 172, 173, 221, 222–28, 233, 234, 237–39, 241, 242
international law, 264, 276, 296
internet, 48, 51–54, 56, 57, 60–65, 68, 99, 101, 103, 116, 276, 298
investigations, 34, 64, 87, 88, 92, 223, 260

investigative journalism, 240

Joh, E., 4, 6, 9, 74, 79, 100, 104, 108–11, 113, 128
jurisdiction, 78–81, 83, 88, 91, 128, 138, 182, 232, 241, 260, 271, 275, 277, 281
justice, iii, v, vi, vii, viii, ix, xi, 3–9, 12, 13, 15, 17, 48, 52, 54, 55, 58, 59, 60, 67, 68, 79, 81, 86, 92, 100, 101, 102, 105, 109, 111, 112, 115, 117, 118, 153–57, 163, 168, 172, 173, 176, 185, 191–93, 198–10, 213, 214, 222, 225, 227, 250, 259, 267, 272, 273, 290, 291, 295–99

Kilty, J.M., 176–81, 188–93

labour, 7, 252, 256–58
law, v, vii, ix, 5, 6, 8, 10–12, 14, 15, 30, 31, 33, 36–40, 49, 54–61, 63, 64, 66, 67, 80, 85, 99, 103, 106, 113, 117, 153–55, 163, 164, 168, 171, 173, 185, 203, 207, 208, 212, 213, 224, 250, 252, 253, 255, 258, 259, 264, 270, 276, 277, 280, 290, 291, 295, 297, 298, 299
law enforcement, v, 10, 30, 31, 33, 37–40, 49, 54–57, 59–61, 63, 64, 66, 67, 99, 103, 106, 203, 207, 208, 213, 259, 290, 291
liability, 15, 75, 85, 89–92, 249
legislation, 14, 35–37, 49, 82, 86, 262, 265, 280, 281
legitimacy, 32, 42, 43, 61, 77, 128, 132, 241, 299

machine learning, 103, 104, 108, 113, 153–58, 171, 172
media, 14, 48–50, 53, 55, 57, 64, 68, 100, 105–8, 112, 117, 130, 176, 185, 186, 231, 238, 240, 261, 275
mental health, 75, 130, 261, 262, 268, 270, 274, 275, 278
methods, 79, 93, 103, 104, 110, 111, 113, 128, 158, 180, 204, 238, 296

migration, 108, 247–50, 252, 253, 258, 264, 265, 281, 297, 299
misconduct, 86–89, 259, 260, 277
moral panic, 48

national security, vi, 4, 8, 10, 13, 16, 219, 221–24, 226, 229–32, 234, 235, 237–42, 247, 257, 280
neo-liberalism, 102, 127, 199, 200, 202, 205, 292
networks, 6, 9, 10, 15, 30, 38, 56, 58, 103, 108, 109, 127, 202, 203, 231, 292
non-governmental organization (NGO), 52, 249, 279
norm violations, 15, 74, 75, 78–80, 85, 88, 90, 92

obfuscation, 100, 110, 112, 113
Ontario, 7, 16, 80, 100, 105, 110, 112, 176, 177, 182–86, 188, 191–93, 203, 208, 214, 236, 257, 269, 273–77, 280
Ottawa, vi, 7, 10, 16, 80, 106, 108, 111, 116, 176, 179, 182, 184–86, 188, 191, 236, 238, 295, 297
outsourcing, ix, 5, 35, 55, 102, 113, 141, 184, 198, 199, 222, 225, 236–38, 241, 252, 253, 255, 264, 291, 292
oversight, 61, 82, 92, 129, 142, 227, 259, 260, 279

paid-duty policing, 12
Parliament, 51, 60, 260
partnerships, 5, 8–10, 14, 16, 17, 30, 31, 38, 49, 55, 56, 58, 64, 68, 102, 129, 130, 191, 198–200, 202–6, 214, 234, 236, 249, 254, 257, 258, 264, 273, 297
penal systems, 7, 183
platform/platformization, 15, 57, 100–3, 105–12, 114–18, 137, 297
plea courts, 16, 199, 202, 203, 205, 207–14
pluralization, vi, 17, 221, 222, 223, 225–29, 233–36, 238–42
police foundation, 10

policing, v, vi, 4, 7, 9–17, 27–32, 35, 37–42, 48–51, 53, 55–61, 63–70, 74, 75–83, 85, 86, 90–93, 99–104, 106–9, 112–15, 117, 118, 126–30, 132, 136, 140, 143, 146, 183, 199, 206, 221–36, 238–42, 253, 256, 257, 280, 291, 292, 296–98
Porter, M., 184, 186–88, 190, 191
postsecondary systems, v, 14, 15, 74–93
prisons, 7, 156, 158, 160, 163, 165–67, 169, 176, 178–81, 183, 186, 192, 198, 225, 227, 250, 261, 268, 280, 292
privacy, 55, 65, 85, 92, 112, 153, 158, 241, 279, 280
private actors, v, vi, 3–5, 7, 8, 10, 11, 15–17, 29, 31, 40, 58, 97, 101, 102, 126, 127, 177, 219, 222, 225–28, 233, 234, 238, 240, 248, 252–55, 264, 265, 274, 280, 281
private security, v, 4, 5, 7, 9, 12, 13, 15, 27–42, 55, 75, 86, 126, 130, 222, 248–50, 252, 256–58, 260–62, 265, 273, 290, 292, 297, 299
privatization, iii, v, vi, vii, viii, ix, 3–7, 11–13, 15–17, 27, 29, 32, 55, 68, 100–2, 105, 114, 115, 117, 118, 127, 146, 151, 176, 179, 181–85, 191–93, 198–200, 213, 214, 222, 225, 247–50, 252–54, 263, 265, 277, 281, 290, 291–93, 296, 299
procurement, 6, 8, 9, 16, 111, 222, 223, 226–33, 240, 257
professionalization, 29, 38, 39
proprietary, 110, 111, 113, 118, 137, 138, 155, 158, 160–62, 164, 166, 167, 172, 173
provincial jails, 17, 176, 181, 183, 249, 257, 258, 265, 267–70, 273–77, 281
public goods, 6, 30, 77, 80, 82, 83, 91, 103
public police, 10, 12, 13, 28, 29, 35, 37, 40–42, 50, 54, 57, 60, 62–65, 68, 75, 76, 78–80, 86–89, 91, 92, 132
public–private partnership, 5, 8, 9, 31, 38, 55, 102, 129, 191, 234, 236, 249, 254, 258, 264, 273

race, v, viii, 17, 99, 100, 118, 163, 164, 170, 171
responsibilization, 58, 86, 127, 132, 136, 140, 146, 199, 214
rights, iv, viii, 16, 65, 78, 81, 83, 90, 105, 110, 112, 116, 130, 155, 162, 165, 168, 171, 176, 177, 185, 191, 241, 247, 248, 250–53, 256, 260, 264, 265, 274, 276, 280, 281, 291, 297
risk, 50, 58, 77, 78, 81, 85, 89, 90, 103, 104, 113, 126, 135, 166, 191, 199, 201, 222, 230, 237, 261, 266, 271–73, 275, 278–80, 298; assessment of, vi, 13, 15, 153–65, 167–73, 268, 270; mitigation of, 48
Robertson, K., 9, 13, 100, 104, 106, 107, 112, 230
Royal Canadian Mounted Police (RCMP), 10, 11, 104, 107, 108, 110–12, 114, 117, 223, 224, 229, 231, 233, 235, 241, 242, 260, 268

secrecy, 4, 8, 10, 59, 84, 87, 222, 229, 231, 233, 235, 238, 240, 241, 260
securitization, 140, 212, 251, 265, 280
security, v, vi, viii, 4, 5, 7–16, 25, 27–42, 54–59, 61, 64, 66, 74–89, 91–93, 100, 108, 126, 129, 130, 132, 135–37, 146, 153, 156, 163–67, 169, 181, 198, 212, 219, 221–24, 226, 229–42, 247–52, 256–63, 265–67, 270–73, 275, 280, 281, 290–92, 296–99
security agents, 32, 33, 35–38
sentencing, 4, 13, 103, 156, 158–62, 164, 167, 170–72, 210, 214
sexual exploitation, 14, 49–52, 54, 57, 58, 63, 64, 66–68
sexual violence, 76, 78, 81, 104, 256
Shearing, C., ix, 4–6, 10, 27, 28, 30, 39, 55, 75, 86, 222, 250
Sidewalk Toronto, 99, 101
Smart City, 15, 100, 101, 103, 109, 114–18, 127, 135, 141
social media, 57, 106–8, 112, 117
sociology, xi, 4, 6, 127, 193, 207, 297, 298

sovereignty, 115, 247, 248, 264, 281
space, 30–32, 37, 42, 61–63, 65, 68, 105, 112, 182, 209, 265
Supreme Court, 65, 90, 130, 159–62, 164–69, 252, 267
surveillance, v, 8–10, 13, 15, 17, 78, 97, 99, 103, 105–12, 114–18, 128, 129, 138, 206, 239, 252, 279, 280, 292, 296, 297
symbolism, 16, 33, 42, 43, 49, 61, 64, 68, 82, 176–79, 181, 186–88, 191–93, 211

task force, 184, 185
technology, v, 8, 9, 13, 31, 51, 53, 56, 61, 62, 65, 66, 85, 92, 99, 100–3, 108–11, 113, 115, 116, 118, 137, 145, 172, 233, 234, 239, 252, 279, 280, 296–99
terror/terrorism, 10, 69, 212, 238, 239, 251, 266, 270, 290
third sector, 54, 58, 200, 201
threat, 52, 69, 81, 91, 113, 153, 231, 256, 292
Toronto, xi, 12, 16, 33, 59, 66, 99, 101, 105, 108, 109, 111, 112, 199, 200, 202, 205, 207–9, 213, 214, 258, 267, 278, 279, 295–97, 299
training, 7, 10, 12, 30, 36, 38, 39, 42, 157, 171, 203, 209, 222, 226, 239, 242, 255, 256, 261–63, 277
transparency, 4, 5, 16, 17, 55, 92, 109, 111, 118, 138, 155, 163, 164, 171–73, 225, 227, 229, 231, 232, 241, 249, 250, 259, 260, 263, 264, 280, 281

unions, 7, 12, 88, 185, 236, 238, 241, 242, 247, 256, 263, 269
United Kingdom, ix, 3, 12, 13, 33, 36, 37, 52, 57, 200, 202, 248, 250, 251, 254, 256, 257, 263
United Nations, 247–50, 252, 257, 260, 264, 276, 277
United States, vi, 3, 7, 9, 10, 15–17, 29, 33, 37, 38, 76–78, 80, 81, 90, 100, 108, 110, 154–59, 167, 170–73, 202, 212, 221–23, 225–28, 235, 236,

238–42, 248, 250, 251, 256, 263, 290, 291, 292, 298
urban/urbanism, 15, 35, 36, 37, 100, 101, 103, 106, 109, 117, 118, 126–29, 135, 141, 142, 144–46, 256, 278, 290, 297
user-pay policing, 12, 34

Valverde, M., 27, 127
VanConnect (app), 15, 127, 128, 130, 132–39, 141, 142, 145–47

video, 10, 78, 107, 109, 115, 238, 291, 296
violence, vi, 16, 17, 76, 78, 81, 90, 104–6, 116, 186, 198–200, 202–14, 256, 290–92, 295, 298
visuals, 55, 58, 61, 141, 145, 297
visibility, 28, 33, 37, 67, 139, 140, 240

Waterfront Toronto, 99

Zedner, L., 4, 5, 27, 28, 42, 102, 105